THE STYLE AND LITERARY METHOD OF LUKE

BY

HENRY J. CADBURY
LECTURER IN THE NEW TESTAMENT, ANDOVER THEOLOGICAL SEMINARY

Wipf and Stock Publishers
150 West Broadway • Eugene OR 97401
2001

The Style and Literary Method of Luke

By Cadbury, Henry J.

ISBN: 1-57910-681-1

Reprinted by *Wipf and Stock Publishers*
150 West Broadway • Eugene OR 97401

Previously published by Harvard University Press, 1920.

PREFACE

The recent linguistic study of the New Testament has been following two lines, both of which have made such terms as "Biblical Greek," "the language of the New Testament," seem inappropriate. On the one hand the several canonical writers have come to be treated as individual authors, each possessing his own characteristics of style and diction. It has been recognized that each wrote with a great degree of freedom and independence and that their present association in the New Testament is due to other causes than similarity in language. We may speak of the style of Luke or the vocabulary of Paul, but if we would include in a grammar or lexicon all the New Testament phenomena, we must remember that we are dealing with a collection of writers, not with a homogeneous volume.

In another direction the category of "New Testament Greek" has been broken down by the comparison of secular contemporary writings. Especially the study of the papyri has shown that the early Christians were not using a special "language of the Holy Ghost," but an idiom which, apart from personal idiosyncrasies and from the special Christian and Semitic influences under which they wrote, was the common language of the Roman empire. Even the more formal and literary productions of the age are not to be excluded from comparison, since they also embody in varying degree the same ordinary language.

The following studies, in accordance with the two tendencies mentioned, aim to examine the work of the *auctor ad Theophilum* as an individual writer of the Hellenistic age. Attention is centered upon his language, as compared with that of the literary men of his time, or as displayed in his correction and paraphrase of Greek sources which he used.

It is fitting that philological inquiries should avoid as far as possible all presuppositions of a theological or historical kind, especially such assumptions as rest upon the questionable basis of early church tradition or upon the conjectures of modern historical criticism. As a rule the linguistic study should precede rather than follow the theological and historical study. Instead of explaining a writer's language in the light of a theory about his identity and interests, we should test the theory by an independent study of the language. It is hoped that these studies may serve as a basis for such tests.

Yet even for strictly philological investigations some hypotheses derived from literary criticism are necessary, and for the following pages two assumptions have been adopted. Both of them are all but universally accepted by competent scholars, and both of them have been justified by the fresh study of the linguistic evidence. The first is the assumption that the third gospel and the Acts of the Apostles were the work of the same author approximately in their present form. The second is the assumption, which accords with prevailing views on the Synoptic Problem, that the Gospel of Luke is based upon a Greek source substantially identical with our Mark and also upon further Greek memorabilia (commonly called Q) which were also used by Matthew. But all further theories about the unity, origin and history of this latter common material, or about other sources for the writings of Luke, have been avoided. Who was the author or editor of these two anonymous books has been left an open question, although for convenience his traditional name, Luke, is often used. The attempts of others to show on linguistic grounds that he was a physician have been separately considered and confuted.

The negative results of these studies, so far as the question of authorship is concerned, will doubtless be disappointing to many, — both those who, out of a desire to maintain the apostolic authority and historical accuracy of these two writings, cling to the tradition of Luke's authorship as supporting them, and those who, under the temptation that besets us all, dislike to admit that such interesting problems are unsolved or insoluble. But the restraint is good for us, and perhaps these studies, with their confession of ignorance on the one hand and their limitation to the tangible facts of language on the other, may prove a wholesome warning against extravagances in the use of linguistic "evidence."

The aim of this book was to investigate the subjects afresh, without full consultation of the many predecessors in the same fields. The notes and text will indicate some use of earlier works for which acknowledgment should be made. To Professor James H. Ropes, who has given his encouragement and guidance since these studies were first undertaken ten years ago as part of a thesis submitted for the degree of Doctor of Philosophy in Harvard University, and to Professor George F. Moore, who has made important contributions not only to the accuracy but also to the substance of the book, the author would express his gratitude.

HENRY J. CADBURY.

CAMBRIDGE, MASS., December, 1919.

CONTENTS

PART I

THE DICTION OF LUKE AND ACTS

PART II

THE TREATMENT OF SOURCES IN THE GOSPEL

PREFATORY NOTE

The investigation of which the First Part is here published was made in the years 1911 to 1913, and submitted as a thesis for the degree of Doctor of Philosophy in Harvard University in 1913. Publication has been unavoidably delayed, and it seems best not to postpone longer the issue of the present part, on the Diction of Luke, which has a certain unity and completeness of its own. The Second Part will deal with Luke's treatment of his sources, Mark and "Q," especially from a literary point of view, and with the style of Luke as illustrated by parallels in the Gospel and Acts. This second and larger part of the work will be published as soon as conditions growing out of the war permit; if the hopes of the editors are fulfilled, within the next few months. It will contain the author's preface and a table of contents to the whole, which can then be bound in one volume.

G. F. M.
J. H. R.
K. L.

CONTENTS

THE STYLE AND LITERARY METHOD OF LUKE

PART I

THE DICTION OF LUKE AND ACTS

1. SIZE OF LUKE'S VOCABULARY

THE size of Luke's vocabulary has been reckoned several times in various ways, with results which approximately agree. According to the latest count, by Professor Goodspeed, the Gospel of Luke contains 2080 different words, Acts 2054. Luke and Acts use in common 1014 words, and the total vocabulary of Luke and Acts together is 3120.[1] The earlier count by J. Ritchie Smith [2] to which Professor Goodspeed refers is in some ways more satisfactory. It omits proper names, and includes the figures for the other New Testament writers. According to this the total vocabulary of Luke and Acts is 2697.

Smith's complete table is as follows:

	Whole number of words	Total vocabulary	Words peculiar to each
Luke	35,239	2,697	715
Paul	31,457	2,446	797
John	27,185	1,396	212
Matthew	17,921	1,542	111
Mark	10,720	1,259	77
Hebrews	4,965	984	150
Peter	2,689	756	115
James	1,728	644	58
Jude	432	203	14

These figures enable us at a glance to compare Luke's vocabulary with that of the other New Testament writers; but, as Professor Goodspeed remarks, " they are disappointing to the critical student because they do not distinguish between Luke and Acts, between the

[1] *Journal of Biblical Literature*, XXXI (1912), pp. 92 ff.

[2] *Presbyterian and Reformed Review*, II (1891), pp. 647 ff.

Pastorals and the ten letters of the primary Pauline canon, or even between the Revelation and the Fourth Gospel."

For the book of Acts alone Blass's edition supplies a convenient lexicon and an enumeration of words. Excluding variant readings of the β-text and not counting proper names, there appear to be in Acts 1787 different words. For the Gospel of Luke by itself no exact count, excluding proper names, appears to be accessible. But the number of different words is very nearly the same as in Acts — approximately 1800. For the letters of Paul an independent count was made by Myron W. Adams.[1]

These figures show that Luke's vocabulary is greater than that of any other New Testament writer. This is only natural, since he is the most voluminous writer (see the figures in the first column of the table above). The only fair test is to compare the figures for the Gospel of Matthew with those for Luke or Acts separately. These three works are of very nearly the same size, and yet either Luke or Acts has a vocabulary about one-sixth larger than that of Matthew.

The last column of Smith's table gives the number of words peculiar to each writer. The lists in Thayer's Lexicon differ somewhat from those in Smith, and as they make distinctions which Smith ignores, their totals are here given, together with some other counts of the same kind:

Number of Words Peculiar to Individual Writers

	Thayer			Smith	Hawkins[2]	Various
	Total	Dubious[3]	Minimum			
Matt.	137	21	116	111	112	
Mark	102	32	70	77	71	80[4]
Luke						
Gospel	312	52	260		261	
Acts	478	49	429		413	414[5]
Gospel and Acts both	61		61		58	53[5]
Totals	851	101	750	715	732	

[1] *St. Paul's Vocabulary*, Hartford, 1895. His total of 2478, like Smith's, includes the Pastoral Epistles, but by means of his lists we have calculated that about 300 of the words he counts occur only in the Pastoral Epistles, so that the total for the ten primary letters is very nearly 2180.

[2] *Horae Synopticae*, 2d edit., pp. 198 ff.

[3] Uncertainty due to various readings.

[4] Swete, *St. Mark*, p. xl.

[5] Blass, *Acta Apostolorum, Editio philologica*, p. 334.

Pauline	Total	Thayer Dubious[3]	Minimum	Smith	Hawkins[2]	Various
Except Pastoral Epistles	627	34	593			
Pastoral Epistles	197[1]	10	187			
Both groups	53	6	47			
Totals	877	50	827	797		816[2]
Johannine						
Gospel and Epistles	133	13	120			
Revelation	156	33	123			108[3]
Both groups	9	1	8			
Totals	298	47	251	212		
Hebrews	169	11	158	150		
James	73	9	64	58		
Peter	121	7	114	115		
Jude	20	1	19	14		

From these tables it appears that the words peculiar to Luke are more numerous than those peculiar to any other New Testament writer, unless the Pastoral Epistles with their great number of words not occurring elsewhere in the New Testament be included in the Pauline canon. Comparing books of equal size only we discover that in Matthew, Luke, and Acts the words peculiar to each book number respectively 116, 260, and 429, or thereabouts. Mr. Adams, using Mr. Smith's figures, calculates the ratio of words peculiar to each writer to his whole vocabulary. He says: "Of the total vocabulary of St. Paul the percentage of words peculiar to him, as far as the New Testament is concerned, is nearly 33. In the case of St. Luke it is nearly 27; in St. John and the author of Hebrews it is between 15 and 16; in the others, still less." [4]

This calculation, however, includes under Paul the Pastoral Epistles, which contain a large proportion of ἅπαξ λεγόμενα. If, following Thayer's figures, we exclude these, the percentages will be both about the same, between 27 and 28, as the following figures show:

	Total vocabulary	Words peculiar to either
Luke	2697	750
Paul	2170	593

1 Thayer makes a mistake in the addition of his list.

2 Adams, *op. cit.* p. 27.

3 Swete, *Apocalypse*, p. cxix.

4 *Op. cit.* p. 28.

Outside of the New Testament a few writers whose works are about the size of either or of both of Luke's works and whose vocabularies could be readily counted were examined with the following result:

About the Size of Luke or Acts Singly

	Teubner pages	Vocabulary
Luke	about 75	1800[1]
Acts	" 75	1787
Letter of Aristeas	" 65	1968
Deuteronomy	" 75	1200 (estimated)

About the Size of Luke and Acts Together

	Teubner pages	Vocabulary
Luke and Acts	150	2697
Xenophon, Memorabilia	142	2404
Xenophon, Anabasis i–iv	135	2431
Aeschines	190	*ca.* 3000
Antiphon	129	1550

2. LITERARY STANDARD OF LUKE'S VOCABULARY

The vocabulary of an author probably affords the best test for comparing him with the various degrees of education and elegance in contemporary speech and writing. In matters of orthography the corrections or corruptions of scribes obscure the original spelling of the autograph. Points of syntax can be more safely used to test a writer's style, but here anything like a statistical comparison is out of the question. But in the vocabulary of an ancient writer scribal changes play the smallest part, and a rough classification is to some extent possible. To estimate the literary standing of Luke it is very desirable to examine the character of his vocabulary.

This subject has already been studied in some connections; chiefly either as part of an investigation of the language of the New Testament, which has been compared as a whole rather than by separate writers with the classical Greek language, or in comparison with the diction of the other New Testament writers. These two methods have led to the following conclusions: *First*, that the Greek of the New Testament in general differs greatly from classical Greek and is on the whole of a more popular and uncultivated style, and,

[1] The figures are exclusive of proper names.

second, that the writings of Luke are rather more elegant in diction than most of the other writings in the New Testament. But both these methods of study have their limitations, and further and more definite judgments are possible in regard to the vocabulary of Luke. It should be studied separately, and not merely as part of the vocabulary of that very heterogeneous collection, the New Testament, and it should be compared with the vocabularies of other writers beside the few comprised in the Christian canon.

The simplest way of comparing the vocabularies of two writers is to discover how many words they have in common. Where lexica are available this is easily ascertained. The following list gives the approximate proportion of Luke's vocabulary found in several Hellenistic writers or collections:

Greek Comedy	67%
LXX, excluding Apocrypha	80
LXX, including Apocrypha	90
New Testament (exclusive of Luke and Acts)	70
Papyri	65
Lucian	70
Plutarch	85

Vogel [1] has made further observations in this field. Of the various parts of the Greek Old Testament, Judges, Samuel, and Kings show the closest resemblance in vocabulary to Luke; with Second Maccabees the likeness is very striking.[2] Among profane writers akin to Luke, Vogel notes especially Polybius, Dioscorides, and Josephus. The lexical relations between Luke and Josephus have been studied with especial fulness by Krenkel.[3] In the New Testament Paul and Hebrews show the closest likeness to Luke in vocabulary.[4]

Such facts and figures may perhaps show some relationship and are therefore not without significance, but they have decided limitations of value. Whether a word used by Luke occurs in another writing depends far more on the chance of subject matter and the size of the writings compared than on any real affinity of language.

[1] Vogel, *Zur Charakteristik des Lukas nach Sprache und Stil*, 2d edit., p. 11.

[2] *Ibid.*, p. 54.

[3] M. Krenkel, *Josephus und Lucas. Der schriftstellerische Einfluss des jüdischen Geschichtsschreibers auf den christlichen nachgewiesen*, 1894.

[4] See for example the lists in Plummer, *Luke*, pp. liv ff.; Hawkins, *Horae Synopticae*, 2d edit., pp. 189 ff.

Furthermore, such collections as the Septuagint, the New Testament, the Apocrypha, and the papyri are of miscellaneous contents and character, the works of many authors, and do not represent a common standard of culture. Probably half of every writer's vocabulary is made up of words of such frequent occurrence that any other writer is likely to use them. It is only the unusual or uncommon words that can be expected to have much significance.

It is often inferred that for New Testament writers such words are to be found in the list of words peculiar to each writer, i. e., not found elsewhere in the New Testament. Such a notion is quite erroneous, and the emphasis usually placed upon these words in New Testament study seems to the present writer inappropriate. In a collection like the New Testament the occurrence of a word in only one writer is often merely an accident, and the words so distinguished are not characteristic of him.[1] On the other hand, some really unusual words or words of significance for a writer's vocabulary are thus left out of account because another writer in the New Testament happened to use the word.

If the fact that two writers have many words in common can not be used as a reliable evidence of affinity in vocabulary, it is still more dangerous to use this fact as a proof of literary dependence. Nowhere can this be more clearly seen than in the subject we are here considering, the vocabulary of Luke. Coincidence of vocabulary has been used at various times to prove that Luke wrote Hebrews, that he was familiar with Paul's letters, and that he had read Josephus or the Greek medical writers. Even the evidence of peculiar words is unsafe in such arguments, though it is used very effectively by both Krenkel and the believers in Luke's medical language. Krenkel, for example, to support his thesis that Luke had read Josephus, collects a large number of words which in the Greek Bible occur only in Luke and are also used by Josephus.[2]

The uncertainty of all such arguments may be illustrated by the following comparison of the vocabularies of Mark and Second Mac-

[1] The evidence that this is true may be seen by a glance at the lists in Part IV of the Appendix to Thayer's Lexicon. See what is said on this point below, p. 62, n. 78.

[2] *Josephus und Lucas*, pp. 304 ff. It is to be observed that Krenkel excludes from his investigation First and Second Maccabees. Were they included, many words would disappear from this list.

cabees as related to that of Luke. The two books are of about the same size. Mark we know was not only read by Luke but was made the chief source of his Gospel and in places copied verbatim; Second Maccabees may not even have been known to him. Yet according to the following figures, both in his general vocabulary and in the words peculiar to him, Luke has more in common with Second Maccabees than with Mark.

	Luke and Mark	Luke and 2 Macc.
Whole number of words in common (α–ε).....	383(15 ?)	451(12 ?)
Words not elsewhere in New Testament (α–ε)..	20(1 ?)	74(5 ?)
Words not elsewhere in the Greek Bible (α–ω) .	9(1 ?)	21(5 ?)

The last comparison is of sufficient interest to justify giving the lists in full.

Peculiar to Mark and Luke in the Greek Bible

ἀρχισυνάγωγος	
ἀνάγαιον	Mark 14, 15 = Luke 22, 12.
βλητέον	Mark 2, 22 (*v. l.*) = Luke 5, 38.
ἐκπνεῖν	Mark 15, 37, 39 = Luke 23, 46.
ἱματίζειν	Mark 5, 15 = Luke 8, 35.
λεπτόν	Mark 12, 42 = Luke 21, 2; also Luke 12, 59.
πρύμνα	
συνζητεῖν	
συσπαράσσειν	Mark 9, 20 = Luke 9, 42.

It will be noted that more than half of the cases are in parallel passages.

Peculiar to Second Maccabees and Luke in the Greek Bible

ἀγωνία	Luke 22, 44 (*v. l.*).	εὔθυμος	
ἀνάπηρος	also Tobit 14, 2 (*v. l.*).	ἱερόσυλος	
ἀντιβάλλειν		μετρίως	
ἀσκεῖν		περιρηγνύναι	
ἄτερ		πρεσβεία	
αὐστηρός		προσκλίνειν	
διανύειν		συνελαύνειν	Acts 7, 26 (*v. l.*).
εἰστρέχειν		σύντροφος	also *v. l.* in 1 Macc. 1, 6; 3 Reg. 12, 24.
ἐκπλήρωσις			
ἐπιτροπή		συντυγχάνειν	
ἔσθησις	3 Macc. 1, 16 (*v. l.*).	ὑποζωννύναι	

Vogel gives a list of more than fifty words and expressions peculiar to Luke in the New Testament and found in 2 Maccabees but not in the canonical books of the Old Testament. But many of these are found in the other apocryphal books and are therefore omitted from the foregoing list. On the other hand Vogel overlooks some of the words cited here. Further coincidences between Luke and 2 Maccabees in the use of words will be found in the word lists below under ἀναλύω, ἀνατίθημι, διανοίγω, διερμηνεύω, ἐπανάγω, ἐπίστασις.[1]

In view of the dangers that have attended the study of Luke's vocabulary in the past it may well be asked whether any examination of it can be safely made. Probably it can be done if the method of procedure is selected with some care, and if the results are not treated too mathematically or made to prove too much. The following methods were adopted only after due consideration and testing, and both the results and the methods by which they are reached are submitted here only tentatively and as the means of a rough estimate of the character of Luke's vocabulary.

The natural way to compare the vocabularies of two authors seemed to be to confine attention in each author to words of unusual occurrence in Greek literature, or at least to those not found in all grades of Greek prose, and to classify these in accordance with the class or age of Greek writing to which they seem to belong; then by counting the number of words of each class used by each author to discover which of the two writers inclined in his distinctive vocabulary towards the educated, Attic, and older words, which towards the more vulgar, less classical, and later words.

Such a comparison involves the analysis of two vocabularies, for example in our case, the vocabulary of Luke and that of at least one other Hellenistic author. Unfortunately most of the numerous linguistic studies in Hellenistic literature deal only with grammar. For Polybius, Strabo, Diodorus Siculus, Dionysius of Halicarnassus, and Plutarch we possess no thorough or well-sifted analysis of vocabulary, as Schmid has already noted with regret.[2] The same is true of the two most extensive Jewish writers, Josephus and Philo, for neither of whom even a lexicon is available. The vocabularies of Jewish and Christian writings, whether canonical or apocryphal, are either unclassified or have been studied in groups that include several different authors. A noteworthy exception is Nägeli, *Der Wortschatz des Apostels Paulus*.[3] The most thorough and satis-

[1] See also W. K. L. Clarke, "Acts and the LXX" in *Christian Origins* (to be published shortly).

[2] Schmid, *Der Atticismus*, IV, 634.

[3] Göttingen, 1905. The study includes only the rarest words, and continues down the alphabet part way through the letter ε.

factory work of the kind desired was found to be the analyses of vocabulary in Schmid's *Atticismus* [1] for Dio Chrysostom, Lucian, Aristides, Aelian, and the younger Philostratus. That a comparison of the New Testament language with the later Greek has been greatly facilitated by this elaborate work was recognized several years ago by Professor J. H. Thayer,[2] but apparently it has never been methodically used for this purpose.

The method of Schmid is as follows: [3]

Words that are of frequent occurrence in the Attic and the better literature of all periods are altogether omitted from consideration as being of no value for estimating "stilistische Neigungen" of the writer. Of the remaining words Schmid makes five classes according to their occurrence in extant authors:

A. Common Attic words, or words occurring in several Attic writers.
B. Words found only or principally in one prose writer before Aristotle.
C. Words found in poetry but not in Attic prose.
D. Words belonging to the post-classical prose, including Aristotle.
E. Words found first in the author under investigation.

In the lists which follow the same classification has been made of the vocabulary of Luke and Acts, extending down the alphabet through the letter ε. As about three-fourths of Luke's vocabulary occurs in the writings of the five authors treated by Schmid, we can follow his authority for nearly all the words which are to be omitted altogether from classification and for a great many of the words that fall into the first four classes. Where Schmid's estimate of a word is obtainable the reference to his work is given. The other words are classified as much in accordance with his methods as possible. As the date of Luke's work is uncertain it seemed safest to include in the last class only words in Luke and Acts that are found in no other writer before 200 A.D., which is about the lower limit for

[1] *Der Atticismus in seinen Hauptvertretern von Dionysius von Halikarnass bis auf den zweiten Philostratus* (4 vols. and index, 1887–1897).

[2] Hastings, *Dictionary of the Bible*, III, 43 ("Language of the New Testament").

[3] *Op. cit.* I, 103 n., 400.

the Atticists treated by Schmid. But of course it is quite possible that the words in list D marked only Josephus or Plutarch are also, strictly speaking, words first used by Luke. The enumeration does not aim to be complete except in the case of the Septuagint[1] (as represented by the texts underlying Hatch and Redpath's Concordance) and the New Testament.[2] In addition, words found in the papyri (except those found only in Christian papyri or papyri of the Byzantine period) are marked by the simple abbreviation, "Pap." In view of the promised lexicon to the papyri it did not seem worth while in most cases to give the references for the occurrence of these words.[3]

WORD LISTS

A. Common Attic Words or Words Occurring in Several Attic Writers[4]

† ἄγνωστος 'unknown.' Schmid IV, 118. — Hom., Pind., Thuc., Plat., LXX (Wisd., 2 Macc.), Joseph., Pap., Inscr.

† ἀγοραῖος Schmid I, 251. — Ar., Arist. *et al.*, Joseph., Strab., Luc., Inscr., Pap.

ἀγρυπνέω Schmid IV, 118. — Plat., Xen., Theognis, LXX, Mk. *al.*, Luc., Philostr., Inscr., Pap.

† [ἀηδία] Schmid II, 72. — Plat., Oratt., Hipp., Arr., Pap. (See Moulton and Milligan, *Vocabulary s. v.*, who call it a vernacular word.)

[1] The symbol LXX is used for the Greek Old Testament, but if a word occurs only in the Apocrypha that fact is shown by adding in parenthesis the exact reference or "Apocr."

[2] The obelus (†) is used to mark words occurring in the New Testament only in Luke or Acts, but is enclosed in round brackets if it occurs in another New Testament writing as a variant reading. Words enclosed in square brackets are variant readings in Luke or Acts.

[3] For a list of the principal collections, see Moulton, *Grammar of New Testament Greek*, I, index; Moulton and Milligan, *Vocabulary of the Greek Testament*.

[4] The customary abbreviations are employed. Note that "Ar." stands for Aristophanes, "Arist." for Aristotle. Abbreviations for the Gospels (in these lists) Mt., Mk., Jn. When the word occurs in Luke only in a context derived from Mark or Q, or in quotation or reminiscence from the Old Testament, the source is noted in brackets at the end of the entry, *e. g.* — [Q]

αἰγιαλός — Schmid IV, 120. — Att. poetry and prose, LXX, Mt., Jn., Luc., Philostr., Pap. (" common, " Moulton and Milligan).

† αἰτέω — with inf. but not acc. of person. Schmid III, 98 (" bewusster Atticismus "). — Trag., Plat., Ar., Isocr.

† αἴτιον — = *αἰτία*. Dem., Plat., Joseph., Pap.

ἀκοή — = *οὖς*. Schmid I, 104 (" diesen Sinn scheint das Wort im N.T. nicht zu haben "; but cf. Luke 7, 1, Mark 7, 35, Acts 17, 20, Heb. 5, 11). — LXX (2 Macc. 15, 39) *al.*

ἄλευρον — Schmid IV, 122. — Hdt., Att. prose., LXX, Joseph., Mt., Luc., Philostr., Pap. — [Q]

† ἀλλόφυλος — Thuc., Plat., Hipp., Aesch., Com., Polyb., Diod., LXX, Joseph., Philo, Pap.

† ἀμάρτυρος — Schmid IV, 123. — Thuc., Dem., Callim., Joseph., Luc., Plut., Hdn., Pap.

ἄμεμπτος — Schmid I, 208; II, 75. — Trag., Plat., Xen., Dem., LXX, Paul, Heb., Aristides, Pap.

† ἀμπελουργός — Schmid IV, 123. — Ar., Alex., Amphis, Luc., Plut., Philostr., LXX, Inscr., Pap.

ἀναβλέπω — Schmid IV, 126. — Plat., Xen., LXX, Mk., Philostr.

† ἀναβολή — Schmidt IV, 126. — Att., Dion. Hal., Joseph., LXX, Arr., Plut., Philostr., Pap.

† ἀνάγω — 'vow to gods.' Schmid II, 76. — Ionic and older Attic, Aristides, Inscr.

† ἀναζητέω — Schmid III, 100 f. — Hdt., Thuc., Ar., Xen., Dem., Plat., Polyb., LXX, Joseph., Luc., Ael., Babr., Pap.

† ἀνακαθίζω — intransitive. Xen., Plut., Hipp., Galen, Pap. (OP. 939, iv A. D., a Christian letter).

ἀνακρίνω — in forensic sense. Att. (Thayer, *s. v.*), Paul (Nägeli, p. 22), LXX (Susanna), Inscr.

† ἀνάκρισις — Xen., Plat., Oratt., LXX (3 Macc. 7, 5), Inscr., Pap.

ἀνακύπτω — Schmid IV, 126. — Hdt., Plat., Ar., Xen., LXX, Joseph., Aristeas, [John 8, 7 10], Luc., Pap.

† ἀναπείθω	Schmid I, 253 *al.* — Hdt., Thuc., Plat., Xen., *al.*, LXX, Joseph., Arr., Luc., Ael., Philostr., Plut., Pap.
† ἀνάπηρος	Schmid III, 101. — Att. prose, Joseph., Ael., LXX (2 Macc. 8, 24).
ἀνασείω	Schmid IV, 128. — Hymn. Hom., Att. prose, Eur., Ar., Diod., Dion. Hal., Mk., Philostr., Plut., Inscr., Pap.
† ἀνασκευάζω	Thuc., Xen., Polyb., Joseph., Plut., Pap. (OP. 745 i A. D., the nearest parallel to Acts 15, 24).
† ἀνασπάω	Schmid IV, 128. — Att. prose, LXX, Joseph., Luc., Philostr., Alciphr., Pap.
† ἀναφαίνομαι	Schmid IV, 272. — Att. prose, LXX, Joseph.
ἄνεσις	Schmid I, 253; IV, 128. — Thuc., Plat., Arist., Polyb., Theophr., LXX, Aristeas, Paul, Inscr., Pap.
† ἀνευρίσκω	Hdt., Plat., Xen., Trag., LXX (4 Macc. 3, 14), Joseph., Arr., Plut., Inscr.
ἀνέχομαι	with genitive. Schmid II, 77. — Plat., Eur., Mt., Mk., LXX, Arr.
† ἀνοικοδομέω	Thuc., Xen., Diod., Joseph., LXX, Plut., Hdn., Inscr., Pap. — [LXX]
ἄνομος	Att. prose and poetry, LXX, Paul (see Nägeli, p. 14) *al.*, Pap.
ἄνωθεν	temporal. Schmid III, 102; IV, 131. — Dem. *al.*, LXX, N. T., Joseph., Pap.
† ἀξιόω	'ask,' with infin. Hdt., Oratt. *al.* (cf. Blass, N. T. Gramm., p. 226), LXX, Pap.
[ἀπαντάω]	with personal subject. Schmid II, 80; III, 102. — Att., LXX, Mk. 14, 13, Pap.
ἀπαρνέομαι	Plat., Hdt., Thuc., Hipp., Trag., LXX, Mt., Mk., Arr., Plut.
ἀπειθής	Pind., Thuc., Xen., LXX, Philo, Paul, Past. Epp., Inscr., Athen.
ἀποβαίνω	'turn out.' Schmid II, 80. — Hdt., Thuc., Plat., Isocr., LXX, Phil. 1, 19, Pap. (PP. III, 42 H).
ἀποβολή	Plat., Arist., Rom. 11, 15, M. Anton., Arr., Plut.
† ἀποστρέφω	intrans. Hdt., Xen., Thuc., LXX (Ecclus. 8, 6 *al.*), Plut.

ἀποχωρίζω — Plat., Lys., LXX., Diod., Rev. 6, 14.

ἅρπαξ — Schmid I, 256. — Ar., Xen., LXX, Mt., Paul.

ἀρχηγός — Thuc., Plat., Isocr., Aesch., Arist., Polyb., Diod., LXX, Heb., Hdn., Inscr., Pap.

† ἀσιτία — Eur., Hdt., Hipp., Arist., Joseph., Plut., Galen.

† ἀσμένως — Schmid II, 87; IV, 138. — Plat., Dem., Polyb., Diod., Dion. Hal., LXX, Joseph., Aristides, Alciphr., Pap.

ἀσπασμός — Theognis, Plat., LXX, Aristeas, Mt., Mk., Paul, Arr., Pap. (OP. 471, 67, ii A. D.)

ἀτιμάζω — Schmid II, 88. — Poets and Attic prose., LXX, Mk. *v. l.*, Jas., Paul, Jn., Dio Chrys., Luc., Aristides, Pap.

ἄτοπος — Schmid IV, 139. — Plat. *et al.*, LXX, 2 Thess. 3, 2, Luc., Philostr., Pap.

αὐλίζομαι — Schmid IV, 139. — Hom., Hdt., Att., LXX, Mt. 21, 17, Arr., Luc., Philostr., Inscr.

† αὐστηρός — of men. Plat., Polyb., Dion. Hal., LXX (2 Macc. 14, 30), Plut., Diog. Laert., Pap.

αὐτόματος — Schmid IV, 140. — Hom., Hdt., Att. prose, LXX, Philo, Mk. 4, 28, Philostr., Diod., Arr., Pap.

† αὐτόπτης — Hdt., Plat., Xen., Oratt., Polyb. and later Gk. writers, Joseph., Pap.

† αὐτόχειρ — Schmid I, 112, 257; II, 90. — Att., Joseph., Arr., Dio Chrys., Luc., Aristides.

ἀφανίζω — Schmid I, 112; II, 90; III, 106. — Thuc., Plat., Ar., LXX, Mt., Jas., Pap. — [LXX]

[ἀφορμή] — Schmid IV, 141 f. — Att. prose, Polyb., LXX, Paul (see Nägeli, p. 15), Luc., Philostr., Pap.

ἄχυρον — Schmid IV, 142. — Hdt., Xen., Com., LXX, Mt. 3, 12, Pap. ("very common," Moulton and Milligan). — [Q]

† βαθύνω — Hom., Xen., Theophr., Dion. Hal., LXX, Joseph.

† βάσις — 'foot.' Schmid III, 107 *al.* — Plat., Arist., Joseph., Philostr., Ael., LXX (Wisd. 13, 18), Apollod.

βόθυνος	Xen., Lys., Solon, Cratin., Theophr., LXX, Mt. 12, 11; 15, 14, Galen. — [Q]
† βολή	(cf. Schmid IV, 282). Thuc., Xen., LXX, Joseph.
βούλημα	Schmid II, 91. — Plat., Arist., LXX (2 and 4 Macc.), Aristeas, Rom. 9, 19, Arr., Pap.
βρῶμα	Schmid IV, 143. — Hipp., Thuc., Xen., LXX, Paul *et al.*, Arr., Alciphr.
γεύομαι	metaphorically. Schmid I, 113. — Hom., Hdt., Soph., Plat. *al.*, LXX, Mt., Mk.
γνωστός	Plat., Xen., Trag. *al.*, LXX, Rom. 1, 19, Jn.
γόμος	Hdt., Dem., Aesch., Mosch. *al.*, LXX, Rev. 18, 11 f., Inscr., Pap.
δεινῶς	Schmid III, 108; IV, 147. — Att., LXX, Mt. 8, 6.
δέρω	Schmid IV, 147. — Hom., Soph., Com., Plat., Xen., LXX, Mt., Mk., Paul, Jn., Pap.
δέσμιος	Trag., Att. (Bekker, *Anecdota Graeca*, I, 90), LXX, Diod., Paul (Nägeli, p. 26) *et al.*, Pap.
† δευτεραῖος	Hdt., Xen., Polyb., Diod., Inscr.
† δημηγορέω	Schmid IV, 148. — Ar., Xen., Plat., Dem., Joseph., LXX, Alciphr.
† διαβάλλω τινά τινι	Schmid IV, 149. — Hdt., Thuc., Plat., Pap. (TbP. I, 23, ii B. C.), Theodotion (Dan. 3, 8).
† διάγνωσις	Plat., Hipp., Dem., LXX (Wisd. 3, 18), Joseph., Arr., Plut., Dio Cass., Inscr., Pap.
† διακούω	Schmid IV, 150. — Xen., Plat. *al.*, LXX, Joseph., Luc., Philostr., Inscr., Pap.
διαλογίζομαι	Schmid II, 93. — Att. prose, LXX, Mt., Mk., Pap.
διαμαρτύρομαι	Schmid II, 94. — Xen. and especially Dem., LXX, Paul *al.*
διαμερίζω	Schmid I, 259. — Plat., Menand., LXX, Aristeas, Mt., Mk., Jn., Luc.
† διανόημα	Schmid II, 94. — Xen., Plat., Arr., Aristides, LXX.

† διασείω	Schmid II, 94 *al.* — Plat., Xen., Dem., Polyb., LXX, Joseph., Luc., Aristides, Ael., Inscr., Pap.
διασπάω	Schmid IV, 151. — Hdt., Att. prose and poetry, LXX, Mk. 5, 4, Philostr., Luc.
† διατηρέω	Plat., Oratt., Com., Arist., Polyb., LXX, Aristeas, Plut., Inscr., Pap.
† διαφεύγω	Schmid IV, 152. — Hdt. *al.*, LXX, Joseph., Arr., Luc., Philostr., Pap.
† διαχλευάζω	Plat., Dem., Aeschin., Polyb., Joseph.
† διαχωρίζομαι	Schmid IV, 152. — Ar., Plat. Xen. *al.*, LXX, Diod., Joseph., Plut.
† διερωτάω	Plat., Xen., Dem., Polyb., Joseph., Plut., Dio Cass. *al.*
† διισχυρίζομαι	Oratt., Plat., Joseph., Dio Cass. *al.*
δικαίωμα	Plat., Arist., LXX, Paul (Nägeli, p. 22) *al.*, Pap.
† διόρθωμα	Hipp., Arist., Polyb., Plut., Diog. Laert., Pap.
διορύσσω	Schmid IV, 153. — Att. prose, LXX, Mt., Inscr., Pap. — [Q]
διχοτομέω	Plat., Arist., Mt. 24, 51, LXX — [Q]
δυνατοί, οἱ	'the rich, prominent.' Schmid IV, 155. — Hdt., Att. prose, Joseph., Philostr.
δυσκόλως	Plat., Isocr., Dem., Mt. 19, 23 = Mk. 10, 23. — [Mk]
† ἐγκάθετος	Plat., Dem., Hyperides, Polyb., LXX, Joseph.
† ἔγκυος	Hdt., Hipp., Arist., Anth., Diod., LXX (Ecclus. 42, 10), Joseph., Plut., Pap.
† ἔδαφος	Schmid II, 98. — Att. prose and poetry, LXX, Aristeas, Inscr., Pap.
εἰσπορεύομαι	Xen. *et al.*, LXX, Mt., Mk., Inscr., Pap.
† εἰστρέχω	Xen., Thuc., Theocr., LXX (2 Macc. 5, 26), Joseph., Lycophron.
† ἐκβολή	Schmid I, 262. — Dem., Arist., LXX, Luc., Pap.
ἐκκόπτω	Schmid IV, 158. — Hdt. *al.*, LXX, Mt., Paul, Pap.
† ἐκκρέμαμαι	Schmid IV, 158. — Eur., Thuc., Philo, Joseph., LXX.

† ἐκλαλέω	Schmid IV, 159. — Eur., Dem., Philo, Joseph., Philostr., Dio Cass., LXX (Jud. 11, 9 *v. l.*)
ἐκλεκτός	Plat., Thuc., LXX, Enoch, Mt., Mk. *al.*, Pap.
ἐκλογή	Plat., Arist., Polyb., Diod., Dion. Hal., Joseph., Aristeas, Paul *al.*, Aquila, Symm., Theodot., Pap.
ἐκπνέω	Plat., Aesch., Eur., Soph., Arist., Mk. 15, 37 39, Philostr. — [Mk]
ἐκπορεύομαι	Schmid IV, 160. — Xen., Polyb., Aeneas Tact., LXX, Mt., Mk., Paul, Rev.
† ἑλκόομαι	Hipp., Xen., Eur., Com., Plut.
ἐμβλέπω	Schmid IV, 161. — Plat., Xen., Polyb., LXX, Mt., Mk., Jn., Pap.
ἐμφανίζω	Schmid II, 103. — Xen., Plat., Dem., Aeschin., LXX, Mk., Jn., Heb., Inscr., Pap.
† ἔνεος	Schmid III, 120. — Plat., Arist., LXX, Joseph.
† ἐντόπιος	Plat., Soph.,[1] Dion. Hal., Hdn., Inscr., Pap.
ἐνυπνιάζω	Hipp., Arist., LXX, Jude 8, Plut. — [LXX]
ἐξαίφνης	Hom., Pind., Plat., Dem. *al.*, LXX., Mk. 13, 36, Arr., Plut., Galen., Babr., Pap.
ἐξαλείφω	Schmid IV, 163. — Att. prose and poetry, Paul, Rev., Luc., Philostr., Inscr., Pap.
† ἐξάλλομαι	Hom., Xen. *al.*, LXX, Joseph.
† ἐπάναγκες	Schmid I, 264. — Hdt., Aeschin., Plat., Dem. *al.*, Arist., Dion. Hal., Joseph., Arr., Luc., Plut. *al*, Pap.
ἐπάνω	with gen. Schmid I, 119 ("seit Hdt. in allen Schichten der Sprache verbreitet"). — LXX, Mt. *al.*, Pap.
† ἔπαυλις	Schmid III, 123. — Hdt., Plat., Diod., Polyb., Philo, Ael., Plut., LXX, Pap. — [LXX]
† ἐπειδήπερ	Plat., Thuc., Ar., Arist., Dion. Hal., Philo, Joseph.
† ἐπέκεινα	Schmid II, 108 f. — Soph., Eur., Thuc., Plat., Xen., Isocr., Strabo, Luc. *al.*, LXX. — [LXX]
† ἐπιβιβάζω	Thuc., Plat., Diod., LXX.

[1] *Oed. Col.* 841 (MSS. not editions).

ἐπιγινώσκω — 'recognize.' Schmid IV, 166. — Hom., Aesch., Thuc., Plat., Xen., LXX, Mt. *al.*

† ἐπικρίνω — Plat., Dem., Arist., Theophr., Dion. Hal., LXX (Apocr.), Joseph., Plut., Hdn. *al.*, Pap.

† ἐπινεύω — Schmid IV, 167. — Hom. and other poets, Att. prose, LXX, Aristeas, Joseph., Luc. *al.*, Pap.

† ἐπίνοια — Schmid II, 109 *al.* — Soph., Ar., Thuc., Xen., Plat., LXX, Joseph., Aristeas, Arr., Luc. *al.*, Pap.

† ἐπισίτισμος — 'supplies.' Dem., Xen., LXX, Joseph., Hdn., Inscr.

† ἐπιστρέφω — transitive. Schmid IV, 169. — Xen. *al.*, LXX.

† ἐπιτροπή — Dem., Hipp., Thuc., Polyb., Dion. Hal., Diod., LXX (2 Macc. 13, 14), Joseph., Aquila, Pap.

† [ἐπιφανής] — 'illustrious.' Schmid IV, 169. — Att. prose, LXX, Philostr., Pap. — [LXX]

ἐρημόω — Hdt., Thuc., Plat., Xen., Andocid., poets, LXX, Philo, Mt. 12, 25, Rev., Pap. — [Q]

εὐαγγελίζομαι — Schmid IV, 173. — Ar., Dem., Lycurg., Theophr., LXX, Joseph., Paul *al.*, Luc., Plut., Paus.

† [εὖγε] — Schmid IV, 173. — Ar., Plat., LXX, Philostr.

† εὔθυμος — Plat., Xen., Att. poets, LXX (2 Macc. 11, 26), Joseph., Plut., Pap.

† εὐθύμως — Xen., poetry, Polyb., Joseph., Plut.

εὐκαιρία — Schmid III, 126. — Plat., Isocr. *al.*, Mt. 16, 26 (the parallel passage), Pap.

εὐλογέω — 'praise.' Schmid I, 267. — Ar., Att., Polyb., Aristeas, Luc.

† εὐπορία — Thuc., Plat., Xen., Oratt., LXX (4 Reg. 25, 10 A), Philo, Joseph., Arr., Plut., Aquila, Pap.

† εὐτόνως — cf. Schmid I, 267. — Ar., Xen., Menand., Diod., LXX, Joseph., Pap. (TbP. 678, medical; Petr. P.)

ἐχθές — Schmid IV, 176; Lobeck, *Phryn.* 323. — LXX, Jn. 4, 52; Heb. 13, 8, Pap. — [LXX]

B. Words from the Vocabulary of Individual Writers before Aristotle

1. *From Plato*

ἀνάγνωσις	'reading.' Schmid I, 299. — Plat., LXX, Aristeas, Paul *al.*, Arr., Luc., Pap.
† ἀνάλημψις	Schmid I, 299. — Plat., Hipp., Polyb., Luc., Com., Pap.
ἀπολύτρωσις	Plat., Polyb., LXX, Aristeas, Philo, Joseph., Diod., Paul (Nägeli, p. 30), Heb., Plut.
ἄφεσις	'forgiveness.' Plat., Diod., Dion. Hal., Philo, Enoch, Paul (Nägeli, p. 55) *al.*, Pap.
βαπτίζω	Schmid I, 299. — Plat., Polyb., Diod., Strabo, LXX, Mt., Mk., Jn., Paul, Arr., Plut., Luc., Pap.
γεννητός	Schmid I, 299. — Plat., Diod., LXX., Mt. 11, 11, Luc. — [Q]
† διαμερισμός	Plat., Diod., LXX, Joseph.
διανοίγω	Schmid I, 300. — Plat., Arist., LXX, Mk., Luc., Plut.
† διαπραγματεύομαι	Plat., Dion. Hal.
† ἐπισφαλής	'dangerous.' Schmid I, 300. — Hipp., Plat., Polyb., LXX (Wisd. 9, 14), Joseph., Aristeas, Luc., Pap. (?)

2. *From Xenophon*

† ἀντικαλέω	Xen.
† βλέπω	in geographical sense (*specto*). Xen., LXX (Ezek. 11, 1 *al.*), Diog. Laert., Hdn., Pap.
ἑκατονταπλασίων	Xen., LXX, Mk. 10, 13. — [Mk]
† ἐπανάγω	'put to sea.' Xen., LXX (2 Macc. 12, 4), Pap.
† [ἑσπερινός]	Xen., LXX, Dio Cass., Athen., Pap.

3. *From Herodotus*

ἀθέμιτος	Hdt., Dion. Hal., LXX (2 and 3 Macc.), 1 Pet. 4, 3, Plut., Vett. Val., Pap.
† *ἀναβαθμός*	Schmid III, 171. — Hdt., Ael., LXX, Dio Cass., Inscr. (*αναβαζμους* Syll. 587, 308, iv B.C.)

4. *From Hippocrates*

† *ἀνάψυξις*	Hipp., LXX, Philo, Strabo, Galen, Eccles.
† *ἀνωτερικός*	Hipp., Galen, Epiphan.
† *ἐκδιηγέομαι*	Hipp., Arist., LXX, Philo, Joseph., Galen.
† *ἐκψύχω*	Hipp., Herond., Aretaeus, Galen, LXX, Plut., Babr., Iambl.
† [*ἐνισχύω*]	transitive. Hipp., LXX.

5. *From Thucydides*

† *ἀγωνίζομαι*	with infinitive. Schmid IV, 256, 389. — Thuc., Diod., Plut., Philostr.

6. *From Demosthenes*

† *ἀσώτως*	Dem., Joseph., Polyaen., Dio Cass., Athen.
† *δανιστής*	Schmid I, 309. — Dem., LXX, Joseph., Plut., Luc., Pap.

7. *From Isocrates*

† *ἐκταράσσω*	Schmid I, 311. — Isocr., LXX, Plut., Joseph., Dio Cass., Luc., Alciphr.

8. *From Hyperides*

† *ἀνέκλειπτος*	Hyperides, Diod., Aristeas, Plut., Sext. Emp., Inscr., Pap.

C. Poetic Expressions

ἀγέλη	Schmid II, 187. — Hom., Trag., Pind., Plat., Xen., Mt., Mk., LXX, Luc. *al.*, Pap. — [Mk]
† *ἀγκαλή*	Schmid I, 318 *al.* — Hdt., Eur., Plat., Joseph., LXX, Luc., Philostr., Pap.

ἁγνίζω	Soph., Eur., Diphil., Apoll. Rhod., Diod., LXX, Jn. *al.*, Plut., Pap.
αἷμα	'murder.' Schmid IV, 268. — Trag., LXX, Rev. *al.*
αἰνέω	("poetic and Ionic," Liddell and Scott) — Plat., LXX, Rev., Plut., Insc. (Syll. 835, 8, iv B.C.)
(†) αἶνος	("Greek poets," Thayer). — LXX, Mt. 21, 16 (LXX), Inscr.
ἀλέκτωρ	Schmid I, 319. — Poets, LXX, Mt., Mk., Jn., Pap. — [Mk.]
ἀλήθω	Theophr., Com., Anth., Diod., LXX, Mt. 24, 41 (from Q), Pap. — [Q]
ἀμνός	Ar., Soph., LXX, Jn., Pap. — [LXX]
ἀναβλέπω	'see again.' Schmid IV, 270. — Eur., Hdt., Plat., Ar., Mt., Mk., Jn., Paus., Inscr., LXX.
† ἀναδείκνυμι	Schmid IV, 271 *al.* — Soph., Hdt., Xen., Polyb., LXX, Joseph., Luc., Philostr., Inscr.
ἀνακράζω	Schmid I, 320. — Hom., Com., Xen., Polyb., LXX, Mk., Luc., Philostr., Pap. (B G U IV, 1201, 11, ii A.D.)
† ἀναφαίνω	active.[1] Schmid IV, 273. — Hom., Aesch., Eur., Plat.
ἄνυδρος	Schmid IV, 275. — Hdt., Eur., Theophr., LXX, Mt. 12, 43 *al.*, Pap. — [Q]
ἀπόκρυφος	Eur., Callim., Xen., Anth., LXX, Mk. 4, 22, Col. 2, 3, Vett. Val., Pap. (Jewish magic). — [Mk]
† ἀπομάσσομαι	Schmid IV, 276 *al.* — Com., Dem., Polyb., Theocr., LXX (Tob. 7, 17, *v. l.*), Luc.
† ἀποτινάσσω	cf. Schmid I, 348. — Eur., LXX, Galen.
† ἀποψύχω	Schmid I, 149 *al.* — Ar., Bion, Hipp., LXX (4 Macc. 15, 18), Joseph., Arr., Dio Chrys. *al.*, Pap.
† ἀργυρόκοπος	Phryn. (Com.), LXX, Plut., Inscr. (CI 3154), Pap.
† ἀρήν	Hom., Com., Inscr., LXX, Joseph., Pap.

[1] Schmid indicates that this word is absent from the New Testament, evidently an oversight.

ἀρτύω [1] Schmid II, 190. — Hom. and the other poets, Arist., Theophr., Polyb., LXX, Mk. *al.*, Pap. — [Mk]

ἀσάλευτος Schmid I, 149. — Eur., LXX, Anth., Diod., Heb. 12, 28, Dio Chrys., Plut., Polemon, [Plat.] *Axioch.* 370D, Inscr.

ἄσβεστος Schmid I, 322. — Poets, Dion. Hal., LXX (Job. 20, 26 *v. l.*), Philo, Mt. 3, 12, Mk., Strabo, Luc., Ael., Plut. — [Q]

† *ἄσημος* metaphorically. Schmid I, 322. — Eur. and other poets, Hdt., LXX (3 Macc. 1, 3), Joseph., Dion. Hal. *al.*

† *ἀστράπτω* Schmid IV, 278. — Trag., Ar., late epic, Plat., Xen., LXX, Philostr., Pap. (magic).

† *ἄτερ* Poets and late prose, LXX (2 Macc. 12, 15), Plut., Inscr., Pap.

† *αὐγή* Schmid IV, 279 *al.* — Poets, Plat., Xen., LXX, Joseph.

† *ἄφαντος* Schmid II, 191. — Hom., Pind., Soph., Diod., Aristides, Plut.

† *ἄφνω* Schmid III, 186. — mostly poetical; Thuc., Dem., LXX, Joseph., Ael., Arr.

† *ἀχλύς* Schmid I, 323 *al.* — Epic, Polyb., Arist., Aquila, Symm., Joseph., Luc., Philostr.

βαρέω Schmid I, 322. — Hom., Plat., Theocr., Paul (Nägeli, p. 26), Luc., Ael., Plut., Pap.

βαστάζω Schmid I, 323. — Trag., Com., Polyb., LXX (rare), Mt., Mk., Paul, Rev., Arr., Luc., Pap.

βάτος Schmid I, 323. — Hom., Theophr., Ar., Luc., Philostr., LXX, Mk.

βλέπω Schmid IV, 281. — chiefly poetical, and then in late prose; LXX, Mt., Paul *al.*, Pap.

† *βουνός* Com., Polyb., LXX, Philo, Joseph., Strabo, Plut., Paus., Inscr., Pap. — [LXX]

[1] Schmid indicates that this word is absent from the New Testament, evidently an oversight.

(†) βραχίων	Hom., Eur., Arist., LXX, Joseph., Jn. 12, 38 (from LXX.), Pap.
βρέφος	Hom., Pind., Anth., LXX (Apocr.), 2 Tim. 3, 15 *al*, Pap.
βρέχω	Schmid II, 192. — originally poetical; Polyb., Mt. *al.*, LXX., Arr., Aristides, Pap.
βρυγμός	Eupolis, Ephipp. (?), LXX, Mt., Galen, Eccles. — [Q]
† βρύχω or βρύκω	Hom., Hermipp., Hipp., LXX.
† βρώσιμος	Aesch., Diphilus (Bekker, *Anecd.* I, 84), LXX.
γέν(ν)ημα	Schmid II, 293. — Soph., Plat., LXX, Mt., Pap. — [Q]
† γλεῦκος	Schmid I, 324. — Nicand., Arist., LXX, Joseph., Luc., Plut., Pap.
γογγυσμός	Anaxandrides, LXX, Paul (Nägeli, pp. 26 f.) *al.*, M. Anton.
δαιμονίζομαι	'be possessed.' Philemon, Mt. *al.*, Aquila, Plut., Pap. (PLeid. W vi. 30, Jewish).
δεσμεύω	Schmid III, 190. — Hymn. Hom., Hes., Eur., Plat., Xen., Polyb., LXX, Mt. 23, 4, Arr., Pap.
† διαλαλέω	Schmid IV, 285. — Eur., Polyb., Symm., Joseph., Philostr., Alciphr.
† διαλεκτός	'language.' Ar., Com., Arist., Polyb., Diod., LXX, Philo, Joseph., Plut.
† διανεύω	Schmid I, 314. — Alexis, Polyb., Diod., LXX, Luc.
† διανύω	Schmid I, 325 *al.* — Hom., Eur., Xen., Polyb., LXX (2 Macc. 12, 17), Joseph., Luc. *al.*
† διοπετής	(cf. Schmid I, 325) — Eur., Dion. Hal., Luc., Hdn., Aristopho, Plut.
διωγμός	Aesch., Soph., Xen., LXX, Mt., Mk., Paul (Nägeli, p. 26) *al.*, Plut.
† δοχή	'reception.' Machon, LXX, Plut. ('receptacle,' Hipp.; 'receipt,' Pap.)
δῶμα	Schmid III, 193. — "Poetic and Alexandrian prose." LXX, Mt., Mk., Ael., Pap.

† ἔα	Aesch., Soph., Ar., Plat., LXX.[1]
εἰσακούω	Hom., Soph., Eur., Hdt., Arist., LXX, Mt. *al.*, Pap.
† ἔκθετος	Eur., Manetho, Vett. Val.
† ἐκκολυμβάω	Eur., Ar., Diod., Dion. Hal.
† ἐκτελέω	Schmid II, 195. — Hom., Hes., Pind., Soph., Eur., Plat., LXX, Joseph., Luc., Aristides, Pap.
ἐκτενῶς	Machon, Diod., LXX, 1 Pet. 1, 22, M. Anton., Polyb., Inscr.
ἐκτινάσσω	Trag., Pind., Hipp., Mt. 10, 14 = Mk. 6, 11, Plut., LXX, Pap.
ἐμπαίζω	Schmid I, 327.—Soph., Eur., Anth., LXX, Mt., Mk., Arr., Luc.
† ἐννεύω	Schmid I, 314. — Ar., LXX, Luc.
ἐντυλίσσω	Ar., Com. frag., Mt. 27, 59, Jn. 20, 7 (the parallel passages), Arr., Athen., Ev. Nicod., Pap. (BM I, p. 110, 826, iii A.D.).
ἐξαυτῆς	Theognis, Arat., Polyb., Joseph., Mk. 6, 25; Phil. 2, 23, Opp., Pap.
ἐπαινέω	Schmid III, 197; IV, 294. — Hom. *al.*, LXX, Paul, Luc., Aristides, Philostr., Alciphr., Pap.
† ἐπαιτέω	Schmid I, 328. — Hom., Soph., LXX, Joseph., Pap.
† ἐπακροάομαι	Schmid I, 314 *al.*[2] — Plato Comicus, Test. XII Patr., Luc., Philostr.
† ἐπεγείρω	Schmid II, 196. — Hom., Soph., Eur., Plat., LXX, Joseph., Luc., Aristides, M. Anton.
† ἐπέρχομαι,	with dative. Schmid IV, 295. — chiefly poetical, LXX, Pap.
ἐπίβλημα	Nicostratus, LXX, Mt. 9, 16 = Mk. 2, 21, Arr., Plut. — [Mk]
ἐπίκειμαι	'press upon.' Schmid I, 329. — Hom., Eur., Hdt., Ar., Theocr., Paus., LXX, Joseph.
† ἐπικέλλω	Hom., Apoll. Rhod., Numen.

[1] From Mk. 1, 24 if the reading is accepted there.

[2] Schmid assigns this word to the LXX by mistake.

(†) *ἐπιρρίπτω* Schmid I, 329. — Hom., Arist., Polyb., LXX, Joseph., 1 Pet. 5, 7 (LXX), Luc., Plut., Pap.

ἐπισκιάζω Schmid I, 329. — Hdt., Soph., Arist., Theophr., LXX, Philo, Mt. 17, 5 = Mk. 9, 7, Luc.

† *ἐπιστάτης = διδάσκαλος* Antiphon (Bekker, *Anecd.* I, 96).

ἐπιφαίνω Schmid IV, 296. — Theognis, Theocr., Dion. Hal., Plut., LXX, Tit. 2, 11; 3, 4.

ἐργάτης Schmid I, 329. — Eur., Soph., Xen., Polyb., LXX (Apocr.), Mt., Paul *al.*, Arr., Luc., Pap.

† *ἐρείδω* Schmid II, 197 *al.* — Poets, Plato, Polyb., LXX, Joseph., Aristides, Philostr., Plut.

ἔριφος or *ἐρίφιον* Schmid I, 329. — Bacch., Com., LXX, Joseph., Aristeas, Mt. 25, 32 f., Luc., Pap.

ἑρπετόν Schmid I, 330. — Hom., Ar., Pind., Eur., Callim., Theophr., LXX, Rom. 1, 23; Jas. 3, 7, Luc., Philostr.

ἑτοιμάζω active. Schmid IV, 298. — chiefly poetic and late prose; LXX, Paul *al.*, Arr., Philostr., Pap.

εὐθυμέω intransitive. Eur., Theocr., Anth., Symm., Jas. 5, 13, Plut., M. Anton., Pap.

† *εὐσεβέω* Trag., LXX (4 Macc. 11, 5), Joseph., 1 Tim. 5, 4.

† *εὐφροσύνη* Schmid I, 331. — chiefly poetical; Xen., LXX, Luc., M. Anton., Pap.

† *ἐφάλλομαι* Hom., Pind. ("rare in prose," Liddell and Scott), LXX, Plut., Alciphr.

ἔχιδνα Schmid I, 331. — Trag., Hdt., Plat., Hes., Aquila, Mt., Luc.

D. Expressions used by the Later Writers

ἄβυσσος substantive; cf. Schmid I, 318. — LXX, Enoch, Paul (Nägeli, p. 46), Pap. (magic), Diog. Laert., Iambl. (the adj. in Aesch., Hdt., Eur., Ar., Luc.).

ἀγαθοποιέω LXX, Mk. *al.*, Aristeas, Sext. Emp.

ἀγαλλίασις LXX, Heb. 1, 9, Jude 24, Clem. Rom., Justin *al.*

ἀγαλλιάω	LXX, Mt. *al.*, Eccles.
ἀγαπή	LXX, Aristeas, Philo, Paul *al.*, Test. XII Patr., Pss. Sol.
ἄγγελος	'angel.' LXX, Philo, Joseph., Mt. *al.*
ἁγιάζω	LXX, Anth., Mt., Paul *al.*, Eccl.
† ἁγνισμός	Dion. Hal., LXX, Plut., Inscr.
† ἀγραυλέω	Arist., Strabo, Plut.
ἀδυνατέω	with impersonal subject; cf. Schmid III, 98 *al.* — LXX, Mt. 17, 20. — [LXX]
τὰ ἄζυμα	LXX, Mt. *al.* (the adj. in Plat., Galen, Athen.)
ἀθετέω	Schmid I, 353. — Polyb., Diod., Dion. Hal., LXX, Mk., Paul *al.*, Arr., Luc., Plut., Pap.
† αἵρεσις	'sect.' Schmid IV, 716.—Epicurus, Dion. Hal., Philo, Arr., Diog. Laert., Sext. Emp., Joseph., Plut., Strab.
αἰχμαλωτίζω	Diod., LXX, Joseph., Aristeas, Paul, Arr., Plut., Inscr. — [? LXX]
ἀκαταστασία	Polyb., Dion. Hal., LXX, Paul *al.*, Arr., Clem. Rom., Pap. (G 1, ii B.C. literary).
† ἀκροατήριον	Plut., Philo, Arr., Tatian.
ἀκροβυστία	LXX, Philo, Paul.
† ἀκωλύτως	Schmid I, 353. — Symm., Joseph., Arr., Plut., Luc., Hdn., Pap. (but in Plat.).
ἀλάβαστρον or -ος	for the earlier ἀλάβαστος. LXX, Mk. *al.*, Luc.,[1] Plut., Inscr.
† ἀλλογενής	LXX, Joseph., Inscr. (Jewish).
ἅλων	Arist., LXX, Mt. 3, 12, Babr. (?), Pap. — [Q]
ἁμαρτωλός,	substant. Arist., LXX, Paul *al.*, Plut., Inscr. (the adj. in Ar., Arist., Plut.).
ἀμήν	LXX, Mt. *al.*
† ἀνάβλεψις	Schmid III, 231. — Arist., Demetr. *de elocut.*, LXX, Ael., Eccles. — [LXX]
† ἀνάδειξις	Diod., LXX (Ecclus. 43, 6), Strabo, Plut., Eccles.
[ἀναζάω]	Rom. 7, 9, Eccles., Artemidorus, Sotion, Nilus, Inscr. (C. I. 2566), (an epic form is quoted from Nicander).

[1] Lucian, *Dial. Mer.* 14, 2, not classified by Schmid.

ἀνάθεμα	'a curse.' LXX, Paul, Anth., Plut., Inscr.
ἀναθεματίζω	LXX, Mk. 14, 71, Inscr.
ἀναθεωρέω	Schmid I, 353 *al.* — Theophr., Diod., Heb. 13, 7, Luc., Philostr., Plut.
ἀναλύω	intransitive. Schmid IV, 340. — Polyb., LXX (2 Macc. 8, 25 *al.*), Diod., Phil. 1, 23, Luc., Ael., Philostr., Pap.
† ἀναντίρ(ρ)ητος	Polyb., Joseph., Plut., Symm.
† ἀναντιρ(ρ)ήτως	Polyb., Inscr. (OGIS. 335, 138, ii B.C.), Diod., Pollux, Hesych.
ἀναπίπτω	'*accumbo.*' Schmid I, 354. — Alexis, LXX, Diod., Jn., Rev., Joseph., Luc., Pap.
ἀναστατόω	LXX, Gal. 5, 12, Justin, Pap.
ἀνατίθημι	'set forth, declare' (mid.). LXX (2 Macc. 3, 9), Gal. 2, 2, Artemidor., Plut., Pap (?).
† ἀναφωνέω	Schmid I, 354. — Arist., Polyb., LXX, Arr., Luc., Plut., Pap.
ἀνεκτός	without a preceding negative. Schmid I, 354. — "im älteren Griechisch nicht gebräuchlich." Thuc., Dem., Ar., LXX, Mt., Luc., Philostr., Inscr. — [Q]
† ἀνένδεκτος	Artemidorus, Eccles., Diog. Laert.
† ἀνετάζω	LXX (Judges 6, 29 A), Theodotion (Susanna 14), Justin, Anaphora Pilati, Pap. (OP 34, i, 13, 127 A.D.)
† ἀνεύθετος	Moschion.
† ἀνθομολογέομαι	'give thanks.' LXX, Test. XII Patr., ('agree,' Dem., Polyb., Plut., Pap.).
(†) ἀνταπόδομα	LXX, Rom. 11, 9 (LXX), Barnab., Didache.
ἀνταποκρίνομαι	Nicomachus Math., Philo, LXX, Rom. 9, 20, Schol. Pind., Schol. Hom., Justin.
† ἄντικρυς	Hellenistic equivalent for ἀντικρύ in Hom., καταντικρύ in Att. Prep., 'opposite.' Philo, Pap., LXX (3 Macc. 5, 16).
† ἀντιμετρέω	Luc.,[1] Eccles. (cf. ἀντικαταμετρέω TbP.)
† ἀντιπαρέρχομαι	Anth., LXX (Wisd. 16, 10), Galen, Eccles.

[1] Schmid does not classify. Lucian, *Amor.* 19.

† ἀντιπίπτω — Schmid II, 215. — Arist., Theophr., Polyb., LXX, Strabo., Aristides, Plut., M. Anton., Pap. (LP, D, 21, ii B.C.).

† ἀντοφθαλμέω — Polyb., Diod., LXX (Wisd. 12, 14), Clem. Rom., Barnab., Apoc. Baruch, Pap.

ἀνώτερον — adv., cf. Schmid III, 102. — Arist., Polyb., Ael., Diod., LXX, Joseph., Heb. 10, 8, Xen. Ephes., Inscr.

ἀπάντησις — Polyb., Diod., LXX., Aristeas, Mt., 1 Thess. 4, 17, Plut., Diog. Laert., Pap.

† ἀπαρτισμός — Herondas, Dion. Hal., Apollon. Dysc., Pap.

† ἀπασπάζομαι — LXX (Tob. 10, 12 א), Himer.

† ἀπειλέομαι (= ἀπειλέω) — Dion. Hal., App., Polyaen., Clem. Alex. (the active in 1 Pet. 2, 23).[1]

† ἀπελπίζω — Schmid I, 156. — Epicur., Anth., Polyb., Diod., LXX, Joseph., Dio Chrys., Plut., M. Anton., Alciphr., Inscr.

ἀπέναντι — cf. Schmid II, 176. — Polyb., LXX, Mt., Inscr., Pap.

† ἀπεριτμητός — 'uncircumcised.' LXX, Philo, Joseph. (in a different sense, Plut.)

ἀποδεκατόω — LXX, Mt. 23, 23, Heb. 7, 5. — [Q]

† ἀποθλίβω — Schmid IV, 342. — Theophr., Diphil., Diod., LXX, Joseph., Luc., Philostr., Alciphr., Pap.

ἀποκάλυψις — LXX, Paul (Nägeli, p. 43) *al.*, Plut.

† ἀποκατάστασις — Arist., Epicur., Polyb., Diod., Joseph., Aristeas, Aretaeus, Plut., Galen, Inscr., Pap. (Liddell and Scott cite [Plat.] *Axioch.* 370 B.)

ἀποκεφαλίζω — LXX, Mt., Mk., Arr., Artemidorus, Dio Cass. — [Mk]

ἀποκυλίω — LXX, Mt. 28, 2 = Mk. 16, 3, Joseph., Luc.,[2] Diod. — [Mk]

ἀποστασία — Diod., Archimedes, LXX, Joseph., 2 Thess. 2, 3 (Nägeli, p. 31), Plut., Justin.

ἀποστολή — 'apostleship.' Paul, Eccles. (in other senses in Thuc., Plat., Polyb., LXX, Plut., Pap.).

[1] Thackeray, *Grammar*, I, 260 cites cases from MSS. of LXX.

[2] Schmid (I. 380) classes as first used by Lucian.

ἀποτάσσομαι	'say farewell.' LXX, Philo, Joseph., Mk., 2 Cor. 2, 13, Aesop, Liban., Jambl., Pap.
† ἀποφορτίζομαι	Philo, Joseph., Athen., Cyril. (cf. εκφορτιζω, OP, 36, ii, 7, 9; ii–iii A. D.).
ἀπρόσκοπος	LXX (Apocr.), Paul (Nägeli, p. 43), Aristeas, Sext. Emp., Clem. Alex., Pap. (cf. απροσκοπτος, Inscr.).
ἀπωλεία	Schmid III, 233 *al.* — Arist., Polyb., LXX, Mt., Paul (Nägeli, p. 35) *al.*, Arr., Luc., Ael., Philostr., Plut., Alciphr., Diog. Laert., Pap.
ἀροτριάω	Callim., Theophr., LXX, 1 Cor. 9, 10 (Nägeli, p. 31), Dio Chrys., Luc.,[1] Babr., Pap.
† ἀρχιερατικός	Joseph., Justin, Inscr. (CIG. 4363). ('episcopal,' Eccles.)
ἀρχισυνάγωγος	Mk., Inscr. (Jewish), Pap. (gentile; see *Archiv*, II, 430).
ἀσσάριον	Anth., Dion. Hal., Plut., Mt. 10, 29, Inscr. — [Q]
† ἀσύμφωνος	'at variance.' Schmid I, 356. — Theophr., Diod., LXX (Wisd. 18, 10), Joseph., Arr., Luc., Plut., Vett. Val. (in diff. sense, Plat.).
ἀσφαλίζω	Polyb., Diod., LXX, Joseph., Mt., Inscr., Pap.
ἀτενίζω	Schmid I, 356 *al.* — Hipp., Arist., Polyb., Diod., LXX (Apocr.), Joseph., Paul (Nägeli, p. 23), Luc., Philostr., Plut., Pap., Arist., and later writers.
αὐξάνω,	intransitive. Schmid I, 156.—Arist. and later writers, Aristeas, Mt., Paul *al.*
ἀφορίζω	'choose, appoint.' Arist., Diod., Dio Cass., LXX, Paul (Nägeli, p. 35) *al.*, Pap. ('define,' Att.)
† ἀφυπνόω	'fall asleep.' Hermas *al.* ('awaken,' Anth.)
βάπτισμα	Mt., Mk., Paul *al.*, Eccles.
βαπτιστής	Joseph., Mt., Mk., Justin *al.*
† βάτος,	the Hebrew measure (also spelled βαδος), LXX (2 Esd. 7, 22 A), Enoch, Joseph.

[1] *Philopatr.* Schmid does not classify, as the piece is probably not genuine. See I, 225.

βδέλυγμα — LXX, Mt. 24, 15 = Mk. 13, 14, Rev., Eccles.

βεβηλόω — LXX, Mt. 12, 5, Heliod., Pss. Sol., Hermas, Justin.

† βίωσις — LXX (Ecclus. Prol.). [Justin] *Quaest. ad Orth.* 124.

βιωτικός — Arist., Polyb., Diod., Philo, Paul (Nägeli, pp. 31 f.), Strabo, Arr., Plut., M. Anton., Pap.

βλασφημέω — with acc. of pers. LXX, Paul (Nägeli, p. 44), Joseph., App., Plut., M. Anton., Babr.

† βραδυπλοέω — Artemid. *Oneir.* 4, 30.

βυθίζω — Schmid IV, 344 f. — Arist., Polyb., LXX (2 Macc. 12, 4), 1 Tim. 6, 9 (Nägeli, p. 32), Dio Chrys., Philostr., Arr., Luc., Alciphr. (cf. Syll. 324, 7, καταβυθίζω).

† βυρσεύς — Artemid. *Oneir.*, Inscr. (CIG 3499), Pap. (FP 121, 15, *c.* 100 A.D.)

† γάζα — Theophr., Polyb., Diod., LXX, Plut., Inscr.

γαζοφυλάκιον — LXX, Joseph., Mk., Jn. 8, 20, Strabo, Inscr. — [Mk]

γαμίζω — Mt., Mk., Paul (Nägeli, p. 44), Apollon. *De Constr.*—[Mk. or Q]

† γαμίσκομαι — Arist., Callicratidas.

γέεννα — Mt., Mk., Orac. Sibyll., Justin *al.* — [Q]

† γνώστης — LXX, Plut.

γογγύζω — Schmid I, 357. — LXX, Mt. 20, 11, Jn., Paul, Arr., Luc., M. Anton., Pollux, Pap.

γρηγορέω — Arist., LXX, Joseph., Mt., Mk., Paul (Nägeli, p. 44) *al.*, Achil. Tat., Inscr.

† δεισιδαιμονία — Schmid I, 357.[1] — Theophr., Polyb., Diod., Joseph., Luc., Plut., M. Anton., Inscr.

† δεκαοκτώ — Schmid IV, 701. — Strabo, LXX, Inscr., Pap.

δεκαπέντε — Schmid IV, 24. — Polyb., Diod., LXX, Gal. 1, 18, Jn. 11, 18, Strabo, Plut., Inscr., Pap.

δεκτός — LXX, Paul, Alciphr., Hermas, Justin.

† δεσμοφύλαξ — Schmid I, 357.— Joseph., Luc., Artemid., Test. XII Patr., Pap.

[1] Schmid marks "not in New Testament," by mistake.

δηνάριον	Mt., Mk., Jn., Rev., Arr., Plut., Pap.
διαβλέπω	Schmid I, 357.[1] — Arist., Mt. 7, 5, Mk. 8, 25, Luc., Philostr., Plut., M. Anton. — [Q]
διάβολος	'devil.' Mt. *al.*, Eccles. ('adversary,' or 'slanderous,' Xen., Andocid., Eur., Arist., LXX, Past. Epp., Plut.)
† διαγογγύζω	LXX, Clem. Alex., Heliod.
† διαγρηγορέω	Hdn., Nilus.
διαθήκη	'covenant.' LXX, Mt., Paul *al.*, also once in Ar. (*Birds* 439). ('testament,' Att., Paul, Heb., Pap.)
διακρίνομαι	'doubt.' Mt. 21, 21 = Mk. 11, 23, Jas. 1, 6.
διαλογισμός	'thought.' Dion. Hal., LXX, Paul (Nägeli, p. 32) *al.*, Plut.
† διανοίγω	'explain.' Dion. Hal., Themist. Cf. LXX (2 Macc. 1, 4).
† διαπονέομαι	'be troubled.' LXX, Joseph., Aquila, Hesych., Pap.
διασκορπίζω	Schmid III, 236. — Polyb., LXX, Joseph., Mt. *al.*, Ael. (cf. διασκορπισμος, TbP 24, 55).
διαστέλλομαι	'command.' Arist., LXX, Mk., Pap., (active, 'define,' Schmid I, 300; Plat. Polyb., Luc., Diod., Strabo, Plut., Pap.).
διαταγή	LXX (2 Esd. 4, 11), Philo, Rom. 13, 2, Clem. Rom., Justin, Inscr., Pap.
† διαχειρίζομαι	'slay.' Polyb., Diod., Dion. Hal., Joseph., Plut., Hdn. (active, 'manage,' Schmid I, 115 *al.*; Att., Pap.)
διεγείρω	Schmid III, 236. — Hipp., Arist., Anth., LXX, Joseph., Mk. 4, 39, Jn. *al.*, Arr., Ael., Plut., Hdn. *al.*, Pap. (magic). — [Mk]
διερμηνεύω	'translate.' Polyb., LXX (2 Macc. 1, 36), Aristeas. 'explain,' Philo, Paul (Nägeli, p. 32).
† διετία	Philo, Inscr., Pap.
† διθάλασσος	Dio Chrys.,[2] Clem. Hom. (in a different sense, Strabo, Dion. Perieg.)

[1] Cf. Schmid, IV, 345: "vor Arist. hat das Wort, aber in anderem Sinn, nur Plat. *Phaed.* 86 D."

[2] Schmid fails to classify.

† διοδεύω	Schmid I, 358.—Arist., Polyb., LXX, Joseph., Anth., Arr., Luc., Plut., Inscr., Pap.
δόμα [1]	LXX, Aristeas, Jos., Paul, Mt. 7, 11, Plut. —[Q]
δόξα	'glory.' LXX, N. T., Eccles.
δοξάζω	'clothe with splendor.' Polyb., LXX, Paul *al.*
(†) δυσβάστακτος [2]	LXX, Philo, Plut., Cyril., John Chrys.
† δωδεκάφυλον	Clem. Rom., Prot. Jac. (the adj. in Orac. Sibyll. ii, 171 *v. l.*).
ἐγγίζω	intransitive. Schmid I, 158.—Arist., Polyb., Diod., LXX, Paul (Nägeli, p. 36) *al.*, Arr., Dio Chrys., Pap.
ἐγκακέω	Polyb., Symm., Philo, Paul (Nägeli, p. 32), [Clem. Rom.], Euseb., Pap. (BU 1043, iii A.D.).
ἐγκόπτω	'hinder.' Polyb., Paul, 1 Pet. 3, 7. (in other senses, Hipp., Theophr.).
† ἐδαφίζω	'raze.' LXX, Eccles. ('pave,' Arist., Polyb.). —[LXX]
τὰ ἔθνη	'Gentiles.' LXX, Paul (Nägeli, p. 46) *al.* (for a similar use in profane writers, see Schmid II, 217, and cf. CIA, II, 445 ff).
εἰδωλόθυτος	LXX (4 Macc. 5, 2), Paul, Rev., Didache *al.*
ἐκδικέω	Apollod., Diod., Paul, Rev., Athen., LXX, Plut., Inscr., Pap.
ἐκδίκησις	Polyb., LXX, Test. XII Patr., Paul (Nägeli, p. 33) *al.*, Inscr.
ἐκζητέω	Schmid II, 217 *al.*—LXX, Aristeas, Heb. *al.*, Aristides, Ael.
† ἔκθαμβος	Polyb., Theodot., Symm., Hermas *al.*
ἐκκλησία	'church.' Mt., Paul *al.* (cf. LXX).
ἐκμάσσω	Schmid I, 359.—Hipp., Trag., Ar., Arist., LXX, Jn., Luc., Plut., Philostr.
† ἐκμυκτηρίζω	LXX, Evangg. Apocr.
ἐκπειράζω	LXX, Philo, Mt. 4, 7 (from Q), 1 Cor. 10, 9.
† ἐκπλήρωσις	Dion. Hal., LXX (2 Macc. 6, 14), Philo, Strabo, Dioscor., Arr.

[1] [Plat.] *Def.* 415B is not of early date. [2] Also Mt. 23, 4 according to text. rec.

ἐκριζόω	LXX, Sibyll. frag., Test. XII Patr., Mt., Jude 12, Babr.
ἔκστασις	'wonder.' LXX, Philo, Mk., Longinus, Stob.
† ἐκτένεια	Cicero, LXX (Apoc.), Joseph., Athen., Inscr. (IMA. 1032, 10).
ἐκχύννομαι	Schmid I, 359. — LXX, Mt. *al.*, Luc.
ἐλαία	for ἐλάα. Schmid I, 360 *al.* — LXX, N. T., Luc. *al.*, Pap. (also in MSS. of Xen. and Lys.).
† ἐλαιών	LXX, Joseph., Pap.
ἐλεημοσύνη	'alms,' Mt., Diog. Laert. ('mercy,' Callim., LXX).
† ἔλευσις	Dion. Hal., Clem. Rom., Polycarp, Iren., Pap.
† ἐμμαίνομαι	Joseph. *Antt.* xvii, 6, 5.
ἔμφοβος	'frightened.' Theophr., LXX (Apocr.), Rev. 11, 13. ('inspiring fear,' Schmid IV, 291; Soph., Philostr.).
† ἔναντι	LXX, Pap. (OP. 495, 5, ii A. D.), Inscr. (Syll. 300, 52, ii B.C.).
(†) ἐνδιδύσκω	LXX, Joseph., Mk. 15, 17 *v. l.*, Hermas, Inscr. (Syll. 857, 13, ii B.C.).
ἔνδυμα	LXX, Menand., Joseph., Mt., Strabo, Plut., Alciphr., Pap. (FP. 12, 20; LipsP 34). — [Q]
ἐνδυναμόω	LXX, Paul, Past. Epp., Hermas, Justin *al.*
† ἐνισχύω	intransitive. Arist., Theophr., Diod., Diosc., LXX, Joseph., Arr.
(†) ἔντρομος [1]	LXX, Plut., Anth., Justin.
ἐνώπιον	LXX, Paul, Rev. *al.*, Enoch, Inscr., Pap.
† ἐνωτίζομαι	LXX, Test. XII Patr., Eccles.
ἐξαποστέλλω	Polyb., Diod., LXX, Joseph., Paul, Apollon. Perg., Pap. (TbP 22, 18, ii B.C.)
ἐξαρτίζω	Schmid I, 361. — Joseph., 2 Tim. 3, 17, Arr., Luc., Pap.
† ἐξαστράπτω	LXX, Tryphiodorus.
ἔξοδος	'decease.' LXX (Wisd.), Philo, Joseph., 2 Pet. 1, 15, Justin *Dial.* 105.
† ἐξολεθρεύομαι	LXX, Test. XII Patr., Joseph., Plut. — [LXX]
ἐξομολογέομαι	Schmid I, 361. — LXX, Philo, Joseph.. Mt.,

[1] Occurs also in Heb. 12, 21, with *v.l.* ἔκτρομος.

Mk. 1, 5, Paul, Jas. 5, 16, Luc., Plut., Pap.

† ἐξορκιστής — Schmid I, 383.[1] — Joseph., Luc., Anth., Eccles.

ἐξουθενέω — LXX, Paul, Eccles. (cf. ἐξουδενέω, -όω Mk. 9, 12 *v. l.*, LXX).

ἐξουσιάζω — Arist., LXX, Dion. Hal., Paul, Inscr. (CIA. 4584).

† ἐξοχή — metaphorically. Cicero, Joseph., Strabo. (literal, Schmid I, 158 *al.*; Arist., Diosc., Dio Chrys., Ael., Babr., Sext. Emp., LXX).

† ἔξυπνος — LXX (1 Esd. 3, 3), Joseph., Test. XII Patr.

† ἐπαθροίζω — Plut.

ἐπαναπαύω — LXX, Rom. 2, 17, Ael.,[2] Arr., Hdn., Artemid., Barnab., Didache.

† ἐπαρχεία — Schmid I, 361. — Polyb., Diod., LXX, Joseph., Arr., Luc., Plut., Dio Chrys., Inscr., Pap.

ἐπαύριον — Polyb., LXX., Mt. 27, 62, Mk. 11, 12, Jn., Pap.

ἐπίθεσις — 'putting on.' Arist., LXX, Aristeas, Heb. 6, 2 *al.*, Plut., Inscr. ('attack,' Plat. *al.* Diod., Dion. Hal., Aristeas, Inscr., Pap. (TbP 15).

ἐπιούσιος — Mt. 6, 11. — [Q]

† ἐπιπορεύομαι — Polyb., LXX, Joseph., Plut., Pap.

ἐπισκοπή — in various senses. LXX, 1 Pet. 2, 12; 1 Tim. 3, 1, Luc.[3] (cf. επισκοπεια TbP 5, 189, 118 B.C.).

† ἐπίστασις[4] — 'attack,' LXX (2 Macc. 6, 3). ('care,' Schmid I, 362; Polyb., Diod., Luc., Pap.).

† ἐπιστηρίζω — Schmid I, 362 *al.* — Arist., LXX, Luc., Philostr.

† ἐπιστροφή — 'conversion.' LXX (Ecclus. 18, 21; 49, 2). In other senses Thuc., Joseph., LXX, Arr., Philostr., M. Anton., Pap.

ἐπισυνάγω — Polyb., LXX, Aristeas, Mt., Mk., Plut., Vett. Val., Pap. (GH 72, iii A. D.).

† ἐπισχύω — intrans. Theophr., Diod., LXX (1 Macc. 6, 6 A), (transit., Xen., Ecclus. 29, 1).

[1] Schmid classes as among the words used first or only by Lucian in List E.

[2] Schmid does not classify.

[3] *Dial. deor.* 20, 6, the only occurrence of the word noted in profane authors; but Schmid does not mention it in his word lists.

[4] The word occurs also in 2 Cor. 11, 28, possibly in this sense.

ἐπιφώσκω	LXX, Mt. 28, 1 (the parallel passage), Inscr. (CI. 9119), Pap. (BM. I p. 132, a horoscope dated 81 A. D.; GH 112, 15, Christian).
ἐρήμωσις	LXX, Mt. 24, 15 = Mk. 13, 14, Arr., Greg. Nyss. — [Mk]
† ἔσθησις	Arist., LXX (2 Macc. 3, 33), Philo, Pollux, Athen., Pap. (BU 16 R, 12, ii A.D.).
ἐσώτερος	Symm., Heb. 6, 19, Pap.
εὐαγγελίζομαι	with acc. pers. Paul *al.*, Justin, Euseb., Heliod., Alciphr.[1]
εὐαγγέλιον	'good news.' Schmid I, 363.—Menand., LXX, Mt., Mk., Paul, 1 Pet. 4, 17, Rev. 14, 6, App., Luc., Plut., Inscr.
εὐαγγελιστής	Eph. 4, 11; 2 Tim. 4, 5, Eccles.
εὐδοκέω	Polyb., Diod., Dion. Hal., LXX, N. T. (except Johannine writings), Pap.
εὐδοκία	LXX, Mt. 11, 26, Paul, Inscr. (CI. 5960).
† εὐθυδρομέω	Philo.
εὐκαιρέω	Schmid I, 363. — Polyb., Mk. 6, 31; 1 Cor. 16, 12, Diod., Plut., Luc., Cleom., Pap.
εὔκοπος	Polyb., LXX (Apocr.), Aristeas, Mt., Mk., Joseph., Anth. — [Mk, Q]
εὐλογητός	LXX, Philo, Pss. Sol., Mk. 14, 61, Paul, 1 Pet. 1, 3.
† εὐπορέομαι	Schmid I, 363. — Arist., LXX, Joseph., Luc. (the active is Attic).
εὐσχήμων	'wealthy,' 'prominent.' Mk. 15, 43, Joseph., Plut., Pap. ('comely,' Att. prose and poetry, LXX, Paul[2]).
† εὐφορέω	'be fruitful.' Schmid IV, 358.— Hipp., Joseph., Philostr., Geopon., Galen, Greg. Nyss. ('sail well,' Luc.)
εὐχαριστέω	'give thanks.' Schmid I, 159.—Polyb., Posidon., Diod., LXX, Philo, Joseph., Aristeas, Paul, Arr., Dio Chrys., Luc., Plut., Inscr., Pap.

[1] *Epist.* ii, 9 [iii, 12], 2 (codd., not in editions).

[2] 1 Cor. 7, 35; 12, 24. Schmid (II, 113) overlooks these instances in the New Testament.

εὐχαριστία	Polyb., Diod., LXX (Apocr.), Com., Philo, Paul *al.*
† ἐφημερία	LXX (cf. ἐφήμερις in Philo, Joseph., Pap.).

E. Expressions used first or only by Luke

† [ἀγαθουργέω]	Eccles. (cf. 1 Tim. 6, 18, ἀγαθοεργέω).
† αἰτίωμα	Pap. (FP 111, 8, 95–6 A.D.)
† ἀκατάκριτος	
† ἀλίσγημα	(cf. ἀλισγέω, LXX).
† ἀνατάσσομαι	'set in order.' (in other senses, Aristeas, Dio Cass., Plut., Iren.)
† ἀπελεγμός	
† [ἀποδεκατεύω][1]	
† ἀποστοματίζω	'urge to speak.'
† ἀρτέμων [2]	
† ἀρχιτελώνης	
† ἀφελότης	Vett. Val., Eccles.
† ἄφιξις	'departure.'[3] ('arrival,' 'journey,' Xen., Dem., LXX (3 Macc. 7, 18), Aristeas, Dion. Hal., Joseph., Luc., Tatian, Pap.)
† βλητέον [4]	Basil.
† βολίζω	Eustath., Geopon.
† δεξιολάβος	Byzantine writers.
† διακατελέγχομαι	
† διαπρίομαι	'be enraged.' Euseb. (in other senses, Plat., Hipp., Ar., LXX).
† διενθυμέομαι	Eccles.
† δυσεντέριον	Moeris.

[1] Lk. 18, 12 א* B; cf. ἀποδεκατόω above, p. 27. The Attic form of the simple verb is δεκατεύω.

[2] The Latin form is used in Vitruv. 10, 5, as 'pulley,' and as a nautical term (probably 'foresail') by other writers, e. g., Javolenus, *Dig.* 50, 16, 242, Schol. on Juvenal, *Sat.* 12, 69, and (restored by editors) in Sen., *Contr.* 7, 1, 2; Statius, *Silv.* 3, 2 30. Whether originally Latin or Greek the word was taken by Luke from current usage.

[3] But the meaning 'departure' is often possible in earlier occurrences, and in Joseph. *Antt.* ii, 2, 4; Diod. 13, 112 is perhaps probable.

[4] Also Mark 2, 22 according to text. rec.

† ἐξομολογέω [1] ‘promise, agree.’
† ἐπιλείχω Longus (*v. l.*).
† [εὐρακύλων]

As analysed by these lists the part of Luke's vocabulary taken as significant for the purposes of the present investigation divides itself in the following proportions:

A.	Common Attic words or words affected by the Atticists	137
B.	Words used chiefly by one of the ancient writers	27
C.	Words found first or chiefly in poetry	87
D.	Words belonging to the post-classical prose, including Aristotle	202
E.	Words first used by Luke	22

These figures may be compared with those of Schmid by means of the following tables. Table I shows the number of words in each of the above classes for the several authors. Table II affords a better means of comparison by giving the same facts reduced to percentages, 100 per cent in each case being the total number of words in the writer's vocabulary that are considered significant, *i. e.* not of common occurrence in all grades and all ages of ancient Greek writing.

TABLE I

Class	Dio Chrysostom	Lucian	Aristides (Schmid, II, 244)	Aelian (Schmid, III, 272)	Philostratus II (Schmid, IV, 428)	Luke and Acts
A	364	1825	805	673	1498	137
B	98	619	162	246	326	27
C	117	1736	350	861	1216	87
D	164	1300	143	575	728	202
E	26	891	101	319	757	22
Total	769	6371	1561	2674	4525	475

[1] Ebeling finds a parallel in TbP 183, ii B. C.

TABLE II

Class	Dio Chrysostom	Lucian	Aristides	Aelian	Philostratus II	Luke and Acts
A	47%	29%	52%	25%	33%	29%
B	13	10	10	9	7	6
C	16	27	23	32	27	18
D	21	20	9	23	16	42
E	3	14	6	11	17	5
Total	100%	100%	100%	100%	100%	100%

The result at first sight is quite as would be expected. Every element of a Hellenistic vocabulary appears in Luke, but the post-classical element is considerably larger than in any of the Atticists which Schmid studies.

There are, however, some considerations that make the difference between Luke and the Atticists really less than appears. For on examining the list of post-classical words we notice:

1. There are a number of words found in it which occur in Luke only in passages derived from the LXX, Mark, or Q. It is true that these words are part of his vocabulary, but in view of their obvious origin, especially those in formal quotations from the Old Testament, it would perhaps be fairer to leave them out of consideration.

2. A number of the words in this list are found before 200 A.D. only in Jewish and Christian writers, and may therefore be considered part of a special local or technical vocabulary of Jewish Christian writers rather than a really typical part of Luke's normal Greek style. Some of them are plainly Jewish Greek terms as *τὰ ἄζυμα, ἀμήν, ἀπερίτμητος*. They also may be subtracted or at least discounted in considering Luke's Greek vocabulary. Schmid himself affords some precedent for omitting such words from list D or transferring them to E.[1] In fact his whole attitude towards the New Testament — treating its vocabulary as a test of the un-Attic

[1] For example, from the vocabulary of Lucian, which is the most fully treated of all (I, 400), Schmid omits entirely

ἀντιμετρέω .... New Testament.
ἐπισκοπή .... LXX, New Testament.
πλάξ .... LXX.

and vulgar,[1] indicates that the margin of error is likely to be on the side of underrating the classical element in its writers.

But the significant fact about the comparisons is that, in spite of this large dilution of Luke's vocabulary with post-classical words, it includes also a large number of Attic words — a number quite as large in proportion as the same element in at least two of Schmid's authors, Lucian and Aelian.

Of course too much confidence must not be placed upon these numerical comparisons of vocabulary. The great variety exhibited by the proportions in the vocabularies of the five authors studied by Schmid warns us against making too much of slight differences of proportion. Apparently the Atticists themselves gathered their vocabulary from the different sources in very different ways.

The value of the study of Luke's vocabulary which we have been here undertaking seems rather to lie, first, in the endeavor to select from it those words which may be looked on as significant, and, second, in arranging those words so as to show the different elements in Luke's vocabulary. Besides, it makes possible a safe comparison of Luke's vocabulary with that of various other writers. While the results of such a comparison can not be stated more definitely than the general impressions of every reader of Luke's work, they are at least better founded. And in particular it justifies itself by showing that the vocabulary of Luke, while it has its natural affiliations with the Greek of the Bible, is not so far removed from the literary style of the Atticists as to be beyond comparison with them.

The question may be pertinently asked whether the gulf between New Testament Greek in general and Attic or Atticistic Greek is not

while he lists among the words first used by Lucian

ἀποκυλίω .... LXX, New Testament, Josephus.
ἀμετανόητος .... New Testament, Philo.
ἐξορκιστής .... New Testament, Josephus.

Note also his omission of these rare words:

διθάλασσος .... New Testament, Strabo, Dio Chrys.
ἐπαναπαύω .... LXX, New Testament, Aelian.

[1] This is shown by his use of a special sign (†) throughout his lists for words absent from New Testament Greek, and by his omitting altogether from his summaries of lists A, B, and C, in IV, 635–679, words occurring in the New Testament.

being exaggerated in our day owing to our fresh knowledge of the vernacular Greek through the papyri. If so, the exaggeration is probably due to two factors, namely, the overrating of the purely imitative and classical element in the so-called Atticists, and the underrating of the literary element in the vocabulary of the New Testament writers. I am inclined to revolt slightly also from the extreme view of Deissmann and Moulton, who minimize the Semitic or Biblical or Jewish element in the New Testament and ascribe such phenomena to the vernacular Greek of the time. I have already indicated that much of Luke's post-classical vocabulary appears to be due to a distinctly Jewish-Christian language. This is probably even more true of his post-classical syntax. And still more allowance must be made if it is assumed that in some parts of his work he consciously imitates the LXX or Mark.

3. THE ALLEGED MEDICAL LANGUAGE OF LUKE*

In the year 1882, W. K. Hobart published under the title "The Medical Language of St. Luke," an elaborate investigation into the vocabulary of Luke, aiming to show, mainly by quoting parallels from medical writers, that the language of the third Evangelist has a distinctly medical tinge. Some attempts in the same direction had been made before Hobart,[1] though he was acquainted with only one, an article that appeared in the *Gentleman's Magazine* for June, 1841. To the large mass of material which Hobart collected no additions seem to have been made since,[2] though Zahn and Harnack [3] have greatly strengthened the argument by selecting from Hobart only the most convincing examples.

Hobart summarizes his argument as follows:

"We have in the account of the miracles of healing, or their opposites, in the third Gospel and the Acts of the Apostles, medical language employed.

"In the general narrative, outside of medical subjects, we find, wherever we have an opportunity of comparing it with the other New Testament writers, that Luke strongly inclines to the use of medical language.

* For the Notes on this Chapter see below, pp. 51 ff.

"Even where in the general narrative a comparison cannot be instituted with other New Testament writers, we find words occurring uniformly throughout which were in use in medical phraseology, and which from habit and training a physician would be likely to employ.

"In estimating the weight of the argument it should be remembered that the evidence is *cumulative*, and that the words adduced as examples are very numerous, considering the extent of St. Luke's writings." [4]

The evidence of Hobart and the thesis for which it was compiled seem to have been very widely accepted by New Testament scholars. Of recent English writers alone who accept this argument (with more or less caution) the following may be mentioned: Plummer,[5] Hawkins,[6] Knowling,[7] Ramsay,[8] Chase,[9] Peake,[10] Stanton,[11] Moffatt.[12] Among German scholars Zahn and Harnack [13] have become the active champions of the theory, and now Harnack [14] claims even P. W. Schmidt and Clemen as converts, though their conversion is apparently hardly complete. The former considers that "a good acquaintance with medical art and terminology is the most that can be asserted of 'Luke.'" [15] The latter limits medical characteristics to the "We" sections.[16]

The arguments of Hobart need testing. A careful examination of them was recommended some years ago by Johannes Weiss,[17] but has not been forthcoming. Some writers treat Hobart's work with respectful attention, others with contempt.[18] A few protests have been raised against it,[19] but apparently none by English or American scholars. What is needed is a complete consideration of all the factors involved. This may be a thankless task, but in view of the importance attached to the argument from the alleged medical language in upholding the traditional authorship of Luke and Acts it is a necessary one.

A great deal of the material so assiduously collected by Hobart has of itself no independent value. There are many words so common in all kinds of Greek that their appearance in Luke and Acts and in the medical writers is inevitable, e.g., *ἀναιρεῖν*, *ἀπαιτεῖν*, *ἀπορεῖν*, *ἀσφαλής*, *βία*, and the like. Hobart attributes Luke's use of *σύν* to the fact that "in his professional practice, St. Luke would have been in the constant habit of employing this word, as it was almost always used in the formula of a prescription, etc., and thus became an almost indispensable word to a physician."[20]

Plummer has pointed out that of Hobart's long list of words:

"More than eighty per cent are found in LXX, mostly in books known to St. Luke, and sometimes occurring very frequently in them. In all such cases it is more reasonable to suppose that Luke's use of the word is due to his knowledge of LXX, rather than to his professional training. . . . If the expression is also found in profane authors, the chances that medical training had anything to do with Luke's use of it become very remote. It is unreasonable to class as in any sense medical such words as *ἀθροίζειν*, *ἀκοή*, *ἀναιρεῖν*, *ἀναλαμβάνειν*, *ἀνορθοῦν*, *ἀπαιτεῖν*, *ἀπαλλάσσειν*, *ἀπολύειν*, *ἀπορεῖν*, *ἀσφάλεια*, *ἄφεσις*, etc., etc. All of these are frequent in LXX, and some of them in profane authors also."[21]

The figures for Josephus are no lower. From Krenkel's lists[22] it appears that of the 400 words in Hobart's index about 300 occur in both LXX and Josephus, 27 in LXX but not in Josephus, while 67 are in Josephus but not in LXX.[23] So that Josephus, who as a single author makes a fair parallel to Luke, uses ninety per cent of the "medical words" listed by Hobart. A comparison of Hobart's list with the lexica of two profane authors of the same period, Plutarch and Lucian,[24] shows that over ninety per cent of the list is found in one or both of these two authors. Of the remaining thirty or forty words few seem to have any strikingly medical signification in Luke. It is clear, therefore, that Hobart's list contains very much that is without significance, many of his words being common words without any special medical use. While he shows most diligently that the words he catalogues are employed by the medical writers, he does *not* show that they are *not* employed by other writers with no professional training. Even those who accept his argument realize this. "He has proved only too much," says Harnack.[25]

Yet it is frequently argued that even when the worthless examples are subtracted from Hobart's list the residue is still quite sufficient to prove his point, that when the material is thoroughly sifted, as Weiss recommended, cogent proofs will still remain. For this reason Zahn and Harnack have selected the most striking examples, and it will evidently be more just for us to confine our argument to their selections. For further examination we shall divide their examples into four general groups:

A. General words
B. Medical words
C. Ordinary words used in a medical sense
D. Longer expressions

In the following lists " H " means that the example is cited by Harnack, " Z " that it is cited by Zahn. Since most of this chapter was written, a similar list of selections has appeared in Moffatt's *Introduction to the Literature of the New Testament* (1911). Many of them are coincident with the selections of Harnack and Zahn, the others are generally less convincing.[26] Some of them are referred to incidentally throughout this chapter and in the Excursus appended to it by the letter "M."

In these lists the occurrence of words in Lucian, Plutarch, Josephus, and LXX is noted, but the citations from Josephus are not exhaustive as there is no complete lexicon of his works. A few other notes are appended to the words and expressions in all the lists. A complete account of the occurrences of these terms in non-medical writers would occupy a great deal of space.

A. General Words

[ἀγωνία] (HZ)	LXX, Joseph., Plut., Luc.
ἀνακαθίζω [27] (HM)	Plut.
ἀνάψυξις (HMZ)	LXX.
ἀποψύχω (HMZ)	LXX, Joseph., Luc.
ἀσιτία (HMZ)	Joseph., Plut., Luc. (*Gallus* 23 *v. l.*)
ἄσιτος (HZ)	Joseph., Plut., Luc.
ἀτενίζω (Z)	LXX, Joseph., Plut., Luc.
βοήθεια (H)	LXX (freq.), Joseph., Plut., Luc.
ἐκπνέω [28] (HZ)	Joseph., Plut.
ἐκψύχω [29] (HMZ)	LXX, Plut.
ἐμπνέω (HZ)	LXX, Joseph., Plut., Luc.
ἐνοχλέω (MZ)	LXX, Joseph., Plut., Luc. (freq.)
ἐξαιφνής (Z)	LXX, Joseph., Plut.
ἐπιμελῶς (HM)	LXX, Joseph., Plut., Luc.
ζωογονέω [30] (HZ)	LXX, Plut., Luc.

ἡμιθανής [31] (HZ)	LXX (4 Macc. 4, 11)
θέρμη (HM)	LXX, Joseph., Plut., Luc.
ἰκμάς (MZ)	LXX, Joseph., Plut., Luc.
κατακλείω (Z)	LXX, Joseph., Plut., Luc.
καταψύχω (HMZ)	LXX, Joseph., Plut.
κλινάριον [32] (H)	
κλίνη (H)	LXX, Joseph., Plut., Luc.
κλινίδιον [32] (H)	Joseph., Plut. (freq.), Luc. (*Asin.* 2)
κράββατος (H)	
ὀθόνη (HZ)	Joseph., Plut., Luc.
ὀθόνιον (HZ)	LXX, Joseph., Plut., Luc.
ὀχλέω (MZ)	LXX, Joseph., Plut.
παρενοχλέω (Z)	LXX, Joseph., Plut., Luc.
πλήμμυρα (MZ)	LXX, Joseph., Plut.
πνοή (HZ)	LXX, Plut.
προσδοκάω (HMZ)	LXX, Joseph., Plut., Luc.
προσδοκία (MZ)	LXX, Joseph., Plut., Luc.
προσρήγνυμι (MZ)	Joseph.
τὰ σιτία (Z)	LXX, Joseph., Plut., Luc.
στηρίζω (H)	LXX, Plut., Luc.
συκάμινος (MZ)	LXX, Joseph. (*Antt.* viii. 7, 4 *v. l.*), Plut.
συκομορέα [33] (MZ)	
συμπίπτω (MZ)	LXX, Joseph., Plut., Luc.
τραυματίζω (Z)	LXX, Joseph., Plut., Luc.
ὑποζώννυμι (HM)	LXX, Joseph., Plut., Luc.

B. Medical Words

ἀνάπηρος (HMZ)	LXX, Joseph., Plut.
ἄτεκνος (Z)	LXX, Joseph., Plut., Luc.
δυσεντέριον [34] (Z)	
ἔγκυος (Z)	LXX, Joseph., Plut.
ἕλκος (HZ)	LXX, Plut.
ἑλκόομαι (HZ)	Plut.
ἱδρώς (Z)	LXX, Joseph., Plut., Luc.
κραιπάλη (HMZ)	Plut., Luc.
ὁλοκληρία [35] (HZ)	LXX, Plut.
παραλελυμένος (HMZ)	LXX, Joseph., Plut.
ῥῆγμα (MZ)	LXX, Joseph., Plut., Luc.

σπαργανόω (Z)	LXX, Plut.
στεῖρα (Z)	LXX, Joseph., Plut., Luc.
σφυδρόν [36] (H)	
τραῦμα (Z)	LXX, Joseph., Plut., Luc.
ὑδρωπικός (H)	Plut.
χάσμα (H)	LXX, Joseph., Plut., Luc.
χρώς (HMZ)	LXX, Joseph., Plut., Luc.

C. Ordinary Words Used in a Medical Sense

ἀδύνατος (H)	'crippled,' LXX, Plut., Luc.
ἀνακύπτω (HM)	of recovery, LXX, Joseph., Plut.
ἀνορθόω (HM)	of recovery, LXX, Luc.
ἀπαλλάσσω (MZ)	of recovery,[37] Joseph., Luc.
ἀπολύω (H)	of recovery, LXX, Joseph.
ἀποχωρέω (Z)	of recovery.
ἀρχαί = πέρατα [38] (HZ)	LXX, Plut.
ἀχλύς (HMZ)	of blindness,[39] Joseph., Plut., Luc.
βλάπτω (HMZ)	of physical injury, LXX, Joseph., Plut.
ἔκστασις (HMZ)	'fit, trance,' LXX, Plut.
ἐπιβλέπω (HMZ)	'examine,' [40] Plut.
ἐπιμελέομαι (HMZ)	of medical care, Luc.
ἐπιμέλεια (HZ)	of medical care, LXX,[41] Plut., Luc.
θηρίον = ἔχιδνα [42] (HZ)	Plut., Luc.
ἵστημι (HZ)	'stop, stanch,' [43] Plut.
καθάπτω (H)	'infect.' [44]
[καταβαίνω] (HZ)	'fall,' of liquids, LXX, Joseph.[45]
καταδέω (Z)	'bandage,' LXX (Ecclus. 27, 21), Joseph.
καταπίπτω (HMZ)	'fall,' of persons, LXX, Joseph., Luc.
ὀδυνάομαι (HZ)	of pain, LXX, Joseph., Plut., Luc.
παραχρῆμα (HZ)	of sudden change in health, Joseph.
πιμπράομαι (HMZ)	'swell,' LXX, Joseph., Plut., Luc.
ῥίπτω (HMZ)	of convulsions.
σκότος (H)	of blindness, LXX, Joseph., Plut., Luc.
συλλαμβάνω (Z)	'conceive,' LXX, Plut., Luc.
συνέχομαι (HZ)	'be afflicted with,' [46] LXX, Joseph., Plut.
συστέλλω (H)	'shroud.' [47]

D. Longer Expressions

πυρετὸς μέγας (HMZ)	
πλήρης λέπρας (HM)	
ἔχω ἐν γαστρί [48] (Z)	LXX
συλλαμβάνω ἐν γαστρί (Z)	LXX (Gen. 25, 21 *v. l.*).[49]
[θρόμβοι αἵματος] (H)	"frequent from Aesch. down."
ἐπιχέω ἔλαιον καὶ οἶνον (HZ)	(ἐπιχέω ἔλαιον, LXX, Plut.) [50]
εἰς μανίαν περιτρέπω [51] (HZ)	Luc.
καταφέρομαι ὕπνῳ, etc. (HMZ)	Joseph., Plut., Luc.
πυρετοί (HZ) (plural)	Joseph., Plut., Luc.
ἀπέπεσαν λεπίδες (HMZ)	(ἀποπίπτω, LXX, Joseph., Plut., Luc.) (λεπίς, LXX, Joseph., Plut.)
ἄσιτοι διατελεῖτε [52] (HMZ)	
τρῆμα βελόνης [53] (HMZ)	(τρῆμα, Polyb., Joseph., Plut.) (βελόνη, Plut., Luc.)
οὐδὲν ἄτοπον, τί ἄτοπον (HZ)	LXX, Joseph., Plut.
ἀναδίδωμι ἐπιστολήν (MZ)	
οὐκ ἄσημος πόλις (HMZ)	

In reviewing these lists anyone familiar with the common vocabulary of Hellenistic Greek will easily see that there are few words in them that are of unusual occurrence. The notes indicate that for several of these even the medical writers do not offer satisfactory parallels. List B can not be given too much weight, as it is natural that any writer's description of purely medical matters should find parallels in the books of medicine. And if there is any argument from the cases (List C) where Luke uses words in the same technical sense as do the doctors, this argument is more than offset by the many cases quoted by Harnack, Hobart, Moffatt, and Zahn themselves in which words that have a special technical meaning among the doctors are used by Luke in an entirely different sense.[54]

List D is no doubt the most specious of all. The first two examples, which Harnack calls *termini technici* for "great fever" and "acute leprosy," are not very convincing when Luke's fondness for the adjectives μέγας and πλήρης is remembered; [55] οὐδὲν ἄτοπον, τί ἄτοπον, seem to be regular expressions for something "out of the way," i.e., either criminal or disastrous; [56] ἀναδίδωμι ἐπιστολήν and similar expressions are common in the papyri.[57] οὐκ ἄσημος was evidently a common litotes and perhaps especially applied to a man's origin.[58] Is it likely that Luke got these last two phrases from the letters of Hippocrates, five hundred years old ? [59]

Hobart, Zahn, and Harnack all group together the differences between Luke and the parallel passages in Matthew and Mark, and make a special point of them.[60] These differences, it is claimed, show the marks of a physician. The examples are of two kinds:

1. Substitution by Luke of synonyms of medical character.

2. Additions, omissions, or changes in the description of patients or cures that show an interest in medicine.

1. In comparing the language of Luke with the synonyms in Mark or Matthew, the fact that the term in Luke is found in the medical writers does not prove that he was a physician, for a well educated person such as Luke evidently was, even without special medical training would use more technical terms than a less educated person. The general difference between Luke and the other synoptists is shown elsewhere to be a marked difference in culture.[61] Harnack admits that three of the examples that he quotes as substitutions of medical synonyms are also verbal improvements, viz.:

ῥίψαν	Luke 4, 35	for σπαράξαν	Mark 1, 26
παραλελυμένος	Luke 5, 18	for παραλυτικός	Mark 2, 3
γενόμενος ἐν ἀγωνίᾳ	[Luke] 22, 44	for ἤρξατο ἐκθαμβεῖσθαι ("unclassical")	Mark 14, 33

Zahn recognizes verbal improvements in two: [62]

κλινίδιον	Luke 5, 19, 24	for κράββατος	Mark 2, 4, 11
ἰκμάς	Luke 8, 6	for ῥίζαν	Mark 4, 6

Three other examples are in accord with the known preferences of the Atticists:

βελόνη	Luke 18, 25	for ῥαφίς	Mark 10, 25,	Matt. 19, 24 [63]
κακῶς ἔχων	Luke 7, 2	for βασανιζόμενος		Matt. 8, 6 [64]
πλήμμυρα	Luke 6, 48	for βροχή		Matt. 7, 25 [65]

The only other examples of this kind in Harnack and Zahn are:

προσρήγνυμι	Luke 6, 48,49	for προσπίπτω	Matt. 7, 25–27
προσρήγνυμι		προσκόπτω	
συμπίπτω		πίπτω	

ῥῆγμα		πτῶσις	
ἵστημι	Luke 8, 44	for ξηραίνω	Mark 5, 29 [66]
ῥύσις		πηγή	
τραυματίζω	Luke 20, 12	for δέρω	Mark 12, 5

But ῥύσις is found in the parallel in Mark (5, 25), and δέρω is used by Luke in the same context (20, 11). The remaining examples have been considered in the lists above. Note that both Josephus (*B. J.* i. 17, 4) and Lucian (*Philopseud.* 31) use συμπίπτω, as does Luke (6, 49), of a house falling in.

On the other hand a number of good medical terms are found in Matthew and Mark but not in Luke. Here are a few examples, those limited in the New Testament to one or both of these evangelists being marked as in Hobart by an asterisk. *

* ἄγκιστρον	Matt., name of a surgical instrument.
* αἱμορροέω	Matt., substituted for οὖσα ἐν ῥύσει αἵματος in Mark, Luke.
* ἄνηθον	Matt. (Hippocr., Theophr *et al.*)
* ἀφρίζω	Mark.
ἄρρωστος	Matt., Mark, once elsewhere in New Testament (1 Cor. 11, 30).
βρυγμός	Matt. (once in Luke also, from Q)
* διυλίζω	Matt. (Dioscor., *et al.*)
* ἐρεύγομαι	Matt.
* κολοβόω	Matt., Mark, "properly to amputate" (Swete on Mark 13, 20).
* κυλλός	Matt., Mark (Hippocr.)
* κύμινον	Matt.
* κώνωψ	Matt.
* μυρίζω	Mark.
ξηραίνω	of paralysis, Mark. [67]
* προσκεφάλαιον	Mark.
* πυρέσσω	Matt., Mark.
πώρωσις	Mark, Paul (see J. A. Robinson, *Ephesians*, p. 264).
* σκώληξ	Mark (for the medical use of the word, see Hobart, p. 43.)[68]
* σμυρνίζω	Mark (Dioscor. and very late writers only).

2. The other arguments for the medical language of Luke based on a comparison with Matthew and Mark are such general differences as the following:

"In the description of Jesus' healing work Luke sometimes writes more fully than does Mark, and with greater vividness." (Zahn, p. 146.)

"Luke often indicates how long the person healed had been afflicted." (Zahn, p. 147.)

"In the cure of the epileptic boy (St. Luke, 9, 38 ff. = St. Mark 9, 17 ff.) St. Luke adds in the description of the patient: ἐξαίφνης κράζει (*scil.* the evil spirit) . . . καὶ μόγις ἀποχωρεῖ ἀπ' αὐτοῦ συντρῖβον αὐτόν." These "interpolations elucidate the description of the disease by telling of symptoms that are characteristic of epilepsy." (Harnack, pp. 183, 186 f.)

"The addition in both these cases (Luke 6, 6; 22, 50 f.) that it was the right hand and the right ear respectively is a token of exactness which is specially intelligible in a physician." (Harnack, p. 185.)[69]

But there are some converse facts in a comparison of the synoptic Gospels that these writers do not mention:

In Luke 4, 39 = Mark 1, 31 = Matt. 8, 15, Luke alone omits the fact that in curing the woman Jesus took (Matt. touched) her hand.[70] In fact Luke frequently omits reference to touching or laying on of hands where Matthew and Mark mention it.[71] Again with all his "special interest in methods of healing" Luke does not mention (9, 6) as does Mark (6, 13) that the twelve on their mission of preaching and practicing anointed their patients with olive oil. In Matthew (8, 6) the patient healed at the request of a Capernaum centurion is plainly described as παραλυτικός, but in Luke (7, 2) merely as one very sick and about to die (κακῶς ἔχων ἤμελλεν τελευτᾶν). It is Matthew (5, 39), not Luke (6, 29), that says "*right* cheek" in Jesus' dictum on non-resistance.[72]

Even in the healing of the epileptic boy referred to by Harnack, as just quoted, the facts turn quite the opposite way. As in the case of another demoniac (Luke 8, 26 ff. = Mark 5, 1 ff.), Luke omits or explicitly contradicts all reference to a self-destructive tendency on the part of the patient. Here he also omits such symptoms as deafness, dumbness, foaming, grinding the teeth, pining away, falling and rolling, death-like coma on the ground.[73] He also omits from Mark the question and answer in reference to the duration of the disease (παιδιόθεν, Mark 9, 21), and the statement that Jesus took the patient by the hand (Mark 9, 27), and commanded the spirit not only to leave him but never to return.[74] Still Harnack asserts (p. 187); "Very nearly all of the alterations and additions which the third Evangelist has made in the Markan text are most simply and surely explained from the professional interest of a physician. Indeed, I cannot see that any other explanation is even possible." [75]

Examples of medical language in an author to have their fullest weight should be words that are used elsewhere only or mainly in medical writers. Hobart not only includes many words used frequently by other than medical writers, but apparently is at no pains to show that many of Luke's words are used principally or exclusively by medical writers.[76] Zahn speaks of his examples as "words and turns of phrase found elsewhere only in the medical books," [77] but does not make plain which of them fulfil this description. It is certain that nearly all of them do not.[78]

The selected examples of Harnack, Moffatt, and Zahn do not impress us with their technical character. Yet even if we accepted them as medical terms, the argument derived from them would not be fully convincing. It is still possible that they could have been used by a non-medical man. We have no way of knowing how far medical language had penetrated into the vocabulary of every day life. The vocabulary of the doctor and the layman always coincide to a considerable degree. We know how many of the simpler medical terms are found in common speech to day, especially on the lips of educated men, and we may well think of conditions in the first century as in this respect much like our own. It is entirely possible, then, that much medical language had already become part of common speech.[79] If we are to accept the definition of Hobart as to what constitutes a medical term, we have already seen that many such words are found in the LXX, Josephus, Plutarch, and Lucian. Kennedy indicates that about ten per cent of the more uncommon words in the LXX are to be found also in Hippocrates. His proportion for the New Testament as a whole is nearly as large.[80] In his study of the Atticists Schmid finds constant affiliations in vocabulary between them and Hippocrates and the other medical writers.[81] Medical borrowings have been asserted for Polybius [82] and even for Xenophon's Anabasis.[83] Many Latin authors also use medical terms.[84]

Any sound argument for the medical bias of Luke's vocabulary not only must show a considerable number of terms possibly or probably medical, but must show that they are more numerous and of more frequent occurrence than in other writers of his time and degree of culture. Even were we to accept Hobart's long list of medical terms, it remains to be proved that the examples are more abundant and more strikingly coincident with medical language as we know it than those which could be collected from Josephus, Philo,[85] Plutarch, or Lucian. "The evidence is cumulative,"[86] but it must also be comparative. Otherwise the conclusions will be thoroughly subjective.[87] The question that presents itself, therefore, is not whether there are many parallels between the diction of Luke and that of the medical writings, but whether these parallels are more numerous or more striking than those which can be found in non-professional men, writing with the same culture as Luke and on similar subjects. If not, the argument of Hobart and the rest is useless.

So far as I know this test has never been applied to the question of the medical language of Luke. To apply it fully for only one other author would be a large task, requiring the "remarkable industry" of another Dr. Hobart. Yet at least a rough test should be made. In an excursus appended to this chapter is given the result of a preliminary investigation of the "medical language" of Lucian, carried on in the manner of Hobart, Harnack, and Zahn. Lucian was chosen as being nearly a contemporary and a fair parallel to Luke. Both writers have a large vocabulary[88] and a ready command of Greek. Lucian was an Asiatic Greek who travelled into the western world. This is also the tradition about Luke the physician.[89] But otherwise the test was chosen entirely at random.

The results given are very incomplete. But a complete study is here not necessary, as we are trying to learn, not whether Luke is a little more medical in diction than his nonprofessional contemporaries, but whether the difference is *striking*. And the test case quite sufficiently proves that it is not. The style of Luke bears no more evidence of medical training and interest than does the language of other writers who were not physicians. This result, it must be confessed, is a purely negative one. It is probably futile to try to carry the argument further, as Clemen does, and to argue from the language of Luke and Acts that a physician *could not* have written them.[90] One cannot know to-day what an ancient physician could not have written. Of course the absence of marked medical traits does not prove that a doctor did not write Luke and Acts. To judge from the fragments that remain, Ctesias, the physician, uses no more medical language in his historical work than did his contemporary Xenophon, the soldier and historian.[91] So Luke, " the beloved physician " and companion of Paul, may have written the two books which tradition assigns to him, though their Greek be no more medical than that of Lucian, " the travelling rhetorician and show-lecturer "; but the so-called medical language of these books cannot be used as a proof that Luke was their author, nor even as an argument confirming the tradition of his authorship.

NOTES

[1] *Editorial Note.* — The earlier discussion turned on the question whether "Luke the physician" (Coloss. 4, 14) was the same Luke to whom tradition ascribed the third Gospel and the Acts (Iren., Euseb., Jerome), or, as Erasmus, Calvin, and others surmised, another person, expressly distinguished from the Evangelist by the designation "the physician." The titles of two 18th century dissertations belong to the bibliographical inventory; viz., J. G. Winckler, *Dissertatio de Luca Evangelista medico* (Lips. 1736, 4⁰), and B. G. Clauswitz, *De Luca Evangelista medico ad Coloss. iv. 14* (Halae Magdeburg. 1740, 4⁰). The former is duly catalogued in the long list of this multitudinous author's publications (*e.g.*, in Meusel), and down to the middle of the 19th century it was regularly cited in the " literature " on Luke, but I discover no evidence that anybody had seen it in the meanwhile. Clauswitz is likewise unattainable, but some of his illustrations of the Evangelist's medical knowledge are quoted by others.

Wettstein, in his edition of the New Testament (1751; I, 643) wrote: "Exercuisse medicinam Paulus ad Colossenses testatur. Eusebius autem et Hieronymus addunt fuisse natione Syrum Antiochensem: utriusque non obscura prodit indicia in scriptis suis." The evidences he adduced of Luke's professional use of terms (especially in Luke 4, 38, Acts 13, 11) became classical, and those who plough with his heifer have, as usual, such faith in him that they deem it superfluous to look up his references or even read his quotations; otherwise some one would have discovered that Galen does not say that physicians make a technical distinction between big fevers and small ones, but — in two places — that " big fever " is an inaccurate expression (since the nature of a fever is not defined in quantitative terms), though common among physicians (*De comp. medic. per genera*, iii. 2, Vol. XIII, pp. 572 f. Kühn; *De different. febrium*, i. 1, Vol. VII, p. 275; see also his commentary on Hippocrates, *Aphorism.* i, ad *Aphor.* 11, Vol. XVII. ii. p. 388). Inaccurate expressions are quite as likely to be in popular use as to be exclusively professional. In fact, in the 17th century a physician (Guil. Ader, *De aegrotis et morbis Evangelicis*, Toulouse, 1621; reprinted in *Critici Sacri*, Lond. 1660, Vol. IX, col. 3679 f.), writing about the miracles of healing in the Gospels, remarked on Luke 4, 38, *συνεχομένη πυρετῷ μεγάλῳ*, "Evangelista loquitur ut vulgus, qui *magnas febres* vocat, quas Hippocrates in Epidem. & com. 4. sec. 13. acut. dicit *acutas, continuas, causonides, ardentes*. Quarum fecit duo genera Galenus: Exquisitam nempe, vel notham."

Till after the beginning of the 19th century, Luke's medical language was a standing topic in the principal Introductions to the New Testament. J. D. Michaelis (*Einleitung in die göttlichen Schriften des Neuen Testaments*, 4 Ausg., Göttingen, 1788, pp. 1078 f.), citing Clauswitz, adduces *πυρετὸς μέγας* (Luke 4, 38), *ἀγωνία* (Luke 22, 43), and *ἀχλύς* (Acts 13, 11), as examples of the author's professional knowledge. J. G. Eichhorn (*Einleitung in das Neue Testament*, 2 Ausg., Leipzig, 1820, p. 625) disposes of these instances with a commonsense observation. See also Winer, *Biblisches Realwoerterbuch*, 3 Aufl., Leipzig, 1848, II, 34 f.

In the collections from Greek authors to illustrate the New Testament, of which the 18th century was prolific, many of the supposed technical medical terms in Luke and Acts are illustrated from authors not suspected of medical learning; it would perhaps be possible to match in them all the words in Hobart's list which have even a superficial plausibility.

Learned physicians, who should be the best judges, have seldom contributed even their opinions on the question whether Luke was of their guild. The few pages which Dr. John Freind (1675–1728) gives to the subject have therefore an especial interest, for Freind knew the Greek medical writers not through indexes or by skimming their pages for an extraneous purpose, but as both a practitioner, and a historian of ancient medicine, and was besides one of the most accomplished Grecians of his time. In his *History of Physick from the Time of Galen to the beginning of the Sixteenth Century* (1725–26), the first part of which deals with the Greek physicians, Freind remarks that "St. Luke's Greek comes nearer to the ancient standard than that of any other of the Evangelists"—a superiority which he attributes to Luke's Greek medical reading; and that "no doubt merely because he was a physician, when there is occasion to speak of distempers or the cure of them [he] makes use of words more proper for the subject than the others do." Of these peculiarities of Luke's diction Freind gives several illustrations (4 ed., London, 1750, I, 222–225). It is noteworthy that among these none of the words and phrases which have recently been signalized by laymen as technical terms of Greek medicine are mentioned; in fact, no instance of a technical term or technical use of terms is adduced. Luke writes *παραλελυμένος* instead of *παραλυτικός*, "a word never used by the ancient Greek Writers" (not particularly medical writers; compare the popular use of *νεφριτικός*, Galen, *De nat. fac.* i. 13 [II, 31 Kühn]; *ὑστερικός*, Galen, *De loc. affect.* vii. 5 [VIII, 414] — midwife's and woman's word); *ἔστη ἡ ῥύσις*, "more simple and more direct as well as more Physical"; *ἰᾶτο πάντας* (instead of *διεσώθησαν, ἐσώζοντο*), "the word that is peculiarly proper for healing"; of the centurion's servant, "St. Luke tells us that they found him not only *recover'd*, but *ὑγιαίνοντα, in perfect health*"; so also in Luke 8, 55, *ἐπέστρεψε τὸ πνεῦμα* [her breath came back], "which he puts in, no doubt as being the first sign of coming to life." "The same accuracy of expression we may see in regard to the lame" (Acts 3, 7). In Luke's account of the woman who had the issue of blood (Mark 5, 26, *παθοῦσα ὑπὸ πολλῶν ἰατρῶν καὶ δαπανήσασα τὰ παρ' ἑαυτῆς, καὶ μηδὲν ὠφεληθεῖσα ἀλλὰ μᾶλλον εἰς τὸ χεῖρον ἐλθοῦσα*), Luke gives these particulars "quite another turn, and softens the passage very much in regard to his faculty, and instead of relating how much she *suffered* by the several Physicians, or how she grew *worse* upon her remedies, he says only that her distemper was above the reach of any of them to remove it; *οὐκ ἴσχυσεν ἀπ' οὐδενὸς θεραπευθῆναι*." So also *προσαναλώσασα* is a more "proper expression" for paying a doctor's bill than Mark's *δαπανήσασα* ("squandered." The miser in *Anthol.* xi. 171, reckons the doctor's pay and *τί νοσῶν δαπανᾷ*, and concludes that it is cheaper to die).

Freind observes that Basil, "whom his own continual illness made a physician," has a great many allusions and similes taken from the art; and he is inclined to think — as others had done — that the historian Procopius had a medical education, "for in some things relating to Physick he is remarkably more minute and circumstantial than we find any other historian is," as he shows by numerous examples.

Mr. J. K. Walker, in the "Gentleman's Magazine" for 1841 (Part I, pp. 585–587), refers to Freind as "Frend, a medical writer" (!), and repeats some of Freind's illustrations, adding others "which show with equal certainty the professional bias of the learned Evangelist, that have, *as far as I know, escaped attention*." His list contains: *ὑδρωπικός, παραλελυμένος, ἀχλύς, παροξυσμός* (!), *κραιπάλη, συνεχομένη* (Luke 4, 38), *ἴασις, πυρετοῖς καὶ δυσεντερίᾳ συνεχόμενος*; Luke's manipulation of the story of the woman with the issue of blood (from "Frend's essays"); and the manner of Herod's (Antipas) death, *σκωληκόβρωτος* (Acts 12, 23). James Smith (*Voyage and Shipwreck of St. Paul*, 1 ed. 1848; 4 ed. 1880, pp. 1 ff.) regards Luke 4, 38 (*συνεχομένη πυρετῷ μεγάλῳ*), Acts 13, 11 (*ἀχλύς*), and the woman with the issue of blood as conclusive; and Lightfoot (on Coloss. 4, 14) deems a reference to Smith sufficient. Hayman (Smith's Dictionary of the Bible, art. "Medicine," Vol. II [1863], pp. 298 f. n.) quotes part of Freind's examples, without reference to the source. Thus the matter stood when Hobart undertook his painstaking investigation, designed to prove that the third Gospel and Acts were written by a physician, therefore by Luke the companion of Paul, thus giving the discussion a new, apologetic turn.

In his book, and in the subsequent discussion, one consideration of fundamental importance is overlooked. Modern medical terminology is a barbarous artificial jargon, consisting partly of terms that have come down from the Greeks, in Greek or translated into Latin, partly of invented terms, coined after the pattern of the ancient, in a Greek or Latin which is often palpably counterfeit. Many medical terms, especially the older ones, have come into common use, frequently supplanting, at least in polite discourse, native English words that mean exactly the same thing; and in recent times various agencies of vulgarization have made the lay public acquainted with hundreds of doctor's words, which they use — or abuse — with a self-satisfied feeling that they are talking the professional lingo.

Greek scientific terminology is the contrary of all this. Its technical terms were native, not foreign; they were not invented, but were real words of the living language, and in considerable part the everyday names for the thing, more exactly defined, if necessary, but not diverted from their meaning. When the teachers of medicine had occasion to designate things for which the common speech had no satisfactory name, they made descriptive terms from common words by derivation or composition, conformably to the genius of the language, with that creative freedom in which Greek surpasses all other tongues. The meaning of such words, if not their technical definition, was at once evident to every Greek. These were real words, too, and could come into general use unhampered by barbarous form or occult significance.

Wilamowitz-Moellendorff ("Die griechische Literatur," in *Die Kultur der Gegenwart*, I, 8, 2 edit. 1907, p. 59), writing of Hippocrates, justly says: "Offenbar muss sich erkennen lassen, dass bereits eine ganz scharfe Terminologie ausgebildet ist. Das kann das Griechische (oder vielmehr Ionische) schon so früh, zweifellos für viele Teile der Naturwissenschaft. Das Latein hat es zu einer Terminologie überhaupt nur in der Jurisprudenz gebracht; die modernen Sprachen bringen es zu keiner, es sei denn, sie borgten bei diesen beiden: sie brauchen Kunstwörter, Surrogate, statt der lebendigen, unmittelbar bezeichnenden, die das griechische Sprachgefühl nicht erfindet, sondern findet."

The ignoring—or should I say the ignorance?—of this elementary fact has ludicrous consequences. Thus Walker, Hobart, Harnack, Zahn, and Moffatt, put down *κραιπάλη* among the words which show Luke to be versed in Greek medical literature. But *κραιπάλη* is not a technical term coined by physicians to designate mysteriously the puking and the dizzy headache that come after a big dinner and much wine; it is — as these scholars might have read in Galen in so many words (*κραιπάλας . . . πάντες οἱ Ἕλληνες ὀνομάζουσι τὰς ἐξ οἴνου βλάβας τῆς κεφαλῆς*, actually quoted in full by Wettstein on Luke 21, 31, the verse in which Hobart and his *pedisequi* discover it to be a medical word!) — the vulgar word for that very vulgar experience. Luke did not have to go to medical literature on the diagnosis and treatment of the ailment to pick up a word that was, so to speak, lying in the gutter, any more than Aristophanes consulted Hippocrates to know what to call the consequences of a protracted symposium. And *κραιπάλη* is only a peculiarly crass example of a pervasive fallacy in the discussion of Luke's "technical language." — G. F. M.]

---

[2] See, however, Plummer on Luke 6, 1 (ψώχω); 6, 40 (καταρτίζω) and 8, 23 (ἀφυπνόω, 'fall off to sleep'). As a recently added example should perhaps be mentioned πρηνής, Acts 1, 18, which according to Chase, Harnack, and Rendel Harris is to be understood not in the sense of 'headlong' but as 'swollen,' like the form πρησθείς from πίμπρημι 'swell,' which has been conjectured for the passage. (See F. H. Chase in *Journal of Theological Studies*, XIII (1912), 278 ff.; Rendel Harris in *American Journal of Theology*, XVIII (1914), 127–131, and the references there given.) But Chase admits that "in a cursory search, I have not discovered any instance of the adjective πρηνής in medical writers in the sense of 'swollen,' 'inflamed.'" Hobart (p. 186) had already collected a number of examples that show the use of the adjective by the doctors in the sense of 'headlong,' frequently connected by them with ὕπτιος. It is obvious that little weight can yet be give to this example. As curiosities may be mentioned the arguments drawn from alleged medical language to maintain Luke's authorship of Hebrews (Franz Delitzsch, *Commentary*, 1857 [Eng. trans., 1868–70]), of the Pastoral

Epistles (R. Scott, *The Pauline Epistles*, 1909, pp. 339–341), or of Second Peter (Selwyn, *St. Luke the Prophet*, 1901, p. 150 n. 1) and Ephesians (*ibid.*, p. 103).

[3] Zahn, *Einleitung in das Neue Testament*, 3d edit. Quoted hereafter (with some reference to the German) chiefly from the English translation, New York, 1909. See especially III, 160 ff., 82 f. Harnack, *Lukas der Arzt*, Leipzig, 1906. Quoted (with some reference to the German) from the English translation, *Luke the Physician*, London, 1907. See pp. 13–17 and Appendix I.

[4] Hobart, pp. xxxv f.

[5] *St. Luke* (International Critical Commentary), 1896, pp. lxiii f.

[6] *Horae Synopticae*, 1899, p. 154; 2d edit., p. 189.

[7] *Expositor's Greek Testament*, 1900, II, 9–11.

[8] *S. Paul the Traveller*, 1900, p. 205; *Luke the Physician*, 1908, chap. i.

[9] *Credibility of Acts*, 1902, pp. 13 f.

[10] *Critical Introduction to the New Testament*, 1909, p. 127.

[11] *The Gospels as Historical Documents*, Part II, 1910, pp. 261 ff. (very guarded).

[12] *Introduction to the Literature of the New Testament*, 1911, pp. 263 f., 298 ff.

[13] Harnack, *Luke The Physician*, p. 14, n. 2; "I subscribe to the words of Zahn [*Introduction*, III, 146], 'Hobart has proved for every one who can at all appreciate proof that the author of the Lukan work was a man practised in the scientific language of Greek medicine — in short, a *Greek physician*.'"

[14] *Neue Untersuchungen zur Apostelgeschichte*, 1911, p. 15. (Eng. trans., *The Date of Acts*, 1911, pp. 1 ff.)

[15] *Festschrift zur Feier des 450-jährigen Bestehens der Universität Basel*, 1910, pp. 16 f. This is about the position taken by Stanton.

[16] C. Clemen, *Hibbert Journal*, VIII (1910), 785 f. Compare the earlier and more direct answer of the same author to Harnack's *Lukas* in *Theologische Rundschau*, X (1907), 97 ff.

[17] Meyer's Commentary, *Lukas*, 8th edit., p. 74. "Eine methodische Sichtung des Materials und Zusammenstellung des wirklich Beweisenden wäre erwünscht."

[18] Jülicher, *Einleitung*, pp. 407 f. (Eng. trans., pp. 447 f.).

[19] See the articles of P. W. Schmidt and Clemen cited above (notes 15 and 16), and the protest of Thumb, quoted below (note 79). See also a few pertinent criticisms by Preuschen in *Berliner philol. Wochenschrift*, XXVIII (1908), col. 1429 ff.

[20] P. 253. Examples could be multiplied indefinitely; e.g., on *ὑπερῷον* Hobart says (p. 185), "This word was very familiar to a physician, being the neuter of *ὑπερῷος*, the feminine of which, *ὑπερῴη*, was the name of the palate," etc.; (p. 272) "*ὑποζώννυμι* is peculiar to St. Luke. . . . He is the only writer who employs this particular compound of *ζώννυμι* for undergirding a ship. . . . The word *ὑποζώννυμι* was a very common one with medical men" — apparently in the participle, *ὁ ὑπεζωκώς* (*ὑμήν*), the membrane lining the thorax (pleura).

[21] Plummer, *op. cit.*, p. lxiv. J. Naylor, "Luke the Physician and Ancient Medicine," in *Hibbert Journal*, VII (1909), p. 29. says: "three hundred and sixty out of Hobart's four hundred words were to be found in the Septuagint, and many of them would have been used by any intelligent Greek writing on the same themes." His figures, amounting to ninety per cent, probably include the Apocrypha.

[22] *Josephus und Lucas*, lists II and III, pp. 302 ff.

[23] Thus 40 more of Hobart's words, or ten per cent more of his list, appear in Josephus than in LXX. Krenkel does not include 1 and 2 Macc. with the LXX, and his lists are otherwise not quite reliable, but they give a simple and approximate answer to our question.

[24] D. Wyttenbach, *Index graecitatis in Plutarchi opera*, Leipzig, 1835. *Lucianus ex recensione Caroli Jacobitz*, Leipzig, 1836–1841. Vol. IV. Index Graecus.

[25] *Lukas der Arzt*, p. 122 n.

[26] One of them, ἐπέπεσεν, rests on an inferior reading in Acts 13, 11.

[27] "In this intransitive sense its use seems, with a few exceptions, to be almost altogether confined to the medical writers, who employ it to describe patients sitting up in bed." (Hobart, p. 11.) But laymen used it in the same way as is shown by the scene at the death-bed of Socrates (Plato, *Phaedo*, 60 B, ἀνακαθιζόμενος εἰς τὴν κλίνην συνέκαμψε τὸ σκέλος) and of Philopoemen (Plut. 368 A, συναγαγὼν μόλις ἑαυτὸν ὑπ' ἀσθενείας ἀνεκάθιζεν). Cf. Plut. *Alex.* 671 D; Xen. *Cyneg.* 5, 19 (of a hare).

[28] Occurs twice in the parallel passage in Mark and frequently in Greek writers, see p. 16.

[29] "Almost altogether confined to the medical writers, and very seldom used by them." (Hobart, p. 37.) To judge from the examples cited by Hobart it means in medical writers to cool off, to have a chill; in Luke it means to expire. So in LXX (Judg. 4, 21 *v. l.*, Ezek. 21, 7); Babr. 115, 11; Herodas 4, 29.

[30] "Used in medical language to signify 'producing alive, enduing with life.'" (Hobart, p. 155.) In this sense the word is common in all "profane" Greek, but Luke, in accordance with the idiom of the LXX, uses the word in the sense of 'keep alive, preserve.'

[31] ἡμιθανής occurs in Dion. Hal., Diod., and Strabo; ἡμιθνής is a much commoner word, used by Thuc., Aristoph., Polyb., Luc., Dion. Hal., Dio Cass., Alciphr. *al.*, and by Galen in the two passages cited by Hobart, p. 27.

[32] "Besides this passage in St. Luke, κλινάριον appears to be found in only two other Greek authors, viz. Aristophanes and Arrian." (Hobart, p. 116.) But Hobart does not cite medical parallels for κλινάριον, κλίνη, κλινίδιον or κράββατος. Both diminutive forms occur in M. Anton., Artemidor., and Pollux.

[33] No example of this word is quoted by the lexica or by Hobart, p. 152. The latter cites Diosc. *Mat. med.* i. 181, but he uses συκόμορον and μορέα = συκαμινέα.

[34] The word in this spelling is not quoted from the doctors by Hobart, p. 52 f., nor is it found elsewhere except in Moeris who condemns it. But δυσεντερία is found in Polyb., Joseph., etc., as well as the doctors.

[35] "The noun ὁλοκληρία does not seem to be used in the medical writers." (Hobart, p. 193.)

[36] Acts 3, 7 (Tisch., W. H.). Found elsewhere only in Hesychius. Harnack (p. 191) says: "Σφυδρόν is a very rare word (e.g., Passow does not give it);" but he then emends (?) σφυρόν in Hobart's example (Galen, *Medicus*, 10 *bis*) to σφυδρόν and quotes it as a parallel. Σφυρόν, the reading of Text. Recept. in Acts, *l.c.* is found in LXX, Joseph., Plut., Luc., and other non-medical writers as well as in Galen, *l. c.*

[37] In some of Hobart's examples the disease is the subject of ἀπαλλάσσω as in Acts 19, 12; [Plato] *Eryx.* 401 C; cf. Soph. *Antigone*, 422. But in most of them the disease is in the genitive as in Joseph. (e.g. *Antt.* vii. 8, 1, ταχέως ἀπαλλαγήσεσθαι τῆς νόσου), Luc. (e.g. *Abdic.* 26, ἰῶ καὶ ταύτην καὶ ἀπάλλαττε ἤδη τῆς νόσου), and other writers.

[38] Eurip., *Hipp.* 762; Herodot. iv. 60; Plut. *Cicero*, 47, *Cato*, 38; LXX (Judges 9, 34); and in Philo, Diod., *et al.* Used in Acts 10, 11; 11, 5 of the corners of the sheet. "The technical expression in medical language for the ends of bandages." (Hobart, p. 218.)

[39] Cf. Erotian, *Lexicon Hippocrat.* s.v. ἀχλυῶδες· ἀχλὺς λέγεται ποιά τις ἀμαύρωσις καὶ σκοτία περὶ τοὺς ὀφθαλμούς, ὡς καὶ Ὅμηρος ἐν τῇ ε' τῆς Ἰλιάδος φησίν· [l. 127] ἀχλὺν δ' αὖ τοι ἀπ' ὀφθαλμῶν ἕλον, ἣ πρὶν ἐπῆεν.

40 Luke 9, 38. But the word here means rather 'pity' as in Luke 1, 48 and often (over 100 times) in LXX, as is shown by the parallels, Mark 9, 22, βοήθησον σπλαγχνισθείς, Matt. 17, 15, ἐλέησον. For the medical use, see Plut. *Quaest. conviv.* 682 E, quoting Hippocrates.

41 Used in Prov. 3, 8 as parallel to ἴασις.

42 Cf. Suidas: θηρία καὶ τὰ δάκετα, ἔχιες, φαλάγγια, ὄφεις.

43 Luke 8, 44, where it is an intransitive verb. So Plutarch, *Consol. ad Apoll.* 106 F (of a river). To judge from the examples in Hobart, pp. 14 ff., repeated by Harnack, p. 186, the medical writers used the verb in this sense transitively. Cf. Pollux, IV, 178.

44 It is to be noted that Ramsay (*Luke the Physician*, pp. 63 f.) disputes this meaning of the verb and the argument drawn from it. It means, he says, simply 'fasten upon.' Preuschen also notes that apparently Acts uses the active, but the doctors, when they mean 'infect,' use the middle.

45 E.g. Job 38, 30, πάχνην . . . ἣ καταβαίνει ὥσπερ ὕδωρ ῥέον; Ps. 132, 2 ὡς μύρον . . . τὸ καταβαῖνον ἐπὶ πώγωνα . . . 3 ὡς δρόσος Ἀερμὼν ἡ καταβαίνουσα ἐπὶ τὰ ὄρη Σιών; Joseph. *Antt.* ii. 16, 3 ὄμβροι τ' ἀπ' οὐρανοῦ κατέβαινον.

46 "Many exx. in Passow *s.v.* συνέχω, I. a." Grimm-Thayer. Cf. note 55.

47 Hobart (pp. 37 f.) says that this word "is found only once in classical Greek in the sense it bears in this passage [Acts 5, 6], 'to shroud.' Eurip. *Troad.* 378: πέπλοις συνεστάλησαν." But the doctors use the word to mean 'bandage,' 'compress,' 'contract.' In these or other senses the word occurs in LXX, Luc., Plut., and other writers, and in the New Testament in 1 Cor. 7, 29, but not in Luke or Acts.

48 Luke 21, 23. But it is also in the two parallel passages, Mark 13, 17 and Matt. 24, 19, and twice besides in Matt.

49 λαμβάνω ἐν γαστρί and συλλαμβάνω alone are common in LXX in this sense.

50 LXX (Gen. 28, 18, ἐπέχεεν ἔλαιον); Plut. *Pericl.* 16, ἔλαιον ἐπιχέουσι.

51 "This compound of τρέπειν, though often used in medical language, is not employed exactly in the same sense as in this passage." (Hobart, p. 268.) Cf. Joseph. *Antt.* ii. 14, 1 εἰς ὀργὴν (περι)τραπέν; ix. 4, 4 τοὺς παρόντας εἰς χαρὰν περιέτρεψε.

52 This exact phrase occurs in Galen, where it applies to voluntary fasting or dieting. In Acts 27, 33 it applies to an enforced fast, perhaps sea-sickness. See Madan in *Journal of Theological Studies*, VI (1904), p. 116.

53 No exact parallel of this phrase is given by Hobart, p. 60; the nearest, τοῦ κατὰ τὴν βελόνην τρήματος, means the puncture made by the needle (Galen, *Sang. in. arter.* 2 [II, 708]).

54 See for examples, the notes above on ἀρχαί, ἐκψύχω, ἐπιβλέπω, ζωογονέω, περιτρέπω, συστέλλω and compare the following:

	Medical Use	Luke's Use
ἀνασκευάζω	cure (Hobart)	subvert
βοήθεια	"a current medical term which is applied to all conceivable objects." (H)	apparently a nautical term
διαχειρίζω	operate (Hobart)	(middle) slay
ἐκλείπω	failure of pulse, etc. (M)	see Luke 16, 9; 22, 32.
ἐπακροάομαι	of auscultation (M)	hear
ἐπιδημέω	be epidemic (Hobart)	sojourn
πτύσσω	roll up a bandage (M)	roll up a book
ῥῆγμα	laceration, rupture (MZ)	fall of a house, ruin
συνδρομή	concurrence of symptoms (Hobart)	concourse of people
τιμωρέω	treat medically, relieve, succour (Hobart)	punish

The evidence of such words as these is ambiguous, to say the least. Granting that the words had a technical sense in the medical profession, would not a doctor be the least likely to use them with a different signification ? Would an English physician be more, or less, likely than a layman to use in their non-medical sense such common words as appendix, eruption, operate, pulse, stool, ward ?

[55] With *ἦν συνεχομένη πυρετῷ μεγάλῳ* substituted by Luke (4, 38) for *πυρέσσουσα* (Mark 1, 30); compare *φόβῳ μεγάλῳ συνεἰχοντο*, Luke 8, 37. On the former passage Harnack, p, 184, says, " the medical writers distinguish between 'slight' and 'great' fevers; therefore, the epithet 'great' in St. Luke is by no means insignificant." In reply to this we may quote B. Weiss, *Das Leben Jesu* (Eng. trans., 1894, II, 89 n.): " This is generally regarded as suggestive of Luke's calling of physician, without considering that by no diagnosis could he determine from Mark's laconic account under which of the kinds of fever distinguished by his Galen this case was to be classed. [See note 1. — Ed.] The consideration was much more likely to occur to him that a fever to cure which Jesus employed miraculous aid could not be an easy one to get rid of." To judge from quotations in Hobart the doctors used for severe fevers the adjectives *ὀξύς* (pp. 32, 53, 127 *τῶν ὀξέων ὀνομαζομένων πυρετῶν*, 178 *bis*, 210, 233) and *σφοδρός* (pp. 56, 71, 178) rather than *μέγας*. *Συνέχομαι πυρετῷ* is found in Joseph. *Antt.* xiii. 15, 5; Oxy. Pap. 896, 33 (316 A.D.)

The argument for *πλήρης λέπρας* is stated thus by Hobart (p. 5): " It would seem that St. Luke by employing two distinct terms *πλήρης λέπρας* and *λεπρός* in his account of these two miracles intended to draw a distinction between the diseases in each case, either that the disease was of a more aggravated type in one case than in the other, or else of a different variety. Now we know that leprosy, even as early as the time of Hippocrates, had assumed three different forms (*ἀλφός*, *λεύκη*, and *μέλας*), 'and it is probable that in the time of our Lord the disease, as it existed in Palestine, did not materially differ from the Hippocratic record of it.' (See *Dict. of the Bible*, Art. 'Leper.') *Πλήρης*, in this connection peculiar to St. Luke, is frequently thus used in the medical writers. Hipp. *De arte*, 5, *καὶ πλήρεες τῆς νόσου*, Hipp. *Coac. progn.* 187, *πλήρεες οὗτοι εἰσὶ πύου*." Few of Hobart's examples are, however, really parallel. Cf. Soph. *Antig.* 1052, *τῆς νόσου πλήρης ἔφυς*.

[56] LXX, Prov. 24, 55 (30, 20), 2 Macc. 14, 23; Joseph. *Antt.* xi. 5, 2, and often; Polyb. viii. 27 (29), 6 *et al.*; Plut. *De Alex. fortuna*, 341 C *et al.;* Philostr. *Apollon.* vii. 11, vii. 39; Epictet. iii. 2, 17; Theophr. *Hist. plant.* i. 1, 3; Dion. Hal. *De comp. verb.* 25 *ter*, *et al.*, illustrating both uses of the word as applied by Luke. For a number of other examples, see Wettstein on Luke 23, 41 and Acts 28, 6. (The reference Judith 11, 11, should be Job 11, 11; add Job 27, 6), Moulton and Milligan, *Vocabulary*, *s. v.*

[57] *ἀναδιδόναι ἐπιστολήν* Oxy. Pap. 237 *bis*; Fay. Pap. 130; *ἀναδιδόναι ἐπιστόλιον* Oxy. Pap. 63, 532; 1295, 15; Tebt. Pap. 448; Giss. Pap. I, 69, 4; *ἀναδιδόναι πιττάκιον* Oxy. Pap. 1063, and scores of other expressions for delivering receipts, contracts, wills, agreements, etc. With Acts 23, 33, compare Oxy. Pap. 486, 11, *ἀνέδωκα τῷ κρατίστῳ ἡγεμόνι ἀναφόριον*. Cf. Joseph. *Antt.* xvi. 10, 9; Diod. xi. 45, *ἀνέδωκε τοῖς ἐφόροις τὰς ἐπιστολάς*.

[58] Strabo has *οὐκ ἄσημος πόλις* several times; Plutarch has *οὐκ ἄσημοι [ἄνθρωποι]* Philo, *φυλὴ οὐκ ἄσημος*, and *ἐξ ἐλευθέρων ἴσως καὶ οὐκ ἀσήμων [πατέρων]*, Dion. Hal. *οὐκ ἀσήμων πατέρων, οὐκ ἄσημοι πόλεις*, Achilles Tatius *ἐλεύθερός τε ὢν καὶ πόλεως οὐκ ἀσήμου*. If the expression in Acts 21, 39, must be considered the echo of something, it is much more natural to compare it with *ἔστιν γὰρ οὐκ ἄσημος Ἑλλήνων πόλις* at the beginning of a famous play (Eur. *Ion*, 8) than with the less similar phrase in the

Hippocratean Epistles (*Epist.* 10, Hercher, μία πολίων οὐκ ἄσημος). See W. Nestle, "Anklänge an Euripides in der Apostelgeschichte," in *Philologus*, LIX (1900), pp. 46 ff. Of Josephus Krenkel (p. 249) says that, "bei ihm die Litotes οὐκ ἄσημος sehr beliebt ist," and gives nine examples. Cf. Lucian, *Pseudol.* 4, θεὸς οὐχ ὁ ἀσημότατος, Eurip. *Herc. Fur.* 849, ἀνὴρ δ' οὐκ ἄσημος.

[59] Of course the letters of Hippocrates are not genuine any more than are the letters of other literary and political figures of the classical era in Greece. But in confuting the argument of Hobart and his followers I have taken no advantage of the fact that a large part of the Hippocratean writings are spurious (Alfred Gudeman, "Literary Frauds among the Greeks," in *Classical Studies in Honour of Henry Drisler*, pp. 56 f., 69). Galen recognized only eleven as genuine (*Comm. in Epidem.*, *Praef. ad lib.* vi.), and speaks of the forgeries as of quite recent date (*Comm. in Hippocr. De offic. med.*, p. 2, χθὲς καὶ πρῴην). The other medical writers from whom Hobart quotes are "Aretaeus, who lived in the first century after Christ, probably in the reign of Nero or Vespasian; Galen, A.D. 130–200; and Dioscorides, who lived in the first or second century of the Christian era." (Hobart, p. vii.) It is not likely that their writings were known to the almost contemporary evangelist. These objections would probably be met by the assertion that "Greek medical language was particularly conservative in its character, the same class of words being employed in it from the time of Hippocrates to that of Galen" (*ibid.*, p. xxx), and that Luke and the other medical writers of his time were drawing on the current terminology of their profession. If anything like literary dependence is to be thought of between Luke and the doctors it must be remembered that at least in the case of Galen, from whom so many of the examples are quoted, the relationship will have to be the other way, for Galen's date was about 200 A.D. Harnack himself recognizes this. In quoting two striking parallels from Galen to the parable of the Good Samaritan he says (p. 190 f.): "One might almost imagine that Galen had read St. Luke. This is not impossible for he had to do with Christians." Norden, *Antike Kunstprosa*, pp. 518 f., thinks it probable that Galen read the Gospels, and he quotes a very interesting fragment in which Galen himself refers to the parables of the Christians.

[60] Hobart, pp. 54–85; Zahn, p. 147; Harnack, pp. 182–188.

[61] See below, Part II, *passim*.

[62] *Introduction*, III, 136, n. 13.

[63] Lobeck, *Phryn.* p. 90.

[64] Lucian, *Soloec.* 6. But κακῶς ἔχοντας of Mark 1, 32, 34 becomes ἀσθενοῦντας in Luke 4, 40, and ἐσχάτως ἔχει of Mark 5, 23 becomes ἀπέθνησκεν, Luke 8, 42.

[65] Lobeck, *Phryn.* p. 291.

[66] In the same passage, Luke substitutes θεραπεύω for Mark's ὠφελέω, though the latter was according to Hobart (p. 2) "in constant use in medical writers as opposed to βλάπτω," and the former "in the strict sense as a medical term means 'received medical treatment'" (Ramsay, *Luke the Physician*, p. 17), a meaning that it will not possibly bear in this passage in Luke. Note the correct use of these two words in the two texts of Tobit 2, 10.

[67] See Ropes, *James*, p. 305.

[68] For some others of these words in Matt. and Mark Hobart himself supplies medical examples, e.g. ἄνηθον (p. 37), ἄρρωστος (pp. 22, 46, 203), διυλίζω (p. 239), κύμινον (p. 230), πυρέσσω (pp. 31, 33, 85, 98, 121, 196, 213, 272).

[69] Note also the suggestion of Burkitt, *Gospel History and its Transmission*, p. 159 n, in regard to Matt. 5, 29, 30: "It seems to me probable that Luke the Physician preferred to leave out the metaphor of amputation."

[70] It is of just this verse that Harnack (p. 184) says that Luke "has, therefore, an interest in methods of healing." It is of the next verse that Zahn (p. 147) says, "It is Luke alone . . . who notes that the healing was accomplished by the laying on of hands (4, 40), where mention of this act is not made in Matthew (8, 16) or in Mark (1, 34)."

[71] This point will be discussed in Part II.

[72] Notice also that the reed which in Mark 15, 19 is used to beat Jesus on the head is in Matt. 27, 29 put in his *right* hand as a mockery of the regal sceptre. In the saying on offences occurring twice in Matthew, once the warning is against an offending eye or hand (18, 8, 9), once against an offending *right* eye or *right* hand (5, 29, 30). The first version of the doublet is apparently from Mark (9, 43–47), the second form presumably from Q. Shall we say then that Q here shows a doctor's interest, or that John does because in the account of Malchus' ear he like Luke names it as the right ear (John 18, 10)? John (5, 5; 9, 1) also indicates the duration of diseases that Jesus cured, and exact data relative to recovery (4, 52, cf. 11, 39).

And even were such details more numerous in Luke than in the parallels the motive might well be literary rather than medical. So the Chronicler in editing the books of Kings adds the exact year when Asa "was diseased in his feet" (1 Kings 15, 23 = 2 Chron. 16, 12), and the fact that Uzziah's leprosy "broke forth in his forehead" (2 Kings 15, 5 = 2 Chron. 26, 19), all of which embellishments are purely literary according to Torrey, *Ezra Studies*, p. 234. Such changes of Mark by Luke, Wernle calls simply legendary. See his comments in *Die synoptische Frage*, pp. 28, 29, 33, on Luke 4, 33; 6, 6; 22, 50 respectively.

[73] The best parallels to the features of Mark not found in Luke in these two cases of possession are in the two authorities on epilepsy that Harnack (p. 187, n. 1) refers to in Hobart (p. 17 f.), viz. Hippocrates, *Morb. sacr.*, I, 592 f., Kühn, and Aretaeus, *Sign. morb. acut.* i. 5, cf. *Sign. morb. diut.* i. 4. The following are the Greek words:

MARK (but not Luke)	HIPPOCRATES
ἄλαλον	ἄφωνός ἐστιν
ἀφρίζει, ἀφρίζων (Luke μετὰ ἀφροῦ)	ἀφρέει, ἀφρὸς ἐκ τοῦ στόματος ἐκρέει
τρίζει τοὺς ὀδόντας	οἱ ὀδόντες συνηρείκασι
ἐπὶ τῆς γῆς ἐκυλίετο	τοῖσι ποσὶ λακτίζει
ὡσεὶ νεκρός	ἀναβλύει ὥσπερ ἀποθνήσκων
διὰ παντὸς νυκτὸς καὶ ἡμέρας . . . ἦν κράζων	ἐκ νυκτῶν βοᾷ καὶ κέκραγεν τὰ μὲν νύκτωρ τὰ δὲ μεθ' ἡμέραν
κατακόπτων ἑαυτὸν λίθοις	
πολλάκις καὶ εἰς πῦρ αὐτὸν ἔβαλεν καὶ εἰς ὕδατα	ἀεί τι ἄκαιρον δρῶντες
	ARETAEUS
κῶφον	βαρυήκοοι
ξηραίνεται	πείρωσίς τινος αἰσθήσιος
διὰ παντὸς νυκτὸς καὶ ἡμέρας	ἄγρυπνοι
ἐκ τῶν μνημείων (Luke ἐκ τῆς πόλεως)	ἐξάνθρωποι, ἀμίκτοι

Hippocrates also describes the effects of the "sacred disease" on patients of different ages, including those "with whom it has grown up and increased since youth (ἀπὸ παιδίου)." Cf. ἐκ παιδιόθεν in Mark. Note also that Luke 9, 39, substitutes the simple λαμβάνει for Mark's technical term for catalepsy καταλάβῃ (9, 18; see references to Celsus in Swete *ad loc.*).

[74] Wernle, *Die synoptische Frage*, p. 24, says of this passage; "Die Erzählung vom Epileptischen, die bei Mr 16 Verse umfasst, erzählt Lc in 7 Versen, da ihre Einzelheiten ihn nicht interessierten."

[75] Ramsay in general accepts the medical language of Luke, but the proof of it drawn from Luke's changes in Mark he does not "remember to have seen adequately discussed." His own treatment of these will scarcely supply the want. He says (*Luke the Physician*, p. 57 f.):

"Even in passages that have been taken over by Luke from the Source which we still possess almost in its original form in the Gospel of Mark, wherever there occurs any reference to illness or to the medical treatment of sick persons, Luke almost invariably alters the expression more or less, as in v, 18 he changes the term "a paralytic" of Mark ii, 3 to "a man who was paralysed." He could hardly ever rest satisfied with the popular untrained language used about medical matters by Mark.

"In some cases the change does not imply really more than is contained in the original Source, and amounts only to a more scientific and medically accurate description of the fact related in the Source. But in other cases a real addition to knowledge is involved, as appears, e.g., from the following examples:

"1. Mark iii, 1 speaks of a man with a withered hand; Luke vi, 6, adds that it was the right hand: the medical mind demands such specification.

"2. Luke viii, 27 adds to Mark v, 2 that the possessed man had for a long time worn no clothes: this was a symptom of the insanity that a physician would not willingly omit.

"3. In Luke viii, 55, the physician mentions that Jairus' daughter called for food (cf. Mark v, 42). Various other examples occur."

Of the three examples given by Ramsay in this passage the first has been considered above; the second is a case where Luke according to his custom (see Part II) anticipates a detail which needs explanation in the sequel, the symptom of nakedness is implied in the ἱματισμένον of Mark 5, 15; the last is apparently a mistake, for the request that food be given to the girl is found in Mark 5, 43, as well as in Luke. Pfleiderer has curiously enough made just the converse mistake by overlooking the passage in Luke. He says (*Primitive Christianity*, II, 23) that Mark alone has preserved this little touch of realism. It is moreover Jesus, not Jairus' daughter, who in both Gospels calls for food for her.

[76] Out of Hobart's list of more than 400 words I find only five which he speaks of as altogether or nearly limited in use to medical writers. In three of them he is followed by Harnack (pp. 188, 193 f.). These three have already been examined above: ἀνακαθίζω (note 27); ἐκψύχω (note 29); συστέλλω (note 47), and found unsatisfactory. Another case of Hobart's is ἐνισχύω, of which he says (pp. 80 f.): "With respect to this word it is remarkable that outside of the LXX its use in the transitive sense, 'to strengthen,' is confined to Hippocrates and St. Luke. All other writers who employ it do so in the intransitive sense, 'to prevail,' 'be strong.'" But in its transitive sense the word occurs apparently only once in Hippocrates (*Lex*), but in the LXX more than fifteen times, while in Luke it is found only in the very doubtful passage, [Luke] 22, 43, 44. In Acts 9, 19, on the other hand, it is used in its common intransitive sense. The fifth example is εὐφορέω, Luke 12, 16, 'be fruitful,' of which Hobart (p. 144) says, "used in this sense by St. Luke, Hippocrates and Galen only." But it is used in this sense in Josephus *B. J.* ii. 21, 2 and Philostratus, *Apollon.* vi. 39; *Imag.* ii. 34 (cited by Schmid, *Atticismus*, IV, 358), and in Geopon., Greg. Nyss., and other later writers. In Lucian (*Lexiph.* 15) it is used in a different sense of ships (though Passow confuses this with the New Testament passage).

Harnack makes this claim of one other word, but with as little foundation as the cases already considered. He says (p. 178; cf. Moffatt, p. 299 n.): "Nor is it without significance that the heat is described as θέρμη; for this word, rare, I believe, in ordinary use, and only found here in the New Testament, is among physicians the general term used for θερμότης, as Hobart (p. 287) shows by very numerous examples." But an investigation of the actual occurrence of the two synonyms shows that while in Plato and Aristotle θέρμη occurs less often than θερμότης, it occurs more often than θερμότης in Greek comedy and lyric poetry, in LXX, in Plutarch and Lucian (see p. 66); it occurs also in Josephus, Aristides and Aelian, and according to Lobeck (*Phryn.* p. 331) in Ctesias, Pherecrates, Philo, Arrian, etc. It should be observed also that θερμότης occurs frequently in medical writings, as in Galen, *Humor. comm.* ii. 22 (XVI, 283) *bis*, and passages cited in Hobart, pp. 67, 81, 82, 83, etc.

With regard to the expressions καταφερόμενος ὕπνῳ βαθεῖ and κατενεχθεὶς ἀπὸ τοῦ ὕπνου, Acts 20, 9, Harnack (p. 180), says: "Hobart has (pp. 48 ff.) pointed out that this word, peculiar to St. Luke in the New Testament, is so usual in medical phraseology (and only in it) for 'falling asleep' that the word 'sleep' is often omitted. . . . Passow also only gives medical authorities for καταφέρεσθαι and καταφορά in the sense of sleep." But Wettstein alone gives examples from Aristotle, Josephus, Diodorus, Plutarch, Lucian, Alexander, Herodian, Parthenius, and Eustathius. On the other hand Thayer (*s. v.*) considers both expressions in Acts to have a different meaning from that found in the doctors and other "profane authors."

The best illustrations of words not found outside the writings of Luke and the doctors, συγκυρία ("rare," Hobart, p. 30) and ἀνωτερικός ("very rare," Hobart, p. 148), appear to have been overlooked by Hobart's followers. Except for later writers these words are cited from no other sources. See also List 4, p. 19.

[77] *Introduction*, III, 162, n. 5. In the German, "Worten und Redewendungen die nur auch bei den Medicinern gebräuchlich sind."

[78] It is doubtful whether the argument for the medical language of Luke gains much from the fact that the examples used are sometimes found only in Luke among New Testament writers. It is with particular emphasis that Hobart and Moffatt star words peculiar to Luke, and Harnack and Zahn remark frequently, "occurs in the New Testament only in the Lukan writings," "is not met again in the New Testament," "here only in the New Testament.," etc. It must be confessed that in all lexical study of the New Testament such facts have played an important part; but it seems to the present writer that their significance has been greatly overestimated. It must be remembered that the New Testament is, linguistically at least, a merely accidental collection of a very limited number of books, on a considerable variety of subjects. As a result the words peculiar to any New Testament writer (as may be seen from the lists in the Appendix to Thayer's Lexicon) are many of them words common in all periods of Greek writing, and typical neither of the vocabulary nor even of the grade of culture of the author. The words *characteristic* of a New Testament writer are a very different kind of list, and cannot be determined without reference to the LXX and profane Greek as well as to the other writers in the New Testament. If Luke's medical knowledge is to be proved by his diction, the proof examples should be shown to be both characteristically Lukan in this sense and characteristically medical. What words belong to the latter category it is difficult for us to know to-day. Perhaps it is safe to assume that the early glossaries to Hippocrates include the terms in his works which would be obscure to a layman in the age of Luke. Of over 1700 such words in the combined index of Franz's edition (Leipzig, 1780) of the glossaries by Erotian, Galen, and Herodotus,

only one word, διατρίβειν, is cited as a medical term in Luke by Hobart (p. 221; on p. 16 f. he declines to take πνεῦμα, Luke 8, 55, in the sense of "respiration" which the glossaries give it for Hippocrates). See also note 39.

[79] Cf. A. Thumb, *Die griechische Sprache im Zeitalter des Hellenismus*, Strassburg, 1901, pp. 225 f.

"Für Quellenuntersuchungen innerhalb der hellenistichen Literatur ergibt sich noch ein anderer Grundsatz: man darf den Wortschatz zweier oder mehrerer Schriftsteller, sofern er dem Bestand der κοινή zugeschrieben werden muss, nicht benützen, um die Abhängigkeit des einem von anderen daraus zu folgern. . . . Dass Lukas eine Reihe medicinischer Ausdrücke gebraucht, die bei Hippokrates und andern Aerzten sich finden, beweist kein Studium der medicinischen Schriften, sondern höchstens die Kenntnis der üblichen medicinischen Terminologie: aber manche der Ausdrücke wie ἔχειν ἐν γαστρί (vgl. neugr. ἐγγαστρώνομαι), ἔγκυος (neugr. ebenso), στεῖρα, oder βελόνη (letzeres statt ῥαφίς für die Nadel des Chirurgen, neugr. βελόνι) sind jedenfalls so allgemein gebrauchte Bestandteile der gesprochenen Sprache gewesen, dass ihnen überhaupt kein Wert für quellenkritische Feststellungen zukommt."

[80] Kennedy, *Sources of New Testament Greek*, pp. 32 f.; cf. pp. 63 f.

[81] See the word lists throughout this work. Schmid says (*Atticismus*, IV, 659): "Dass die Schriften des Hippokrates auch von Nichtmedicinern in der Atticistenzeit noch gelesen wurden, zeigen mehrfache Entlehnungen einzelner Ausdrücke des H. bei unseren Autoren; sie waren nie vergessen; aber einen stärkeren Einfluss auf die Diktion der Atticisten hat H. nicht geübt; nur eine *vox Hippocratea*, ἀραιότης, kommt bei mehreren von ihnen vor."

[82] Götzeler, *De Polybii elocutione*, p. 15 f., cited by Schmid, *l. c.* Wunderer in his *Polybios-Forschungen*, Part I (Leipzig, 1898), pp. 88 f., also finds evidence of medical knowledge in phrases and proverbial expressions of the historian. Although he confesses that the Hellenistic age was characterized by a "Verallgemeinerung der medicinischen Kentnisse," even among the laymen, he adds, "Polybios legt überall, wie ich an den bemerkenswerten Vergleichen zeigen werde, besonderes Interesse für medicinische Fragen an den Tag und muss in der That eingehende medicinische Studien nicht bloss in der Jugend, sondern auch während der Abfassung seines Geschichtswerkes gemacht haben."

[83] Th. Beck in *Correspondenz-Blatt für Schweizer. Aerzte*, XXXV (1905), No. 24.

[84] On medical language in Seneca, for example, see K. F. H. Marx, "Uebersichtliche Anordnung der die Medizin betreffenden Aussprüche des Philosophen L. Ann. Seneca," in *Abhandl. d. königl. Gesellschaft der Wissensch. zu Göttingen*, XXII (1877); C. S. Smith, *Metaphor and Comparison in the Epistulae ad Lucilium of L. Annaeus Seneca*, Baltimore, 1910, pp. 39 ff., 100 ff.; D. Steyns, *Etude sur les métaphores et les comparaisons dans les œuvres en prose de Sénèque le philosophe*, Gand, 1907.

[85] Wendland, *Urchristliche Literaturformen*, p. 335, asserts: "Aber diese [ärztlichen] Kenntnisse gehen nicht über das Mass hinaus, das bei gebildeten Laien vorauszusetzen ist. Eine umfassende, meist für ein weites Publikum bestimmte medizinische Literatur, darunter zahlreiche von Laien verfasste Schriften, auch öffentliche medizinische Vorträge haben eine gewisse Vertrautheit mit ärztlicher Kunst und Terminologie verbreitet. Philos Kenntnisse auf dem Gebiete gehen erheblich weiter als die unseres Autors [Lukas], und doch ist er kein Arzt gewesen."

[86] Hobart, p. xxxvi; cf. Plummer, p. lxiv.

[87] The necessity of comparative evidence is recognized by Zahn (*Introduction*, III, 130 n. 1) in a similar linguistic argument — the alleged dependence of Luke on Jose-

phus — but he does not seem to have applied the principle to his own arguments on the dependence of Luke on the medical writers. In refuting the argument of Krenkel, he says: "His method is not to be commended. . . . The only list of words which really belongs here is that of the words common to Luke and Josephus, not found in the LXX. And this would be significant only if very familiar words were excluded, such as are found quite universally in literature since Homer." And he suggests that "it would be necessary to compare other authors known not to be dependent on Josephus, who might show points of resemblance to Luke in content and form," such as Philo, Polybius, and the historians that followed, down to Herodian. "If this extended investigation should show a special resemblance between Luke and Josephus in language and style," it still could be explained otherwise than by interdependence.

Zahn goes so far in this inconsistent attitude toward the theories of Krenkel and Hobart that he even rejects the same example when proposed by the former, but accepts it as an argument from the latter. I refer to his treatment of parallels to αὐτόπται γενόμενοι, Luke 1, 2. He says (*Introduction*, III, 82 f., n. 5): "Luke's language does show the most striking resemblance to that of the medical writers from Hippocrates to Galen, as has been conclusively shown by Hobart. This is noticeably true in the prologue. . . . Hobart cites from Galen not less than 11 instances of αὐτόπτης γενόμενος, γίνεσθαι, γενέσθαι." But a few pages later (p. 130, n. 1) he rejects Krenkel's list of parallels to Luke from Josephus because it contains very familiar words, "such as are found quite universally in literature since Homer. . . . In this class belongs also αὐτόπτης, Luke 1, 2, upon which Krenkel (pp. 55, 56, 305) lays weight; whereas it is used by Herodotus, iv. 16; Polybius, i. 4, 7, iii. 4, 13, and frequently — generally with γίνεσθαι, as in Luke."

[88] Schmid, *Atticismus*, I, 431 n., says: "Es giebt wahrscheinlich keinen griechischen Prosaiker, dessen Wortvorrat reichhaltiger wäre, als derjenige des Lucian. Die Zahl der von ihm angewendeten Wörter beträgt beiläufig 10,400 (bei Plato etwa 9,900, bei Polybius etwa 7,700)." For the size of Luke's vocabulary, see above, Chapter I. Schmid is, however, scarcely right in assigning to Lucian a larger vocabulary than any other Greek prose writer. Plutarch apparently uses more than 15,000 words according to a rough calculation in Wyttenbach's Lexicon.

[89] Hobart (p. xxxi) notes that both Luke and the medical writers came from Asia Minor.

[90] Some of Clemen's arguments are of interest:

"Truly the author of these writings employs some medical terms in their technical sense, but in a few cases he uses them in such a way as no physician would have done. E.g. in the description of Christ's prayer in Gethsemane his sweat is compared with θρόμβοι αἵματος καταβαίνοντες ἐπὶ τὴν γῆν, i.e. not with great drops of blood, as the English version has it, but with clots of blood, which here of course not even for comparison's sake can be thought of." "Could a Greek physician represent the good Samaritan (Luke 10, 34) as pouring on the wounds of the man who had fallen among robbers oil and wine?" (*Hibbert Journal*, VIII (1910), pp. 785 f.). On ἀπέπεσαν λεπίδες, Acts 9, 18, he writes: "Ein Arzt musste doch wissen, dass dabei nichts vom Auge abzufallen braucht." (*Theol. Rundschau*, X (1907), p. 102.)

[91] At the beginning of his treatise "On the Natural Faculties" Galen explicitly deprecates and renounces the use of technical terms: "We, however, for our part, are convinced that the chief merit of language is clearness, and we know that nothing detracts so much from this as do unfamiliar terms; accordingly we employ those terms which the bulk of people (οἱ πολλοί) are accustomed to use." [Brock's translation, in *Loeb Classical Library*, p. 3.]

EXCURSUS

MEDICAL TERMS IN LUCIAN *

THE object of this study is to investigate the diction of Lucian for medical terms after the manner adopted by Hobart, Harnack, and Zahn for Luke.

Of the 400 words in Hobart's index, 300 appear in the index to Lucian. It would be natural to suppose that there are 100 words in Lucian but not in Luke that could with equal propriety be called medical terms, so that the total size of his medical vocabulary would be no smaller than that of Luke.[1]

Of the 100 specially selected examples chosen by Zahn and Harnack, nearly half are found in Lucian's works. They are so marked "Luc." in the lists above, but it will be worth while to quote a few of the cases in full:

ἀποψύχειν is used in Luke 21, 26 in the meaning 'faint, fail,' and is cited by Harnack (p. 197) and Zahn (p. 161) as a medical term. "But medical writers use *ἀποψύχειν* of *being chilled*, not of swooning or expiring." (Plummer, *ad. loc.*) See the examples in Hobart, p. 166. So Lucian, *Vit. auct.* 25, and elsewhere, uses it of limbs growing cold or stiff, like Niobe's.

Lucian, *Dial. mar.* 7, *ἀνορθώσας δὲ αὐτὴν ὁ Ἑρμῆς γυναῖκα παγκάλην αὖθις ἐποίησε*, referring to the restoration of the heifer Io to the form of a woman. "*ἀνορθοῦν* likewise is the usual medical word for the restoring of the members or parts of the body to their natural position." (Harnack, p. 189, referring to the story of Luke 13, 11 ff.)

In Lucian, *Ocyp.* 45, the lame (*χωλός* 41) attendant is called *ὑπηρέτης*[2] *ἀδύνατος γογγύζων γέρων*. "The man of Lystra, lame from his mother's womb, is described as an *ἀνὴρ ἀδύνατος τοῖς ποσίν* (Acts xiv, 8). See the medical examples for *ἀδύνατος* in Hobart, p. 46." (Harnack, p. 193.)

Lucian, *Herm.* 86, *τοσαύτην ἀχλὺν ἀποσεισάμενος*[3] *τῶν ὀμμάτων*. "Hobart, pp. 44 f. shows that *ἀχλύς*, according to Galen, is a distinct disease of the eyes." (Harnack, p. 193).

Lucian, *Tox.* 43, *ὁ λέων ἀφεὶς ἐκεῖνον ἡμιθνῆτα*. Cf. Luke 10, 30, *οἱ λῃσταὶ ἀπῆλθον ἀφέντες ἡμιθανῆ*. On *ἡμιθνής*, see above, p. 56, note 31. This, and not *ἡμιθανής* as Harnack says (p. 190), is the word used by Galen.

Lucian, *Philopseud.* 11, *ὑπὸ ἐχίδνης δηχθέντα . . . τὸ θηρίον δακεῖν*. "The fact that the viper (*ἔχιδνα*) is called *θηρίον* is not without significance; for this is just the medical term that is used for the reptile. . . . Hobart further

* For the notes on this chapter see below, pp. 71 f.

remarks (*loc. cit.*, p. 51) that 'Dioscorides uses θηριόδηκτος to signify bitten by a serpent' " (Harnack, p. 178). Similarly in Lucian's *Dipsades* a reptile like the ἔχιδνα (4) is called θηρίον (6), πίμπρασθαι is used of the swelling from the bite (4) as in Acts 28, 6 (cf. Hobart, p. 50, Harnack, p. 179), and other medical details are mentioned with apologies to the medical poet Nicander (9).

Lucian, *Dial. mar.* 11, 2, ἡ θέρμη ἀπὸ τοῦ πύρος. Cf. Acts 28, 4. "Nor is it without significance that the heat is described as θέρμη; for this word, rare, I believe, in ordinary use, and only found here in the New Testament, is among physicians the general term used for θερμότης, as Hobart (p. 287) shows by very numerous examples." (Harnack, p. 178.) As a matter of fact the doctors use θερμότης also, e.g. Galen, *Humor. comm.* ii. 22 (XVI, 283 *bis*). See above, p. 62, note 76.

Lucian, *Dial. mort.* 28, 2, στεῖρα καὶ ἄγονος διετέλεσας. On στεῖρα see Zahn, p. 160. With the construction of διατελέω (" very much used in medical language " — Hobart, p. 278) compare ἄσιτοι διατελεῖτε, Acts 27, 33 in List D above (p. 45).

Lucian, *Dial. meretr.* 2, 4, ἐς ὕπνον κατηνέχθην. Cf. Acts 20, 9, καταφερόμενος ὕπνῳ βαθεῖ[4] . . . κατενεχθεὶς ἀπὸ τοῦ ὕπνου. "Passow only gives medical authorities for καταφέρεσθαι in the sense of sleep; cf. the multitude of instances quoted by Hobart (from Hippocrates to Galen), some of which closely coincide with the passage we are considering." (Harnack, p. 180.) One of Hobart's instances has κατενεχθέντας εἰς ὕπνον, but none use ὕπνῳ or ἀπὸ τοῦ ὕπνου.

"Let it be observed that Luke avoids the following terms for sickness which are not customary with medical men, μαλακία, βάσανος, βασανίζεσθαι (Matt. iv, 24, viii, 6, ridiculed by Lucian, *Soloec.* 6)." (Zahn, p. 160.)

Lucian, *Vera hist.* i. 22, συλλάβῃ τὸ ἔμβρυον. For συλλαμβάνω without ἐν γαστρί of conception see Luke 1, 24, 36; Zahn, p. 160.

Lucian speaks of lunatics, *Philopseud.* 16, καταπίπτοντας πρὸς τὴν σελήνην . . . καὶ ἀφροῦ[5] πιμπλαμένους τὸ στόμα. *Tox.* 24, ἐλέγετο δὲ καὶ καταπίπτειν πρὸς τὴν σελήνην αὐξανομένην. "Καταπίπτω — here only in the New Testament — can also be vouched for from medical language (Hobart, pp. 50 f.)." (Harnack, p. 179.) "Καταπίπτειν, peculiar to St. Luke, is used of persons falling down suddenly from wounds, or in epileptic fits." (Hobart, p. 50.)

Though all these general observations are significant, yet for any comparison of Lucian with Luke it would not be fair to match the whole extent of Lucian's writings against Luke's work of only 150 pages. One point in Hobart's argument is that his " examples are very numerous considering the extent of St. Luke's writings." Are the " medical terms " of Lucian as numerous *proportionately* as the medical terms of Luke ?

To answer this question a small section of Lucian was examined more minutely for comparison. Three pieces, the *Alexander*, the second part of the *True History*, and the *Death of Peregrinus* were chosen purely on the basis of subject matter as forming a kind of parallel to Luke's stories of miracles and travel and martyrdom.

The total extent of these three writings of Lucian is about half that of the works of Luke.

In this limited section of Lucian were found about 115 of the words considered medical by Hobart, or over one-fourth of his entire list. It was also found that these words occur about half as often in this section of Lucian as they do in Luke's work of twice the size. In other words, the frequency of occurrence of these words is about the same in the two writers. And this fact is all the more remarkable in view of the fact that many words are included which are distinguished by Hobart as especially frequent in Luke and used by him much oftener than by other New Testament writers.[6]

Still more remarkable are the figures for that other class of words on which Hobart lays so much weight — the words peculiar to Luke in the New Testament. About 75 of this class, or about one-fourth of all the words starred by Hobart, are found in the section of Lucian examined, and, as for frequency of occurrence, it actually appears that these words "peculiar to Luke" occur at least twice as often in Lucian as they do in Luke himself. The times of occurrence of these 75 words in the three writings are very nearly as follows:

Luke	50
Acts	75
Lucian (section the size of Luke *or* Acts)	150

But of course it is not necessary to limit our study of medical terms in Lucian to those words which happen also to occur in Luke. The parallel should be made quite independently of Luke, but after the manner and method of Hobart, Harnack, and Zahn, especially the two last. Accordingly, from the 75 pages of Lucian examined, I have formed four lists of words corresponding to the four lists formed for Luke from the examples of Harnack and Zahn. In addition I have compiled a fifth list of the kind already suggested,[7] of words whose use in extant writers seems to connect Lucian with Hippocrates and the doctors. It will be remembered that such a list has not been produced for Luke. Those who put weight on the evidence of words in Luke but not in the other New Testament writers will observe that these words occur neither in Luke nor, with few exceptions, elsewhere in the New Testament.[8]

A. General Words

1. Words of rare occurrence but found in medical writers.
2. Words used frequently by doctors, or akin to such words.
3. Words used by doctors as technical terms.

ἀναχαίνω, cf. Hobart, p. 33.
ἀνιμάω, Aret. *al.*
ἀπαρτάω
γαλακτώδης, Hipp.
γερόντιον, Hipp. *al.*
δίαιτα, 'diet,' Hipp.
διαπνέω, cf. Hobart, p. 236.
διασήπω, Theophr. *Hist. plant.*
διερείδω, cf. Hobart, p. 280.
ἐγχρίω, of eye salve, Rev. 3, 18.
ἐντεριώνη, Hipp., Arist., Theophr.
ἔξωρος, Hipp. *al.*
ἐπιδημία, cf. Hobart, p. 188.
κατακλίσις, 'a way of lying in bed,' Hipp., cf. Hobart, p. 69.
κατόπιν, Hipp. *al.*
καῦσις, 'cautery,' Heb. 6, 8.
κοιλαίνω, of ulcers, Hipp.
κόλλα, cf. Hobart, p. 128.
κορώνη, 'apophysis of a bone' (term. tech.).
κρᾶσις
μολύβδινος, Hipp. *al.*
ὀθόνινος, cf. Hobart, pp. 218 f.
ὁμιχλώδης, Theophr., *Caus. plant.*
παραβύω
περιπνέω, cf. Hobart, p. 236.
σκέψις, of medical examination, Hipp.
σκευαστός, cf. Hobart, p. 232.
σκίλλα, Hipp. *al.*
συγκολλάω, cf. Hobart, p. 128.
συναγωγεύς, a kind of muscle, Hipp.
τρυπάω, Hipp. *al.*
τύρβη, Hipp. *al.*
ὑπερπίμπλημι, Hipp. *al.*, cf. Hobart, p. 107.
ὑποπίμπλημι, cf. Hobart, p. 107.
ὑποτύφω
ὑποφρίττω, rare outside of Lucian, but found in Galen.
χαίνω, cf. Hobart, p. 33.

B. Medical Words *

ἀλεξιφάρμακον, medical writers
ἀναφλάω
ἄσαρκος, Hipp. *al.*
γομφίος
ἐλλέβορος (ἐλλεβορίζω)
ἐμέω, Rev. 3, 16
θηλή
κιννάμωμον (κινναμώμινος), Rev. 18, 13
κολοκύνθη (κολοκύνθινος), Diosc. *al.*
κυτμίς
κύω
λύζω
μαλάχη, medical writers
μελαγχολέω
μηρός, Rev. 19, 16
πύελος
πώγων

* Diseases, medicines, and parts of the body.

C. Ordinary Words Used in a Medical Sense *

ἄκοπον (sc. φάρμακον), 'painkiller,' *Alex.* 22. Cf. Galen's work, περὶ ἀκόπων, and elsewhere in Galen.

ἁρμογή, 'joint' of the body, *Alex.* 14. Only Galen XIX, 460, cf. II, 734, ed. Kühn, are cited in the lexica for this meaning.

ἀρτηρία, 'wind pipe,' *Alex.* 26. Frequently so in the doctors.

διηγέομαι, of the *post mortem* account, *Peregr.* 44. Cf. Hobart, pp. 229 f.

δριμύς, of drugs, *Peregr.* 45. Hipp., Theophr., Diosc., Galen. In Hipp. *Fract.* 769 it is used without φάρμακον in the same sense.

ἐπισκοπέω, of medical examination, *Peregr.* 44. So used by Galen.[9]

στρουθίον, as name of a plant, *Alex.* 12. "Name of plant in Hipp., Theophr., Diosc., *et al.*" (Passow, *s.v.*). Contrast Luke 12, 6.

ψυχρόν (without ὕδωρ), 'cold water,' *Peregr.* 44. Hippocr. *et al.* So Matt. 10, 42, but not Mark 9, 41, nor in Luke.

D. Longer Expressions

πυρετὸς μάλα σφοδρός, *Peregr.* 44.

λευκὸς τὴν χρόαν, *Alex.* 3.

νεκρικῶς τὴν χρόαν ἔχειν, *Peregr.* 33.

κοιλὴ ἡ χείρ

εἰς μανίαν ἐμβάλλω, *Alex.* 30.[10]

ἄσιτος ἐκαθέζετο, *Vera hist.* ii. 24. Cf. Acts 27, 33.

διατελέω χρώμενος, *Alex.* 5. Cf. Galen, *Comp. med. sec. loc.* vii. 2 (XII, 19, Kühn), φαρμάκοις χρώμενοι διατελῶσιν, cited by Hobart, p. 278.

σκωλήκων ζέσας, *Alex.* 59. "σκώληξ is used both of worms in sores and of intestinal worms," Hobart, p. 43, quoting this passage.

ἀναισθητῶς ἔχειν, *Vera hist.* ii. 1. Hipp.

συμμύω τὸ στόμα, *ibid.*, ii. 1. Hipp.

ὁ ἰατρὸς μετακληθείς, *Peregr.* 44. "These two compounds of καλέω [εἰσκαλέω, μετακαλέω], peculiar to St. Luke, were used in medical language for 'to call in' or 'send for' a physician," Hobart, pp. 219 f.[11]

* By both Lucian and the medical writers.

E. Special List Connecting Lucian and the Medical Writers [12]

1. Words apparently found elsewhere only in the medical writers.

2. Words found in no writer before Polybius except Hippocrates.

ἀλέα	Hipp. *al.*
ἀμβλυωπέω	Hipp., not in Attic writers.
ἐπιβρέχω	Theophr., Diosc.
ἐπιχλιαίνω	Stephanus quotes only Hipp. besides.
ἡμιτόμιον	Diosc.; Passow cites no other authors.
καταθηλύνω	Lexica refer only to Luc. (*ter*) and Hipp.
καταρράπτω	Hipp., Galen.
κολλύριον	Hipp., Galen., Diosc., Rev. 3, 18.
κορύζη	Lexica refer only to medical writers besides.
μαστίχη	Theophr., Diosc.
προσοκέλλω	Aretaeus and later writers.
συλλείβομαι	Hipp., Arist.
φλογμός	frequent in Hipp.

The following observations may also be made:

1. Hippocrates is directly referred to in *Vera hist.* ii. 7, Ἱπποκράτει τῷ Κῴῳ ἰατρῷ.

2. *Vera hist.* ii. 47 closes in much the same way as Galen makes his transitions between the seventeen books of his *De usu partium*, e.g., Book vi, *ad fin.*, περὶ ὧν ἁπάντων ὁ ἐφεξῆς τῷδε λόγος ἐξηγήσεται.

3. The preface to the *Alexander* has a certain resemblance to the preface of Dioscorides' *Materia medica*. This, it will be remembered, is the preface that Luke is said to have imitated.[13] Its resemblance to Luke and Lucian is equally close.

4. If the medical coloring of certain passages is to be examined, as Harnack, pp. 15 f, 176 ff., examines the story of Acts 28, 3–10, probably *Alex.* 21, or *Peregr.* 44, 45, would make a sufficient parallel.

5. Harnack (p. 175) suggests as one of the traces of the author's medical profession that " the language may be coloured by the language of physicians (medical technical terms, metaphors of medical character, etc.)." For medical technical terms, see Lists

B and C; for metaphors of medical character, see O. Schmidt, *Metapher und Gleichnis in den Schriften Lukians*, 1897, pp. 13 ff.

6. Harnack (p. 176) says that these signs will " compel us to believe that the author was a physician if . . . in those passages where the author speaks as an eyewitness medical traits are especially and prominently apparent." In *Peregr.* 44, 45, and in many other places where the medical traits are most numerous, Lucian also is writing as an eyewitness — even in the *True History*!

These suggestions do not exhaust the passages in Lucian, but probably they are enough for our purpose. Already they match in nearly every detail the evidence produced for the medical profession of Luke. And if the amount of Lucian examined should be doubled so as to equal in extent the writings of Luke, and if we then should " spend a lifetime " in going through the twenty-five volumes containing the writings of Hippocrates, Galen, Dioscorides, and Aretaeus, with occasional glimpses at Theophrastus, to collect the occurrences of words and note coincidences in their usage or combination with this part of Lucian, there can be no doubt that such an investigation could produce a volume quite as large as Hobart's, and that the best examples selected from it would be found quite as cogent as those of Harnack, Moffatt, and Zahn, to prove by his " medical language " that Lucian was a physician.

NOTES

[1] The following words occurring in Lucian but not in Luke or Acts are explicitly mentioned as medical terms by Hobart himself in the course of his book (pages of Hobart in brackets): *ἀγών* (81), *ἀθυμία* (280), *ἀνάδοσις* (260), *ἀνανεύω* (240), *ἀναπνέω* (236), *ἀναρπάζω* (244), *ἄσκησις* (263), *ἄτακτος* (222), *ἄτονος* (241), *ἄφορος* (144), *βιβρώσκω* (42), *διοχλέω* (232), *δοχεῖον* (158), *ἐξαρπάζω* (244), *ἐφεδρεύω* (260), *ἐπιταράττω* (93), *εὔφορος* (144), *καταναλίσκω* (16), *κατορθόω* (262), *ὁλόκληρος* (193), *πιέζω* (62), *πήρος,* *-όω*, *-ωσις* (148 f), *πρόχειρος* (202), *σκευάζω*, (232), *συνεδρεύω* (260), *συνταράσσω* (93), *συντρέφω* (223), *συντυχία* (30), *ταραχώδης* (93), *ὑποδοχή* (158), *ὑποταράσσω* (93), *φορός* (144), *ψαύω* (62).

[2] *ὑπηρέτης* is a medical term, according to Hobart, p. 88.

[3] " The compounds of *σείειν* were used by the medical writers." (Hobart, p. 103.)

[4] " Hobart also makes an attempt to prove by examples that *ὕπνος βαθύς* is a specific medical phrase; but I pass this by." (Harnack, p. 180, n. 1). The phrase occurs in Lucian, *Tim.* 6.

[5] " *ἀφρός* is used by Hippocrates and Aretaeus in describing the symptoms of epilepsy." (Hobart, p. 17.)

[6] E.g.,

Times in	Luke	Acts	Lucian
ἀναιρέω	2	18	4
διέρχομαι	10	21	3
ἰάομαι	11	4	2
καταβαίνω	14	19	2
πίμπλημι	13	9	1
πλῆθος	7	16	9
σύν	23	32	2
σώζω	15	13	1
ὑπάρχω	15	25	3
	110	157	27
But excluding these nine words the 108 other words occur approximately			
	102	149	226
or nearly twice as often in Lucian as in either half of Luke's work.			
Totals	212	306	253

[7] See p. 49.

[8] The exceptions are marked on the lists by the New Testament references. Five out of the eight are in Revelation. It should be observed that in compiling these lists "medical terms" actually occurring in Luke as well as in Lucian have been excluded.

[9] Cf. ἐπιβλέπω, above p. 44.

[10] Cf. Acts 26, 24, τὰ πολλά σε γράμματα εἰς μανίαν περιτρέπει, which Hobart (p. 268) considers medical, though he confesses that περιτρέπω is not employed exactly in this sense by medical writers. But ἐμπίπτω and ἐμβάλλω, which Hobart also considers medical words (pp. 130, 137), are probably used by the doctors as in Lucian. Note Hobart's quotation from Galen: ὥσπερ καὶ τοὺς εἰς ἐπιληψίαν τε καὶ ἀποπληξίαν ῥᾳδίως ἐμπίπτοντας.

The nearest parallel to Acts, *l.c.*, is not in the doctors but in Lucian's *Abdicatus* 30. This passage has apparently been overlooked by commentators (Wettstein does not use it, though he illustrates περιτρέπειν by two other passages in Lucian). In referring to the countless forms of madness (μυρία εἴδη; cf. Aretaeus, cited by Hobart, p. 267, μανίης τρόποι εἴδεσι μὲν μυρίοι) and its various causes he says: γέροντας δὲ καὶ διαβολὴ ἄκαιρος καὶ ὀργὴ ἄλογος πολλάκις κατ' οἰκείων ἐμπεσοῦσα τὸ μὲν πρῶτον διετάραξεν, εἶτα κατ' ὀλίγον ἐς μανίαν περιέτρεψε. Not only is this passage full of other words which Hobart would call medical (besides διαβολή, ἄλογος, ἐμπίπτω, διαταράσσω, occur in equally medical connections in the next few lines λύπη, ἀποτελέω, σωτηρία, ἀπαλλάσσω, θεραπεία, ὁμότεχνος ἐπανέρχομαι), but the whole piece is written from the doctor's view point with the most delicate sympathy for his professional sensitiveness.

[11] εἰσκαλέω also is used in this sense in Lucian: ὁ ἰατρὸς εἰσκληθεὶς, *Pseudol.* 23; but not by Luke, εἰσκαλεσάμενος οὖν αὐτοὺς ἐξένισεν, Acts 10, 23, the only occurrence in the New Testament.

[12] This list of words, intended to illustrate the criticism of the examples used for the medical language of Luke, contains words "found elsewhere only or mainly in the medical writers" (see above, p. 49). Of course the cases given are only those found in the 75 pages of Lucian examined for this purpose. The total number of words of this kind to be found in all Lucian's works may be estimated with the help of the word lists in Schmid's *Atticismus* as considerably over 100.

[13] Lagarde, *Psalterium juxta Hebraeos Hieronymi*, 1874, p. 165.

THE STYLE AND LITERARY METHOD OF LUKE

PART II

THE TREATMENT OF SOURCES IN THE GOSPEL

Introductory

The starting point for any study of Luke's method of using sources is a comparison of Luke and Mark. In the second Gospel is preserved to us, substantially as it was in the hands of our Evangelist, one of those " accounts concerning the things fulfilled among us," to which he refers, and the one which he used as his chief single source. The survival of this source gives us an unusually secure basis for the study of editorial method. In most other cases the source is known only through the derivative work, and the editorial method can be inferred only from the finished product. In the Gospel of Luke we can confront the author's work with his source, so that the changes, rearrangements, and additions which he has made can be certainly known.

The advantage of this field for the study of redactorial method is increased by another fact. The closeness with which Luke follows Mark, as compared with the freedom of paraphrase and embellishment in other ancient writers, gives us a sustained assurance throughout extensive sections of his work that this dependence is really there; for whenever (as in a few cases in Luke and usually in ancient writers) the divergence from known sources becomes quite considerable, the suspicion always arises that some unknown source is being used to supplement or even supplant the main source; or at least that the latter has gone through some intermediate stage before reaching our author.

There is no reason to suppose that Luke knew any later form of Mark than that which we possess. But an element of uncertainty would be introduced into our comparison of Luke and Mark, if, as some have maintained, the copy of Mark used by Luke was an earlier form of that Gospel, a so-called "Urmarcus." This is not the place for the discussion of a theory which synoptic study has practically destroyed, though it is still kept alive by a few scholars in a kind of artificial respiration. The differences between the "Urmarcus" and our Mark are probably so small that they would be sufficiently accounted for by scribal changes in a few successive copyings. They are to be sought where Matthew and Luke agree against Mark, their common source.[1] But these cases are not very numerous, and many of them may equally well be ascribed to identical corrections of Mark made independently by both Matthew and Luke.

In all cases of agreement of Matthew and Luke against Mark, whatever the presumed cause, great caution must be used in postulating the primitive form of the Marcan text,[2] and these cases are so few that they justify us in supposing that elsewhere Luke and Matthew followed a text that is substantially our Mark. And here the general accuracy that we may presume of all the New Testament text is an additional advantage possessed by the comparison of Mark and Luke over the comparison of any other two ancient books outside the New Testament, either or both of which rest on less trustworthy textual tradition.

The comparison of our Gospels is not a new problem, nor is the special relation of Luke and Mark an unexplored part of the more general field. But the examination of this question has often been made in a fragmentary way, and the results have often been left so unclassified that there is good reason for collecting at least some of the phenomena in such a way that some general observations can be made on the editorial method of Luke. In harmonies and commentaries, Luke's changes in the matter derived from Mark, no matter how fully they are indicated, necessarily follow the order of

[1] For a list see Allen, *Matthew*, pp. xxxvi–xl.

[2] For an attempted classification see, Stanton, *Gospels as Historical Documents, II*, pp. 207–219; Wernle, *Synoptische Frage*, pp. 45–61. Especially noteworthy is the list of passages where Matthew and Luke agree with the Western text of Mark but differ from the current text.

the text and fail of general classification. There are, no doubt, many changes that allow of no classification, or could be classified in more than one way, but there remain a great number of phenomena that allow of collective treatment, and they should be so treated.[1]

It must of course be confessed from the start that the relation of Luke to Mark is not merely a literary problem. There can be no doubt that some of the changes made by Luke in Mark are due to historical reasons, others are due to the general motives of the author — to his so-called " tendencies " — i.e. for doctrinal reasons. In so far as these changes are not of a stylistic or literary character, they lie outside the scope of these studies. But the exclusion must not be too strictly made. On the other hand the discovery of non-literary tendencies in New Testament writers is made entirely too easy in some schools of criticism, and should be attempted only after the literary habits of the writer have been carefully examined. The question may often be raised whether a single detail, or even a repeated phenomenon in Luke, supposed to show some special religious or social interest, may not be merely stylistic or artistic. In the following investigation of Luke's relation to Mark it will therefore be best to limit the examination to matters that may be only of the latter type, including, however, cases for which the motive may also be different.[2] Only on such a basis can the further motives of the editor be separated and established. And whatever the classification of the changes, it must not be assumed that they are necessarily due to conscious motives. An ancient author in paraphrasing a source naturally used his own style and language, and even his own

[1] Short but valuable lists of literary changes in his sources made by Luke are to be found in Norden, *Die Antike Kunstprosa*, pp. 486–492, and in Wernle, *Die Synoptische Frage*, pp. 9 ff. The most complete study of the sort here attempted is the work of J. H. Scholten, *Het paulinisch Evangelie*, 1870; quoted here from the German translation (with considerable additions and changes by the author), *Das Paulinische Evangelium*, 1881. Although the value of this work is somewhat lessened by the author's addiction to certain theories of Synoptic criticism now generally abandoned, and by excessive emphasis on the " heidenchristliche paulinische Tendenz " of the third Gospel, it may still be recommended as a mine of interesting and suggestive material. And, as it is but little known to modern English reading students of the question, the publication of similar investigations made independently does not seem superfluous. A few of Scholten's lists have been added with proper acknowledgment, and references have been given to some others.

[2] A single exception to this limitation is made in the section below on pp. 90–96.

religious prepossessions, without realizing in every case of change the significant contrasts. Such a study reveals most strikingly the subconscious, spontaneous workings of the mind. Nor must it be supposed that changes of this sort are carried out with regularity and uniformity throughout the work. The author will sometimes correct his source in a certain way, and sometimes leave the same expression or thought in his source unchanged. The many exceptions that we shall find to what is plainly the usual literary practice of Luke will abundantly illustrate this point. Not infrequently in a single passage Luke will leave unchanged at its second occurrence a word or expression in his source that he has just modified.[1]

Changes in the Order of Sections

It is well known that sections of Luke derived from Mark and those of other origin are arranged in continuous blocks and not interspersed as in the Gospel of Matthew. Thus, in general: Luke 1–2 are peculiar to Luke; Luke 3, 1–6, 19 are from Mark; Luke 6, 20–8, 3 are not from Mark; Luke 8, 4–9, 50 are from Mark; Luke 9, 51–18, 14 are not from Mark; Luke 18, 15–24, 11 are from Mark.

Our present study has to do with the order of the material in the three sections derived from Mark, viz., 3, 1–6, 19; 8, 4–9, 50; 18, 15–24, 11.

In the first place we may observe that these three sections represent three consecutive and almost continuous sections in Mark, viz., Mark 1, 1–3, 19; 3, 20–9, 41; 10, 1 to the end — that is, substantially the whole Gospel. Of course there are some omissions

[1] Scholten comments particularly on this phenomenon, e.g., p. 19, n. 3, on the change of *πνεῦμα ἀκάθαρτον*, Mark 5, 2, 13, to *δαιμόνιον*, Luke 8, 27, 33: "Da sich Lucas hierin selber nicht gleich bleibt (s. 8, 29), so wird noch sichtlicher, dass er nicht selbstständig schreibt, sondern als Corrector den Text des Mc. verändert hat;" p. 38, "Mt. 8, 6, *ὁ παῖς μου* . . . Lucas setzt dafür 7, 2, 10: *δοῦλος*, lässt jedoch *παῖς* in der Rede des Hauptmannes stehen. Ein Beweis, dass er corrigierte;" p. 47, "Bei der Vergleichung von Stellen, welche Lc. mit Mt. gemein hat, fällt ferner die Vertauschung des *μισθός*, Mt. 5, 46, mit der paulinischen *χάρις* 6, 32, 33, 34, ins Auge, welche jedoch bei dem Evangelisten (6, 23, 35), aus leicht erklärlicher und öfter vorkommender Unachtsamkeit, unterblieb"; p. 56, "Zu beachten ist die Veränderung der 'Vögel des Himmels' Mt. 6, 26 in 'Raben' Lc. 12, 24a . . . Dass die Veränderung absichtlich ist, geht daraus hervor, dass Lc. 24b in Übereinstimmung mit Mt. 26 'Vögel' schreibt." See also p. 113, on Mark 2, 6, and the references there.

from Mark by Luke, especially the great omission of Mark 6, 45–8, 26; but as these do not disturb Mark's order, they may be left out of account here, and, considering the sections dependent on Mark in blocks, we may state this as our first observation on order, namely, that neither the great insertions in Luke nor its great omissions from Mark disturb Mark's general order. Within the large blocks, also, the sections of Mark generally succeed one another in the same order in Luke, even when additions or omissions in the latter Gospel might be expected to change the order. A detailed list of the parallels need not be given here, for they can be readily found in harmonies, e.g., in the "Parallelenregister" in Huck's *Synopse*. The regular coincidence in order is most striking.

The exceptions to this order are, therefore, few, and demand special notice. They are principally the following: [1]

1. The account of the imprisonment of John the Baptist, which occurs in Mark 6, 17–29, is found in Luke, greatly abbreviated, after the account of John's preaching (Luke 3, 19–20).

2. The saying about the true kindred of Jesus in Mark 3, 31–35 is found in Luke 8, 19–21 after, not before, the parable of the sower and its sequel (Mark 4, 1–25 = Luke 8, 4–18).

3. The call of the Twelve in Luke 6, 12–16 precedes, in Mark 3, 13–19 follows, the summary of travel and healing in Mark 3, 7–12 = Luke 6, 17–19.

4. The prediction of the traitor in Luke 22, 21–23 follows, in Mark 14, 18–21 precedes, the Last Supper (Mark 14, 22–25 = Luke 22, 15–20).

5. The denial of Peter in Luke 22, 56–62 precedes, in Mark 14, 66–72 follows, the trial before the Sanhedrin (Mark 14, 55–65 = Luke 22, 63–71).

The motive in at least two of these cases is clearly the desire to conclude at once a subject when it has been introduced. Thus Luke anticipates the actual imprisonment of John the Baptist by inserting it immediately after the account of John's teaching. Again, Luke anticipates the denials of Peter by bringing them in at once upon Peter's entrance into the court of the high priest, while Mark

[1] Omitting such passages as Luke 4, 16–30 and 5, 1–11, which do not appear to be derived from Mark 6, 1–6 and 1, 16–20, though somewhat akin to them in subject matter.

narrates the trial to its conclusion before coming back to Peter and his denials.

But the infrequency of such transpositions only emphasizes the general parallelism of order between Mark and Luke.

Changes of Order within the Sections

Within the several sections Luke adheres as faithfully to the order of Mark as he does in the order of the sections themselves. As a rule the details follow each other in much the same succession, even in cases when the structure of the sentence has been considerably changed.

In the following cases Luke, in introducing an incident, brings in explanatory details which Mark gives only later:

In Luke 5, 17 the presence of the Pharisees and lawyers is mentioned at the beginning of the story of the man cured of paralysis; in Mark 2, 6 the hostile spectators are mentioned only after Jesus has aroused their ire.

At the healing of the withered hand the Pharisees are only mentioned by name as they leave the synagogue to plot with the Herodians (Mark 3, 6), but in Luke 6, 7 these spectators are named before the cure.

Mark tells the age of Jairus' daughter after she was healed (Mark 5, 42), Luke before (Luke 8, 42).

The number fed by the miracle of the loaves is stated by Mark (6, 44) after, by Luke (9, 14) before, the miracle takes place.

Luke 8, 23 mentions Jesus' sleep before the storm rose, Mark 4, 38, only afterward.

Luke 4, 31–37 adds πόλιν τῆς Γαλιλαίας to Καφαρναούμ (Mark 1, 21) at the beginning of the story of the demoniac in the synagogue, but omits τῆς Γαλιλαίας from περίχωρον in the concluding summary.

Luke 4, 42 mentions the pursuit of the crowd before the arrival of the disciples, Mark 1, 37 mentions it afterward.

The women who followed Jesus from Galilee are mentioned by Luke in his company during the Galilean ministry (Luke 8, 1–3); in Mark they are first mentioned at the cross (Mark 15, 40, 41 = Luke 23, 49). In Luke 24, 10 = Mark 16, 1 the situation is nearly the reverse, for Luke mentions by name the women at the grave only after their visit.

Bethsaida, Luke 9, 10, whether correctly used or not, is without doubt from Mark 6, 45, a later section, which Luke omits when he comes to it.

In Luke 23, 2 the priests accuse Jesus before Pilate puts the question, "Art thou the king of the Jews?" In Mark 15, 3 their accusation is told only afterwards.

There are a number of minor transpositions in Luke's narrative of the Passion, when it is compared with Mark. A list of twelve has been collected and carefully discussed by J. C. Hawkins in *Oxford*

Studies in the Synoptic Problem, pp. 81 ff. He attributes them to the use by Luke of an account of the Passion other than Mark's. But the transpositions enumerated by Hawkins are generally cases where Luke has anticipated something which is mentioned later in Mark. The frequency of this phenomenon seems to warrant the inference that he habitually read a whole section of Mark, and indeed perhaps the whole Gospel, before composing the corresponding section, or his own Gospel.[1] Thus he was able to rearrange the details of a story so that such explanatory matters as the age of Jairus' daughter or the number of men who shared the bread and fishes can be given before the miracle itself is described.

Perhaps further evidence of the same import is furnished by places where Luke distinctly prepares the way for something that in Mark is sudden and unexplained. Thus in Mark 3, 2 (= Luke 6, 7) it is said that they "watched to see if Jesus would heal on the sabbath," but Luke 6, 6 has already dated the incident on the sabbath. Again in Mark 5, 15 (= Luke 8, 35) it is said that they found the demoniac cured and clothed,[2] but Luke alone had prepared the way for this by mentioning (8, 27) as a symptom of his madness that he had not worn a garment for a long time.[3]

Abbreviations and Omissions

A number of instances may be quoted where Luke by omission, by combination, or by putting into indirect form, considerably shortens the dialogue of his source.

1 Wernle, *Synoptische Frage*, p. 9: "Daraus wird deutlich, wie vollständig Lc seine Quelle beherrscht, bevor er sie aufnimmt. Er ist kein Abschreiber, der Seite nach Seite seiner Vorlage umschlägt und abschreibt. Er hat sie erst vollständig von Anfang bis zu Ende studiert und in sich aufgenommen." *Ibid.*, p. 26: "Er hat jede Erzählung erst völlig durchgelesen und dabei kleine Züge, die wir bei Mr erst allmählich kennen lernen, hervorgeholt und an den Anfang gestellt." Wernle suggests that Luke's ἄρχων, 18, 18, is due to the fact that he read through Mark 10, 17–22 to the end before writing his parallel.

2 This addition by Luke is one of those changes in Mark which Harnack (*Luke the Physician*, p. 182) attributes to his medical interest. But it is plain from ἱματισμένον in Mark 5, 15 that the second evangelist also had this symptom in mind (see above p. 61).

3 For converse phenomena, i.e., cases where Luke's transpositions or omissions make him more obscure than Mark, see below pp. 101 ff.

Mark 1, 37 *καὶ λέγουσιν αὐτῷ ὅτι πάντες ζητοῦσίν σε.*	Luke 4, 42 omits; cf. *οἱ ὄχλοι ἐπεζήτουν αὐτόν.*
Mark 1, 44 *καὶ λέγει αὐτῷ ὅρα μηδενὶ μηδὲν εἴπῃς.*	Luke 5, 14 *καὶ αὐτὸς παρήγγειλεν αὐτῷ μηδενὶ εἰπεῖν.*
Matt. 8, 6 [Q] *καὶ λέγων· κύριε, ὁ παῖς μου βέβληται . . . 7 λέγει αὐτῷ ἐγὼ ἐλθὼν θεραπεύσω αὐτόν.*	Luke 7, 3 *ἐρωτῶν αὐτὸν ὅπως ἐλθὼν διασώσῃ τὸν δοῦλον αὐτοῦ.*
Mark 4, 39 *καὶ εἶπεν . . . σιώπα, πεφίμωσο.*	Luke 8, 24 omits.
Mark 5, 8 *ἔλεγεν γὰρ αὐτῷ· ἔξελθε τὸ πνεῦμα τὸ ἀκάθαρτον ἐκ τοῦ ἀνθρώπου.*	Luke 8, 29 *παρήγγελλεν γὰρ τῷ πνεύματι τῷ ἀκαθάρτῳ ἐξελθεῖν ἀπὸ τοῦ ἀνθρώπου.*
Mark 5, 9 *λέγει αὐτῷ· λεγιὼν ὄνομά μοι, ὅτι πολλοί ἐσμεν*	Luke 8, 30 *ὁ δὲ εἶπεν· λεγιών, ὅτι εἰσῆλθεν δαιμόνια πολλὰ εἰς αὐτόν.*
Mark 5, 12 *καὶ παρεκάλεσαν αὐτὸν λέγοντες· πέμψον ἡμᾶς εἰς τοὺς χοίρους, ἵνα εἰς αὐτοὺς εἰσέλθωμεν.*	Luke 8, 32 *καὶ παρεκάλεσαν αὐτὸν ἵνα ἐπιτρέψῃ αὐτοῖς εἰς ἐκείνους εἰσελθεῖν.*
Mark 5, 23 *παρακαλεῖ . . . λέγων ὅτι τὸ θυγάτριόν μου ἐσχάτως ἔχει, κ.τ.λ.*	Luke 8, 42 *παρεκάλει . . . ὅτι θυγάτηρ μονογενὴς ἦν αὐτῷ, κ.τ.λ.*
Mark 5, 28 *ἔλεγεν γὰρ ὅτι ἐὰν ἅψωμαι κἂν τῶν ἱματίων αὐτοῦ σωθήσομαι.*	Luke 8, 44 omits.
Mark 6, 31 *καὶ λέγει αὐτοῖς· δεῦτε ὑμεῖς αὐτοὶ κατ' ἰδίαν εἰς ἔρημον τόπον καὶ ἀναπαύσασθε ὀλίγον.*	Luke 9, 10 omits.
Mark 6, 37, 38 *Disciples* — Shall we go and buy bread? *Jesus* — How many loaves have ye? go and see. *Disciples* — Five and two fishes.	Luke 9, 13. *Disciples* — We have not more than five loaves and two fishes, unless we go and buy bread.
Mark 8, 29 *λέγει αὐτῷ· σὺ εἶ ὁ χριστός.*	Luke 9, 20 *εἶπεν· τὸν χριστὸν τοῦ θεοῦ.*
Mark 9, 16 *καὶ ἐπηρώτησεν αὐτούς· τί συνζητεῖτε πρὸς αὐτούς;*	Luke 9, 37 omits.
Mark 9, 21–25 *Jesus* — How long has he had this? *Father* — From childhood, etc. *Jesus* — If possible! all things are possible to one who believes. *Father* — I believe, help my unbelief. *Jesus* (to the spirit) — Deaf and dumb spirit, I bid thee come out of him and enter him nevermore.	Luke 9, 42 omits.
Mark 9, 33 *ἐπηρώτα αὐτούς· τί ἐν τῇ ὁδῷ διελογίζεσθε;*	Luke 9, 47 omits.
Mark 10, 24 *πάλιν ἀποκριθεὶς λέγει αὐτοῖς· τέκνα, κ. τ. λ.*	Luke 18, 24 omits.
Mark 10, 49 *ὁ Ἰησοῦς εἶπεν· φωνήσατε αὐτόν. καὶ φωνοῦσιν τὸν τυφλὸν λέγοντες αὐτῷ· θάρσει, ἔγειρε, φωνεῖ σε.*	Luke 18, 40 *ὁ Ἰησοῦς ἐκέλευσεν αὐτὸν ἀχθῆναι πρὸς αὐτόν.*
Mark 11, 33 *ἀποκριθέντες . . . λέγουσιν· οὐκ οἴδαμεν.*	Luke 20, 7 *ἀπεκρίθησαν μὴ εἰδέναι πόθεν.*
Mark 13, 1 *λέγει αὐτῷ εἷς τῶν μαθητῶν αὐτοῦ· διδάσκαλε, ἴδε ποταποὶ λίθοι καὶ ποταπαὶ οἰκοδομαί.*	Luke 21, 5 *καὶ τινων λεγόντων περὶ τοῦ ἱεροῦ ὅτι λίθοις καλοῖς καὶ ἀναθέμασιν κεκόσμηται.*

Mark 14, 2 *ἔλεγον γάρ· μὴ ἐν τῇ ἑορτῇ, μήποτε ἔσται θόρυβος τοῦ λαοῦ.*	Luke 22, 2 *ἐφοβοῦντο γὰρ τὸν λαόν.*
Mark 14, 19 *ἤρξαντο . . . λέγειν . . . μήτι ἐγώ;*	Luke 22, 23 *ἤρξαντο συνζητεῖν . . . τὸ τίς ἄρα εἴη.*
Mark 14, 45 *προσελθὼν αὐτῷ λέγει· ῥαββεί, καὶ κατεφίλησεν αὐτόν.*	Luke 22, 47 *ἤγγισεν τῷ Ἰησοῦ φιλῆσαι αὐτόν.*
Mark 15, 14 *οἱ δὲ περισσῶς ἔκραξαν· σταύρωσον αὐτόν.*	Luke 23, 23 *οἱ δὲ ἐπέκειντο . . . αἰτούμενοι αὐτὸν σταυρωθῆναι.*

Note also the omission of dialogue parts in Mark 9, 28 f., Mark 12, 33–34a, Mark 14, 31.

Somewhat similar is Luke's condensation of sentences in dialogue even when no change of speakers is involved. This is shown in his treatment of questions (mainly rhetorical), especially when the questions are associated with their immediate answer or with another question. Both these arrangements Luke to some extent avoids.[1]

Mark 1, 27 *τί ἐστιν τοῦτο; διδαχὴ καινή· κατ' ἐξουσίαν κ. τ. λ.*	Luke 4, 36 *τίς ὁ λόγος οὗτος, ὅτι ἐν ἐξουσίᾳ κ. τ. λ.*
Mark 2, 7 *τί οὗτος οὕτω λαλεῖ; βλασφημεῖ.*	Luke 5, 21 *τίς ἐστιν οὗτος ὃς λαλεῖ βλασφημίας.*
Mark 2, 19 *μὴ δύνανται οἱ υἱοὶ τοῦ νυμφῶνος, ἐν ᾧ ὁ νυμφίος μετ' αὐτῶν ἐστιν, νηστεύειν; ὅσον χρόνον ἔχουσιν τὸν νυμφίον μετ' αὐτῶν, οὐ δύνανται νηστεύειν.*	Luke 5, 34 *μὴ δύνασθε τοὺς υἱοὺς τοῦ νυμφῶνος, ἐν ᾧ ὁ νυμφίος μετ' αὐτῶν ἐστιν, ποιῆσαι νηστεύειν [-εῦσαι];*
Mark 3, 33 *τίς ἐστιν ἡ μήτηρ μου καὶ οἱ ἀδελφοί μου;* 34 . . . *ἴδε ἡ μήτηρ μου καὶ οἱ ἀδελφοί μου.* 35 *ὃς ἂν ποιήσῃ τὸ θέλημα τοῦ θεοῦ, οὗτος ἀδελφός μου καὶ ἀδελφὴ καὶ μήτηρ ἐστίν.*	Luke 8, 21 *μήτηρ μου καὶ ἀδελφοί μου οὗτοί εἰσιν οἱ τὸν λόγον τοῦ θεοῦ ἀκούοντες καὶ ποιοῦντες.*
Mark 4, 13 *οὐκ οἴδατε τὴν παραβολὴν ταύτην; καὶ πῶς πάσας τὰς παραβολὰς γνώσεσθε;*	Luke 8, 11 *ἔστιν δὲ αὕτη ἡ παραβολή.*
Mark 4, 40 *τί δειλοί ἐστε; οὔπω ἔχετε πίστιν;*	Luke 8, 25 *ποῦ ἡ πίστις ὑμῶν;*
Mark 8, 36 *τί γὰρ ὠφελεῖ ἄνθρωπον κερδῆσαι τὸν κόσμον ὅλον καὶ ζημιωθῆναι τὴν ψυχὴν αὐτοῦ;* 37 *τί γὰρ δοῖ ἄνθρωπος ἀντάλλαγμα τῆς ψυχῆς αὐτοῦ;*	Luke 9, 25 *τί γὰρ ὠφελεῖται ἄνθρωπος κερδήσας τὸν κόσμον ὅλον, ἑαυτὸν δὲ ἀπολέσας ἢ ζημιωθείς;*
Mark 9, 19 *ἕως πότε πρὸς ὑμᾶς ἔσομαι; ἕως πότε ἀνέξομαι ὑμῶν;*	Luke 9, 41 *ἕως πότε ἔσομαι πρὸς ὑμᾶς καὶ ἀνέξομαι ὑμῶν;*

[1] Twice in the parable of the wicked husbandmen, Luke does not follow this practice. In 20, 15, 16, following Mark 12, 9, he writes, "What then will the lord of the vineyard do to them? He will come and destroy these husbandmen," etc. In 20, 13 the proprietor says, "What shall I do? I will send my son." The question here added by Luke (*τί ποιήσω*) is characteristic of Luke's parables; cf. 12, 17; 16, 3.

Mark 12, 14 *ἔξεστιν δοῦναι κῆνσον Καίσαρι ἢ οὔ; δῶμεν ἢ μὴ δῶμεν;*	Luke 20, 22 *ἔξεστιν ἡμᾶς Καίσαρι φόρον δοῦναι ἢ οὔ;*
Mark 14, 37 *Σίμων, καθεύδεις; οὐκ ἴσχυσας μίαν ὥραν γρηγορῆσαι;*	Luke 22, 46 *τί καθεύδετε;*
Mark 14, 63 *τί ἔτι χρείαν ἔχομεν μαρτύρων;* 64 *ἠκούσατε τῆς βλασφημίας· τί ὑμῖν φαίνεται;*	Luke 22, 71 *τί ἔτι ἔχομεν μαρτυρίας χρείαν; αὐτοὶ γὰρ ἠκούσαμεν ἀπὸ τοῦ στόματος αὐτοῦ.*

Note also Mark 11, 32, compared with Luke 20, 6.

Even single questions disappear under Luke's recension, being changed to commands or statements.

Mark 2, 18 *διατί οἱ μαθηταὶ Ἰωάννου . . . νηστεύουσιν κ. τ. λ;*	Luke 5, 33 *οἱ μαθηταὶ Ἰωάννου νηστεύουσιν κ. τ. λ.*
Mark 4, 38 *οὐ μέλει σοι ὅτι ἀπολλύμεθα;*	Luke 8, 24 *ἀπολλύμεθα.*
Mark 5, 35 *τί ἔτι σκύλλεις τὸν διδάσκαλον;*	Luke 8, 49 *μηκέτι σκύλλε τὸν διδάσκαλον.*
Mark 5, 39 *τί θορυβεῖσθε καὶ κλαίετε;*	Luke 8, 52 *μὴ κλαίετε.*
Mark 11, 17 *οὐ γέγραπται ὅτι ὁ οἶκός μου κ. τ. λ.*	Luke 19, 46 *γέγραπται· καὶ ἔσται ὁ οἶκός μου κ. τ. λ.*
Mark 12, 26 *οὐκ ἀνέγνωτε ἐν τῇ βίβλῳ Μωϋσέως ἐπὶ τοῦ βάτου κ. τ. λ*	Luke 20, 37 *Μωϋσῆς ἐμήνυσεν ἐπὶ τῆς βάτου κ. τ. λ.*

Compare also the questions in Mark 12, 15; 12, 24; 15, 12; 16, 3, which are altogether omitted by Luke. The saying of the lamp and lampstand occurs in Mark (4, 21) as two rhetorical questions, and in the corresponding verse of Luke (8, 16) as a statement. But the saying was also in Q, as is shown by its occurrence in Matt. (5, 15) and its recurrence in Luke (11, 33), so that its affirmative form may be due to this source rather than to Luke himself.

In passages derived from Q also Harnack finds a tendency in Luke to avoid rhetorical questions. In his *Sayings of Jesus*, p. 6, referring to the three instances in Luke 12, 23, 24, 28, where Luke has no rhetorical question parallel to those of Matt. 6, 25, 26, 30, he says, "St. Luke removes the rhetorical question for the sake of smoothness (a correction which, as we shall see, he makes in other places)." Cf. also, p. 69. The "other places" appear to be Luke 6, 32, 33 = Matt. 5, 46, 47; Luke 6, 44 = Matt. 7, 16; Luke 15, 4 = Matt. 18, 12;[1] Luke 17, 4 = Matt. 18, 21, 22.

Therefore in cases where the situation is reversed, Matthew having the declarative and Luke the interrogative form, there is possibly

[1] In Matt. 18, 12 = Luke 15, 4 the double question of Matthew can hardly be original as Harnack (*Sayings*, 92) thinks. For the first question *τί ὑμῖν (σοι) δοκεῖ;* is Matthean as shown by its addition to Mark in Matt. 22, 17, 42; 26, 66 (where Mark 14, 64 has *τί ὑμῖν φαίνεται;*). Note also Matt. 17, 25.

a presumption that Luke is more original (cf. Harnack, *Sayings*, pp. 26, 86), as Matthew also has some tendency to remove questions (see Allen, *Matthew*, p. xxxiii).

The passages are Matt. 15, 14 = Luke 6, 39; Matt. 7, 21 = Luke 6, 46; Matt. 10, 34 = Luke 12, 51; Matt. 13, 31 = Luke 13, 18, 19 (so also Mark 4, 30); Matt. 13, 33 = Luke 13, 20, 21. But in three of these cases Nicolardot (*Les procédés de rédaction*, pp. 148 f.), and in two of them even Harnack (*Sayings*, on Matt. 7, 21 = Luke 6, 46; Matt. 15, 14 = Luke 6, 39), prefers the declarative form as original.

Avoidance of Repetition

In a great many ways Luke avoids repetition. Often instead of repeating the noun a pronoun is used:

Mark 1, 34 δαιμόνια ἐξέβαλεν καὶ οὐκ ἤφιεν λαλεῖν τὰ δαιμόνια.	Luke 4, 41 ἐξήρχοντο δαιμόνια . . . οὐκ εἴα αὐτὰ λαλεῖν.
Mark 2, 3–10 παραλυτικός (-όν, -ῷ), five times.	Luke 5, 18 παραλελυμένος . . . 19 αὐτὸν . . . 24 παραλελυμένῳ.
Mark 2, 18b οἱ μαθηταὶ Ἰωάννου καὶ οἱ μαθηταὶ τῶν Φαρισαίων . . . οἱ δὲ σοὶ μαθηταί.	Luke 5, 33 οἱ μαθηταὶ Ἰωάννου . . . καὶ οἱ τῶν Φαρισαίων, οἱ δὲ σοί.
Mark 2, 22 ὁ οἶνος . . . ὁ οἶνος.	Luke 5, 37 ὁ οἶνος . . . αὐτός.
Mark 3, 1 ἄνθρωπος . . . 3 τῷ ἀνθρώπῳ . . . 5 τῷ ἀνθρώπῳ.	Luke 6, 6 ἄνθρωπος . . . 8 τῷ ἀνδρὶ . . . 10 αὐτῷ.
Mark 5, 35 ἀπὸ τοῦ ἀρχισυναγώγου . . . 36 τῷ ἀρχισυναγώγῳ . . . 38 εἰς τὸν οἶκον τοῦ ἀρχισυναγώγου.	Luke 8, 49 παρὰ τοῦ ἀρχισυναγώγου . . . 50 αὐτῷ . . . 51 εἰς τὴν οἰκίαν.
Mark 5, 39 τὸ παιδίον . . . 40 τοῦ παιδίου . . . τὸ παιδίον . . . 41 τοῦ παιδίου.	Luke 8, 51 τῆς παιδός . . . 52 "she" (in verb) . . . 54 αὐτῆς.
Mark 5, 41 τὸ κοράσιον . . . 42 τὸ κοράσιον.	Luke 9, 54 ἡ παῖς . . . 55 "she" (in verb).
Mark 6, 41 τοὺς πέντε ἄρτους καὶ τοὺς δύο ἰχθύας . . . τοὺς ἄρτους . . . καὶ τοὺς δύο ἰχθύας . . . 43 τῶν ἰχθύων . . . 44 τοὺς ἄρτους.	Luke 9, 16 τοὺς πέντε ἄρτους καὶ τοὺς δύο ἰχθύας . . . αὐτούς.
Mark 8, 27 οἱ μαθηταὶ αὐτοῦ . . . τοὺς μαθητὰς αὐτοῦ.	Luke 9, 18 οἱ μαθηταί . . . αὐτούς.
Matt. 5, 25 [Q] τῷ ἀντιδίκῳ . . . μήποτέ σε παραδῷ ὁ ἀντίδικος.	Luke 12, 58 τοῦ ἀντιδίκου . . . μήποτε κατασύρῃ σε.
Mark 10, 13 προσέφερον . . . τοῖς προσφέρουσιν.	Luke 18, 15 προσέφερον . . . αὐτοῖς.
Mark 10, 46 τυφλός . . . 49 τὸν τυφλὸν . . . 51 ὁ δὲ τυφλός.	Luke 18, 35 τυφλός . . . 40 αὐτὸν . . . 41 ὁ δέ.

Luke does not, however, in avoiding the repetition of nouns, fall into the equally awkward superabundance of pronouns. On the contrary, he not infrequently improves on his sources by leaving out superfluous pronouns (e. g. *αὐτός*), as, for instance, in Mark 1, 40; 5, 12–14, 18–19; 8, 29; 10, 17; 12, 8, 37; Matt. 4, 5 (= Luke 4, 9).

In the following passages from Mark, Luke avoids repetition by omission or other changes. The words which have no equivalent in Luke are in brackets:

Mark 2, 9 *ἔγειρε [καὶ ἆρον τὸν κράββατόν σου] . . .* 11 *ἔγειρε, ἆρον τὸν κράββατόν σου.*
Mark 2, 15 *πολλοὶ τελῶναι καὶ ἁμαρτωλοὶ συνανέκειντο τῷ Ἰησοῦ . . .* 16 *[ἰδόντες ὅτι ἤσθιεν μετὰ τῶν τελωνῶν καὶ ἁμαρτωλῶν] . . . ὅτι μετὰ τῶν τελωνῶν καὶ ἁμαρτωλῶν ἐσθίει καὶ πίνει.*
Mark 2, 18 *[ἦσαν οἱ μαθηταὶ Ἰωάννου καὶ οἱ Φαρισαῖοι νηστεύοντες] . . . λέγουσιν αὐτῷ διατί οἱ μαθηταὶ Ἰωάννου καὶ οἱ [μαθηταὶ] τῶν Φαρισαίων νηστεύουσιν;*
Mark 2, 19, see above p. 81.
Mark 3, 7 *[πολὺ πλῆθος] . . .* 8 *πλῆθος πολύ.*
Mark 3, 14 *καὶ ἐποίησεν δώδεκα . . .* 16 *[καὶ ἐποίησεν τοὺς δώδεκα].*
Mark 3, 33–35, see above p. 81.
Mark 4, 5 *τὸ πετρῶδες [ὅπου οὐκ εἶχεν γῆν πολλήν] . . . [διὰ τὸ μὴ ἔχειν βάθος γῆς] . . .* 6 *διὰ τὸ μὴ ἔχειν ῥίζαν.*
Mark 5, 2 *ὑπήντησεν αὐτῷ [ἐκ τῶν μνημείων] ἄνθρωπος . . .* 3 *ὃς τὴν κατοίκησιν εἶχεν ἐν τοῖς μνήμασι. . . .* [5 *ἐν τοῖς μνήμασιν καὶ ἐν τοῖς ὄρεσιν ἦν κράζων].*
Mark 5, 3 *[οὐδὲ ἁλύσει οὐκέτι οὐδεὶς ἐδύνατο αὐτὸν δῆσαι]* 4 *διὰ τὸ αὐτὸν πολλάκις πέδαις καὶ ἁλύσεσιν δεδέσθαι, καὶ διεσπάσθαι ὑπ' αὐτοῦ τὰς ἁλύσεις καὶ τὰς πέδας συντετρῖφθαι, [καὶ οὐδεὶς ἴσχυεν αὐτὸν δαμάσαι].*
Mark 5, 9 *τί ὄνομά σοι; . . . λεγιὼν [ὄνομά μοι].*
Mark 5, 13 *εἰς τὴν θάλασσαν . . . [ἐν τῇ θαλάσσῃ].*
Mark 6, 35 *καὶ ἤδη ὥρας πολλῆς γινομένης . . . ἔλεγον ὅτι . . . [ἤδη ὥρα πολλή].*
Mark 6, 41 *καὶ λαβὼν τοὺς πέντε ἄρτους καὶ τοὺς δύο ἰχθύας ἀναβλέψας εἰς τὸν οὐρανὸν εὐλόγησεν καὶ κατέκλασεν τοὺς ἄρτους καὶ ἐδίδου τοῖς μαθηταῖς ἵνα παρατιθῶσιν αὐτοῖς [καὶ τοὺς δύο ἰχθύας ἐμέρισεν πᾶσιν]. . . .* 43 *καὶ ἦραν κλασμάτων δώδεκα κοφίνων πληρώματα, [καὶ ἀπὸ τῶν ἰχθύων].*
Mark 9, 38 *εἴδομέν τινα ἐν τῷ ὀνόματί σου ἐκβάλλοντα δαιμόνια, [ὃς οὐκ ἀκολουθεῖ ἡμῖν,] καὶ ἐκωλύομεν, ὅτι οὐκ ἠκολούθει ἡμῖν.*
Mark 10, 23 *πῶς δυσκόλως οἱ τὰ χρήματα ἔχοντες εἰς τὴν βασιλείαν τοῦ θεοῦ εἰσελεύσονται* 24 *. . . [πῶς δύσκολόν ἐστιν εἰς τὴν βασιλείαν τοῦ θεοῦ εἰσελθεῖν.]*
Mark 10, 27 *[παρὰ θεῷ] . . . παρὰ τῷ θεῷ.*
Mark 10, 29 *οὐδείς ἐστιν ὃς ἀφῆκεν οἰκίαν ἢ ἀδελφοὺς ἢ ἀδελφὰς ἢ μητέρα ἢ πατέρα ἢ τέκνα ἢ ἀγροὺς . . .* 30 *ἐὰν μὴ λάβῃ ἑκατονταπλασίονα . . . [οἰκίας καὶ ἀδελφοὺς καὶ ἀδελφὰς καὶ μητέρας καὶ τέκνα καὶ ἀγροὺς μετὰ διωγμῶν].*
Mark 11, 28 *ἐν ποίᾳ ἐξουσίᾳ ταῦτα ποιεῖς; ἢ τίς σοι τὴν ἐξουσίαν ταύτην ἔδωκεν [ἵνα ταῦτα ποιῇς]; . . .* 29 *[καὶ ἐρῶ ὑμῖν ἐν ποίᾳ ἐξουσίᾳ ταῦτα ποιῶ].*
Mark 12, 41 *[κατέναντι τοῦ γαζοφυλακίου] . . . εἰς τὸ γαζοφυλάκιον . . .* 43 *[εἰς τὸ γαζοφυλάκιον].*
Mark 13, 8 *ἔσονται σεισμοὶ κατὰ τόπους, [ἔσονται] λιμοί.*
Mark 14, 43 *ὄχλος [μετὰ μαχαιρῶν καὶ ξύλων] . . .* 48 *ὡς ἐπὶ λῃστὴν ἐξήλθατε μετὰ μαχαιρῶν καὶ ξύλων.*
Mark 15, 33 *ἕως ὥρας ἐνάτης.* 34 *[καὶ τῇ ἐνάτῃ ὥρᾳ].*

Sometimes repetition is avoided by the insertion of a synonym for the repeated word, as in

Mark 10, 47 ἤρξατο κράζειν . . . 48 ἔκραζεν: Luke 18, 38 ἐβόησεν . . . 39 ἔκραζεν.
Mark 12, 42 χήρα πτωχή . . . ἡ χήρα αὕτη ἡ πτωχή: Luke 21, 2 χήραν πενιχράν . . . ἡ χήρα ἡ πτωχὴ αὕτη.
Mark 14, 37 καθεύδοντας . . . καθεύδεις: Luke 22, 45 κοιμωμένους . . . καθεύδετε.
Mark 15, 37 ἐξέπνευσεν . . . 39 ἰδὼν ὁ κεντυρίων . . . ὅτι οὕτως ἐξέπνευσεν: Luke 23, 46 ἐξέπνευσεν . . . 47 ἰδὼν δὲ ὁ ἑκατοντάρχης τὸ γενόμενον (cf. Matt. 27, 54 τά γινόμενα).
Matt. 11, 8 ἐν μαλακοῖς . . . τὰ μαλακά: Luke 7, 25 ἐν μαλακοῖς ἱματίοις . . . ἐν ἱματισμῷ ἐνδόξῳ [Q].

Compare also the changes noted on page 76, note 1, and on p. 157.

Even the article is not repeated by Luke in these parallels (see also examples on p. 197):

Mark 8, 31 τῶν πρεσβυτέρων καὶ [τῶν] ἀρχιερέων καὶ [τῶν] γραμματέων: Luke 9, 22 (so Matt. 16, 21).
Mark 9, 2 [τὸν] Πέτρον καὶ [τὸν] Ἰάκωβον καὶ [τὸν] Ἰωάννην: Luke 9, 28 (cf. Matt. 17, 1).

In Q passages, also, Luke shows himself less repetitious than Matthew, e.g.:

Matt. 7, 16 [Q] ἀπὸ τῶν καρπῶν αὐτῶν ἐπιγνώσεσθε αὐτούς . . . [20 ἄραγε ἀπὸ τῶν καρπῶν αὐτῶν ἐπιγνώσεσθε αὐτούς].
Matt. 12, 35 [Q] ὁ ἀγαθὸς ἄνθρωπος ἐκ τοῦ ἀγαθοῦ θησαυροῦ ἐκβάλλει τὰ ἀγαθά, καὶ ὁ πονηρὸς [ἄνθρωπος] ἐκ τοῦ πονηροῦ [θησαυροῦ] ἐκβάλλει πονηρά.[1]
Matt. 6, 22 [Q] ἐὰν ᾖ ὁ ὀφθαλμός σου ἁπλοῦς, ὅλον τὸ σῶμα . . . 23 ἐὰν δὲ [ὁ ὀφθαλμός σου] πονηρὸς ᾖ [ὅλον] τὸ σῶμα κ. τ. λ.
Matt. 6, 32 [Q] πάντα γὰρ ταῦτα τὰ ἔθνη ἐπιζητοῦσιν . . . χρῄζετε τούτων [ἁπάντων] 33 . . . καὶ ταῦτα [πάντα] προστεθήσεται ὑμῖν. (See by way of contrast, pp. 115 f.)
Matt. 23, 37 [Q] ἠθέλησα ἐπισυναγαγεῖν τὰ τέκνα σου, ὃν τρόπον ὄρνις [ἐπισυνάγει].
Matt. 19, 28 [Q] καθήσεσθε . . . ἐπὶ [δώδεκα] θρόνους κρίνοντες τὰς δώδεκα φυλὰς τοῦ Ἰσραήλ.

That all differences of this sort are due to Luke cannot be maintained. Matthew is fond of formulas, and may have been scrupulous in rounding out the parallel members of comparisons. But Luke's Greek instinct would lead him to avoid distinctly Semitic parallelisms. Norden (*Agnostos Theos*, pp. 357 ff.) has recently called attention to this feature of Jesus' sayings and to the difference in form given them by Matthew and Luke. Two extensive examples are given below in a form suitable for comparison:

[1] Harnack does not include this verse in the *Sayings of Jesus*, but it plainly belongs there; see Luke 6, 45.

Matt. 7, 24, 25	Matt 7, 26, 27	Luke 6, 47, 48	Luke 6, 49
πᾶς οὖν	καὶ πᾶς	πᾶς	ὁ δὲ
		ὁ ἐρχόμενος πρός με	
ὅστις ἀκούει μου	ὁ ἀκούων μου	καὶ ἀκούων μου	ἀκούσας
τοὺς λόγους τούτους	τοὺς λόγους τούτους	τῶν λόγων	
καὶ ποιεῖ αὐτούς,	καὶ μὴ ποιῶν αὐτοὺς	καὶ ποιῶν αὐτούς,	καὶ μὴ ποιήσας
		ὑποδείξω ὑμῖν τίνι	
ὁμοιωθήσεται	ὁμοιωθήσεται	ἐστὶν ὅμοιος.	
ἀνδρὶ φρονίμῳ,	ἀνδρὶ μωρῷ,	ὅμοιός ἐστιν ἀνθρώπῳ	ὅμοιός ἐστιν ἀνθρώπῳ
ὅστις ᾠκοδόμησεν	ὅστις ᾠκοδόμησεν	οἰκοδομοῦντι	οἰκοδομήσαντι
αὐτοῦ τὴν οἰκίαν	αὐτοῦ τὴν οἰκίαν	οἰκίαν,	οἰκίαν
		ὃς ἔσκαψεν καὶ	
		ἐβάθυνεν	
		καὶ ἔθηκεν θεμέλιον	
ἐπὶ τὴν πέτραν.	ἐπὶ τὴν ἄμμον.	᾽πὶ τὴν πέτραν·	ἐπὶ τὴν γῆν.
			χωρὶς θεμελίου, ᾗ
καὶ κατέβη ἡ βροχὴ	καὶ κατέβη ἡ βροχὴ	πλημμύρης δὲ γενομένης	
καὶ ἦλθον οἱ ποταμοὶ	καὶ ἦλθον οἱ ποταμοὶ	προσέρηξεν ὁ ποταμὸς	προσέρηξεν ὁ ποταμός,
καὶ ἔπνευσαν οἱ ἄνεμοι	καὶ ἔπνευσαν οἱ ἄνεμοι		
καὶ προσέπεσαν	καὶ προσέκοψαν		
τῇ οἰκίᾳ ἐκείνῃ,	τῇ οἰκίᾳ ἐκείνῃ,	τῇ οἰκίᾳ ἐκείνῃ,	
καὶ οὐκ ἔπεσεν·	καὶ ἔπεσεν,	καὶ οὐκ ἴσχυσεν	καὶ εὐθὺς συνέπεσεν,
		σαλεῦσαι αὐτὴν	
τεθεμελίωτο γὰρ		διὰ τὸ καλῶς	
ἐπὶ τὴν πέτραν.		οἰκοδομῆσθαι αὐτήν.	
	καὶ ἦν ἡ πτῶσις		καὶ ἐγένετο τὸ ῥῆγμα
	αὐτῆς μεγάλη.		τῆς οἰκίας ἐκείνης μέγα.

Matt. 25, 20, 21	Matt. 25, 22, 23	Luke 19, 16, 17	Luke 19, 18, 19
καὶ προσελθὼν	προσελθὼν δὲ [καὶ]	παρεγένετο δὲ	καὶ ἦλθεν
ὁ τὰ πέντε τάλαντα λαβὼν	ὁ τὰ δύο τάλαντα	ὁ πρῶτος	ὁ δεύτερος
προσήνεγκεν ἄλλα πέντε τάλαντα			
λέγων·	εἶπεν·	λέγων·	λέγων·
κύριε,	κύριε,	κύριε,	
πέντε τάλαντά μοι παρέδωκας,	δύο τάλαντά μοι παρέδωκας,	ἡ μνᾶ σου	ἡ μνᾶ σου,
			κύριε,
ἴδε ἄλλα πέντε τάλαντα ἐκέρδησα.	ἴδε ἄλλα δύο τάλαντα ἐκέρδησα.	δέκα προσηργάσατο	ἐποίησεν πέντε
		μνᾶς.	μνᾶς.
ἔφη αὐτῷ ὁ κύριος αὐτοῦ·	ἔφη αὐτῷ ὁ κύριος αὐτοῦ·	καὶ εἶπεν αὐτῷ·	εἶπεν δὲ καὶ τούτῳ·
εὖ, δοῦλε ἀγαθὲ καὶ πιστέ,	εὖ, δοῦλε ἀγαθὲ καὶ πιστέ,[1]	εὖγε, ἀγαθὲ δοῦλε,	
ἐπὶ ὀλίγα ἦς πιστός,	ἐπὶ ὀλίγα ἦς πιστός,	ὅτι ἐν ἐλαχίστῳ	
		πιστὸς ἐγένου,	
ἐπὶ πολλῶν σε καταστήσω·	ἐπὶ πολλῶν σε καταστήσω·	ἴσθι ἐξουσίαν	καὶ σὺ ἐπάνω
		ἔχων ἐπάνω δέκα	γίνου πέντε
		πόλεων.	πόλεων.
εἴσελθε εἰς τὴν χαρὰν	εἴσελθε εἰς τὴν χαρὰν		
τοῦ κυρίου σου.	τοῦ κυρίου σου.		

[1] With the pair of adjectives in Matthew compare:

Matt. 25, 26 πονηρὲ δοῦλε καὶ ὀκνηρέ	Luke 19, 22 πονηρὲ δοῦλε
Matt. 24, 45 ὁ πιστὸς δοῦλος καὶ φρόνιμος	Luke 12, 42 ὁ πιστὸς οἰκονόμος ὁ φρόνιμος
Matt. 16, 4 = 12, 39 γενεὰ πονηρὰ καὶ μοιχαλίς	Luke 11, 29 γενεὰ πονηρά (Mark 8, 12 γενεά, but cf. 8, 38)
Matt. 17, 17 γενεὰ ἄπιστος καὶ διεστραμμένη	Mark 9, 19 γενεὰ ἄπιστος

But in the last case Luke agrees with Matthew against Mark. Observe further the pairs of antithetical adjectives in Matt. 5, 45 πονηροὺς καὶ ἀγαθοὺς . . . δικαίους καὶ ἀδίκους (contrast Luke 6, 35) and the following pairs of similes:

Matt. 10, 16 γίνεσθε οὖν φρόνιμοι ὡς οἱ ὄφεις καὶ ἀκέραιοι ὡς αἱ περιστεραί. Matt. 17, 2 ἔλαμψεν . . . ὡς ὁ ἥλιος . . . λευκὰ ὡς τὸ φῶς (cf. Mark 9, 3 = Luke 9, 29). Matt. 28, 3 ὡς ἀστραπή . . . λευκὸν ὡς χιών.

In several cases one of two parallel or antithetical clauses is absent from Luke, as is shown by the brackets in the following parallel passages in Matthew:

Matt. 5, 43 [Q] [*ἠκούσατε ὅτι ἐρρέθη· ἀγαπήσεις τὸν πλησίον σου καὶ μισήσεις τὸν ἐχθρόν σου.*] 44 *ἐγὼ δὲ λέγω ὑμῖν, ἀγαπᾶτε τοὺς ἐχθροὺς ὑμῶν κ. τ. λ.* Cf. Luke 6, 27. So Matt. 5, 38 = Luke 6, 29; Matt. 5, 31 = Luke 16, 18.

Matt. 10, 24 *οὐκ ἔστιν μαθητὴς ὑπὲρ τὸν διδάσκαλον,* [*οὐδὲ δοῦλος ὑπὲρ τὸν κύριον αὐτοῦ*]. 25 *ἀρκετὸν τῷ μαθητῇ ἵνα γένηται ὡς ὁ διδάσκαλος αὐτοῦ,* [*καὶ ὁ δοῦλος ὡς ὁ κύριος*]. Cf. Luke 6, 40.

Matt. 7, 17 [Q] [*πᾶν δένδρον ἀγαθὸν καρποὺς καλοὺς ποιεῖ, τὸ δὲ σαπρὸν δένδρον καρποὺς πονηροὺς ποιεῖ.*] 18 *οὐ δύναται δένδρον ἀγαθὸν καρποὺς πονηροὺς ἐνεγκεῖν, οὐδὲ δένδρον σαπρὸν καρποὺς καλοὺς ἐνεγκεῖν.* Cf. Luke 6, 43, also Matt. 12, 33.

Matt. 13, 16 [Q] *ὑμῶν δὲ μακάριοι οἱ ὀφθαλμοὶ ὅτι βλέπουσιν* [*καὶ τὰ ὦτα ὑμῶν ὅτι ἀκούουσιν*]. Cf. Luke 10, 23.

Matt. 6, 13 [Q] *καὶ μὴ εἰσενέγκῃς ἡμᾶς εἰς πειρασμόν,* [*ἀλλὰ ῥῦσαι ἡμᾶς ἀπὸ τοῦ πονηροῦ*]. Cf. Luke 11, 4.

Matt. 6, 19 [Q] [*μὴ θησαυρίζετε ὑμῖν θησαυροὺς ἐπὶ τῆς γῆς, ὅπου σὴς καὶ βρῶσις ἀφανίζει, καὶ ὅπου κλέπται διορύσσουσιν καὶ κλέπτουσιν·*] 20 *θησαυρίζετε δὲ ὑμῖν θησαυροὺς ἐν οὐρανῷ, ὅπου οὔτε σὴς οὔτε βρῶσις ἀφανίζει, καὶ ὅπου κλέπται οὐ διορύσσουσιν οὐδὲ κλέπτουσιν.* Cf. Luke 12, 33.

Matt. 7, 13 [Q] [*ὅτι πλατεῖα ἡ πύλη καὶ εὐρύχωρος ἡ ὁδὸς ἡ ἀπάγουσα εἰς τὴν ἀπώλειαν, καὶ πολλοί εἰσιν οἱ εἰσερχόμενοι δι' αὐτῆς·*] 14 *ὅτι στενὴ ἡ πύλη καὶ τεθλιμμένη ἡ ὁδὸς ἡ ἀπάγουσα εἰς ζωήν, καὶ ὀλίγοι εἰσὶν οἱ εὑρίσκοντες αὐτήν.* Cf. Luke 13, 24.

Matt. 10, 37 [Q] *ὁ φιλῶν πατέρα ἢ μητέρα ὑπὲρ ἐμὲ οὐκ ἔστιν μου ἄξιος, καὶ ὁ φιλῶν υἱὸν ἢ θυγατέρα ὑπὲρ ἐμὲ οὐκ ἔστιν μου ἄξιος.* Cf. Luke 14, 26, which combines all into one clause and uses *τέκνα* for the more symmetrical *υἱὸν ἢ θυγατέρα* (cf. p. 189).

The following list of expressions in Mark omitted by Luke because they repeat either a word or an idea found in the context has been drawn up from Hawkins' lists of "context supplements," and synonymous and duplicate expressions (*Horae Synopticae*, pp. 100 f., 110 ff.). Additional cases will be found in the lists of double expressions of time and of place below, pp. 151 f.[1]

Mark 1, 12 [*εἰς τὴν ἔρημον*] . . . 13 *ἐν τῇ ἐρήμῳ*
Mark 1, 21 [*ἐδίδασκεν*] . . . 22 *ἦν διδάσκων*
Mark 1, 42 *ἀπῆλθεν ἀπ' αὐτοῦ ἡ λέπρα* [*καὶ ἐκαθαρίσθη*]
Mark 2, 15 *πολλοὶ τελῶναι* . . . [*ἦσαν γὰρ πολλοί*]
Mark 2, 25 [*χρείαν ἔσχεν καὶ*] *ἐπείνασεν*
Mark 4, 8 *ἐδίδου καρπόν* . . . [*καὶ ἔφερεν*]
Mark 5, 15 *τὸν δαιμονιζόμενον* . . . [*τὸν ἐσχηκότα τὸν λεγιῶνα*]
Mark 5, 33 [*φοβηθεῖσα καὶ*] *τρέμουσα*
Mark 5, 39 [*θορυβεῖσθε καὶ*] *κλαίετε*

[1] For similar corrections of Mark by Matthew (many of them parallel to the passages we have considered) see, beside Hawkins *l. c.*, the list in Allen, *Matthew*, pp. xxiv f.

Mark 14, 15 ἐστρωμένον [ἕτοιμον]
Mark 14, 68 οὔτε οἶδα [οὔτε ἐπίσταμαι]
Mark 15, 21 [παράγοντά] τινα Σίμωνα . . . ἐρχόμενον ἀπ' ἀγροῦ

Note also the following (not in Hawkins):
Mark 6, 11 καὶ ὃς ἂν τόπος μὴ δέξηται ὑμᾶς [μηδὲ ἀκούσωσιν ὑμῶν].

Three other classes of expressions unnecessary in Mark and omitted by Luke may be listed.

1. References to the fulfilment of requests when the context alone would imply that the request is fulfilled:

Mark 3, 13 προσκαλεῖται οὓς ἤθελεν αὐτός [καὶ ἀπῆλθον πρὸς αὐτόν].
Mark 5, 23 παρακαλεῖ αὐτὸν πολλά . . . ἵνα ἐλθὼν . . . 24 [καὶ ἀπῆλθεν μετ' αὐτοῦ].
Mark 9, 19 φέρετε αὐτὸν πρός με. 20 [καὶ ἤνεγκαν αὐτὸν πρὸς αὐτόν].
Mark 10, 13 προσέφερον αὐτῷ παιδία, ἵνα ἅψηται αὐτῶν . . . 16 [καὶ ἐναγκαλισάμενος αὐτὰ κατευλόγει, τιθεὶς τὰς χεῖρας ἐπ' αὐτά].
Mark 10, 49 φωνήσατε αὐτόν. [καὶ φωνοῦσιν τὸν τυφλόν].
Mark 11, 6 The messengers ask for the colt from its owners [καὶ ἀφῆκαν αὐτούς].
Mark 12, 15 φέρετέ μοι δηνάριον . . . 16 [οἱ δὲ ἤνεγκαν].
Mark 14, 13 ὑπάγετε εἰς τὴν πόλιν . . . 16 καὶ ἐξῆλθον . . . [καὶ ἦλθον εἰς τὴν πόλιν] καὶ εὗρον κ. τ. λ.
Mark 14, 23 ποτήριον . . . ἔδωκεν αὐτοῖς [καὶ ἔπιον ἐξ αὐτοῦ πάντες].
Mark 15, 43 Ἰωσὴφ . . . ᾐτήσατο τὸ σῶμα τοῦ Ἰησοῦ . . . 44 [ὁ δὲ Πειλᾶτος . . . 45 ἐδωρήσατο τὸ πτῶμα τῷ Ἰωσήφ]. See also Mark 8, 6, Matt. 14, 22 f. = Mark 6, 45 f.

Some instances of the converse occur, e.g.,

Mark 3, 3 ἔγειρε εἰς τὸ μέσον.	Luke 6, 8 ἔγειρε καὶ στῆθι εἰς τὸ μέσον. καὶ ἀναστὰς ἔστη.

But more often when Luke preserves the redundancy of Mark he slightly alters the phraseology. The following cases are instructive:

Mark 3, 5 ἔκτεινον τὴν χεῖρα. καὶ ἐξέτεινεν.	Luke 6, 10 ἔκτεινον τὴν χεῖρά σου. ὁ δὲ ἐποίησεν.
Mark 4, 35 διέλθωμεν εἰς τὸ πέραν 36 καὶ . . . παραλαμβάνουσιν αὐτόν.	Luke 8, 22 διέλθωμεν εἰς τὸ πέραν τῆς λίμνης· καὶ ἀνήχθησαν.
Mark 5, 12 παρεκάλεσαν αὐτὸν λέγοντες· πέμψον . . . 13 καὶ ἐπέτρεψεν αὐτοῖς.	Luke 8, 32 παρεκάλεσαν αὐτὸν ἵνα ἐπιτρέψῃ . . . καὶ ἐπέτρεψεν αὐτοῖς.
Mark 6, 39 ἐπέταξεν ἀνακλῖναι πάντας . . . 40 καὶ ἀνέπεσαν.	Luke 9, 14 κατακλίνατε αὐτοὺς . . . 15 καὶ ἐποίησαν οὕτως καὶ κατέκλιναν ἅπαντας.

2. Notices that people came, saw, heard, or took, when such facts can be easily assumed from the context without special mention:

Mark 2, 18 [ἔρχονται καὶ] λέγουσιν Mark 3, 6 [ἐξελθόντες] . . . συμβούλιον ἐποίησαν Mark 4, 4 [ἦλθεν] τὰ πετεινὰ [καὶ] κατέφαγεν Mark 5, 39 [εἰσελθὼν] λέγει Matt. 13, 32 [Q] [ἐλθεῖν] τὰ πετεινὰ τοῦ οὐρανοῦ [καὶ] κατασκηνοῖν Mark 12, 14 καὶ [ἐλθόντες] λέγουσιν Mark 12, 42 [ἐλθοῦσα] μία χήρα πτωχὴ ἔβαλεν Mark 14, 12 ποῦ θέλεις [ἀπελθόντες] ἑτοιμάσωμεν Mark 14, 66 [ἔρχεται] μία τῶν παιδισκῶν [καὶ] ἰδοῦσα . . . λέγει Mark 5, 22 [ἰδὼν αὐτὸν] πίπτει πρὸς τοὺς πόδας Mark 9, 20 [ἰδὼν αὐτὸν] τὸ πνεῦμα συνεσπάραξεν Mark 10, 14 [ἰδὼν] δὲ ὁ Ἰησοῦς Mark 2, 17 καὶ [ἀκούσας] ὁ Ἰησοῦς λέγει Mark 5, 27 [ἀκούσασα τὰ περὶ τοῦ Ἰησοῦ] Mark 6, 16 [ἀκούσας] δὲ ὁ Ἡρώδης ἔλεγεν Mark 11, 18 καὶ [ἤκουσαν] οἱ ἀρχιερεῖς καὶ οἱ γραμματεῖς [καὶ] ἐζήτουν Mark 14, 11 [οἱ δὲ ἀκούσαντες] ἐχάρησαν Mark 12, 3 καὶ [λαβόντες] αὐτὸν ἔδειραν Mark 12, 8 καὶ [λαβόντες] ἀπέκτειναν αὐτόν Mark 14, 23 καὶ [λαβὼν] ποτήριον Mark 1, 7 οὐκ εἰμὶ ἱκανὸς [κύψας] λῦσαι τὸν ἱμάντα Matt. 4, 9 ἐὰν [πεσὼν] προσκυνήσῃς [Q] Mark 15, 43 [τολμήσας] . . . ᾐτήσατο τὸ σῶμα Mark 15, 46 καὶ [ἀγοράσας σινδόνα] . . . ἐνείλησεν αὐτὸ τῇ σινδόνι

The converse occurs principally in two passages, Mark 10, 17 ff. and 12, 1 ff., with their parallels. Here, the following phrases wanting in Mark are found in Luke (and in several cases in Matthew also):

Luke 18, 22 ἀκούσας Luke 18, 23 ἀκούσας ταῦτα (cf. Matt. 19, 22 ἀκούσας) Luke 18, 24 ἰδὼν δὲ αὐτόν Luke 18, 26 οἱ ἀκούσαντες (cf. Matt. 19, 25 ἀκούσαντες δέ) Luke 20, 14 ἰδόντες αὐτόν (cf. Matt. 21, 38 ἰδόντες τὸν υἱόν) Luke 20, 16 ἀκούσαντες (cf. Matt. 21, 45 ἀκούσαντες) Luke 20, 17 ἐμβλέψας αὐτοῖς.

Compare also the following examples:

Luke 5, 12 ἰδὼν δὲ τὸν Ἰησοῦν, not in Mark 1, 40; Luke 6, 4 ἔλαβεν καί, not in Mark 2, 26; Luke 8, 24 προσελθόντες, not in Mark 4, 38 but in Matt. 8, 25; Luke 18, 15 ἰδόντες, not in Mark 10, 13.

In two passages from Q, however, the phrase ἔρχεται (-όμενος) πρός με (in Luke but not in Matthew) is not without force.

Luke 6, 47 πᾶς ὁ [ἐρχόμενος πρός με καὶ] ἀκούων μου τῶν λόγων καὶ ποιῶν αὐτούς — Matt. 7, 24. Luke 14, 26 εἴ τις [ἔρχεται πρός με καὶ] οὐ μισεῖ τὸν πατέρα αὐτοῦ κ. τ. λ. — Matt. 10, 37.

3. Unnecessary explanatory purpose clauses:

Mark 5, 12 πέμψον ἡμᾶς εἰς τοὺς χοίρους, ἵνα εἰς αὐτοὺς εἰσέλθωμεν — cf. Luke 8, 32.
Mark 11, 28 τίς σοι τὴν ἐξουσίαν ταύτην ἔδωκεν, [ἵνα ταῦτα ποιῇς] — Luke 20, 2.
Mark 12, 15 φέρετέ μοι δηνάριον, [ἵνα ἴδω] — Luke 20, 24.
Mark 14, 12 ποῦ θέλεις ἀπελθόντες ἑτοιμάσωμεν, [ἵνα φάγῃς τὸ πάσχα] — Luke 22, 9. (But cf. Luke 22, 8 πορευθέντες ἑτοιμάσατε ἡμῖν τὸ πάσχα ἵνα φάγωμεν.)
Mark 14, 48 ὡς ἐπὶ λῃστὴν ἐξήλθατε μετὰ μαχαιρῶν καὶ ξύλων [συλλαβεῖν με] — Luke 22, 52
Mark 15, 32 καταβάτω νῦν ἀπὸ τοῦ σταυροῦ, [ἵνα ἴδωμεν καὶ πιστεύσωμεν] — Luke 23, 35, 37

Changes Perhaps Attributable to Religious Motives

A number of changes, chiefly omissions, are made by Luke in passages derived from Mark, which are usually explained as due to Luke's reverence for the person of Jesus. In many of the subjoined examples as well as elsewhere Matthew shows the same tendency (see Allen, *Matthew*, pp. xxxi ff.).

Human emotions and expressions of feeling on Christ's part are omitted by Luke, even when they are love and pity.

Thus Luke omits
Mark 1, 41 σπλαγχνισθεὶς (*v. l.* ὀργισθείς)
Mark 1, 43 ἐμβριμησάμενος
Mark 3, 5 μετ' ὀργῆς συνλυπούμενος ἐπὶ τῇ πωρώσει τῆς καρδίας αὐτῶν
Mark 6, 34 ἐσπλαγχνίσθη ἐπ' αὐτοὺς
Mark 8, 32 καὶ παρρησίᾳ τὸν λόγον ἐλάλει
Mark 8, 33 ἐπετίμησε τῷ Πέτρῳ κ. τ. λ.
Mark 9, 36 καὶ ἐναγκαλισάμενος αὐτό
Mark 10, 14 ἰδὼν δὲ . . . ἠγανάκτησεν
Mark 10, 16 καὶ ἐναγκαλισάμενος αὐτά
Mark 10, 21 ἐμβλέψας αὐτῷ ἠγάπησεν αὐτόν
Mark 11, 11 περιβλεψάμενος πάντα
Mark 14, 33 ἤρξατο ἐκθαμβεῖσθαι καὶ ἀδημονεῖν (cf. [Luke] 22, 44)
Mark 14, 35 ἔπιπτεν ἐπὶ τῆς γῆς (Luke 22, 41 θεὶς τὰ γόνατα).

Luke's omission of the cursing of the fig tree (Mark 11, 12–14, 20–25) may be due to the same motive.

Violent acts of Jesus whether actual, as at the cleansing of the temple, or threatened, as when he is said to have threatened to destroy the temple (Mark 14, 58) are omitted by Luke.

Luke 19, 45 omits Mark 11, 15b, 16 καὶ τὰς τραπέζας τῶν κολλυβιστῶν καὶ τὰς καθέδρας τῶν πωλούντων τὰς περιστερὰς κατέστρεψεν καὶ οὐκ ἤφιεν ἵνα τις διενέγκῃ σκεῦος διὰ τοῦ ἱεροῦ, retaining only ἤρξατο ἐκβάλλειν τοὺς πωλοῦντας. Even ἐκβάλλω itself is omitted by Luke in the following passages: Mark 1, 43 ἐξέβαλεν αὐτὸν 44 καὶ λέγει Mark 5, 40 αὐτὸς δὲ ἐκβαλὼν πάντας

Possibly in the Gospel, as in Acts, he wished to present Christianity as in no way hostile to Judaism, but even as faithful to its requirements. Note the addition Luke 23, 56 καὶ τὸ μὲν σάββατον ἡσύχασαν κατὰ τὴν ἐντολήν.[1]

Luke frequently makes less peremptory and abrupt the commands and requests found in his sources by avoiding such words as ὕπαγε, δεῦτε, ἴδε, and by the subtle use of vocatives. These changes quite accord with motives of style, lending grace and smoothness to the dialogue (cf. p. 147); but they also affect the impression we get of the speakers, both Jesus himself and those who address him. Perhaps something of the same sort is to be seen in the following changes in the words of Jesus:

[1] Cf. Luke 2, 21–24, and see Wernle, *Synoptische Frage*, p. 105.

Mark 11, 3 *εἴπατε*	Luke 19, 31 *οὕτως ἐρεῖτε*
Mark 14, 14 *εἴπατε*	Luke 22, 11 *ἐρεῖτε*
Mark 14, 36 *παρένεγκε* (*v. l.*) *τὸ ποτήριον τοῦτο.*	Luke 22, 43 *εἰ βούλει παρενέγκαι* (*v. l.*) *τοῦτο τὸ ποτήριον*
Mark 12, 15 *τί με πειράζετε*	Luke 20, 24 omits.
Mark 13, 9 *βλέπετε δὲ ὑμεῖς ἑαυτούς.*	Luke 21, 12 omits.

Luke omits not only the symptoms of self-destruction in maniacs (see above, p. 48) but also Jesus' apparent teaching of self-mutilation to avoid offence, Mark 9, 43–48 = Matt. 18, 8–9. Even allusions to Jesus' use of physical contact in working cures are omitted by Luke: Mark 1, 31 *ἤγειρεν κρατήσας τῆς χειρός* Mark 5, 23 *ἐλθὼν ἐπιθῇς τὰς χεῖρας* Mark 9, 27 *κρατήσας τῆς χειρός.* So Luke 18, 15–17 does not say that Jesus actually put his hands upon the children (cf. Mark 10, 16; Matt. 19, 15). It may be for the same reason that Luke so often leaves out what Mark relates about the crowd's hindering or discommoding Jesus and about violent or impertinent conduct of individuals to Jesus or in his presence.

In his account of the woman with the issue of blood, Luke, following Mark, mentions the crowd that pressed about Jesus, for therein lies an essential feature of the story (Luke 8, 42, 45; cf. Mark 5, 24, 31; note however Luke's omission of *ἐν τῷ ὄχλῳ* in Mark 5, 27, 30). But elsewhere his references to crowds are rarer than in Mark, and imply less inconvenience to Jesus. In Luke 5, 1–3 the situation is about the same as in Mark 4, 1. In 12, 1 Luke describes a crowd of myriads who trod one upon another, but elsewhere confines himself simply to such mild expressions as *ὄχλος πολύς, ὄχλοι πολλοί.*

In Mark on the other hand we find a number of expressions indicating the annoying presence of crowds (cf. p. 138):

Mark 1, 33 *καὶ ἦν ὅλη ἡ πόλις ἐπισυνηγμένη πρὸς τὴν θύραν*
Mark 1, 45 *ὥστε μηκέτι αὐτὸν δύνασθαι εἰς πόλιν φανερῶς εἰσελθεῖν*
Mark 2, 2 *καὶ συνήχθησαν πολλοί, ὥστε μηκέτι χωρεῖν μηδὲ τὰ πρὸς τὴν θύραν*
Mark 3, 9 *καὶ εἶπεν τοῖς μαθηταῖς αὐτοῦ ἵνα πλοιάριον προσκαρτερῇ αὐτῷ διὰ τὸν ὄχλον, ἵνα μὴ θλίβωσιν αὐτόν*
Mark 3, 20 *καὶ συνέρχεται πάλιν ὄχλος ὥστε μὴ δύνασθαι αὐτοὺς μηδὲ ἄρτον φαγεῖν*
Mark 6, 31b *ἦσαν γὰρ οἱ ἐρχόμενοι καὶ οἱ ὑπάγοντες πολλοί, καὶ οὐδὲ φαγεῖν εὐκαίρουν*
Mark 10, 1 *καὶ συνπορεύονται πάλιν ὄχλοι πρὸς αὐτόν.*

Accordingly Jesus enjoins silence; see Mark 1, 34; 1, 44; 3, 12; 5, 43; 8, 30; 9, 9; 9, 30 (Luke has parallels to four out of seven of these passages).

Mark uses strong words for the pursuit of Jesus, which Luke softens or omits:

Mark 1, 36 *κατεδίωξεν*	Luke 4, 42 *ἐπεζήτουν*
Mark 1, 45 *καὶ ἤρχοντο πρὸς αὐτὸν πάντοθεν*	Luke 5, 15 *συνήρχοντο ὄχλοι πολλοί*
Mark 2, 13 *καὶ πᾶς ὁ ὄχλος ἤρχετο πρὸς αὐτόν*	Luke 5, 27 omits
Mark 3, 10 *ἐπιπίπτειν αὐτῷ*	Luke 6, 19 *ἐζήτουν*
Mark 4, 1 *ὄχλος πλεῖστος*	Luke 8, 4 *ὄχλου πολλοῦ*
Mark 5, 6 *ἀπὸ μακρόθεν ἔδραμεν*	Luke 8, 28 omits
Mark 5, 21 *συνήχθη ὄχλος πολύς*	Luke 8, 40 *ἀπεδέξατο αὐτόν ὁ ὄχλος*
Mark 6, 33 *πεζῇ ἀπὸ πασῶν τῶν πόλεων συνέδραμον ἐκεῖ καὶ προῆλθον αὐτούς.*	Luke 9, 11 *ἠκολούθησαν*
Mark 9, 15 *πᾶς ὁ ὄχλος . . . προστρέχοντες ἠσπάζοντο αὐτόν*	Luke 9, 37 *συνήντησεν αὐτῷ ὄχλος πολύς*
Mark 9, 25 *ἐπισυντρέχει ὄχλος*	Luke 9, 42 omits.
Mark 10, 17 *προσδραμών*	Luke 18, 18 omits
Mark 10, 50 *ἀναπηδήσας ἦλθεν*	Luke 19, 40 *ἐγγίσαντος αὐτοῦ*
Mark 15, 36 *δραμών*	Cf. Luke 23, 36 *προσερχόμενοι*

The explanation suggested may seem fanciful, but the omission of *τρέχω* and its compounds in six of these passages is certainly striking. Violent or impatient or disrespectful conduct either to Jesus or in his presence is elsewhere avoided by Luke. All the following details found in Mark are omitted or altered in Luke.

In Mark 1, 26 the unclean spirit when summoned to come out tore the patient with spasms and cried with a loud voice; in Luke 4, 35 it cast him in the midst without injuring him. In Mark 5, 7 a possessed man adjures Jesus by God;[1] in Luke 8, 28 he merely begs him. In Mark 9, 26 the unclean spirit when summoned to come out "cried out and tore the patient so much that he became like a corpse and many said that he was dead;" Luke omits this. In Mark 1, 45 the cured leper frankly disobeys the command of Jesus to tell no man; in Luke 5, 15 Jesus' growing fame is not attributed to such direct disobedience. Cf. Mark 7, 36. Possibly a parallel case is found at Mark 16, 7, 8 in which the angel ordered the women to tell the disciples and Peter, but they instead of doing so "said nothing to anyone"; while in Luke (24, 9) the women reported the matter "to the eleven and to all the rest."

[1] Hawkins, *Horae Synopticae*, 2d edit., p. 119, suggests the same reason for the change of Mark 5, 7: "It is only in this one of the three narratives that the unclean spirit dares to adjure Jesus (*ὁρκίζω*)."

In Mark 10, 22 the young man went away *στυγνάσας* ("looking gloomy") at the reply of Jesus. Another young man flees from Jesus in the garden in such haste that his cloak was left behind (Mark 14, 51 f.). Similarly Bartimaeus leaves his cloak in his haste to respond to Jesus' call (Mark 10, 50). Luke omits these features as well as the flight of the disciples from the garden and of the women from the tomb (*ἔφυγον* Mark 14, 50; 16, 8). In all the gospels the violent act of cutting off an ear of the high priest's servant is mentioned. In Luke alone its violence is counteracted by the immediate cure by Jesus (22, 51b).

If Luke objected to having Jesus touch people, he would object as much to having people touch him. Not only does he limit the insistence of crowds, but in Luke 8, 44 the patient touches only the border of his garment (so in Matt. 9, 20, but in Mark 5, 27 the garment). Luke 22, 47 does not say, as does Mark (14, 45), that Judas actually kissed Jesus. In speaking of the plan to arrest Jesus, Luke 22, 2 omits *κρατέω* (Mark 14, 1, cf. Mark 14, 44), and when he describes the actual event he again avoids the word (Luke 22, 48; cf. Mark 14, 46 *οἱ δὲ ἐπέβαλαν τὰς χεῖρας αὐτῷ καὶ ἐκράτησαν αὐτόν*). Even the trial and crucifixion scenes are softened by Luke. He omits not only the whole incident of the mockery (Mark 15, 16–20), but a number of details: the spitting on Jesus (Mark 14, 65, cf. Luke 22, 63–65), the beating with rods by the *ὑπηρέται* (*ibid.*), the binding of Jesus (Mark 15, 1 *δήσαντες*), and the scourging with the *flagellum* (15, 15). In Mark and Matthew the high priest tears his clothes in horror at the blasphemy of Jesus, the passers by revile him on the cross wagging their heads, and both the thieves crucified with him reproach him. Luke avoids all this, except that of the two thieves one is penitent and the other is not. In Luke also Jesus' own persistent silence is not so prominent.

Similar shielding of his hero is perhaps shown by Luke in his omission of the account of John the Baptist's death, Mark 6, 21–29 (although it is implied in Luke 9, 7, 9, 19); and, some would add, in the omission from Acts of the martyrdom of Peter and Paul. In view of the *mortes persecutorum* in Acts 1, 18, 19; 12, 23, it cannot be said that Luke avoids violent death scenes for artistic reasons, or out of sensitiveness.

The conduct of Jesus' disciples and friends towards him in Mark can easily be improved on, and Luke improves it. In Luke his kindred do not come out to seize him, nor are they said to think him mad (Mark 3, 21); they merely wish to see him (Luke 8, 20, cf. Mark 3, 32). Peter does not take Jesus and begin to rebuke him (Mark 8, 32); he does not flatly contradict Jesus when he predicts Peter's denial (Mark 14, 31); nor does he curse and swear when accused of knowing Jesus (Mark 14, 71). The disciples in Luke do not ask Jesus a question so complaining as *οὐ μέλει σοι ὅτι ἀπολλύμεθα;* (Mark 4, 38), so superior as *βλέπεις τὸν ὄχλον συνθλίβοντά σε καὶ λέγεις· τίς μου ἥψατο;* (Mark 5, 31), so ironical as *ἀπελθόντες ἀγοράσωμεν δηναρίων διακοσίων ἄρτους καὶ δώσωμεν αὐτοῖς φαγεῖν;* (Mark 6, 37). They say more respectfully *ἐπιστάτα, ἐπιστάτα, ἀπολλύμεθα* (Luke 8, 24); *ἐπιστάτα, οἱ ὄχλοι συνέχουσίν σε καὶ ἀποθλίβουσιν* (Luke 8, 45); and *οὐκ εἰσὶν ἡμῖν πλεῖον ἢ ἄρτοι πέντε καὶ ἰχθύες δύο, εἰ μήτι πορευθέντες ἡμεῖς ἀγοράσωμεν . . . βρώματα* (Luke 9, 13). They do not refuse to answer when he asks them what they are quarreling about [1] (Mark 9, 34; in Luke 9, 47 Jesus simply knows the reasoning of their hearts without asking it, a fact which Luke 6, 8 again adds to Mark 3, 2). They do not show by their surprise so little credence in Jesus' saying about riches as to cause him to repeat it (Mark 10, 23b, 24b; note the omission of Mark 10, 24a, 26a, in Luke 18, 24–26). Finally, they do not all forsake him and flee (Mark 14, 50; accordingly Luke omits also Mark 14, 27, 31b), but rather remain to watch the crucifixion and to hear the first news of the resurrection (Luke 23, 49; 24, 9, 10).

Many of these omissions could be explained quite as easily as made in the interest of the disciples themselves, for example, the rebuke by Peter and the desertion in the garden, as well as the incident of the sons of Zebedee (Mark 10, 35–40). This motive is seen clearly in Matthew's treatment of Mark (Allen, *Matthew*, pp. xxxiii f.), and in a few further cases Luke avoids emphasizing the ignorance of the disciples or want of faith in them. Instead of *τί δειλοί ἐστε οὕτως; οὔπω ἔχετε πίστιν;* (Mark 4, 40), Jesus asks them *ποῦ ἡ πίστις ὑμῶν;* (Luke 8, 25), and he does not dwell on their inabil-

[1] Again in 6, 9 Luke omits the silence of Jesus' hearers at his question (see Mark 3, 4), but not in the seeming parallel in Luke 14, 3. Cf. p. 99.

ity to cure the epileptic boy (Mark 9, 28), nor declare it to be due to lack of faith (Matt. 17, 20). Their ignorance is not chided as in Mark 4, 13, but Luke explains that the facts were hidden from them (by God), (Mark 9, 32, Luke 9, 45; cf. Luke 18, 34; 24, 16). Even their awe and wonder is omitted (Mark 10, 24, 26, 32). Whatever reason we may assign for Luke's omission of the long passage, Mark 6, 45–8, 26, we cannot help noticing how many of the preferences we have just been discussing might have been at least contributory motives. The section is greatly at variance with Luke's tastes, which is only another way of saying that it is very typical of Mark.

Observe emotions and expressions of feeling, Mark 7, 34 ἐστέναξεν 8, 2 σπλαγχνίζομαι 8, 12 ἀναστενάξας 6, 45 ἠνάγκασεν. Personal contact, 6, 56; 7, 32, 33; 8, 22, 23, 25. The crowd, 6, 55 περιέδραμον; 7, 17, 33 ἀπὸ τοῦ ὄχλου, and often. Jesus' inability to have his will, 6, 48; 7, 24. Disobedience to Jesus' command, 7, 36. Jesus' desire for concealment, 6, 48; 7, 24, 36; 8, 26. Ignorance of disciples, 6, 52; 7, 17; 8, 17, 21. Hardened heart, 6, 52; 8, 17 (cf. Mark 3, 5, omitted in Luke 6, 10). Fright of disciples, 6, 49, 50, 52. Forgetfulness of disciples, 8, 14, 18. Want of food, 8, 1, 14.

Phrases of Mark Misunderstood or Transferred by Luke [1]

It is not without interest to collect those passages in which it is possible that Luke misunderstood Mark, or from intention or carelessness has altered details in Mark or transferred them to another passage. It is not likely that all of the following cases are due to misreading or misunderstanding on the part of Luke; other causes may be suggested, such as deliberate change, possible corruption or obscurity in the text of Mark used by Luke, or at least dependence on a form of Mark different from that found in our best manuscripts, though sometimes still represented in inferior manuscripts of Mark. But it is altogether likely that in using a source so extensively an author should sometimes not follow his source exactly even when it was read with diligence. The very uncertainty of most of the following shows how little these mistakes or negligences in Luke may amount to.

In Mark 2, 15, καὶ γίνεται κατακεῖσθαι αὐτὸν ἐν τῇ οἰκίᾳ αὐτοῦ, the αὐτοῦ could apply either to Jesus (cf. αὐτόν) or to Levi. Matthew understands it of Jesus, and if Mark so meant it, Luke misunderstands him, for he writes (5, 29) καὶ ἐποίησεν δοχὴν μεγάλην

[1] See Scholten, *Das Paulinische Evangelium*, pp. 26 f., 41 f., 143 ff.

Λευεὶς αὐτῷ ἐν τῇ οἰκίᾳ αὐτοῦ. There is much to be said however, in favor of Luke's interpretation of Mark. Following Matthew's interpretation of Mark 2, 15, some (e.g. Pfleiderer) understand Jesus to mean in verse 17, οὐκ ἦλθον καλέσαι δικαίους ἀλλὰ ἁμαρτωλούς, that he calls (i.e., invites to his feasts) not just men but sinners. Luke takes καλέσαι in a different sense, for he writes (5, 32) οὐκ ἐλήλυθα καλέσαι δικαίους ἀλλὰ ἁμαρτωλοὺς εἰς μετάνοιαν. But Luke may be right, and εἰς μετάνοιαν be "a true gloss" (Swete).

In Mark 1, 38, Jesus, having gone out from Capernaum, says to those who overtake him that he must preach in other cities, adding, εἰς τοῦτο γὰρ ἐξῆλθον. If ἐξῆλθον refers to his recent departure from Capernaum, Luke does not so understand it, but of Jesus' mission in general, for he writes (4, 43), ὅτι ἐπὶ τοῦτο ἀπεστάλην.[1]

In Mark 6, 15, Herod is told by some that Jesus is a prophet like one of the prophets; Luke (9, 8) understands this to mean that one of the ancient prophets is risen, an idea parallel to the other suggestions, that he is John the Baptist risen from the dead, or that Elias has appeared.

It is possible that Luke has made the same change in 9, 19, for there he suggests again, ὅτι προφήτης τις τῶν ἀρχαίων ἀνέστη (cf. Mark 8, 28, ὅτι εἷς τῶν προφητῶν). Matthew also apparently understands this phrase of Mark to apply to dead prophets, and here this may even be the view of Mark. But that Mark did not feel that a new prophet was impossible, that the line was finally extinct, is clear from Mark 6, 15 just quoted.

One or two cases can be explained as based on an ill-attested or lost reading of Mark.

Thus, in 9, 7, Luke says, λέγεσθαι ὑπό τινῶν, as if he read (with BD 2 min a b ff[2]), ἔλεγον for ἔλεγεν in Mark 6, 14 καὶ ἤκουσεν . . . Ἡρῴδης . . . καὶ ἔλεγεν, and were avoiding the indefinite "they" in characteristic fashion.[2]

In Luke 19, 35, ἐπεβίβασαν τὸν Ἰησοῦν might have been suggested by a reading like that of ℵ in Mark 11, 7, ἐκάθισαν (transitive) for ἐκάθισεν, but this explanation is not necessary.

In Luke 21, 13, ὑμῖν εἰς μαρτύριον might be due to understanding as reflexive the unpointed αυτοις in Mark 13, 9, εἰς μαρτύριον αὐτοῖς (as it is usually written).

In Luke 8, 13, πρὸς καιρὸν πιστεύουσιν could have arisen from misreading πρόσκαιροί εἰσιν, Mark 4, 17.

Similarly, in Luke 7, 19 [Q] Scholten (p. 41) suggests that the mention of *two* disciples sent by John to Jesus is due to a misreading of δύο for διά in [the source of] Matt. 11, 2, πέμψας διὰ τῶν μαθητῶν αὐτοῦ. So J. H. Moulton, *Grammar*, II, 29.

In the following cases, Luke seems to have transferred a phrase in such a manner as to alter the meaning. In some cases, though certainly not in the last one, this may be accidental.

In Mark 14, 43, Jesus' captors are spoken of as a multitude "from (παρὰ) the high priests and scribes and elders." In Luke 22, 52, they are spoken of as being "high priests and generals of the temple and elders."

[1] For a different explanation of these two changes see below, pp. 117 f.

[2] See p. 165.

Mark 14, 71 οὐκ οἶδα τὸν ἄνθρωπον τοῦτον ὃν λέγετε — Luke 22, 60 ἄνθρωπε, οὐκ οἶδα ὃ λέγεις

In Mark 14, 54 and Luke 22, 56, πρὸς τὸ φῶς is used of Peter, but in Mark the heat of the fire, in Luke the light of the fire, seems to be meant by the context.

In Luke 9, 10 Bethsaida is made the scene of the feeding of the five thousand. Luke no doubt gets this from Mark 6, 45; but according to the latter passage Bethsaida is clearly located on the opposite side of the sea. Cf. also Mark 8, 22.

Mark 10, 13, 14 οἱ δὲ μαθηταὶ ἐπετίμων . . . ἰδὼν δὲ ὁ Ἰησοῦς.	Luke 18, 15, 16 ἰδόντες δὲ οἱ μαθηταὶ ἐπετίμων . . . ὁ δὲ Ἰησοῦς.
Mark 6, 16 ὃν ἐγὼ ἀπεκεφάλισα Ἰωάννην, οὗτος ἠγέρθη.	Luke 9, 9 Ἰωάννην ἐγὼ ἀπεκεφάλισα, τίς δέ ἐστιν οὗτος;
Mark 5, 30 τίς (interrog.) μου ἥψατο τῶν ἱματίων;	Luke 8, 46 ἥψατό μού τις (indef.).

In Mark 4, 9 cares and wealth and other desires, εἰσπορευόμενοι, choke the word. In Luke 8, 14 the construction is so changed that those who are choked by cares and wealth and the pleasures of life become the subject of the sentence, yet in agreement with the subject an unintelligible participle, πορευόμενοι, remains.

Mark 3, 16 ff. Simon, James, John, τὸν ἀδελφὸν τοῦ Ἰακώβου, Andrew.	Luke 6, 14 Simon, Andrew, τὸν ἀδελφὸν αὐτοῦ, James, John.

(Matt. 10, 2 adds ὁ ἀδελφὸς αὐτοῦ to both Andrew and John.)

Mark 14, 71 Peter began ἀναθεματίζειν καὶ ὀμνύναι.	Luke 22, 59 ἄλλος τις (not Peter) διισχυρίζετο.
Mark 16, 7 Tell his disciples and Peter that he goes into Galilee.	Luke 24, 6 Remember how he said to you while still in Galilee.

While the influence of Mark on Luke, outside of the parallel passages, is slight and cannot be estimated as a whole, a few instances may be mentioned here in which an unusual expression in Luke may have been suggested by reminiscence of its occurrence in a neighboring context in Mark. This explanation has a higher degree of plausibility in proportion to the infrequency of the word or phrase and to the proximity of the passage in Mark.[1]

Luke 9, 7 διηπόρει. Herod's perplexity about Jesus (nowhere else in Luke); cf. ἠπόρει of Herod's perplexity about John, Mark 6, 20 (ℵBL; nowhere else in Mark), a passage that immediately follows the one Luke is using, but which Luke omits, having already summarized it in Luke 3, 19, 20.

Luke 9, 18 προσευχόμενον κατὰ μόνας. This thought is not in the parallel (Mark 8, 27); but in Mark 6, 45 f. (cf. Matt. 14, 22 f.), which immediately follows the last passage used by Luke (Mark 6, 44 = Luke 9, 17; Luke omits Mark 6, 45–8, 26), Mark tells us that Jesus dismissed both his disciples and the multitude, and went εἰς τὸ ὄρος (Matt. adds κατ' ἰδίαν) προσεύξασθαι.

[1] See Additional Note at the end of this chapter.

Luke 18, 39 *οἱ προάγοντες*. The verb does not occur in the parallel, Mark 10, 48, and is found nowhere else in Luke nor (except transitively) in Acts; but *οἱ προάγοντες* occurs in Mark 11, 9 (= Matt. 21, 9), the section of Mark immediately following that which Luke is using in 18, 39.

Luke 22, 54 *συλλαβόντες* is not used in the parallel, Mark 14, 53,[1] but just before, in Mark 14, 48 (= Matt. 26, 55) stand the words, *ὡς ἐπὶ λῃστὴν ἐξήλθατε μετὰ μαχαιρῶν καὶ ξύλων συλλαβεῖν με*. In Luke's parallel to this verse (Luke 22, 52) the last two words are omitted, nor does the verb occur in this sense elsewhere in the Gospels except John 18, 12 — again of the arrest of Jesus (cf. Acts 1, 16, *Ἰούδα τοῦ γενομένου ὁδηγοῦ τοῖς συλλαβοῦσι τὸν Ἰησοῦν*, and elsewhere in Acts).

Luke 23, 5 *ἀνασείει τὸν λαόν* — the charge made against Jesus; cf. Mark 15, 11, *ἀνέσεισαν τὸν ὄχλον* (the leaders of the Jews stir up the mob at the trial of Jesus), in the very next section of Mark. *Ἀνασείω* occurs nowhere else in the New Testament.

A transfer by Luke not from an adjacent but from a similar passage in Mark may be illustrated by the following:

In Mark 3, 4 the question of Jesus whether it is lawful to do good on the sabbath is met by silence, *οἱ δὲ ἐσιώπων*. Luke in his parallel (6, 9) omits these words; but in a similar incident after a similar question he writes (14, 3) *οἱ δὲ ἡσύχασαν*.

Under the heading "Words Differently Applied," Hawkins (*Horae Synopticae*, pp. 53–61), collects for all the synoptists cases in which "the same or closely similar words are used with different applications or in different connexions, where the passages containing them are evidently parallel." These phenomena seem to him to point to the influences of oral transmission. "Copying from documents does not seem to account for them; but it is not at all difficult to see how they might have arisen in the course of oral transmission. Particular words might linger in the memory, while their position in a sentence was forgotten; and in some cases they might become confused with words of similar sound."

To the present writer this explanation does not seem more adequate than the view that the changes were made in written transmission. Errors in copying frequently exhibit apparently auditory or vocal traits, while the exact position of words in a sentence is quite as easily forgotten when the sentence is read and copied from memory as when it is simply remembered orally.[2]

In either case some of Hawkins' examples illustrate the subject here discussed and may be added to those already collected.

[1] It is possible that *συλλαβόντες* was originally in Mark 14, 53; for Matt. 26, 57 has *κρατήσαντες*, corresponding to Luke 22, 54.

[2] See Additional Note 2, p. 105.

1. Variations in the reports of sayings of Jesus:

Matt. 10, 27 [Q] *ὃ λέγω ὑμῖν ἐν τῇ σκοτίᾳ, εἴπατε ἐν τῷ φωτί· καὶ ὃ εἰς τὸ οὖς ἀκούετε, κηρύξατε ἐπὶ τῶν δωμάτων.*	Luke 12, 3 *ὅσα ἐν τῇ σκοτίᾳ εἴπατε, ἐν τῷ φωτὶ ἀκουσθήσεται, καὶ ὃ πρὸς τὸ οὖς ἐλαλήσατε, . . . κηρυχθήσεται ἐπὶ τῶν δωμάτων.*
Matt. 5, 45 [Q] *ὅπως γένησθε υἱοὶ κ.τ.λ. . . .* 46 *τίνα μισθὸν ἔχετε;*	Luke 6, 35 *καὶ ἔσται ὁ μισθὸς ὑμῶν πολύς, καὶ ἔσεσθε υἱοὶ κ.τ.λ.*[1]
Matt. 10, 25 [Q] *ἀρκετὸν τῷ μαθητῇ ἵνα γένηται ὡς ὁ διδάσκαλος αὐτοῦ.*	Luke 6, 40 *κατηρτισμένος δὲ πᾶς ἔσται ὡς ὁ διδάσκαλος αὐτοῦ.*
Matt. 11, 27 [Q] *οὐδὲ τὸν πατέρα τις* (indef.) *ἐπιγινώσκει.*	Luke 10, 22 *οὐδεὶς γινώσκει . . . τίς* (interrog.) *ἐστιν ὁ πατήρ.*

2. Attribution of the same words to different speakers:

In Mark 6, 16; Matt. 14, 2 Herod himself says that John was risen from the dead; in Luke 9, 7 others have said so. Cf. Mark 6, 14 and above p. 97.

In Matt. 18, 21 [Q] Peter asks how often he shall forgive, and whether until seven times (*ἕως ἑπτάκις*); in Luke 17, 4 Jesus tells the disciples to forgive seven times (*ἑπτάκις*).

In Matt. 7, 14 [Q] the mention of *ὀλίγοι οἱ* forms part of a warning given by Jesus; in Luke 13, 23 it forms part of a question put to him.

3. Use of the same, or very similar, words as part of a speech and as part of the evangelist's narrative:

In Luke 4, 43 Jesus says, *εὐαγγελίσασθαί με δεῖ τὴν βασιλείαν τοῦ θεοῦ*; in Matt. 4, 23 he is spoken of *κηρύσσων τὸ εὐαγγέλιον τῆς βασιλείας.*

In Luke 8, 46, Jesus says, *ἐγὼ γὰρ ἔγνων δύναμιν ἐξεληλυθυῖαν ἀπ' ἐμοῦ*; in Mark 5, 30, the evangelist says of him, *ἐπιγνοὺς ἐν ἑαυτῷ τὴν ἐξ αὐτοῦ δύναμιν ἐξελθοῦσαν.*[2]

4. Variations in the rest of the synoptic narratives:

Matt. 3, 5 [Q] *ἐξεπορεύετο πρὸς αὐτὸν . . . πᾶσα ἡ περίχωρος τοῦ Ἰορδάνου.*	Luke 3, 5 *καὶ ἦλθεν εἰς πᾶσαν τὴν περίχωρον τοῦ Ἰορδάνου.*
Mark 3, 8 *ἀκούοντες ὅσα ποιεῖ ἦλθαν πρὸς αὐτόν.*	Luke 6, 17 *ἦλθαν ἀκοῦσαι αὐτοῦ καὶ ἰαθῆναι κ.τ.λ.*
Mark 1, 23 *καὶ ἀνέκραξεν . . .* 26 *φωνῆσαν φωνῇ μεγάλῃ ἐξῆλθεν ἐξ αὐτοῦ.*	Luke 4, 33 *καὶ ἀνέκραξεν φωνῇ μεγάλῃ.* [Luke mentions no cry after the command *φιμώθητι.*]
Mark 1, 45 *ὁ δὲ ἐξελθὼν ἤρξατο . . . διαφημίζειν τὸν λόγον.*	Luke 5, 15 *διήρχετο δὲ μᾶλλον ὁ λόγος περὶ αὐτοῦ.*

There must have been similarity in sound between *ἤρξατο* and *-ήρχετο.*

[1] In the adjacent verse may perhaps be found the explanation of *γένησθε* (Matt) = *ἔσεσθε* (Luke), for there we have *ἔσεσθε* (Matt. 5, 48) = *γίνεσθε* (Luke 6, 36). See below, p. 179.

[2] One striking variation of this kind between Matthew and Mark seems to have escaped the notice of Hawkins:

Mark 14, 23 *καὶ λαβὼν ποτήριον εὐχαριστήσας ἔδωκεν αὐτοῖς, καὶ ἔπιον ἐξ αὐτοῦ πάντες.*	Matt. 26, 27 *καὶ λαβὼν ποτήριον καὶ εὐχαριστήσας ἔδωκεν αὐτοῖς λέγων· πίετε ἐξ αὐτοῦ πάντες.*

Mark 5, 31 βλέπεις τὸν ὄχλον συνθλίβοντά σε	Luke 8, 45 οἱ ὄχλοι συνέχουσίν σε καὶ ἀποθλίβουσιν

This, however, is only a different arrangement of parts of words.

Hawkins adds among others these cases:

Mark 6, 35 = Luke 9, 12, where the ὅτι introducing the mention of the desert place is in Mark recitative, in Luke causal; ἀπεκρίνατο οὐδέν, used in Mark 14, 61; Matt. 27, 12; Luke 23, 9 of the silences before the High Priest, Pilate, and Herod respectively (this first aorist middle being used besides in the New Testament only in Luke 3, 16; John 5, 17, 19; Acts 3, 12, instead of the far more common passive forms ἀπεκρίθη, etc.); Mark 3, 30 ὅτι ἔλεγον, compared with Luke 11, 18, ὅτι λέγετε (cf. p. 125).

Note also the following:

Matt 4, 8 [Q] Satan shows him πάσας τὰς βασιλείας τοῦ κόσμου καὶ τὴν δόξαν αὐτῶν, and says ταῦτά σοι πάντα δώσω, ἐὰν κ.τ.λ.	Luke 4, 5 f. Satan shows him πάσας τὰς βασιλείας τῆς οἰκουμένης . . . and says σοὶ δώσω τὴν ἐξουσίαν ταύτην ἅπασαν καὶ τὴν δόξαν αὐτῶν (*sic*), . . . ἐὰν κ.τ.λ.
Matt. 5, 11 [Q] μακάριοί ἐστε ὅταν ὀνειδίσωσιν ὑμᾶς καὶ διώξωσιν καὶ εἴπωσιν πᾶν πονηρὸν καθ' ὑμῶν ψευδόμενοι.	Luke 6, 22 μακάριοί ἐστε ὅταν . . . ὀνειδίσωσιν καὶ ἐκβάλωσιν τὸ ὄνομα ὑμῶν ὡς πονηρὸν.

εἶτα is used by both Mark and Luke in explaining the parable of the sower, but in neither gospel elsewhere except at Mark 8, 25. But in this parable it is very differently applied. In Luke 8, 12 it is said of the seed sown by the wayside, εἶτα (Mark εὐθύς) ἔρχεται ὁ διάβολος καὶ αἴρει τὸν λόγον. In Mark 4, 17 it is said of the seed sown on the rock, εἶτα (Luke καί) γενομένης θλίψεως ἢ διωγμοῦ διὰ τὸν λόγον εὐθὺς σκανδαλίζονται.

καθὼς εἶπεν is used by both Mark and Luke of the disciples who went to get the colt for the triumphal entry, but is applied by Mark 11, 6 to their reply to those who objected to their taking the colt, by Luke 19, 32 to their finding the colt.

Mark 14, 42 ἰδοὺ ὁ παραδιδούς με ἤγγικεν.	Luke 22, 47 ἰδοὺ . . . Ἰούδας . . . ἤγγισεν.

The following parallels, if the reading and punctuation given below is correct, contain other cases of words that Luke has transferred from one word or clause to another:

Mark 3, 26 καὶ εἰ ὁ σατανᾶς ἀνέστη ἐφ' ἑαυτόν, ἐμερίσθη (*v.l.*).
Matt. 12, 26 καὶ εἰ ὁ σατανᾶς τὸν σατανᾶν ἐκβάλλει, ἐφ' ἑαυτὸν ἐμερίσθη· πῶς κ.τ.λ.
Luke 11, 18 εἰ δὲ καὶ ὁ σατανᾶς ἐφ' ἑαυτὸν διεμερίσθη, πῶς κ.τ.λ. [Q]

Mark 12, 21 f. καὶ ὁ τρίτος ὡσαύτως· καὶ οἱ ἑπτά.
Luke 20, 31 καὶ ὁ τρίτος ἔλαβεν αὐτήν· ὡσαύτως δὲ καὶ οἱ ἑπτά.

In this connection may be added a few cases where Luke's omission of details given in Mark makes the situation obscure or abrupt.

In Mark 1, 29 f. four disciples are mentioned in connection with Jesus' visit to the house where Simon's wife's mother was sick, " and straightway they tell him of her."

In Luke 4, 38 Simon alone is mentioned, and yet the plural is retained, "and *they* asked him of her." [1]

In Mark 2, 1 it is said that Jesus was in a house. In Luke 5, 17 this is omitted, and has to be inferred from the sequel (vs. 18 εἰσενεγκεῖν, vs. 19 δῶμα).

In Mark 2, 18 Jesus is asked, apparently by the publicans and sinners, why the disciples of the Pharisees fast; in Luke 5, 33 the same question is asked by the Pharisees themselves but without changing τῶν Φαρισαίων to the first person. (So Scholten, p. 144.) [2]

In Mark 6, 14 and Luke 9, 7 it is implied that John the Baptist is dead, though neither Gospel has thus far mentioned his death. Mark at once explains the reference by narrating (6, 17–29) the circumstances of John's death (note γάρ, vs. 17) but Luke nowhere directly relates it.

Mark 14, 44 is omitted by Luke 22, 47. Wernle says (*op. cit.* p. 33): Dass der Kuss das Zeichen für die Häscher sein sollte, hat Lc ausgelassen, nicht gerade zur Aufklärung der Leser.

The trial of Jesus before the Sanhedrin occurs in Mark before the denial of Peter. Luke reverses this order, but fails to make plain that the chief actor has changed, using in 22, 63 ff. the simple αὐτόν of Jesus although the last antecedent is Peter. Cf. Mark 14, 65.

In Mark 15, 46 is added the note that Joseph rolled a stone to the door of the tomb, so that in 16, 4 we understand what stone is meant when we read that the women found the stone rolled away. In Luke the stone is first mentioned on the resurrection day, 24, 2, εὗρον δὲ τὸν λίθον ἀποκεκυλισμένον ἀπὸ τοῦ μνημείου. Cf. John 20, 1.

The omission of Mark 15, 16–20, describing the maltreatment of Jesus by the soldiers (Matt. 27, 27, the soldiers of the governor), leaves unfulfilled the prediction in Luke 18, 32 ff. which is derived from Mark 10, 34. Note especially in Luke 18, 32 f. ἐμπτυσθήσεται and μαστιγώσαντες and the fulfilment of the prophecy in φραγελλώσας, ἐνέπτυον (Mark 15, 15, 19, but not in Luke). Further, the omission of στρατιῶται (Mark 15, 16) gives a vague or mistaken idea of the subject of the verbs that follow in Luke 23, e.g., vs. 26, ἀπήγαγον, vs. 33, ἐσταύρωσαν, vs. 34, διαμεριζόμενοι ἔβαλον, until in vs. 36 the στρατιῶται are brought in as though they had been mentioned before.

In Luke 23, 18 the demand that Barabbas be released is given as in Mark 15, 11, but by omitting Mark 15, 6–10, Luke has left it unexplained why such a demand was likely to be made (the custom of releasing a prisoner) and what it has to do with Jesus (Pilate's suggestion that Jesus be given the annual pardon).[3]

In Luke 20, 40 we are told that the scribes no longer (οὐκέτι, so Mark 12, 34) dared ask him any question; but Luke has omitted Mark 12, 28–31, where a question of one of the scribes is given. The οὐκέτι has therefore no real meaning in Luke.

Similarly in the trial of Jesus before the Sanhedrin Mark tells of the testimony of witnesses against Jesus, and that after Jesus confessed that he was the Christ the high

[1] Of course the mention in Luke even of Simon is rather abrupt since Luke has omitted the calling of Simon, and the other three disciples in Mark 1, 16–20, or at least has not yet narrated his version of it (Luke 5, 1–11). Compare the premature mention of Capernaum (Luke 4, 23).

[2] So from Mark 12, 35 πῶς λέγουσιν οἱ γραμματεῖς Luke 20, 41 retains the verb in the third person, although the omission of the subject, and Luke's own context imply that the question was addressed to the scribes themselves.

[3] In this passage of Luke as well as at 24, 2 D corrects the awkward omission, and here is supported by ℵ W among others and by several versions: 23, [17] ἀνάγκην δὲ εἶχεν ἀπολύειν αὐτοῖς κατὰ ἑορτὴν ἕνα.

priest cried, τί ἔτι χρείαν ἔχομεν μαρτύρων; (Mark 14, 63). Luke 22, 71 keeps this remark, but the ἔτι has no longer any force, inasmuch as Luke has omitted everything about the witnesses.

In Luke 23, 35 the probable reading is ἐξεμυκτήριζον δὲ καὶ οἱ ἄρχοντες, and the καί is no doubt the καί of Mark 15, 31, meaning "also," for Mark has just mentioned other mockers, "the passers by." As Luke has omitted these mockers, the "also" is with him meaningless.[1]

In Luke 22, 2 we read, καὶ ἐζήτουν οἱ ἀρχιερεῖς καὶ οἱ γραμματεῖς τὸ πῶς ἀνέλωσιν αὐτόν· ἐφοβοῦντο γὰρ τὸν λαόν. The last clause is peculiar to Luke, but is quite natural and in accord with Mark's picture of the conditions of Jesus' life (Mark 11, 32; 14, 2), and characteristic of Luke (see Luke 7, 29; 18, 43; 19, 47 f.; 20, 26; Acts 4, 21; 5, 13, 26). The difficulty is in the use of γάρ. Either καί as at 20, 19 or "but" would seem more appropriate. Γάρ would explain either why they were unable to carry out their plan (as at 19, 48) or why they planned a special method of arrest as in Acts 5, 26. Now, while neither of these is found in Luke in the context, features in Mark which he omits contain both. For Mark says plainly that they planned to make the arrest ἐν δόλῳ (Mark 14, 1; δόλῳ, Matt. 26, 4), and that they were loath to do it at a feast for fear of an uprising of the people (vs. 2, ἔλεγον γάρ (Matt. δέ) μὴ ἐν τῇ ἑορτῇ, μήποτε ἔσται θόρυβος τοῦ λαοῦ. It is this omitted context of Mark which I believe explains the elliptical γάρ in Luke. This is the interpretation of Tatian, who combines Matt., Mark, and Luke in the following instructive manner: "And they took counsel concerning Jesus that they might take him by subtility, and kill him. But they said, not during the feast, lest peradventure a tumult arise among the people; for they feared the people." (*Diatessaron*, 44, 4, 5, Hill's translation.)

A number of other instances of this sort have been collected by Badham, *S. Mark's Indebtedness to S. Matthew*, pp. xv–xxviii, who uses them in telling fashion to show that Luke was familiar with nearly every important passage in our canonical Mark which he does not use. An argument of the same kind may be made from evidences in Matthew that he knew the parts of Mark which he omits (e.g., the parable of the seed growing in secret, see *Oxford Studies in the Synoptic Problem*, p. 432, n. 3).

Note 1 (p. 98)

The process of transferring phrases is still more amply exemplified in Matthew's use of his sources. To it are due many of the doublets in Matthew; for doublets arise from using the same source twice, as well as from using two different sources. Especially the very numerous short expressions found repeatedly in Matthew are to be so explained (Hawkins, *Horae Synopticae*, p. 137), and in transferring and repeating Mark's summaries, Matthew shows great freedom.

[1] Probably some would prefer to include these three cases in the list given above of words differently applied by Luke. It is possible to assign some meaning to οὐκέτι, ἔτι, and καί in these passages of Luke, though not the meaning they bear in Mark.

Thus Mark 1, 22 is transferred to Matt. 7, 28, 29. Matt. 4, 23–25 is made up of many passages in Mark, to nearly all of which Matthew has a doublet in its proper place as is shown below:

Mark		Parallel in Matthew	Elsewhere in Matthew
1, 39	preaching in synagogues of Galilee	4, 23a	9, 35
6, 6	περιῆγεν	9, 35	4, 23a
1, 28	ἐξῆλθεν ἡ ἀκοή		4, 24a
1, 34	τοὺς κακῶς ἔχοντας	8, 16	4, 24b
3, 7a	many followed him	12, 15	4, 25a
3, 7b, 8	list of places		4, 25b

The miracle recorded in Matt. 9, 27–31 has many distinct borrowings from Mark; especially noteworthy are the rare verbs *ἐμβριμάομαι* and *διαφημίζω* found in Mark's account of the leper, Mark 1, 43, 45, but not in Matthew's parallel to it. More nearly parallel are the charge here to the blind men, *μηδεὶς γινωσκέτω*, and that to Jairus and his wife, *μηδεὶς γνοῖ τοῦτο*, Mark 5, 43, since in Matthew the story of Jairus' daughter immediately precedes (Matt. 9, 18–26). Matthew has wedged in this miracle of healing the blind men just before the last verse of the raising of Jairus' daughter in Mark, so that the charge to secrecy now has a new application. The other details are like Mark's account of Bartimaeus, and still more like Matthew's parallel to it (Matt. 20, 29–34). See the following table:

Matthew 9, 27–31	Recurs in Matthew	Occurs in Mark
27 παράγοντι ἐκεῖθεν	9, 9 παράγων ἐκεῖθεν	= 2, 14 παράγων
27 δύο τυφλοί	20, 30 δύο τυφλοί	= 10, 46 τυφλός
27 κράζοντες καὶ λέγοντες	20, 30 ἔκραξαν λέγοντες	= 10, 47 ἤρξαντο κράζειν καὶ λέγειν·
28 ἐλέησον ἡμᾶς, υἱὸς [v.l. υἱὲ] Δαυείδ	20, 30 ἐλέησον ἡμᾶς, υἱὲ [v.l. υἱὸς] Δαυείδ	= 10, 47 υἱὲ Δαυείδ Ἰησοῦ ἐλέησόν με
28 ἐλθόντι εἰς τὴν οἰκίαν		cf. 2, 15; 7, 24
28 πιστεύετε κ.τ.λ.		cf. 9, 23, 24 τῷ πιστεύοντι . . . πιστεύω
29 ἥψατο τῶν ὀφθαλμῶν	20, 34 ἥψατο τῶν ὀμμάτων	
29 κατὰ τὴν πίστιν κ.τ.λ.		10, 52 ἡ πίστις σου κ.τ.λ.
30 ἠνεῴχθησαν οἱ ὀφθαλμοί	cf. 20, 33 ἵνα ἀνοιγῶσιν οἱ ὀφθαλμοὶ ἡμῶν	10, 51 ἵνα ἀναβλέψω
30 ἐνεβριμήθη		1, 43 ἐμβριμησάμενος
30 ὁρᾶτε		1, 44 ὅρα μηδενὶ μηδὲν κ.τ.λ.
31 μηδεὶς γινωσκέτω		5, 43 μηδεὶς γνοῖ τοῦτο
31 ἐξελθόντες διεφήμισαν		1, 45 ἐξελθὼν ἤρξατο . . . διαφημίζειν
31 ἐν ὅλῃ τῇ γῇ ἐκείνῃ	9, 26 εἰς ὅλην τὴν γῆν ἐκείνην	

Note 2 (p. 99)

Sandday (*Oxford Studies in the Synoptic Problem*, p. 5) cites with approval the judgment of Hawkins that these phenomena are to be attributed to "oral transmission," but by his definition that term seems to mean pretty nearly the method of employing written sources we have outlined above. On p. 18 f., after describing the methods of a modern copyist, he contrasts those of an ancient writer like one of the Evangelists: "He would not have his copy before him, but would consult it from time to time. He would not follow it clause by clause and phrase by phrase, but would probably read through a whole paragraph at once, and trust to his memory to convey the substance of it safely from the one book to the other. We see here where the opening for looseness of reproduction comes in. There is a substantial interval between reading and writing. During that interval the copy is not before the eye, and in the meantime the brain is actively, though unconsciously, at work. Hence all those slight rearrangements and substitutions which are a marked feature in our texts as we have them. Hence, in a word, all those phenomena which simulate oral transmission. There is a real interval during which the paragraph of text is carried in the mind, though not a long one. The question may be not one of hours or days but only of minutes . . .

"The phenomena of variation [as between Mark and the succeeding Gospels] in the texts that have come down to us do not require for their explanation any prolonged extension of time or diffused circulation in space; they might be described in homely phrase as just so many 'slips between the cup and the lip.'"

Opening and Close of Sections. Summaries

In the introductions to new sections Luke shows the greatest independence. Where events are closely connected by their inner relation, as in the progress of events from the Lord's Supper to the Resurrection, Luke follows Mark's introductions more exactly; but during the Galilean ministry, when more or less detached scenes are presented, Luke takes the liberty of rewriting the introductions in his own way. Specific indications of time and place are frequently replaced by more general references, and details are added to supply the invisible mental environment of the scene rather than its graphic physical scenery.

A favorite form of preface is the use of *καὶ ἐγένετο, ἐγένετο δέ.* (For lists, see a concordance; for classification according to grammatical construction, see Plummer, *Luke,* p. 45).

In the following list the majority of instances are peculiar to Luke, but the cases that have parallels show that the method throughout is the same.

6, 6 *ἐγένετο δὲ ἐν ἑτέρῳ σαββάτῳ εἰσελθεῖν αὐτὸν εἰς τὴν συναγωγὴν καὶ διδάσκειν* (cf. Mark 3, 1 *καὶ εἰσῆλθεν πάλιν εἰς συναγωγήν*).
7, 11 *καὶ ἐγένετο ἐν τῇ ἑξῆς ἐπορεύθη κ.τ.λ.*
9, 37 *ἐγένετο δὲ τῇ ἑξῆς ἡμέρᾳ* (cf. Mark 9, 9, 14).
8, 1 *καὶ ἐγένετο ἐν τῷ καθεξῆς καὶ αὐτὸς διώδευεν.*
9, 28 *ἐγένετο δὲ μετὰ τοὺς λόγους τούτους ὡσεὶ ἡμέραι ὀκτώ* (cf. Mark 9, 2 *καὶ μετὰ ἡμέρας ἕξ*).
8, 40 *ἐγένετο δὲ ἐν τῷ ὑποστρέφειν τὸν Ἰησοῦν* (cf. Mark 5, 21, gen. abs.).
9, 51 *ἐγένετο δὲ ἐν τῷ συμπληροῦσθαι τὰς ἡμέρας.*
10, 38 *ἐγένετο δὲ ἐν τῷ πορεύεσθαι αὐτούς.*
11, 1 *καὶ ἐγένετο ἐν τῷ εἶναι αὐτὸν ἐν τόπῳ τινὶ προσευχόμενον.*
14, 1 *καὶ ἐγένετο ἐν τῷ ἐλθεῖν αὐτὸν εἰς οἶκόν τινος.*
17, 11 *καὶ ἐγένετο ἐν τῷ πορεύεσθαι εἰς Ἱερουσαλήμ.*
18, 35 *ἐγένετο δὲ ἐν τῷ ἐγγίζειν αὐτὸν εἰς Ἰερειχώ* (cf. Mark 10, 46 *καὶ ἔρχονται εἰς Ἰερειχώ*).

Particularly common are a variety of expressions with *ἐγένετο ἐν μιᾷ.*

5, 12 *καὶ ἐγένετο ἐν τῷ εἶναι αὐτὸν ἐν μιᾷ τῶν πόλεων* (cf. Mark 1, 40).
5, 17 *καὶ ἐγένετο ἐν μιᾷ τῶν ἡμερῶν καὶ αὐτὸς ἦν διδάσκων* (cf. Mark 2, 1).
8, 22 *ἐγένετο δὲ ἐν μιᾷ τῶν ἡμερῶν καὶ αὐτὸς ἐνέβη* (cf. Mark 4, 35).
20, 1 *καὶ ἐγένετο ἐν μιᾷ τῶν ἡμερῶν διδάσκοντος αὐτοῦ τὸν λαόν* (cf. Mark 11, 27).

Cf. Luke 13, 10 (peculiar to Luke). In each of these cases except the last the expression supplants a more definite one, or else creates for Luke a new setting when the preceding sections in Luke and Mark are different.

Characteristic of Luke is the introduction of a parable by *ἔλεγεν* or *εἶπεν παραβολήν.* The other gospels do not use this expression either in the parallels to Luke's examples or elsewhere.

5, 36 *ἔλεγεν δὲ καὶ παραβολὴν πρὸς αὐτούς* (cf. Mark 2, 21).
6, 39 *εἶπεν δὲ καὶ παραβολὴν αὐτοῖς* (cf. Matt. 15, 14).
12, 16 *εἶπεν δὲ παραβολὴν πρὸς αὐτοὺς λέγων.*
13, 6 *ἔλεγεν δὲ ταύτην τὴν παραβολήν.*
14, 7 *ἔλεγεν δὲ πρὸς τοὺς κεκλημένους παραβολὴν . . . λέγων.*
15, 3 *εἶπεν δὲ πρὸς αὐτοὺς τὴν παραβολὴν ταύτην λέγων* (cf. Matt. 18, 12).
18, 1 *ἔλεγεν δὲ παραβολὴν αὐτοῖς . . . λέγων.*
18, 9 *εἶπεν δὲ καὶ πρός τινας . . . τὴν παραβολὴν ταύτην.*

19, 11 προσθεὶς εἶπεν παραβολήν (cf. Matt. 25, 14).
20, 9 ἤρξατο . . . λέγειν τὴν παραβολὴν ταύτην (cf. Mark 12, 1).
21, 29 καὶ εἶπεν παραβολὴν αὐτοῖς (cf. Mark 13, 28).

To a less extent Luke changes the conclusions of sections, the principal changes from Mark being the addition, or intensification, of descriptions of the effect of Jesus' words or deeds. Two favorite expressions are illustrated by the following lists:

4, 15 δοξαζόμενος ὑπὸ πάντων added to Mark 1, 15.
5, 25 δοξάζων τὸν θεόν added to Mark 2, 12.
18, 43 δοξάζων τὸν θεόν added to Mark 10, 52.
23, 47 δοξάζων τὸν θεόν added to Mark 15, 39.
δοξάζω τὸν θεόν occurs also at Luke 2, 20; 7, 16; 13, 13; 17, 15; Acts 4, 21; 11, 18; 21, 20. In Luke 5, 26 it comes from Mark 2, 12 = Matt. 9, 8.
4, 28 καὶ ἐπλήσθησαν πάντες θυμοῦ (cf. Mark 6, 2, 3).
5, 26 καὶ ἐπλήσθησαν φόβου added to Mark 2, 12.
6, 11 αὐτοὶ δὲ ἐπλήσθησαν ἀνοίας added to Mark 3, 6.
Cf. Acts 3, 10 ἐπλήσθησαν θάμβους καὶ ἐκστάσεως; 5, 17 and 13, 45 ἐπλήσθησαν ζήλου.

A variety of other descriptions added to Mark are as follows:

8, 37 ὅτι φόβῳ μεγάλῳ συνείχοντο added to Mark 5, 17.
9, 34 ἐφοβήθησαν δὲ ἐν τῷ εἰσελθεῖν αὐτοὺς εἰς τὴν νεφέλην (cf. Mark 9, 7).
9, 43a ἐξεπλήσσοντο δὲ πάντες ἐπὶ τῇ μεγαλειότητι τοῦ θεοῦ added to Mark 9, 27.
9, 43b πάντων δὲ θαυμαζόντων ἐπὶ πᾶσιν οἷς ἐποίει (cf. Mark 9, 30, 31).
18, 43 καὶ πᾶς ὁ λαὸς ἰδὼν ἔδωκεν αἶνον τῷ θεῷ added to Mark 10, 52.
19, 37 ἤρξαντο ἅπαν τὸ πλῆθος τῶν μαθητῶν χαίροντες αἰνεῖν τὸν θεὸν περὶ πασῶν ὧν εἶδον δυνάμεων (*v.l.*) added to Mark 11, 9.
Note also Luke's additions to Mark in Luke 20, 16, 26; 23, 27, 48.

Luke elaborates on failure to understand:

9, 45 οἱ δὲ ἠγνόουν τὸ ῥῆμα τοῦτο, καὶ ἦν παρακεκαλυμμένον ἀπ' αὐτῶν, ἵνα μὴ αἴσθωνται αὐτό, for Mark 9, 32 οἱ δὲ ἠγνόουν τὸ ῥῆμα.
18, 34 καὶ αὐτοὶ οὐδὲν τούτων συνῆκαν, καὶ ἦν τὸ ῥῆμα τοῦτο κεκρυμμένον ἀπ' αὐτῶν, καὶ οὐκ ἐγίνωσκον τὰ λεγόμενα added to Mark 10, 34.
In the sequel Luke (24, 8) adds καὶ ἐμνήσθησαν τῶν ῥημάτων αὐτοῦ. Cf. 2, 50 αὐτοὶ οὐ συνῆκαν τὸ ῥῆμα.

In a few cases Luke omits a statement of the effect of Jesus' words:

8, 39 omits καὶ πάντες ἐθαύμαζον from Mark 5, 20.
9, 37 omits ἰδόντες αὐτὸν ἐξεθαμβήθησαν from Mark 9, 15.
18, 24 omits ἐθαμβοῦντο ἐπὶ τοῖς λόγοις αὐτοῦ from Mark 10, 24.
18, 25 omits οἱ δὲ περισσῶς ἐξεπλήσσοντο from Mark 10, 26.
18, 31 omits ἐθαμβοῦντο, οἱ δὲ ἀκολουθοῦντες ἐφοβοῦντο from Mark 10, 32.
Mark is little, if at all, stronger than Luke in Mark 11, 18 = Luke 19, 48; Mark 12, 37 = Luke 20, 45. Except Mark 10, 26 all the phrases in Mark above referred to are omitted by Matthew also. On the omission of (ἐκ) θαμβέομαι see p. 172.

As in the prefaces and conclusions of the several sections, so in the brief summaries of Jesus' work and influence we should expect that Luke would show great freedom with the wording of Mark, if not with the actual content of his summaries. With what we know of Luke's tendency to generalization it might be expected, also, that some purely local description or single examples in Mark would become more general in Luke. Yet this is rarely, if ever, the case. With extraordinary fidelity Luke avoids amplifying or exaggerating his source in these summaries of Jesus' work or fame. The following table will show that a large part of the substance of the summaries comes from Mark, but that it is rather loosely borrowed with some re-wording, and that phrases from different parts of Mark are joined together. Passages in Mark which are not parallel to the passage in Luke which appears to use them are enclosed in square brackets.

Luke	Mark
4, 14 καὶ ὑπέστρεψεν ὁ Ἰησοῦς ἐν τῇ δυνάμει τοῦ πνεύματος εἰς τὴν Γαλιλαίαν. καὶ φήμη ἐξῆλθεν καθ' ὅλης τῆς περιχώρου περὶ αὐτοῦ. 15 καὶ αὐτὸς ἐδίδασκεν ἐν ταῖς συναγωγαῖς αὐτῶν, δοξαζόμενος ὑπὸ πάντων.	1, 14 ἦλθεν ὁ Ἰησοῦς εἰς τὴν Γαλιλαίαν [1, 28 καὶ ἐξῆλθεν ἡ ἀκοὴ αὐτοῦ εἰς ὅλην τὴν περίχωρον τῆς Γαλιλαίας.] [1, 21 ἐδίδασκεν εἰς τὴν συναγωγήν. 39 καὶ ἦλθεν κηρύσσων εἰς τὰς συναγωγάς.]
4, 31 καὶ κατῆλθεν εἰς Καφαρναούμ, πόλιν τῆς Γαλιλαίας, καὶ ἦν διδάσκων αὐτοὺς ἐν τοῖς σάββασιν. 32 καὶ ἐξεπλήσσοντο ἐπὶ τῇ διδαχῇ αὐτοῦ, ὅτι ἐν ἐξουσίᾳ ἦν ὁ λόγος αὐτοῦ.	1, 21 καὶ εἰσπορεύονται εἰς Καφαρναούμ, καὶ εὐθὺς τοῖς σάββασι ἐδίδασκεν εἰς τὴν συναγωγήν. 32 καὶ ἐξεπλήσσοντο ἐπὶ τῇ διδαχῇ αὐτοῦ, ἦν γὰρ διδάσκων αὐτοὺς ὡς ἐξουσίαν ἔχων, καὶ οὐχ ὡς οἱ γραμματεῖς.
4, 37 καὶ ἐξεπορεύετο ἦχος περὶ αὐτοῦ εἰς πάντα τόπον τῆς περιχώρου.	1, 28 καὶ ἐξῆλθεν ἡ ἀκοὴ αὐτοῦ εὐθὺς πανταχοῦ εἰς ὅλην τὴν περίχωρον τῆς Γαλιλαίας.
4, 40 δύνοντος δὲ τοῦ ἡλίου πάντες ὅσοι εἶχον ἀσθενοῦντας νόσοις ποικίλαις ἤγαγον αὐτοὺς πρὸς αὐτὸν. ὁ δὲ ἑνὶ ἑκάστῳ αὐτῶν τὰς χεῖρας ἐπιτιθεὶς ἐθεράπευ[σ]εν αὐτούς. 41 ἐξήρχοντο δὲ καὶ δαιμόνια ἀπὸ πολλῶν, κραυγάζοντα καὶ λέγοντα ὅτι σὺ εἶ ὁ υἱὸς τοῦ θεοῦ καὶ ἐπιτιμῶν	1, 32 ὀψίας δὲ γενομένης, ὅτε ἔδυ ὁ ἥλιος, [see 1, 34 below] ἔφερον πρὸς αὐτὸν τοὺς κακῶς ἔχοντας [6, 5 ἐπιθεὶς τὰς χεῖρας ἐθεράπευσεν] καὶ τοὺς δαιμονιζομένους . . . 34 καὶ ἐθεράπευσεν πολλοὺς κακῶς ἔχοντας ποικίλαις νόσοις καὶ δαιμόνια πολλὰ ἐξέβαλεν καὶ [3, 11 καὶ τὰ πνεύματα τὰ ἀκάθαρτα . . . ἔκραζον λέγοντες ὅτι σὺ εἶ ὁ υἱὸς τοῦ θεοῦ. 12 καὶ πολλὰ ἐπετίμα αὐτοῖς ἵνα μὴ αὐτὸν φανερὸν ποιῶσιν.]
οὐκ εἴα αὐτὰ λαλεῖν ὅτι ᾔδεισαν τὸν Χριστὸν αὐτὸν εἶναι.	οὐκ ἤφιεν λαλεῖν τὰ δαιμόνια, ὅτι ᾔδεισαν αὐτόν.
4, 44 καὶ ἦν κηρύσσων εἰς τὰς συναγωγὰς τῆς Γαλιλαίας.	1, 39 καὶ ἦλθεν κηρύσσων εἰς τὰς συναγωγὰς αὐτῶν εἰς ὅλην τὴν Γαλιλαίαν καὶ τὰ δαιμόνια ἐκβάλλων.

Luke	Mark
5, 15 διήρχετο δὲ μᾶλλον ὁ λόγος περὶ αὐτοῦ, καὶ συνήρχοντο ὄχλοι πολλοὶ ἀκούειν καὶ θεραπεύεσθαι ἀπὸ τῶν ἀσθενειῶν αὐτῶν. 16 αὐτὸς δὲ ἦν ὑποχωρῶν ἐν ταῖς ἐρήμοις καὶ προσευχόμενος.	1, 45 ὁ δὲ ἐξελθὼν ἤρξατο κηρύσσειν πολλὰ καὶ διαφημίζειν τὸν λόγον, ὥστε μηκέτι αὐτὸν δύνασθαι εἰς πόλιν φανερῶς εἰσελθεῖν ἀλλ' ἔξω ἐπ' ἐρήμοις τόποις ἦν καὶ ἤρχοντο πρὸς αὐτὸν πάντοθεν. [1, 35 καὶ ἀπῆλθεν εἰς ἔρημον τόπον κἀκεῖ προσηύχετο.]
6, 17 καὶ πλῆθος πολὺ τοῦ λαοῦ ἀπὸ πάσης τῆς Ἰουδαίας καὶ Ἱερουσαλὴμ καὶ τῆς παραλίου Τύρου καὶ Σιδῶνος, οἳ ἦλθον ἀκοῦσαι αὐτοῦ καὶ ἰαθῆναι ἀπὸ τῶν νόσων αὐτῶν, 18 καὶ οἱ ἐνοχλούμενοι ἀπὸ πνευμάτων ἀκαθάρτων ἐθεραπεύοντο· 19 καὶ πᾶς ὁ ὄχλος ἐζήτουν ἅπτεσθαι αὐτοῦ, ὅτι δύναμις παρ' αὐτοῦ ἐξήρχετο [1] καὶ ἰᾶτο πάντας.	3, 7 καὶ πολὺ πλῆθος ἀπὸ τῆς Γαλιλαίας καὶ ἀπὸ τῆς Ἰουδαίας ἠκολούθησαν, 8 καὶ ἀπὸ Ἱεροσολύμων καὶ ἀπὸ τῆς Ἰδουμαίας καὶ πέραν τοῦ Ἰορδάνου καὶ περὶ Τύρον καὶ Σιδῶνα πλῆθος πολύ, ἀκούοντες ὅσα ἐποίει, ἦλθον πρὸς αὐτόν. . . . [see 11 below]. 10 πολλοὺς γὰρ ἐθεράπευσεν, ὥστε ἐπιπίπτειν αὐτῷ, ἵνα αὐτοῦ ἅψωνται, ὅσοι εἶχον μάστιγας. 11 καὶ τὰ πνεύματα τὰ ἀκάθαρτα κ.τ.λ.
7, 17 καὶ ἐξῆλθεν ὁ λόγος οὗτος ἐν ὅλῃ τῇ Ἰουδαίᾳ περὶ αὐτοῦ καὶ πάσῃ τῇ περιχώρῳ. 7, 21 ἐν ἐκείνῃ τῇ ὥρᾳ ἐθεράπευσεν πολλοὺς ἀπὸ νόσων καὶ μαστίγων καὶ πνευμάτων πονηρῶν καὶ τυφλοῖς πολλοῖς ἐχαρίσατο βλέπειν.	[1, 28 καὶ ἐξῆλθεν ἡ ἀκοὴ αὐτοῦ εὐθὺς πανταχοῦ εἰς ὅλην τὴν περίχωρον τῆς Γαλιλαίας.] This occurs in a passage from Q (Luke 7, 19, 22, 23 = Matt. 11, 2–6). Either the summary stood in Q and was omitted by Matthew in accordance with his habit of abbreviation (cf. Luke 7, 20 and Matthew's treatment of Mark), or it was composed by Luke to suit the report of 7, 22 which Matthew has prepared for by his grouping of material (Matt. 8–10): leper 8, 1–4; two paralytics 8, 5–13; 9, 1–8; two demoniacs 8, 28–34; 9, 32–34; two blind 9, 27–31; dead raised 9, 18–26; the gospel preached 9, 35 — 10, 16. For the wording compare Mark 3, 10 πολλοὺς γὰρ ἐθεράπευσεν . . . ὅσοι εἶχον μάστιγας. Luke elsewhere avoids this use of μάστιξ.
8, 1 καὶ αὐτὸς διώδευεν κατὰ πόλιν καὶ κώμην κηρύσσων καὶ εὐαγγελιζόμενος τὴν βασιλείαν τοῦ θεοῦ, καὶ οἱ δώδεκα σὺν αὐτῷ, 2 καὶ γυναῖκές τινες . . . 3 αἵτινες διηκόνουν αὐτοῖς ἐκ τῶν ὑπαρχόντων αὐταῖς. 4 συνιόντος δὲ ὄχλου πολλοῦ καὶ τῶν κατὰ πόλιν ἐπιπορευομένων πρὸς αὐτὸν . . .	[6, 6 καὶ περιῆγεν τὰς κώμας κύκλῳ διδάσκων.] [1, 14 κηρύσσων τὸ εὐαγγέλιον τοῦ θεοῦ . . . 15 ἤγγικεν ἡ βασιλεία τοῦ θεοῦ.] [15, 40 γυναῖκες . . . αἳ ὅτε ἦν ἐν τῇ Γαλιλαίᾳ ἠκολούθουν αὐτῷ καὶ διηκόνουν αὐτῷ.] 4, 1 συνάγεται πρὸς αὐτὸν ὄχλος πλεῖστος. [6, 33 πεζῇ ἀπὸ πασῶν τῶν πόλεων συνέδραμον ἐκεῖ.]

[1] For the thought, see Mark 5, 30 δύναμιν ἐξελθοῦσαν.

Luke	Mark
13, 22 καὶ διεπορεύετο κατὰ πόλεις καὶ κώμας διδάσκων καὶ πορείαν ποιούμενος εἰς Ἱεροσόλυμα. 14, 25 συνεπορεύοντο δὲ αὐτῷ ὄχλοι. 17, 11 καὶ ἐγένετο ἐν τῷ πορεύεσθαι εἰς Ἰερουσαλὴμ καὶ αὐτὸς διήρχετο διὰ μέσον Σαμαρίας καὶ Γαλιλαίας.	10, 1 καὶ ἐκεῖθεν ἀναστὰς ἔρχεται εἰς τὰ ὅρια τῆς Ἰουδαίας καὶ πέραν τοῦ Ἰορδάνου, καὶ συνπορεύονται πάλιν ὄχλοι πρὸς αὐτόν, καὶ ὡς εἰώθει πάλιν ἐδίδασκεν αὐτούς.
19, 28 καὶ εἰπὼν ταῦτα ἐπορεύετο ἔμπροσθεν, ἀναβαίνων εἰς Ἱεροσόλυμα.	10, 32 ἦσαν δὲ ἐν τῇ ὁδῷ ἀναβαίνοντες εἰς Ἱεροσόλυμα, καὶ ἦν προάγων αὐτοὺς ὁ Ἰησοῦς.

Bartlet, in *Oxford Studies in the Synoptic Problem*, p. 346, also believes that these last four references are inserted by Luke, "only following a hint of his source." But he takes that source to be not Mark, but Luke's "Special Source," used in Luke 9, 51, 57; 10, 38. His linguistic arguments are the occurrence of *πορεύομαι*, "a favorite word of Luke's S," in Luke 9, 51 ff., 57; 10, 38; 17, 11, and of Ἱεροσόλυμα in 13, 22; 19, 28, "the more Greek form found in Luke's Gospel only here and in 2, 22; 23, 7 (a parenthetic note by Luke writing as Greek to Greeks)." But *πορεύομαι* is found all through Luke's gospel, and is in some cases clearly due to him rather than his source (see p. 177), while the form Ἱεροσόλυμα occurs (and with *ἀναβαίνω*) in Mark 10, 32. The expression *συνπορεύονται* (*συνεπορεύοντο*) ὄχλοι in Mark 10, 1; Luke 14, 25, is specially noteworthy, as the verb occurs elsewhere in the New Testament only twice (Luke 7, 11; 24, 15). Dependence on Mark seems, therefore, entirely probable.

Even Luke's summary of Jesus' days in Jerusalem is largely dependent on Mark.

Luke	Mark
19, 47 καὶ ἦν διδάσκων τὸ καθ' ἡμέραν ἐν τῷ ἱερῷ . . .	[11, 11 καὶ εἰσῆλθεν εἰς Ἱεροσόλυμα εἰς τὸ ἱερόν. . . . 27 καὶ ἔρχονται πάλιν εἰς Ἱεροσόλυμα. καὶ ἐν τῷ ἱερῷ περιπατοῦντος αὐτοῦ κτλ. (= Luke 20, 1). 12, 35 ἔλεγεν διδάσκων ἐν τῷ ἱερῷ. 14, 49 καθ' ἡμέραν ἤμην πρὸς ὑμᾶς ἐν τῷ ἱερῷ διδάσκων (= Luke 22, 53).]
48 ὁ λαὸς γὰρ ἅπας ἐξεκρέμετο αὐτοῦ ἀκούων.	11, 18 πᾶς γὰρ ὁ ὄχλος ἐξεπλήσσοντο ἐπὶ τῇ διδαχῇ αὐτοῦ. [12, 37 καὶ ὁ πολὺς ὄχλος ἤκουεν αὐτοῦ ἡδέως.]

Luke

21, 37 *ἦν δὲ τὰς ἡμέρας ἐν τῷ ἱερῷ διδάσκων, τὰς δὲ νύκτας ἐξερχόμενος ηὐλίζετο εἰς τὸ ὄρος τὸ καλούμενον ἐλαιών.* 38 *καὶ πᾶς ὁ λαὸς ὤρθριζεν πρὸς αὐτὸν ἐν τῷ ἱερῷ ἀκούειν αὐτοῦ.*

Mark

11, 11 *ὀψὲ ἤδη οὔσης τῆς ὥρας ἐξῆλθεν εἰς Βηθανίαν.*

11, 19 *καὶ ὅταν ὀψὲ ἐγένετο, ἐξεπορεύετο ἔξω τῆς πόλεως.*

[13, 3 *καὶ καθημένου αὐτοῦ εἰς τὸ ὄρος τῶν ἐλαιῶν.*]

11, 20 *καὶ παραπορευόμενοι πρωΐ . . .* 27 *καὶ ἔρχονται πάλιν εἰς Ἱεροσόλυμα. καὶ ἐν τῷ ἱερῷ κ.τ.λ.*

For the equivalence of Bethany to the mount of Olives see further Mark 11, 1 = Luke 19, 29 *εἰς Βηθανίαν πρὸς τὸ ὄρος τὸ καλούμενον ἐλαιῶν*, and cf. Luke 24, 50 with Acts 1, 12. For the equivalence of *πρωΐ* and *ὄρθρος* see Mark 16, 2 and Luke 24, 1. Even *ηὐλίζετο*, though not in our Mark, is presumably due to Luke's source, for it occurs in the parallel in Matt. 21, 17, *ἐξῆλθεν ἔξω τῆς πόλεως εἰς Βηθανίαν καὶ ηὐλίσθη ἐκεῖ.*

Perhaps the chief liberty that Luke takes with Mark's summaries is the liberty of repeating them, so as to apply them to two or three successive stages in his own narrative. Thus, as has already been shown (pp. 108 f.), the substance of Mark 1, 28 is found three times in the early chapters of Luke, viz., Luke 4, 14, 37; 7, 17. So the reference to the disciples' ignorance from Mark 9, 32 is used both in Luke 9, 45 and in 18, 34 (p. 107). In some cases, especially in the sayings of Jesus, Luke's doublets are no doubt due to his use of two sources. But that an editor is likely to use twice a statement found but once and in one source is well proved in the case of Tatian (A. A. Hobson, *The Diatessaron of Tatian and the Synoptic Problem*, chap. vii) and seems extremely likely for Matthew; see especially the list in Hawkins, *Horae Synopticae*, p. 137. For Luke, Hawkins suggests further (p. 136), Luke 5, 20, 21 = Mark 2, 5, 7; cf. Luke 7, 48, 49; Luke 8, 48 = Mark 5, 34 = Matt. 9, 22; Luke 18, 42 = Mark 10, 52; also Luke 7, 50 and 17, 19 and some others.

One is tempted to refer to the same cause certain other repetitions in Luke where not even one source is known to us, such as the repeated statements of the growth of John and of Jesus in Luke 1, 80; 2, 40, 52 (perhaps from 1 Sam. 2, 26), the repeated statements of the growth of the Christian church in Acts, and especially the repetition about the scattering of the church in Acts 8, 1; 11, 19.

Besides the miracle of the healing of the ear of the high priest's servant (Luke 22, 51), Luke, in passages dependent on Mark, adds a few summary references to cures. Before the healing of the paralytic we read (Luke 5, 17) *καὶ δύναμις κυρίου ἦν εἰς τὸ ἰᾶσθαι αὐτόν* (not in Mark 2, 1). In Mark 3, 7–12 we read (vs. 10) *πολλοὺς ἐθεράπευσεν*, but in the parallel passage, Luke 6, 17–19, though it is shorter, three references to his healing are found: the multitude came, 17 *ἀκοῦσαι αὐτὸν καὶ ἰαθῆναι ἀπὸ τῶν νόσων αὐτῶν*, 18 *καὶ οἱ ἐνοχλούμενοι ἀπὸ πνευμάτων ἀκαθάρτων ἐθεραπεύοντο* . . . 19 *δύναμις παρ' αὐτοῦ ἐξήρχετο καὶ ἰᾶτο πάντας*. According to Mark 6, 7 the twelve are given authority over unclean spirits; Luke 9, 1 adds the authority *νόσους θεραπεύειν*, and describes their commission as *κηρύσσειν τὴν βασιλείαν τοῦ θεοῦ καὶ ἰᾶσθαι*. Mark's account of their work (6, 13) *καὶ δαιμόνια πολλὰ ἐξέβαλλον καὶ ἤλειφον ἐλαίῳ πολλοὺς ἀρρώστους καὶ ἐθεράπευον*, becomes in Luke 9, 6, *θεραπεύοντες πανταχοῦ*. In a similar way the charge of Matt. 10, 8 (presumably from Q), *ἀσθενοῦντας θεραπεύετε, νεκροὺς ἐγείρετε, λεπροὺς καθαρίζετε, δαιμόνια ἐκβάλλετε*, becomes in Luke 10, 9, in the charge to the seventy, *θεραπεύετε τοὺς ἐν αὐτῇ ἀσθενεῖς*. Before the feeding of the 5,000 we read only of teaching in Mark 6, 34, only of healing in Matthew 14, 14 (*καὶ ἐθεράπευσεν τοὺς ἀρρώστους αὐτῶν*), in Luke 9, 11 of both — *ἐλάλει αὐτοῖς περὶ τῆς βασιλείας τοῦ θεοῦ καὶ τοὺς χρείαν ἔχοντας θεραπείας ἰᾶτο*. The coincidence of Matthew and Luke in this passage may of course be ascribed to a phrase in the primitive form of Mark not preserved in our present text (note also the word *ἄρρωστος* in Matt. 14, 14, elsewhere in New Testament only in Mark 6, 5, 13; [16, 18]; 1 Cor. 11, 30), but it seems to me more probable that Matthew has here as elsewhere turned teaching into healing (cf. Matt. 19, 2 = Mark 10, 1; Matt. 21, 14, cf. Mark 11, 17, 18; 12, 35, 38), and that Luke quite independently has added one of his characteristic notes of healing.

In the above cases of addition *ἰάομαι* is generally used. An addition with *θεραπεύω* is found in Luke 5, 15, *καὶ συνήρχοντο ὄχλοι πολλοὶ ἀκούειν καὶ θεραπεύεσθαι ἀπὸ τῶν ἀσθενειῶν αὐτῶν*. Cf. Luke 6, 17. As has been already observed, *ἰάομαι* is a common word in Luke (only once in Mark; four times in Matt.; cf. *ἴασεις*, Luke 13, 32). So is *δύναμις* in the sense of healing power. It is found in this sense once in Mark (5, 30 = Luke 8, 46), but is added by Luke in Marcan contexts at Luke 4, 36 and 9, 1 (contrast Mark 1, 27 and 6, 7); it occurs in summaries at Luke 5, 17; 6, 19, and frequently elsewhere in Luke and Acts; ἀσθένεια occurs in Luke 5, 15; 8, 2; 13, 11, 12; Acts 28, 9, but not in Matt. or Mark except in the quotation from the LXX in Matt. 8, 17.

The prefaces and summaries may serve to illustrate certain other characteristics of Luke's account of the life of Jesus. Luke's interest in the prayer-life of Jesus has often been noticed,[1] and this is a feature which he several times introduces into his setting for a scene. Before the baptism (3, 21), before the choice of the twelve (6, 12; note the full description . . . προσεύξασθαι, καὶ ἦν διαννκτερεύων ἐν τῇ προσευχῇ τοῦ θεοῦ), and before the transfiguration (9, 28 f), Luke is the only one of the Gospels to mention that Jesus prayed.[2] In three other pericopes, Luke mentions that Jesus was praying, while the parallels say nothing of it: Luke 5, 16 αὐτὸς δὲ ἦν ὑποχωρῶν ἐν ταῖς ἐρήμοις καὶ προσευχόμενος (cf. Mark 1, 45); Luke 9, 18 καὶ ἐγένετο ἐν τῷ εἶναι αὐτὸν προσευχόμενον κατὰ μόνας (cf. Mark 8, 27); Luke 11, 1 καὶ ἐγένετο ἐν τῷ εἶναι αὐτὸν ἐν τόπῳ τινὶ προσευχόμενον (cf. Matt. 6, 9).

The καὶ προσευχόμενος in Luke 5, 16, though not in Mark 1, 45, is very likely from Mark 1, 35 (κἀκεῖ προσηύχετο), which Luke 4, 42 omits, and προσευχόμενον κατὰ μόνας in Luke 9, 18 may come from Mark 6, 46 as explained above, p. 98. That Luke looked upon prayer as habitual with Jesus may be inferred from his use of the analytical verb form in this and several other of the cases above mentioned, and by the addition, κατὰ τὸ ἔθος, in Luke 22, 39. In the same passage Luke evidently identifies Gethsemane of Mark 14, 32 with the Mount of Olives, and he makes Jesus pass the last nights of his life there regularly in the open (Luke 21, 37; Mark 11, 11 and Matt. 21, 17 say Bethany). Was this due to Luke's conception of Jesus as praying on mountains (Luke 6, 12; 9, 28) ? Is it not further possible that the word προσευχή has something of the local sense of "place of prayer" which it has in Acts 16, 13, 16, both in this passage (Luke 22, 45; with ἀναστὰς ἀπὸ τῆς προσευχῆς in this sense compare Luke 4, 38, ἀναστὰς ἀπὸ τῆς συναγωγῆς. Notice also in 22, 40, γενόμενος ἐπὶ τοῦ τόπου) and at 6, 12 (notice the article).

For the substance of Jesus' teaching Luke does not use the noun εὐαγγέλιον (four times in Matt., seven times in Mark, twice in Acts; not in Luke or John), and twice when it is found in his source

[1] See for example Plummer, p. xlv f.

[2] The book of Acts makes it clear that Luke looked upon prayer as a regular occasion for a voice or vision from heaven (Acts 9, 11; 10, 9 ff., 30; 11, 5; 16, 25; 22, 17; so Luke 1, 10) and as the proper accompaniment of a Christian appointment (Acts 1, 24 ff.; 6, 5 f.; 13, 3; 14, 23).

(Mark 8, 35; 10, 29) he appears to omit it.[1] The verb *εὐαγγελίζομαι* is, however, frequent in both Luke and Acts (10 and 15 times respectively; in the other Gospels only once, Matt. 11, 5 = Luke 7, 22), and in Luke 4, 43; 9, 6, is directly substituted for the *κηρύσσω* of Mark 1, 38; 6, 12; cf. also Luke 3, 18 with Mark 1, 7; Luke 20, 1 with Mark 11, 27. *ἡ βασιλεία τοῦ θεοῦ* is a favorite expression in Luke for the substance of Christian teaching and frequently occurs where it is not found in the parallels. To a less extent the same is true of *ὁ λόγος τοῦ θεοῦ*, a phrase which in this sense is peculiar to Luke (Luke 5, 1; 8, 11; 8, 21; 11, 28; Acts 4, 31; 6, 2, 7; 8, 14; 11, 1; 13, 5, 7, 46; 17, 13; 18, 11, and, with *ὁ λόγος τοῦ κυρίου* as a variant reading, Acts 12, 24; 13, 44, 48; 16, 32). In Mark 7, 13 it is used of the Old Testament legislation. A list of parallel passages for these expressions is subjoined.

Luke	Parallels
4, 43 *εὐαγγελίσασθαι τὴν βασιλείαν τοῦ θεοῦ*	Mark 1, 38 *κηρύξω*
5, 1 *ἀκούειν τὸν λόγον τοῦ θεοῦ*	Cf. Mark 4, 1
8, 1 *κηρύσσων καὶ εὐαγγελιζόμενος τὴν βασιλείαν τοῦ θεοῦ*	Cf. Mark 6, 6.
8, 11 *ὁ σπόρος ἐστὶν ὁ λόγος τοῦ θεοῦ*	Mark 4, 14 *ὁ σπείρων τὸν λόγον σπείρει*
8, 21 *τὸν λόγον τοῦ θεοῦ*	Mark 3, 35 *τὸ θέλημα τοῦ θεοῦ*
9, 2 *κηρύσσειν τὴν βασιλείαν τοῦ θεοῦ*	Cf. Mark 6, 7 and Q (Matt. 10, 7 = Luke 10, 9)
9, 6 *εὐαγγελιζόμενοι*	Mark 6, 12 *ἐκήρυξαν*
9, 11 *ἐλάλει περὶ τῆς βασιλείας τοῦ θεοῦ*	Mark 6, 34 *ἤρξατο διδάσκειν πολλά*
9, 60 *διάγγελλε τὴν βασιλείαν τοῦ θεοῦ*	Cf. Matt. 8, 22
16, 16 *ἡ βασιλεία τοῦ θεοῦ εὐαγγελίζεται*	Matt. 11, 12 *ἡ βασιλεία τῶν οὐρανῶν βιάζεται*
18, 29 *εἵνεκεν τῆς βασιλείας τοῦ θεοῦ*	Mark 10, 29 *ἕνεκεν ἐμοῦ καὶ ἕνεκεν τοῦ εὐαγγελίου*
20, 1 *διδάσκοντος αὐτοῦ .... καὶ εὐαγγελιζομένου*	Cf. Mark 11, 27; 12, 35
21, 29 *ἐγγύς ἐστιν ἡ βασιλεία τοῦ θεοῦ*	Mark 13, 29 *ἐγγύς ἐστιν*

But the words *διδάσκω, διδαχή*, are less frequent in Luke than in Mark. Sometimes the fact that Jesus (or the disciples) taught is

[1] The omission by Matthew also makes it, however, at least possible that in these passages of Mark the word is secondary. For *ἕνεκεν ἐμοῦ καὶ [ἕνεκεν] τοῦ εὐαγγελίου*, Matthew has simply *ἕνεκεν ἐμοῦ* (10, 18; 16, 25) or *ἕνεκεν τοῦ ἐμοῦ ὀνόματος* (19, 29), but Matthew elsewhere supports Mark's use of the word: Matt. 24, 14 = Mark 13, 10; Matt. 26, 13 = Mark 14, 9; Matt. 4, 23 and 9, 35 = Mark 1, 14 (adding *τοῦτο* or *τῆς βασιλείας* or both). Luke has no parallel to these other passages in Mark.

omitted; elsewhere a simple "said" is used for "taught," "began to teach," "taught and said," "said in his teaching." See Mark 2, 13; 4, 1, 2; 6, 30, 34; 8, 31; 9, 31; 11, 17; 12, 35, 38; 14, 49. "It is remarkable that the word [διδαχή] is used most often by Mark, who records so little of what was taught. The verb διδάσκω occurs in Matt. 14 times, in Mark 17 times, in Luke 17 times" (Hawkins, *Horae Synopticae*, p. 10, n.).

Changes Attributable to Literary Predilections

Generalization

The prevailing faithfulness of Luke's reproduction of his source is the more impressive when we observe that in details he inclines to generalization; *ἅπας, πᾶς, ἕκαστος* are favorite words of his, and are sometimes added to his sources as the following cases show:[1]

Mk. 1, 34 ἐθεράπευσεν πολλοὺς	Lk. 4, 40 πάντες . . . ἑνὶ ἑκάστῳ
Mk. 3, 5 καὶ περιβλεψάμενος αὐτοὺς	Lk. 6, 10 adds πάντας
Mk. 3, 7 πλῆθος ἀπὸ τῆς Ἰουδαίας	Lk. 6, 17 adds πάσης
Mt. 5, 42 τῷ αἰτοῦντι	Lk. 6, 30 adds παντί [Q]
Mt. 12, 33 τὸ δένδρον	Lk. 6, 44 ἕκαστον δένδρον [Q]
Mt. 11, 19 ἔργων (*v.l.* τέκνων)	Lk. 7, 35 τέκνων πάντων (*v.l.*) [Q]
Mk. 6, 7 τῶν πνευμάτων τῶν ἀκαθάρτων	Lk. 9, 1 πάντα τὰ δαιμόνια
Mk. 6, 14 ἤκουσεν	Lk. 9, 7 adds τὰ γινόμενα πάντα
Mt. 6, 12 τοῖς ὀφειλέταις	Lk. 11, 4 παντὶ ὀφείλοντι [Q]
Mk. 10, 21 ὅσα ἔχεις πώλησον	Lk. 18, 22 adds πάντα
Mt. 7, 23 οἱ ἐργαζόμενοι	Lk. 13, 27 πάντες ἐργάται [Q]

Further, Luke adds a general term to those already specific:

Mk. 6, 18 ἔλεγεν γὰρ ὁ Ἰωάννης τῷ Ἡρώδῃ ὅτι οὐκ ἔξεστίν σοι ἔχειν τὴν γυναῖκα τοῦ ἀδελφοῦ σου.	Lk. 3, 19 Ἡρώδης . . . ἐλεγχόμενος ὑπ' αὐτοῦ [*sc.* Ἰωάννου] περὶ Ἡρωδιάδος τῆς γυναικὸς τοῦ ἀδελφοῦ αὐτοῦ καὶ περὶ πάντων ὧν ἐποίησεν πονηρῶν ὁ Ἡρώδης.
Mt. 23, 23 ἀποδεκατοῦτε τὸ ἡδύοσμον καὶ τὸ ἄνηθον καὶ τὸ κύμινον	Lk. 11, 42 ἀποδεκατοῦτε τὸ ἡδύοσμον καὶ τὸ πήγανον καὶ πᾶν λάχανον [Q]
Mt. 23, 35 πᾶν αἷμα δίκαιον . . . ἀπὸ τοῦ αἵματος Ἅβελ τοῦ δικαίου ἕως τοῦ αἵματος Ζαχαρίου κ.τ.λ.	Lk. 11, 50f τὸ αἷμα πάντων τῶν προφητῶν . . . ἀπὸ αἵματος Ἅβελ ἕως αἵματος Ζαχαρίου κ.τ.λ. [Q]
Mt. 8, 11 Ἀβραὰμ καὶ Ἰσαὰκ καὶ Ἰακώβ	Lk. 13, 28 Ἀβραὰμ καὶ Ἰσαὰκ καὶ Ἰακὼβ καὶ πάντας τοὺς προφήτας [Q]
Mk. 11, 18 ἤκουσαν οἱ ἀρχιερεῖς καὶ οἱ γραμματεῖς καὶ ἐζήτουν πῶς αὐτὸν ἀπολέσωσιν	Lk. 19, 47 οἱ δὲ ἀρχιερεῖς καὶ οἱ γραμματεῖς ἐζήτουν αὐτὸν ἀπολέσαι καὶ οἱ πρῶτοι τοῦ λαοῦ
Mk. 13, 28 ἀπὸ τῆς συκῆς μάθετε	Lk. 21, 29 ἴδετε τὴν συκῆν καὶ πάντα τὰ δένδρα

[1] See also below, p. 195.

Mk. 15, 39 The centurion exclaims at Jesus' death	Lk. 23, 48 adds, "and all the multitudes that came together to behold this sight, when they beheld the things that were done, returned smiting their breasts."
Mk. 15, 40 *γυναῖκες*	Lk. 23, 49 *πάντες οἱ γνωστοὶ αὐτῷ . . . καὶ γυναῖκες*
Mk. 16, 1 names three women	Lk. 24, 10 adds *καὶ αἱ λοιπαὶ σὺν αὐταῖς*

Notice also that Luke alone in the resurrection narratives joins others to the eleven. 24, 9 *τοῖς ἕνδεκα καὶ πᾶσιν τοῖς λοιποῖς*; 24, 33 *τοὺς ἕνδεκα καὶ τοὺς σὺν αὐτοῖς*. Compare Mark 16, 7 *τοῖς μαθηταῖς αὐτοῦ καὶ τῷ Πέτρῳ*; Matt. 28, 16 *οἱ ἕνδεκα μαθηταί*; John 20, 19 *οἱ μαθηταί* (apparently ten, Thomas being absent, cf. vs. 24), [Mark] 16, 14 *τοῖς ἕνδεκα*. But it is quite probable that his source confined its reference to the eleven (cf. Acts 1, 2, 13).

Without noting here all instances of the use of *πᾶς* in Luke but not in the parallels we may add the following striking series of generalizations where the word is not used in parallels. Compare especially Luke 3, 19; 9, 7 (p. 115) and Matt. 6, 32, 33 (p. 85).

Lk. 3, 16 *προσδοκῶντος δὲ τοῦ λαοῦ καὶ διαλογιζομένων πάντων κ.τ.λ.* — Matt. 3, 11; Mark 1, 7 [Q].

Lk. 7, 18 *καὶ ἀπήγγειλαν Ἰωάννει οἱ μαθηταὶ αὐτοῦ περὶ πάντων τούτων.* — Matt. 11, 2 [Q].

Lk. 8, 40 *ἦσαν γὰρ πάντες προσδοκῶντες αὐτόν.* — Mark 5, 21.

Lk. 9, 43 *ἐξεπλήσσοντο δὲ πάντες ἐπὶ τῇ μεγαλειότητι τοῦ θεοῦ, πάντων δὲ θαυμαζόντων ἐπὶ πᾶσιν οἷς ἐποίει, κ. τ. λ.* — Mark 9, 27, 30.

Lk. 13, 17 *κατῃσχύνοντο πάντες οἱ ἀντικείμενοι αὐτῷ, καὶ πᾶς ὁ ὄχλος ἔχαιρεν ἐπὶ πᾶσιν τοῖς ἐνδόξοις τοῖς γινομένοις ὑπ' αὐτοῦ.*

Lk. 18, 43 *καὶ πᾶς ὁ λαὸς ἰδὼν ἔδωκεν αἶνον τῷ θεῷ.* — Mark 10, 52.

Lk. 19, 37 *ἤρξαντο ἅπαν τὸ πλῆθος τῶν μαθητῶν χαίροντες αἰνεῖν τὸν θεὸν φωνῇ μεγάλῃ περὶ πασῶν ὧν εἶδον δυνάμεων* (*v.l.*). — Mark 11, 9.

Lk. 24, 9 *ἀπήγγειλαν πάντα ταῦτα τοῖς ἕνδεκα καὶ πᾶσιν τοῖς λοιποῖς.* — Mark 16, 8.

A number of other instances of generalization may be found by a comparison of Luke and Matthew. The more picturesque and realistic terms in the first Gospel have in the third more general and vague equivalents, and no doubt the change is often due to Luke:

Matthew	Luke
5, 45 *τὸν ἥλιον ἀνατέλλει . . . καὶ βρέχει*	6, 35 *χρηστός ἐστιν* [Q]
5, 39 *τὴν δεξιὰν σιαγόνα*	6, 29 *τὴν σιαγόνα* [Q]
5, 46f *τελῶναι . . . ἐθνικοί*	6, 32f *ἁμαρτωλοὶ . . . ἁμαρτωλοί* [Q]
5, 46 *τίνα μισθὸν ἔχετε*	6, 32 *ποία ὑμῖν χάρις ἐστίν* [Q]
5, 15 = Mark 4, 21 *μόδιος*	8, 16 *σκεῦος* (but Luke 11, 33 *v.l. μόδιος*) [Q]
23, 25 *παροψίδος, ἀκρασίας*	11, 39 *πίνακος, πονηρίας* [Q] [1]

[1] See Harnack, *Sayings of Jesus*, p. 101.

Matthew	Luke
23, 26 τὸ ἐκτὸς αὐτοῦ [τοῦ ποτηρίου] καθαρόν	11, 41 πάντα καθαρά [Q]
10, 29 οὐ πεσεῖται ἐπὶ τὴν γῆν ἄνευ τοῦ πατρὸς ὑμῶν	12, 6 οὐκ ἔστιν ἐπιλελησμένον ἐνώπιον τοῦ θεοῦ [Q]
Contrast:	
Matt. 6, 26 τὰ πετεινὰ τοῦ οὐρανοῦ	Luke 12, 24 τοὺς κόρακας

The distributive use of κατά *c. acc.* is a grammatical peculiarity of Luke in temporal phrases; καθ' ἡμέραν occurs in Matt. 26, 55 = Mark 14, 49 = Luke 22, 53, but elsewhere only in Luke 9, 23; 11, 3; 16, 19; 19, 47; Acts 2, 46, 47; 3, 2; 16, 5; 17, 11; 19, 9; cf. κατὰ πᾶσαν ἡμέραν Acts 17, 17; κατὰ πᾶν σάββατον Acts 13, 27; 15, 21; 18, 4; κατ' ἔτος Luke 2, 41. But in its local use in summaries κατά may indicate Luke's sense of regular geographical progress or extension.

Luke 8, 1 διώδευεν κατὰ πόλιν καὶ κώμην.

Luke 9, 6 διήρχοντο κατὰ τὰς κώμας.

Luke 13, 22 διεπορεύετο κατὰ πόλεις καὶ κώμας. See also Luke 8, 4; Acts 14, 23; 15, 21, 36; 20, 23; 22, 19.

Narratives which in Mark refer to a single event become more general in Luke. Thus in Mark 1, 21 καὶ εὐθὺς τοῖς σάββασιν ἐδίδασκεν εἰς τὴν συναγωγήν, the reference may be to a single sabbath; but in Luke 4, 31, καὶ ἦν διδάσκων αὐτοὺς ἐν τοῖς σάββασι, it is probably to several; for Luke usually if not always uses the singular σάββατον for a single sabbath.[1] Similarly the question in Mark 11, 28 ἐν ποίᾳ ἐξουσίᾳ ταῦτα ποιεῖς; has reference chiefly to the cleansing of the temple. In Luke 20, 1, 2 the context has been so changed that in the same question ταῦτα must be understood to apply to Jesus' teaching in general. In Mark 2, 18 we read that the disciples of John and the Pharisees were observing a fast (ἦσαν . . . νηστεύοντες); in Luke 5, 33 they (the Pharisees and scribes) said to him, "The disciples of John fast often (νηστεύουσιν πυκνά) and make prayers."

It is possible that two cases above referred to (pp. 96 f.) as misunderstanding of Mark by Luke are intentional generalizations. Thus, when Jesus withdraws from Capernaum and is overtaken in a desert place he tells those who have followed him that he must preach in

[1] See p. 190.

other cities as well, and adds in Mark 1, 38, εἰς τοῦτο γὰρ ἐξῆλθον, "for to this end came I forth" (from Capernaum ?). Luke refers this clause, however, to the whole career of Jesus, his coming forth from God, ἐπὶ τοῦτο ἀπεστάλην (Luke 4, 43). Similarly, perhaps, in Mark 2, 17, οὐκ ἦλθον καλέσαι δικαίους, the verb should be understood merely of inviting to meals; but in Luke 5, 32 the addition of εἰς μετανοίαν gives it a wider meaning.

Twice Luke adds a generalizing summary to specific instances; neither, however, refers to Jesus. To the teaching of John on the Christ (Luke 3, 16–17, from Mark and Q) he adds (3, 18) πολλὰ μὲν οὖν καὶ ἕτερα παρακαλῶν εὐηγγελίζετο τὸν λαόν. To the taunts and mockings of Luke 22, 63, 64 (= Mark 14, 65), Luke adds καὶ ἕτερα πολλὰ βλασφημοῦντες ἔλεγον εἰς αὐτόν. Cf. Acts 2, 40 ἑτέροις τε λόγοις πλείοσιν διεμαρτύρατο, καὶ παρεκάλει αὐτούς.

Freedom from Exaggeration

Instead of making the language of his source stronger, Luke sometimes omits or tones down emphatic words, such as μέγας:

Mk. 4, 37 λαῖλαψ μεγάλη	Lk. 8, 23 λαῖλαψ
Mk. 4, 39 γαλήνη μεγάλη	Lk. 8, 24 γαλήνη
Mk. 4, 41 ἐφοβήθησαν φόβον μέγαν	Lk. 8, 25 φοβηθέντες ἐθαύμασαν
Mk. 5, 11 ἀγέλη χοίρων μεγάλη	Lk. 8, 32 ἀγέλη χοίρων ἱκανῶν
Mk. 5, 42 ἐξέστησαν ἐκστάσει μεγάλῃ	Lk. 8, 56 ἐξέστησαν
Mt. 4, 8 εἰς ὄρος ὑψηλὸν λίαν [1]	Lk. 4, 5 omits [Q]
Mk. 9, 2 εἰς ὄρος ὑψηλόν	Lk. 9, 28 εἰς τὸ ὄρος
Mk. 9, 3 λευκὰ λίαν, οἷα γναφεὺς ἐπὶ τῆς γῆς οὐ δύναται οὕτως λευκᾶναι [2]	Lk. 9, 29 λευκός

πολύς is omitted by Luke:

Mk. 1, 34 ἐθεράπευσεν πολλοὺς	Lk. 4, 40 ἐθεράπευσεν αὐτούς
Mk. 3, 10 πολλοὺς ἐθεράπευσεν	Cf. Lk. 6, 18 οἱ ἐνοχλούμενοι ἐθεραπεύοντο
Mk. 5, 21 ὄχλος πολύς	Lk. 8, 40 ὁ ὄχλος
Mk. 5, 24 ὄχλος πολύς	Lk. 8, 42 οἱ ὄχλοι
Mk. 5, 26 πολλῶν ἰατρῶν	Lk. 8, 43 ἰατροῖς

[1] Harnack supposes that here and elsewhere the word ὄρος in Matthew comes from Q and is purposely omitted by Luke (cf. Matt. 5, 1 = Luke 6, 17, 20; Matt. 17, 20 = Luke 17, 6; Matt. 18, 12 = Luke 15, 4). Compare in the last passage Luke's ἐν τῇ ἐρήμῳ, also Mark 5, 5 ἐν τοῖς ὄρεσιν with Luke 8, 29 εἰς τὰς ἐρήμους (cf. John 6, 2 τὸ ὄρος with Mark 6, 31 etc. ἔρημος τόπος), and note Luke's omission of εἰς τὸ ὄρος τῶν ἐλαιῶν in Mark 13, 3.

[2] Observe further Luke's correction of πρωῒ ἔννυχα λίαν, Mark 1, 35; λίαν πρωΐ, Mark 16, 2 (cf. p. 201).

Mk. 6, 33 πολλοί	Lk. 9, 11 οἱ ὄχλοι
Mk. 6, 34 πολὺν ὄχλον	Lk. 9, 11 omits
Mt. 8, 11 πολλοὶ . . . ἥξουσιν	Lk. 13, 29 ἥξουσιν [Q]
Mk. 10, 31 πολλοὶ ἔσονται πρῶτοι ἔσχατοι	Lk. 13, 30 εἰσὶν ἔσχατοι οἳ ἔσονται πρῶτοι
Mk. 10, 48 ἐπετίμων αὐτῷ πολλοί	Lk. 18, 39 οἱ προάγοντες ἐπετίμων αὐτῷ
Mk. 11, 8 πολλοὶ τὰ ἱμάτια ἔστρωσαν	Lk. 19, 36 ὑπεστρώννυον τὰ ἱμάτια
Mk. 12, 5 καὶ πολλοὺς ἄλλους κτλ.	Lk. 20, 12 omits
Mk. 14, 24 ἐκχυννόμενον ὑπὲρ πολλῶν	Lk. 22, 20 ὑπὲρ ὑμῶν ἐκχυννόμενον

The superlative becomes the positive:

Mk. 4, 1 συνάγεται ὄχλος πλεῖστος	Lk. 8, 4 συνιόντος ὄχλου πολλοῦ

So πολλά (adverbial or cognate accusative) is omitted by Luke (see pp. 199 f.).

The adverbs for "very" are found in the synoptic writers as indicated below:

	Matt.	Mark	Luke	Acts
σφόδρα	7	1	1	1
λίαν	4	4	1	0
περισσῶς	1	2	0	1
πολλά, adv.[1]	[1]	10	0	[1]

Mark has also once each ἐκπερισσῶς, ὑπερπερισσῶς, μᾶλλον περισσότερον and (in some MSS. at 6, 51) λίαν ἐκ περισσοῦ.

Contrast Matthew's method in these cases:

Mk. 13, 19 θλίψις	Mt. 24, 21 θλίψις μεγάλη
Mk. 13, 22 σημεῖα καὶ τέρατα	Mt. 24, 24 σημεῖα μεγάλα καὶ τέρατα
Lk. 9, 34 ἐφοβήθησαν	Mt. 17, 6 ἐφοβήθησαν σφόδρα
Mk. 14, 19 ἤρξαντο λυπεῖσθαι καὶ λέγειν	Mt. 26, 22 λυπούμενοι σφόδρα ἤρξαντο λέγειν
Mk. 15, 5 θαυμάζειν τὸν Πειλᾶτον	Mt. 27, 14 θαυμάζειν τὸν ἡγεμόνα λίαν
Mk. 10, 1 ὄχλοι	Mt. 19, 2 ὄχλοι πολλοί
Mk. 10, 46 ὄχλου ἱκανοῦ	Mt. 20, 29 ὄχλος πολύς
Mk. 14, 43 ὄχλος	Mt. 26, 47 ὄχλος πολύς
Mk. 15, 40 γυναῖκες	Mt. 27, 55 γυναῖκες πολλαί
Mk. 11, 8 πολλοί	Mt. 21, 8 ὁ πλεῖστος ὄχλος

Indication of Setting

If we may judge from his treatment of the matter taken from Q, Luke is inclined to elaborate a situation and to create an audience

[1] The instances of πολλά, adv. are those so marked in Moulton and Geden. The total instances of this neuter plural form, including all doubtful cases, are, Matt. 4, Mark 15, Luke 4, Acts 2.

suitable for the various sayings of Jesus which he records. He has a sense of the fitness of words for particular kinds and conditions of men. His gospel and Acts both illustrate this feeling, but in opposite ways. For in Acts it is the situation that is already supplied to the artist, and the speech which must be made to fit. In the gospel the words of Jesus had been preserved by tradition, the evangelist selects the appropriate frame for them.

Luke takes an especial interest in the nature of the audience to whom words of Jesus are addressed. He interrupts the continuous discourse on watching in 12, 39, 40, 42–46 (= Matt. 24, 43–51) by Peter's question, "Lord, sayest thou this parable to us or to all?"[1]

In characteristic fashion also Luke specifies the different classes of people who came to John the Baptist and received appropriate answers, Luke 3, 10–14, *οἱ ὄχλοι . . . τελῶναι . . . στρατευόμενοι*. So the woes, which in Matt. 23 are all pronounced against scribes and Pharisees collectively, have been divided by Luke (11, 39–52) into two groups. The first group is against Pharisees and is addressed to a Pharisee, 11, 39–44. Then a lawyer interrupts, and to him Jesus addresses the remaining words as woes against lawyers, 11, 46–52. The author looks upon lawyers as forming a class distinct from the Pharisees, with besetting sins of their own.[2]

Observe also Luke's definition of the audience in the following instances, sometimes interrupting a continuous address. In several cases Luke lays the scene at a Pharisee's dinner table:

Luke 7, 36 *ἠρώτα δέ τις αὐτὸν τῶν Φαρισαίων ἵνα φάγῃ μετ' αὐτοῦ· καὶ εἰσελθὼν εἰς τὸν οἶκον τοῦ Φαρισαίου κατεκλίθη.*

Luke 11, 37 *ἐν δὲ τῷ λαλῆσαι ἐρωτᾷ αὐτὸν Φαρισαῖος ὅπως ἀριστήσῃ παρ' αὐτῷ· εἰσελθὼν δὲ ἀνέπεσεν.*

Luke 14, 1 *ἐν τῷ ἐλθεῖν αὐτὸν εἰς οἶκόν τινος τῶν ἀρχόντων τῶν Φαρισαίων σαββάτῳ φαγεῖν ἄρτον.*

[1] I am inclined to think that something similar was in Luke's source (Q?). For Mark 13, 37 has the saying, "But what I say unto you I say unto all, watch," in a context similar to Luke's and paralleled by Q (Mark 13, 33–36 = Matt. 25, 14, 15b; 24, 42; 25, 13 = Luke 19, 12–13; 12, 40; 12, 38). In Luke 9, 23 the transition *ἔλεγεν δὲ πρὸς πάντας* plainly follows the change of audience indicated in Mark 8, 34.

[2] Nicolardot, *op. cit.* p. 157: "Le rédacteur semble considérer les scribes comme formant une catégorie distincte des adeptes du pharisaisme, tandis qu'ils étaient, pour la plupart, pharisiens eux-mêmes." Note also Luke's change of *γραμματεῖς τῶν Φαρισαίων* (Mark 2, 16) to *οἱ Φαρισαῖοι καὶ οἱ γραμματεῖς αὐτῶν* (Luke 5, 30).

In other cases Luke makes Jesus the companion of publicans and sinners, which gives occasion of complaint to the Pharisees (Levi, 5, 29 ff.; Zacchaeus, 19, 1 ff.; and in Luke 15, 1, 2).

Of these six episodes only two have any parallel in Matt. or Mark. But in Matt. and Mark the incident of Luke 5, 29 is placed in Jesus' own house (?),[1] and the anointing of Jesus in the house of Simon the leper. And some of the teaching which has in those gospels a different setting is introduced by Luke quite appropriately in these scenes. The question on fasting which in Mark 2, 18 ff. and Matt. 9, 14 ff. follows the feast with publicans and sinners, but as a separate incident, is in Luke 5, 33 ff., made apparently part of the same incident. The woes to the Pharisees which in Matt. 23, 1 ff. are spoken to the multitudes and the disciples, Luke places at a Pharisee's luncheon, Luke 11, 37 ff. The parable of the lost sheep, which in Matt. 18, 12–14 is in a series of disconnected teachings of Jesus, is joined in Luke 15 with the two companion parables of the lost coin and the lost son and prefaced by the description of an appropriate audience. The parable of the marriage feast, which in Matt. 22, 1–10 is appended to the parable of the wicked husbandmen simply as another parable, is in Luke (14, 15 ff.) told at the dinner table and in answer to the remark of a fellow guest about eating bread in the kingdom of God.

Frequently in Luke the saying of Jesus is called forth by the special situation described, or is in answer to a remark or question of another. Thus, in 3, 15 the wondering of the expectant people whether John the Baptist is the Christ elicits his testimony to Jesus (so in John 1, 20, but not in Mark 1, 7, 8 or Matt. 3, 11, 12). At 19, 11, because they are near Jerusalem and thought the kingdom of God would at once appear, Jesus tells the parable of the pounds. The joy of the seventy on their return becomes the occasion for various warnings and thanksgivings of Jesus (Luke 10, 17–24; contrast Matt. 11, 25–27; 13, 16–17). A report of Pilate's cruelty becomes the text for a sermon of warning, 13, 1–9. The warning of Herod's purpose to kill him leads to Jesus' prophecy of his own death and the lament over the doom of Jerusalem, 13, 31–35.

Requests from the disciples to be taught a prayer (11, 1) and for increase of faith (17, 5) receive appropriate replies (compare Matt.

[1] See above, pp. 96 f.

6, 9–13; and Mark 11, 22, 23 = Matt. 17, 20; 21, 21). As the great apocalyptic section in all three gospels is in response to questions about signs and times (Mark 13, 4 = Matt. 24, 3 = Luke 21, 7), so in Luke 17, 20 another apocalyptic section is introduced by a similar question as to when the kingdom of God is to come; and again, at 13, 23, the question, "Are there few that be saved?" leads to a discourse (the substance of which is derived from Q) of prophetic warning.

The insertion of a question to introduce the teaching of Jesus as an answer to the question is well illustrated by Matt. 18, 1, the passage on greatness in the kingdom of heaven. In Mark 9, 33 ff. = Luke 9, 46 ff., Jesus' teaching on this subject is given of his own accord, because of a controversy among the disciples; in Matt. the disciples come to Jesus, saying, "Who then is greatest in the kingdom of heaven?" The answer in Matt. 18, 2 ff., though in general it is modelled on two passages in Mark (9, 37; 10, 15) and one in Q (Matt. 23, 12; Luke 14, 11; 18, 14), is worded so as to fit exactly the form of question, ". . . he is greatest in the kingdom of heaven" (18, 4b). Another example is Matt. 19, 27. In Mark and Luke Jesus' announcement of rewards to the disciples simply follows Peter's remark, "Lo, we have left all and followed thee;" but Matthew adds to Peter's words the definite question, *τί ἄρα ἔσται ἡμῖν;* Note also the question in Matt. 18, 21, but not in Luke 17, 4; in Matt. 19, 20, but not in Mark 10, 20.

The parable of the good Samaritan is given in reply to the lawyer's question (Luke 10, 29), "Who is my neighbor?" That of the rich fool, with its warning against covetousness, is drawn out by a man's request that Jesus should help him get his share of his inheritance (Luke 12, 13 ff.). Twice (11, 27; 14, 15) a chance beatitude of one near Jesus is corrected, and so becomes the occasion for teaching.

By giving to Christ's teachings a more definite setting Luke does not intend to limit their scope and application. The audience is neither historically reproduced nor artistically delimited, but rather taken as typical and suggestive. Luke has really in mind the Christian church of his own time. Thus, expressions in Mark and Matthew that seem to make Jesus' teaching esoteric are in Luke omitted or modified, as for example the discourse of Mark 13 (Luke 21, 5 ff.), which the first two gospels limit to a private audience of disciples. Compare also Mark 4, 10, 34; 9, 28; 9, 30 ff. (especially the *γάρ* in vs. 31); and Matt. 20, 17. The same motive is assigned by Harnack (*Sayings*, p. 83), following Wellhausen, to explain the difference between Luke 12, 3 and Matt. 10, 27. "Probably he [Luke] wished that our Lord should not appear a mystagogue."

Nicolardot, *Procédés de Rédaction*, p. 157, says: Il arrive que les paroles prêtées au Christ par Luc ou par sa source débordent l'entourage actuel de Jésus. C'est mettre alors du mouvement dans le discours que de marquer le retour de la leçon au cercle réel du Maître qu'elle avait dépassé. Ainsi est suggérée la diversité des perspectives, et la différence des auditoires, le fictif, le prophétique, celui que l'Église prête au Christ et le véritable, l'historique, celui du Nazaréen. Sans doute, Luc n'entend pas cette distinction de façon aussi abrupte. Il sent, du moins, et ne laisse pas de faire sentir que l'horizon de Jésus, à en juger par les discours qui lui sont attribués, était tantôt celui-là même, où il se mouvait actuellement, tantôt le plus vaste horizon des communautés futures.[1]

It will be observed that most of the preceding illustrations are in contexts the source of which is Q, so that we cannot assert positively that the introductions to these sections were added by Luke. They may have been omitted by Matthew. On this point, as in many others respecting Q, scholars differ. Contrast for example the views of Hawkins and Streeter in the *Oxford Studies on the Synoptic Problem*, pp. 124 and 207, respectively. In favor of the view here taken note the suggestion of Streeter: "Particularly significant is the fact that [Luke] imports τότε ἔλεγεν αὐτοῖς, Luke 21, 10, cf. καὶ εἶπεν [παραβολὴν αὐτοῖς] 21, 29, into the middle of the apocalyptic discourse derived from Mark [13], showing that he likes to divide long pieces of discourse as it were into paragraphs by a word or two of narrative." Similarly Luke 5, 36, inserts ἔλεγεν

[1] Wernle, *op. cit.* p. 82, connects with Luke's introduction of prefaces various other changes that tend "die Reden in Erzählung umzusetzen durch lebhaftere Form, Zwischenreden, Einleitungen. Als Mittel für lebhaftere, für die Erzählung passende Gestaltung braucht Lc:

πλήν. Mt schreibt es einmal mit Lc zusammen (11, 22), zweimal für sich allein, Lc 7mal allein in den Redestücken.

ὑποδείξω ὑμῖν 6, 47; 12, 5.

λέγω ὑμῖν in verschiedenen Variationen. Lc schreibt es mit Mt zusammen aus der Quelle 10mal, für sich allein in Stücken der Quelle noch 11mal (6, 27; 11, 9; 12, 4, 5, 8, 51; 14, 24; 15, 7, 10; 17, 34; 19, 26).

Unterbrechung der Reden Jesu oder der Reden im Gleichnis durch Zwischenreden 11, 45; 12, 41 f.; 17, 37; 19, 24 f."

Even where Luke introduces sayings of Jesus by the expression, "He said to the disciples," as at 6, 20; 9, 43; 10, 23; 12, 1, 22; 16, 1; 17, 1, 22; 20, 45 he is not (except at 10, 23) indicating that the teaching is secret; he is reminding the readers of the special group in the audience for which the words were intended. Others are present and listening, e. g. 6, 19; 9, 43; 12, 1; 16, 14; 20, 45. Note also within the sayings themselves Luke's addition to the phrase λέγω ὑμῖν of the words τοῖς ἀκούουσιν (6, 27, contrast Matt. 5, 44) or τοῖς φίλοις μου (12, 4, contrast Matt. 10, 28).

δὲ καὶ παραβολὴν πρὸς αὐτοὺς ὅτι in the middle of the continuous discourse of Mark 2, 19–22.[1]

But the words of Jesus themselves, the *verba ipsissima*, whether reported by Mark or found in the source designated as Q, have rarely been retouched by the author of the third Gospel to give them a wider scope or application. An exception is perhaps found in Luke 8, 21. The true brethren of Christ according to Mark 3, 34 were shown by Jesus' glance to be those seated about him (Matt. 12, 49 is still more distinct: *ἐκτείνας τὴν χεῖρα ἐπὶ τοὺς μαθητάς*); in Luke they are defined as those in general who hear and do God's word. But the solitariness of this instance only makes the general faithfulness of Luke the more impressive.

In a number of passages, especially from Q, Luke's form is in the second person, as addressed directly to Jesus' hearers, while in the parallels the third person is used, as in general or indirect teachings or in the description of persons in a parable.

The most familiar example is in the Beatitudes, which have in Matthew (all but the last) the form:

μακάριοι οἱ πτωχοὶ τῷ πνεύματι, ὅτι αὐτῶν ἐστιν ἡ βασιλεία τῶν οὐρανῶν (5, 3), but in Luke *μακάριοι οἱ πτωχοί, ὅτι ὑμετέρα ἐστὶν ἡ βασιλεία τοῦ θεοῦ* (Luke 6, 20). So Matt. 5, 5, 6 = Luke 6, 21.[2]

Matt. 7, 21 *οὐ πᾶς ὁ λέγων μοι κύριε κύριε, εἰσελεύσεται εἰς τὴν βασιλείαν τῶν οὐρανῶν, ἀλλ' ὁ ποιῶν τὸ θέλημα τοῦ πατρός μου τοῦ ἐν τοῖς οὐρανοῖς.* Luke 6, 46 *τί δέ με καλεῖτε· κύριε κύριε, καὶ οὐ ποιεῖτε ἃ λέγω;*

Matt. 11, 18 *ἦλθεν γὰρ Ἰωάννης μήτε ἐσθίων μήτε πίνων, καὶ λέγουσιν· δαιμόνιον ἔχει,* 19 *ἦλθεν ὁ υἱὸς τοῦ ἀνθρώπου ἐσθίων καὶ πίνων καὶ λέγουσιν κ.τ.λ.* Luke 7, 33, 34 reads in each case *λέγετε* for *λέγουσιν*.[3]

[1] Note the frequent *εἶπεν δέ* in Luke, e.g. 4, 24; 15, 11. In Mark 4 the similar phrases in verses 9, 13, 21, 24, 26, 30 may indicate, what we otherwise suspect, that scattered sayings here are collected into a discourse. Compare "Jesus saith" in the Oxyrhynchus Logia.

[2] Harnack, *Sayings*, p. 49, n. 1, regards Matthew's form as original, against Wellhausen and others.

[3] Here and sometimes elsewhere the change from third to second person serves the additional purpose, which seems to be a feature of Luke's method (see p. 150), of removing the indefiniteness of the subject. So the questions asked in complaint against Jesus or his disciples are directly addressed to them in Luke, while Matthew adopts the other mode of correction by inserting the subject. Thus,

Mark 2, 16 *ἐσθίει καὶ πίνει* (Matt. 9, 11 adds *ὁ διδάσκαλος ὑμῶν*)	Luke 5, 30 *ἐσθίετε καὶ πίνετε*
Mark 2, 24 *ποιοῦσιν* (Matt. 12, 2 adds *οἱ μαθηταί σου*)	Luke 6, 2 *ποιεῖτε*

Mark 12, 38, and from him Luke 20, 46 as well as Matt. 23, 6, warns against the scribes as τῶν θελόντων (φιλούντων Luke, φιλοῦσιν Matt.) . . . ἀσπασμοὺς ἐν ταῖς ἀγοραῖς 39 καὶ πρωτοκαθεδρίας ἐν ταῖς συναγωγαῖς κ.τ.λ. Luke 11, 43 addresses the Pharisees, οὐαὶ ὑμῖν τοῖς Φαρισαίοις, ὅτι ἀγαπᾶτε τὴν πρωτοκαθεδρίαν ἐν ταῖς συναγωγαῖς καὶ τοὺς ἀσπασμοὺς ἐν ταῖς ἀγοραῖς.

Matt. 23, 4 says similarly of the scribes and Pharisees, δεσμεύουσιν δὲ φορτία βαρέα καὶ ἐπιτιθέασιν ἐπὶ τοὺς ὤμους τῶν ἀνθρώπων, αὐτοὶ δὲ τῷ δακτύλῳ αὐτῶν οὐ θέλουσιν κινῆσαι αὐτά. Luke 11, 46 καὶ ὑμῖν τοῖς νομικοῖς οὐαί, ὅτι φορτίζετε τοὺς ἀνθρώπους φορτία δυσβάστακτα, καὶ αὐτοὶ ἑνὶ τῶν δακτύλων ὑμῶν οὐ προσψαύετε τοῖς φορτίοις.

With Matt. 25, 1–13, the parable of the ten virgins, compare Luke 12, 35, ἔστωσαν ὑμῶν αἱ ὀσφύες περιεζωσμέναι καὶ οἱ λύχνοι καιόμενοι 36 καὶ ὑμεῖς ὅμοιοι ἀνθρώποις προσδεχομένοις τὸν κύριον ἑαυτῶν, πότε ἀναλύσῃ ἐκ τῶν γάμων.

Matt. 25, 11 ὕστερον δὲ ἔρχονται καὶ αἱ λοιπαὶ παρθένοι λέγουσαι· κύριε κύριε, ἄνοιξον ἡμῖν. 12 ὁ δὲ ἀποκριθεὶς εἶπεν· ἀμὴν λέγω ὑμῖν, οὐκ οἶδα ὑμᾶς. Luke 13, 25 ἄρξησθε ἔξω ἑστάναι καὶ κρούειν τὴν θύραν λέγοντες· κύριε, ἄνοιξον ἡμῖν, καὶ ἀποκριθεὶς ἐρεῖ ὑμῖν· οὐκ οἶδα ὑμᾶς πόθεν ἐστέ.

Matt. 7, 22 πολλοὶ ἐροῦσίν μοι ἐν ἐκείνῃ τῇ ἡμέρᾳ· κύριε κύριε κ.τ.λ. . . . 23 καὶ τότε ὁμολογήσω αὐτοῖς ὅτι οὐδέποτε ἔγνων ὑμᾶς, ἀποχωρεῖτε ἀπ' ἐμοῦ οἱ ἐργαζόμενοι τὴν ἀνομίαν. Luke 13, 26 τότε ἄρξεσθε λέγειν . . . 27 καὶ ἐρεῖ λέγω ὑμῖν· οὐκ οἶδα πόθεν ἐστέ κ.τ.λ.

Matt. 8, 12 οἱ δὲ υἱοὶ τῆς βασιλείας ἐξελεύσονται εἰς τὸ σκότος τὸ ἐξώτερον· ἐκεῖ ἔσται ὁ κλαυθμὸς καὶ ὁ βρυγμὸς τῶν ὀδόντων. Luke 13, 28 ἐκεῖ ἔσται ὁ κλαυθμὸς καὶ ὁ βρυγμὸς τῶν ὀδόντων, ὅταν ὄψεσθε Ἀβραὰμ . . . ἐν τῇ βασιλείᾳ τοῦ θεοῦ, ὑμᾶς δὲ ἐκβαλλομένους ἔξω.

Matt. 18, 12 ἐὰν γένηταί τινι ἀνθρώπῳ ἑκατὸν πρόβατα κ.τ.λ. Luke 15, 4 τίς ἄνθρωπος ἐξ ὑμῶν[1] ἔχων ἑκατὸν πρόβατα κ.τ.λ.

Mark 13, 12 καὶ παραδώσει ἀδελφὸς ἀδελφὸν εἰς θάνατον καὶ πατὴρ τέκνον, καὶ ἐπαναστήσονται τέκνα ἐπὶ γονεῖς καὶ θανατώσουσι αὐτούς . . . 13b ὁ δὲ ὑπομείνας εἰς τέλος οὗτος σωθήσεται (so Matt. 10, 21; 24, 13). Luke 21, 16 παραδοθήσεσθε δὲ καὶ ὑπὸ γονέων καὶ ἀδελφῶν καὶ συγγενῶν καὶ φίλων καὶ θανατώσουσιν ἐξ ὑμῶν . . . 19 ἐν τῇ ὑπομονῇ ὑμῶν κτήσασθε τὰς ψυχὰς ὑμῶν.[2]

Somewhat different is the contrast between Mark's (3, 30) assigning a statement of Jesus to the cause ὅτι ἔλεγον· πνεῦμα ἀκάθαρτον ἔχει, and the assignment by Jesus himself of a different statement in a passage of Luke, connected with the same passage in Mark but also dependent on Q (Luke 11, 18 compare Matt. 12, 26), ὅτι λέγετε ἐν Βεελζεβοὺλ ἐκβάλλειν με τὰ δαιμόνια. But it is not impossible that the two causal clauses have some literary connection, and that

[1] For τίς (ἐξ) ὑμῶν (ἄνθρωπος) see Matt. 7, 9 = Luke 11, 11; Matt. 6, 27 = Luke 12, 25; Matt. 12, 11 = Luke 14, 5; Luke 14, 28.

[2] In Matt. 23, 34–36 = Luke 11, 49–51 the converse phenomenon (Matt. πρὸς ὑμᾶς . . . ἀποκτενεῖτε . . . διώξετε . . . ἐφονεύσατε, Luke εἰς αὐτοὺς . . . ἀποκτενοῦσιν ἐκδιώξουσιν . . . ἀπολομένου) is perhaps due to the fact that what in Luke is the quotation from "the Wisdom of God" is found in Matthew as the actual words of Jesus to the scribes and Pharisees.

the parallels should be included in the list above as well as in that on page 101.

In the following cases the second person plural is used by Luke parallel to other persons than the third:

Mark 9, 40 *ὃς γὰρ οὐκ ἔστιν καθ' ἡμῶν, ὑπὲρ ἡμῶν ἐστιν* (*v. l.* *ὑμῶν bis*)	Luke 9, 50 *ὃς γὰρ οὐκ ἔστιν καθ' ὑμῶν, ὑπὲρ ὑμῶν ἐστιν*
Matt. 6, 21 *ὅπου γάρ ἐστιν ὁ θησαυρός σου, ἐκεῖ ἔσται καὶ ἡ καρδία σου*	Luke 12, 34 *ὅπου γάρ ἐστιν ὁ θησαυρὸς ὑμῶν, ἐκεῖ καὶ ἡ καρδία ὑμῶν ἔσται* [Q]

Application of Parables

The allegorizing of Christ's figures and parables is another method of adapting his teaching to the later generation. There can be no doubt that this process was active before Luke took in hand to write his gospel, just as it has been continuing ever since. A parable, if originally intended to point but one lesson, can easily be reinterpreted and restated so as to teach several lessons. It is evident from the parables peculiar to Luke that he was aware of their general moral. This is shown by the special setting which he gives them (e.g., 19, 11; 18, 9; 18, 1; 15, 1, etc., see above, pp. 120 f.) and by the way he draws the moral at the end. The parable of the two debtors (7, 41, 42) is directly applied to the case of Simon the Pharisee. To the lawyer who elicited the parable of the Good Samaritan Jesus adds, "Go thou and do likewise." To the story of the rich fool is added the sentence, "So is he who lays up treasure for himself and is not rich toward God." To the parables on counting the cost is added the conclusion, "So therefore every one of you who forsaketh not all his possessions cannot be my disciple." The parables of the lost sheep and the lost coin each conclude with the joy over one repentant sinner. The parable of the unjust steward is followed by the advice it suggests, 16, 9 ff. To the parable of the faithful servant Luke adds as usual an application, "So also ye, when ye," etc. The parable of the unjust judge proves the faithfulness of the avenging God. The parable of the Pharisee and the publican, and the figure of the choice of seats at a feast, lead to the same lesson of humility (Luke 14, 11 = Luke 18, 14).

In these cases it is impossible to determine how far Luke has altered the contents of the parable; but where he is parallel with Mark and Matthew we are better able to judge. The chief illusstrations have been collected and carefully explained by Nicolardot, *op. cit.*, pp. 158–162. Some of them may be briefly summarized as follows:

In Mark 2, 19 the question is asked, "Can the children of the bridechamber fast as long as the bridegroom is with them?" but in Luke 5, 34, it runs, "Can you make the children of the bridechamber fast?" — thus more clearly identifying "the children of the bridechamber" with the disciples of Jesus, whose neglect of fasts was complained of.

In Luke 5, 36 (= Mark 2, 21) the comparison is between old and new coats, rather than between an old coat and a patch of new stuff. The meaning is that John represents a full and complete system of his own, which would be spoiled if one feature of it (e.g., fasting), were removed, just as Christ's system would be spoiled if one feature were added to it. One who is brought up in John's school is naturally content with it (see Luke 5, 39).

The allegorizing of the parable of the sower is carried a step further in Luke by his addition (Luke 8, 15) of ἐν καρδίᾳ καλῇ καὶ ἀγαθῇ as an interpretation of ἐν τῇ καλῇ γῇ (cf. 8, 12 ἀπὸ τῆς καρδίας). Note further the addition ἵνα μὴ πιστεύσαντες σωθῶσιν (8, 12), the substitution of πρὸς καιρὸν πιστεύουσιν for πρόσκαιροί εἰσιν (Mark 4, 17), and the omission of σπειρόμενοι, σπαρέντες (Mark 4, 16, 20).

In the parable of the lamp, Luke twice says the light is for those who enter in (8, 16; 11, 33), while Matt. 5, 15 says it shines for all those in the house. Harnack, *Sayings*, pp. 55 f. writes: "St. Luke evidently intends to improve the sense of the passage; he perhaps also thinks of the missionary aspect of the gospel (though this is doubtful)."

A reference to the Gentile mission may perhaps be found also in Luke's version of the parable of the wedding feast, 14, 16–24. When the original guests refuse, the servants are sent out even to the φραγμοί to get men to partake of the feast. Luke adds that the original guests are definitely excluded (14, 24).

In the parable of the pounds (Luke 19, 11–27), by a variety of touches, the identification of the master with Jesus is made more clear than in the corresponding parable of the talents (Matt. 25, 14–30). See Luke 19, 12, 14, 27; Nicolardot, pp. 160 f.

There can be no doubt that in the parable of the husbandmen the culprits are meant to be the Jewish rulers. So, at least, the hearers understood it according to all synoptists, Mark 12, 12 = Matt. 21, 45 = Luke 20, 19. But in Matt. and in Luke it is made doubly clear; in Matt. by Jesus' direct application (21, 43), in Luke by the self-defending remark of the bystanders, μὴ γένοιτο (20, 16).

Omission of Details

Like Luke's tendency to generalization, so his tendency to omit numerals and proper names leads to loss of definite color and realism. In some cases (see p. 156) the proper names may be omitted because of their barbarous sound, in accord with strictly literary rules; but in others no such reason for the omission exists, and the effect is only to lessen the local Palestinian coloring of the narrative.

Perea (πέραν τοῦ Ἰορδάνου, Mark 3, 8; 10, 1) is not mentioned by Luke by name, not even in his reputed "Perean section," neither is Idumea (Mark 3, 8). Probably they, and sometimes even Galilee, are included in his Judea (see Luke 6, 17, and cf. Luke 1, 5. 7, 17; 23, 5; Acts 2, 9; 10, 37; 11, 1, 29; 26, 20). Decapolis, though found at Matt. 4, 25; Mark 5, 20; 7, 31, is not in Luke, who in 8, 39 substitutes καθ' ὅλην τὴν πόλιν; cf. 8, 27. Caesarea Philippi (Mark 8, 27) is not mentioned in Luke 9, 18. Galilee (Mark 9, 30) is omitted in Luke 9, 43. Samaria, on the other hand, though not mentioned in Matt. or Mark, occurs in Luke 17, 11; and frequently in Acts in connection with the spread of Christianity in Palestine. Samaritans are mentioned in Matt. once (their cities to be avoided, 10, 5), never in Mark, but in Luke 9, 52; 10, 33; 17, 16; Acts 8, 25. Bethany is not mentioned by Luke as being Jesus' lodging place during his last week (cf. Mark 11, 11, 12; 14, 3). Twice when Mark places a scene in Capernaum (2, 1; 9, 33) Luke omits any reference to place (5, 17; 9, 46). Even references to Jesus' being by the sea are omitted (cf. Mark 2, 13; 3, 7; 4, 1; 5, 21).

In the following quotations the names of persons found in Mark but omitted by Luke are enclosed in brackets:

Mark 1, 29 ἦλθον εἰς τὴν οἰκίαν Σίμωνος [καὶ 'Ανδρέου μετὰ 'Ιακώβου καὶ 'Ιωάννου] — Luke 4, 38.
Mark 2, 14 εἶδεν Λευεὶν [τὸν τοῦ 'Αλφαίου] καθήμενον ἐπὶ τὸ τελώνιον — Luke 5, 27.
Mark 2, 26 εἰσῆλθεν εἰς τὸν οἶκον τοῦ θεοῦ [ἐπὶ 'Αβιάθαρ ἀρχιερέως] — Luke 6, 4.
Mark 3, 17 'Ιάκωβον [τὸν τοῦ Ζεβεδαίου] καὶ 'Ιωάννην [τὸν ἀδελφὸν τοῦ 'Ιακώβου] — Luke 6, 14.
Mark 5, 37 'Ιωάννην [τὸν ἀδελφὸν 'Ιακώβου] — Luke 8, 51.
Mark 6, 17 'Ηρωδιάδα τὴν γυναῖκα [Φιλίππου] τοῦ ἀδελφοῦ αὐτοῦ — Luke 3, 19.
Matt. 23, 35 Ζαχαρίου [υἱοῦ Βαραχίου] — Luke 11, 51 [Q].
Mark 10, 46 [ὁ υἱὸς Τιμαίου Βαρτίμαιος] τυφλός . . . — Luke 18, 35.
Mark 13, 1 ἐπηρώτα αὐτὸν . . . [ὁ Πέτρος καὶ 'Ιάκωβος καὶ 'Ιωάννης καὶ 'Ανδρέας] — Luke 21, 7 ἐπηρώτησαν.
Mark 14, 33 [Πέτρον καὶ 'Ιάκωβον καὶ 'Ιωάννην] — Luke 22, 39 οἱ μαθηταί.
Mark 14, 37 λέγει τῷ Πέτρῳ — Luke 22, 46 εἶπεν αὐτοῖς.
Mark 15, 21 Σίμωνα Κυρηναῖον . . . [τὸν πατέρα 'Αλεξάνδρου καὶ 'Ρούφου] — Luke 23, 26.

For examples of the converse see Mark 5, 31 οἱ μαθηταί — Luke 8, 45 ὁ Πέτρος καὶ οἱ σὺν αὐτῷ. Mark 14, 13 δύο τῶν μαθητῶν αὐτοῦ—Luke 22, 8 Πέτρον καὶ 'Ιωάννην

Luke, like Matthew (see Allen, *Matthew*, p. xxxvi), leaves out details of number.

Mark alone mentions (2, 3) that the paralytic was carried by *four* men. Luke does not tell (8, 33), as does Mark (5, 13) that the swine drowned were ὡς δισχίλιοι. Luke 9, 13 speaks of the needed supplies as βρώματα εἰς πάντα τὸν λαὸν τοῦτον rather than as δηναρίων διακοσίων ἄρτους (Mark 6, 37). The companies in Luke 9, 14 are fifty each, not fifty and a hundred (Mark 6, 40). In the parable of the sower and in its interpretation in Mark 4, 8, 20 the good seed brings forth thirty, sixty, and a hundred-fold. In Luke 8, 8, 15 it yields a hundred-fold, or simply "with patience." The recompense of the faithful is changed from ἑκατονταπλασίονα, Mark 10, 30, to πολλαπλασίονα, Luke 18, 30 (ABΔ*al.*; so also in Matt. 19, 29 BL). Note also the ἑβδομηκοντάκις ἑπτά in Matt. 18, 22, but not in the parallel, Luke 17, 4 [Q].

Again, Mark (14, 1, cf. Matt. 26, 2) says that the passover was to occur *μετὰ δύο ἡμέρας*; Luke merely says it was near (22, 1 *ἤγγιζεν*). Luke 22, 34, 61 and Matt. 26, 34, 75 both omit the double cock-crowing of Mark 14, 30, 72. (So even in Mark ℵC*W omit *δίς*. Note further omissions of ℵ *al* in Mark 14, 68, 72.)

The addition of *δύο* in Luke 9, 30 *καὶ ἰδοὺ ἄνδρες δύο . . . οἵτινες ἦσαν Μωϋσῆς καὶ Ἠλείας* (cf. Mark 9, 4 *Ἠλείας σὺν Μωϋσεῖ*) is perhaps due to a kind of formula of Luke for apparitions. See Luke 24, 4 *καὶ ἰδοὺ ἄνδρες δύο ἐπέστησαν αὐταῖς*; Acts 1, 10 *καὶ καὶ ἰδοὺ ἄνδρες δύο παριστήκεισαν αὐτοῖς*. See also p. 178 n.

Characteristic of Luke is his qualification of numbers by *ὡσεί*, e.g.

Mk. 6, 40 *κατὰ πεντήκοντα*	Lk. 9, 14 *ὡσεὶ ἀνὰ πεντήκοντα* (*v.l.*)
Mk. 6, 44 *πεντακισχίλιοι ἄνδρες*	Lk. 9, 14 *ὡσεὶ ἄνδρες πεντακισχίλιοι*
Mk. 9, 2 *μετὰ ἡμέρας ἕξ*	Lk. 9, 28 *ὡσεὶ ἡμέραι ὀκτώ*
Mk. 15, 33 *ὥρας ἕκτης*	Lk. 23, 44 *ὡσεὶ ὥρα ἕκτη*

This use of *ὡσεί* is found elsewhere in the New Testament only in Luke's writings (Luke 3, 23; 22, 41, 59; Acts 1, 15; 2, 41; 10, 3; 19, 7, 34), with the solitary exception of Matt. 14, 21, *ἄνδρες ὡσεὶ πεντακισχίλιοι*, which is thus under suspicion of having been assimilated to Luke 9, 14.[1] In two cases Luke uses it with a more definite phrase substituted for Mark's *μικρόν*, *μετὰ μικρόν*, viz. Luke 22, 41 *ὡσεὶ λίθου βολήν*, 22, 59 *διαστάσης ὡσεὶ ὥρας μιᾶς* (cf. 22, 58 *μετὰ βραχύ*).

Other details of many kinds are omitted by Luke. Beside the examples discussed elsewhere (pp. 151 f.) of indications of time an place which Luke omits, a few others may here be given:

Mark 2, 1 *ἐν οἴκῳ*[2] — Luke 5, 17.
Mark 4, 38 *ἐν τῇ πρύμνῃ ἐπὶ τὸ προσκεφάλαιον* — Luke 8, 23.
Mark 5, 21 *ἐν τῷ πλοίῳ* — Luke 8, 40.
Mark 6, 8 *εἰς τὴν ζώνην* — Luke 9, 3.
Mark 6, 32 *τῷ πλοίῳ* — Luke 9, 10.
Mark 6, 39 *ἐπὶ τῷ χλωρῷ χόρτῳ* — Luke 9, 14.
Mark 8, 27 *ἐν τῇ ὁδῷ* — Luke 9, 18.
Mark 9, 8 *ἐξάπινα* — Luke 9, 36.

[1] Elsewhere numbers are thus qualified by *ὡς*, as by Mark at the feeding of the four thousand (8, 9 = Matt. 15, 38 *v.l.*) and by John at the feeding of the five thousand (6, 10; cf. Mark 6, 44 = Luke 9, 14 above) and elsewhere (e.g. John 19, 14 = Luke 23, 44 above, and Mark 5, 13; John 1, 40; 4, 6; 6, 19; 11, 18; 19, 39; 21, 8). Luke uses it twice in the gospel (1, 56, and 8, 42 where it is added to Mark 5, 42 *ἐτῶν δώδεκα*) and frequently in Acts: 1, 15 *v.l.*; 4, 4 *v.l.*; 5, 7 (*ὡς ὡρῶν τριῶν διάστημα*, cf. Luke 22, 59 above), 5, 36; 13, 18, 20; 19, 34 *v.l.*, 27, 37.

[2] According to Hawkins, *Horae Synopticae*, pp. 11, 28, *οἰκία* and *οἶκος* without mention of the owner occur seven times in Mark, four times in Matthew, but nowhere else in the New Testament.

Mark 9, 33 ἐν τῇ οἰκίᾳ[1] — Luke 9, 46.
Mark 9, 33 ἐν τῇ ὁδῷ — Luke 9, 47.
Mark 10, 32 ἐν τῇ ὁδῷ — Cf. Luke 19, 28.
Mark 10, 52 ἐν τῇ ὁδῷ — Luke 18, 43.
Mark 12, 35 ἐν τῷ ἱερῷ — Luke 20, 41.
Mark 12, 41 κατέναντι τοῦ γαζοφυλακίου — Luke 21, 1.
Mark 13, 1 ἐκ τοῦ ἱεροῦ — Luke 21, 5.
Mark 13, 3 εἰς τὸ ὄρος τῶν ἐλαιῶν κατέναντι τοῦ ἱεροῦ — Luke 21, 7.
Mark 14, 16 εἰς τὴν πόλιν — Luke 22, 13.
Mark 14, 68 ἔξω εἰς τὸ προαύλιον — Luke 22, 58.
Mark 15, 25 ἦν δὲ ὥρα τρίτη, cf. 15, 34 — Luke 23, 33f.
Mark 15, 42 καὶ ἤδη ὀψίας γενομένης — Luke 23, 50; but cf. vs. 54.
Mark 16, 5 ἐν τοῖς δεξιοῖς — Luke 24, 4.

Other details of all sorts omitted by Luke may be illustrated by the following:[2]

Mark 1, 6 Dress and food of John the Baptist — Luke 3, 1–6.
Mark 1, 13 ἦν μετὰ τῶν θηρίων — Luke 4, 1, 2.
Mark 4, 36 καὶ ἄλλα πλοῖα ἦσαν μετ' αὐτοῦ — Luke 8, 22.
Mark 10, 50 ἀποβαλὼν τὸ ἱμάτιον αὐτοῦ (cf. Mark 14, 51, 52) — Luke 18, 40; cf. 22, 53.
Mark 11, 8 ἄλλοι δὲ στιβάδας κόψαντες ἐκ τῶν ἀγρῶν — Luke 19, 36
Mark 11, 15 τὰς τραπέζας τῶν κολλυβιστῶν καὶ τὰς καθέδρας τῶν πωλούντων τὰς περιστερὰς κατέστρεψεν — Luke 19, 45.
Mark 12, 1 περιέθηκεν φραγμὸν καὶ ὤρυξεν ὑπολήνιον καὶ ᾠκοδόμησεν πύργον — Luke 20, 9.
Mark 14, 1 ἐν δόλῳ — Luke 22, 2.

Loss of Palestinian color has been found by some in various other passages, where it is supposed that Luke adapted his sources for readers to whom Palestinian life was unknown. Thus according to Scholten (*op. cit.* p. 22; but see below, p. 197) Luke (8, 16) failed to recognize the force of the articles in Mark 4, 21, where the regular pieces of furniture in a Jewish house are mentioned as *the* lamp, *the* lampstand, *the* bed (cf. also Mark 7, 30, and Luke 11, 7: "my children are with me in *the* bed," εἰς τὴν κοίτην.) The use of mud and thatch in the walls and roof of houses is obscured by Luke's omission of ἐξορύξαντες in Mark 2, 4 (cf. Luke 5, 19, διὰ τῶν κεράμων) and of διορύσσουσι in Matt. 6, 19, 20; cf. Luke 12, 33. (In Luke 12, 39 = Matt. 24, 43 διορυχθῆναι is retained by Luke). According to Lagrange, *Revue Biblique* (1896), p. 31, quoted by

[1] See note 2 on preceding page.

[2] Though only omissions are mentioned here, it must not be overlooked that Luke often adds a short phrase for the sake of fulness and clearness. See Hawkins, *Horae Synopticae*, 2nd edit., pp. 194 ff.

Batiffol, *Credibility of the Gospel,* p. 138, the expression in the parable, Matt. 7, 25, 27 ἦλθαν οἱ ποταμοί, while appropriate enough for Palestine with its sudden freshets and its unsubstantial houses, was changed by Luke (6, 48, 49) as not suitable to conditions elsewhere.

Structure of Sentences and Use of Conjunctions

We come now to consider those changes made by Luke, in passages derived from Mark, which affect neither the order of the paragraphs nor the treatment of the paragraph as a whole, but rather the structure of the sentence, the order of words, and matters of grammar and vocabulary, all of which constitute the minor elements of style. The details here are numerous, and do not always afford a basis for natural classification, so that a complete list of all changes would give no very definite results. Instead, we shall list and group those changes which seem to show the editorial habits of the author, without demanding or expecting that his changes should uniformly be in one direction. For example, if from the expression ταῦτα πάντα in Mark 13, 4 and 13, 30, Luke omits first one word and then the other, the two instances alone furnish us but little information about his method.

To the investigation of Luke's use of Mark would follow as a natural sequel an investigation of his use of Q. The subject no doubt admits of separate treatment, and much of the material is already collected in Harnack's *Sayings of Jesus.* But as the original wording of Q is not certainly discovered by mere comparison with Matthew, and as the changes attributable to Luke are usually to be recognized by his literary habits elsewhere, it seems most instructive, instead of reserving this part of our study for a separate chapter, to add under each class of changes made by Luke in passages derived from Mark similar differences between Luke and Matthew in sections that have no parallels in Mark. This will at the same time strengthen the evidence given by comparison with the sections from Mark alone and confirm by that evidence the suspicion of corresponding changes where Q was the source. As before, these parallels will be distinguished by the sign [Q].

Harnack does not appear to have used for the basis of his reconstruction of Q a full study of the editorial methods of the two subsequent writers in their use of Mark. In a few cases I believe this analogy would have led him to reverse his decision, or at least to speak with less confidence. A few examples will be found in the course of this discussion.

Luke's changes in the text of Mark often find their readiest explanation in his desire for improvement in the structure of sentences. It is true that Luke never equals in his later sections the balanced periodical sentence with which his work begins, yet his sense for the balance of composite sentences is not lost, and in many other ways his constructions approximate more nearly to classical models than do those of his sources. Norden observes this fact and quotes a few cases. He says (*Antike Kunstprosa*, pp. 490 f.): "Einige Perioden bildet Lukas besser als die beiden anderen (ohne dass er durchweg gut periodisierte), doch habe ich mir aus vielem nur weniges notiert," and adds as an example:

Mark 1, 10 f. *καὶ εὐθὺς ἀναβαίνων ἐκ τοῦ ὕδατος εἶδεν σχιζομένους τοὺς οὐρανοὺς καὶ τὸ πνεῦμα ὡς περιστερὰν καταβαῖνον εἰς αὐτόν. καὶ φωνὴ ἐγένετο ἐκ τῶν οὐρανῶν, σὺ εἶ ὁ υἱός μου ὁ ἀγαπητός, ἐν σοὶ εὐδόκησα.*

Luke 3, 21 f. *ἐγένετο δὲ ἐν τῷ βαπτισθῆναι ἅπαντα τὸν λαὸν καὶ Ἰησοῦ βαπτισθέντος καὶ προσευχομένου ἀνεῳχθῆναι τὸν οὐρανὸν καὶ καταβῆναι τὸ πνεῦμα τὸ ἅγιον σωματικῷ εἴδει ὡς περιστερὰν ἐπ' αὐτόν, καὶ φωνὴν ἐξ οὐρανοῦ γενέσθαι κ.τ.λ.*

The most frequent improvement is the substitution of some form of complex sentence for successive co-ordinate verbs, thus reducing the extent of parataxis. This is done in many ways. Norden's example suggests two of these, the construction with *ἐν τῷ* with the infinitive and the use of the genitive absolute.

The construction *ἐγένετο ἐν τῷ* with the infinitive occurs frequently in Luke in various forms (see Plummer, *St. Luke*, p. 45). It appears in a few cases to be substituted for a different expression in Mark:

Mk. 1, 10 (quoted above)	Lk. 3, 21 (quoted above)
Mk. 5, 21 *διαπεράσαντος τοῦ Ἰησοῦ*	Lk. 8, 40 *ἐγένετο ἐν τῷ ὑποστρέφειν τὸν Ἰησοῦν*
Mk. 10, 46 *καὶ ἔρχονται εἰς Ἰερειχώ*	Lk. 18, 35 *ἐγένετο ἐν τῷ ἐγγίζειν αὐτὸν εἰς Ἰερειχώ*

We may also add one case of the infinitive with *ἐν* without preceding *ἐγένετο*, a construction which also is a favorite with Luke:

Mk. 5, 24 *καὶ ἠκολούθει αὐτῷ ὄχλος πολὺς καὶ συνέθλιβον αὐτόν*	Lk. 8, 42 *ἐν δὲ τῷ ὑπάγειν αὐτὸν οἱ ὄχλοι συνέπνιγον αὐτόν*

Participles

In one of the preceding cases (Mark 5, 21 = Luke 8, 40) Luke is supplanting a genitive absolute. More often Luke introduces the genitive absolute in place of a finite verb:

Mk. 1, 9 καὶ ἐβαπτίσθη	Lk. 3, 21 Ἰησοῦ βαπτισθέντος
Mk. 4, 1 συνάγεται . . . ὄχλος	Lk. 8, 4 συνιόντος ὄχλου πολλοῦ
Mk. 10, 50 ὁ δὲ . . . ἦλθεν	Lk. 18, 40 ἐγγίσαντος αὐτοῦ
Mk. 11, 4 λύουσιν αὐτόν	Lk. 19, 33 λυόντων αὐτῶν τὸν πῶλον
Mk. 12, 37 πολὺς ὄχλος ἤκουεν	Lk. 20, 45 ἀκούοντος παντὸς τοῦ λαοῦ
Mk. 13, 1 λέγει εἶς	Lk. 21, 5 τινων λεγόντων
Mk. 14, 13 ὑπάγετε	Lk. 22, 10 εἰσελθόντων ὑμῶν
Mk. 14, 49 ἤμην . . . διδάσκων	Lk. 22, 53 ὄντος μου

When, as occasionally happens, Luke omits a genitive absolute in his source it is sometimes because the subject is already present in the sentence so that a genitive absolute is strictly ungrammatical,[1] as:

Mk. 5, 2 ἐξελθόντος αὐτοῦ . . . ὑπήντησεν αὐτῷ	Lk. 8, 27 ἐξελθόντι αὐτῷ . . . ὑπήντησεν
Mk. 5, 18 ἐμβαίνοντος αὐτοῦ . . . αὐτόν	Lk. 8, 37, 38 αὐτὸς ἐμβὰς . . . ἐδεῖτο δὲ αὐτοῦ
Mk. 10, 17 ἐκπορευομένου αὐτοῦ . . . αὐτόν	Lk. 18, 18 omits
Cf. Mk. 10, 46 ἐκπορευομένου αὐτοῦ	Lk. 18, 35 omits
Mk. 13, 1 ἐκπορευομένου αὐτοῦ . . . αὐτῷ	Lk. 21, 5 omits

In other cases Luke inserts a different genitive absolute of his own in the sentence:

Mk. 1, 32 ὀψίας δὲ γενομένης	Lk. 4, 40 δύνοντος τοῦ ἡλίου
Mk. 15, 33 καὶ γενομένης ὥρας ἕκτης σκότος ἐγένετο	Lk. 23, 44, 45 καὶ ἦν ἤδη ὡσεὶ ὥρα ἕκτη καὶ σκότος ἐγένετο . . . τοῦ ἡλίου ἐκλείποντος

The only other genitive absolute omitted by Luke is:

Mk. 6, 35 ὥρας πολλῆς γινομένης	Lk. 9, 12 ἡ δὲ ἡμέρα ἤρξατο κλίνειν

Luke sometimes uses the genitive absolute for some other expression in Mark's narrative, and frequently adds it, thereby making the situation more definite:

Mk. 1, 35 πρωὶ ἔννυχα λίαν	Lk. 4, 42 γενομένης δὲ ἡμέρας
Mk. 4, 36	Lk. 8, 23 πλεόντων δὲ αὐτῶν
Mk. 5, 31	Lk. 8, 45 ἀρνουμένων δὲ πάντων
Mk. 9, 7	Lk. 9, 34 ταῦτα δὲ αὐτοῦ λέγοντος[2]

[1] Luke does not however completely avoid this ungrammatical genitive absolute. See Luke 12, 36; 15, 20; 17, 12; 18, 40; 22, 10, 53; Acts 4, 1; 21, 17.

[2] Cf. Matt. 17, 5 ἔτι αὐτοῦ λαλοῦντος

Mk. 9, 20	Lk. 9, 42 *ἔτι δὲ προσερχομένου αὐτοῦ*
Mk. 9, 30	Lk. 9, 43 *πάντων δὲ θαυμαζόντων*
Mk. 11, 8	Lk. 19, 36 *πορευομένου δὲ αὐτοῦ*
Mk. 11, 9	Lk. 19, 37 *ἐγγίζοντος δὲ αὐτοῦ κ.τ.λ.*
Mk. 14, 54	Lk. 22, 55 *περιαψάντων δὲ πῦρ κ.τ.λ.*
Mk. 14, 72	Lk. 22, 60 *ἔτι λαλοῦντος αὐτοῦ*
Mk. 16, 5 *ἐξεθαμβήθησαν*	Lk. 24, 5 *ἐμφόβων δὲ γενομένων κ.τ.λ.*

Similar use of the genitive absolute is made by Luke in passages derived from Q or in introducing such passages. (Cf. Harnack, *Sayings*, pp. 39, 113).

Matthew	Luke
Mt. 3, 11	Lk. 3, 15 *προσδοκῶντος δὲ τοῦ λαοῦ καὶ διαλογιζομένων πάντων κτλ.* [Q]
Mt. 7, 25 *κατέβη ἡ βροχή*	Lk. 6, 48 *πλημμύρης δὲ γενομένης* [Q]
Mt. 8, 19	Lk. 9, 57 *καὶ πορευομένων αὐτῶν ἐν τῇ ὁδῷ* [Q]
Mt. 12, 22 *ἐθεράπευσεν αὐτόν*	Lk. 11, 14 *τοῦ δαιμονίου ἐξελθόντος* [Q]
Mt. 12, 38	Lk. 11, 29 *τῶν δὲ ὄχλων ἐπαθροιζομένων* [Q]

The other uses of the participle in Luke are both more numerous and more idiomatic than in Mark. The simplest illustrations of his correction of Mark by participles are found in those pairs of verbs connected in Mark by *καί*, for one of which Luke substitutes a participle.[1] In most cases it is the former of the two verbs that is changed by Luke to the participle, and the temporal sequence is shown by the tense (aorist) of the participle. But in some other cases, notably with verbs of saying where the time of the two verbs is really synchronous the second is changed to the participle.

List of both kinds of changes follow.

Participle for the former of two co-ordinate verbs.

Mk. 1, 35 *ἐξῆλθεν καί*	Lk. 4, 42 *ἐξελθών*
Mk. 2, 11 *ἆρον . . . καί*	Lk. 5, 24 *ἄρας*
Mk. 2, 12 *ἠγέρθη καί*	Lk. 5, 25 *ἀναστάς*
Mk. 4, 5 *ἐξανέτειλεν . . . καί*	Lk. 8, 6 *φυέν*
Mk. 4, 7 *ἀνέβησαν καί*	Lk. 8, 7 *συνφυεῖσαι*
Mk. 4, 20 *ἀκούουσιν . . . καί*	Lk. 8, 15 *ἀκούσαντες*
Mk. 5, 22 f. *πίπτει . . . καί*	Lk. 8, 41 *πεσών*
Mk. 5, 33 *προσέπεσεν . . . καί*	Lk. 8, 47 *προσπεσοῦσα*
Mk. 6, 7 *προσκαλεῖται . . . καί*	Lk. 9, 1 *συνκαλεσάμενος*
Mk. 6, 30 *συνάγονται . . . καί*	Lk. 9, 10 *ὑποστρέψαντες*
Mk. 6, 33 *ἐπέγνωσαν . . . καί*	Lk. 9, 11 *γνόντες*
Mk. 9, 2 *παραλαμβάνει . . . καί*	Lk. 9, 28 *παραλαβών*
Mt. 8, 21 *ἀπελθεῖν καί*	Lk. 9, 59 *ἀπελθόντι* (*v.l.* *-όντα*) [Q]
Mt. 5, 15 *καίουσι . . . καί*	Lk. 11, 33 *ἅψας* [Q]

[1] For an opposite case see Mark 9, 7 *ἐγένετο νεφέλη ἐπισκιάζουσα αὐτοῖς* (Luke 9, 34 *καὶ ἐπεσκίαζεν αὐτούς*).

Mk. 10, 28 ἀφήκαμεν . . . καί	Lk. 18, 28 ἀφέντες
Mk. 10, 34 μαστιγώσουσιν . . . καί	Lk. 18, 33 μαστιγώσαντες
Mk. 11, 2 λύσατε . . . καί	Lk. 19, 30 λύσαντες
Mk. 11, 4 ἀπῆλθον καί	Lk. 19, 32 ἀπελθόντες
Mk. 11, 7 ἐπιβάλλουσι . . . καί	Lk. 19, 35 ἐπιρίψαντες
Mk. 12, 3 ἔδειραν καί	Lk. 20, 10 δείραντες
Mk. 12, 18 ἔρχονται . . . καί	Lk. 20, 27 προσελθόντες
Mk. 12, 20 ἔλαβεν . . . καί	Lk. 20, 29 λαβών
Mk. 14, 16 ἐξῆλθον . . . καί	Lk. 22, 13 ἀπελθόντες
Mk. 14, 35 ἔπιπτεν ἐπὶ τῆς γῆς καί	Lk. 22, 41 θεὶς τὰ γόνατα [1]
Mk. 14, 37 ἔρχεται καί	Lk. 22, 45 ἐλθών
Mk. 14, 65 ἤρξαντο . . . περικαλύπτειν . . . καί	Lk. 22, 64 περικαλύψαντες
Mk. 15, 43 εἰσῆλθεν . . . καί	Lk. 23, 52 προσελθών (So Matt. 27, 58)

Participle for the latter of two co-ordinate verbs:

Mk. 1, 41 καὶ λέγει	Lk. 5, 12 λέγων
Mk. 4, 38 καὶ λέγουσι	Lk. 8, 24 λέγοντες
Mk. 4, 41 καὶ ἔλεγον	Lk. 8, 25 λέγοντες
Mk. 5, 20 καὶ ἤρξατο κηρύσσειν	Lk. 8, 39 κηρύσσων
Mk. 5, 37 f. οὐκ ἀφῆκεν . . . καὶ ἔρχονται	Lk. 8, 51 ἐλθὼν . . . οὐκ ἀφῆκεν
Mk. 8, 31 καὶ ἤρξατο διδάσκειν	Lk. 9, 22 εἰπών
Mk. 10, 14 καὶ εἶπεν	Lk. 18, 16 λέγων
Mk. 10, 47 καὶ λέγειν	Lk. 18, 38 λέγων
Mk. 11, 2 καὶ λέγει	Lk. 19, 30 λέγων
Mk. 11, 17 καὶ ἔλεγεν	Lk. 19, 46 λέγων
Mk. 12, 4 καὶ ἠτίμασαν	Lk. 20, 11 ἀτιμάσαντες
Mk. 12, 8 καὶ ἐξέβαλον	Lk. 20, 15 ἐκβαλόντες
Mk. 14, 22 καὶ εἶπεν	Lk. 22, 19 λέγων
Mk. 14, 24 καὶ εἶπεν	Lk. 22, 20 λέγων
Mk. 14, 36 καὶ ἔλεγεν	Lk. 22, 42 λέγων

It will be observed that this change is chiefly with verbs of saying. In the few other cases where Luke substitutes a participle for the second of two co-ordinate verbs the change reverses also the order in time of the acts mentioned.

The participle, usually with the article, is substituted by Luke for a relative clause:

Mt. 5, 39 ὅστις σε ῥαπίζει	Lk. 6, 29 τῷ τύπτοντί σε [Q]
Mt. 7, 24 ὅστις ἀκούει	Lk. 6, 47 ὁ . . . ἀκούων [Q]
Mt. 7, 24 ὅστις ᾠκοδόμησεν	Lk. 6, 48 οἰκοδομοῦντι [Q]
Mt. 7, 26 ὅστις ᾠκοδόμησεν	Lk. 6, 49 οἰκοδομήσαντι [Q] [2]
Mk. 4, 9 ὃς ἔχει ὦτα	Lk. 8, 8 ὁ ἔχων ὦτα (cf. Matt. 13, 9)
Mk. 3, 35 ὃς ἂν ποιήσῃ	Lk. 8, 21 οἱ . . . ποιοῦντες
Mt. 23, 35 ὃν ἐφονεύσατε	Lk. 11, 51 τοῦ ἀπολομένου [Q]

[1] In this instance, however, the preceding clause shows the converse difference, for Mark has προελθὼν μικρόν, Luke ἀπεσπάσθη ἀπ' αὐτῶν ὡσεὶ λίθου βολὴν καί.

[2] Perhaps Luke 7, 32 = Matt. 11, 16 f. should be added, see full text and variants.

Mt. 10, 33 ὅστις δ' ἂν ἀρνήσηταί με	Lk. 12, 9 ὁ δὲ ἀρνησάμενός με [Q]
Mt. 12, 32 ὃς δ' ἂν εἴπῃ Mk. 3, 29 ὃς δ' ἂν βλασφημήσῃ	Lk. 12, 10 τῷ . . . βλασφημήσαντι [Q?]
Mt. 23, 12 ὅστις δὲ ὑψώσει ἑαυτόν	Lk. 14, 11; 18, 14 πᾶς ὁ ὑψῶν ἑαυτόν [Q]
Mt. 23, 12 ὅστις ταπεινώσει ἑαυτόν	Lk. 14, 11; 18, 14 ὁ δὲ ταπεινῶν ἑαυτόν [Q]
Mt. 5, 32 ὃς ἐὰν ἀπολελυμένην γαμήσῃ	Lk. 16, 18 ὁ ἀπολελυμένην . . . γαμῶν [Q]
Mk. 12, 18 οἵτινες λέγουσι	Lk. 20, 27 οἱ ἀντιλέγοντες
Mk. 15, 41 αἳ . . . ἠκολούθουν	Lk. 23, 49 αἱ συνακολουθοῦσαι

Compare also

Mk. 9, 35 εἴ τις θέλει πρῶτος εἶναι, ἔσται πάντων ἔσχατος καὶ πάντων διάκονος	Lk. 9, 48 ὁ γὰρ μικρότερος ἐν πᾶσιν ὑμῖν ὑπάρχων, οὗτός ἐστιν μέγας
Mk. 10, 43 ὃς ἂν θέλῃ μέγας γενέσθαι ἐν ὑμῖν	Lk. 22, 26 ὁ μείζων ἐν ὑμῖν
Mk. 10, 43 διάκονος	Lk. 22, 26 ὁ διακονῶν
Mk. 10, 44 ὃς ἂν θέλῃ ὑμῶν γενέσθαι πρῶτος	Lk. 22, 26 ὁ ἡγούμενος
Mt. 6, 12 τοῖς ὀφειλέταις	Lk. 11, 4 παντὶ ὀφείλοντι [Q]

The only case of the reverse is

Mk. 12, 40 οἱ κατεσθίοντες	Lk. 20, 47 οἳ κατεσθίουσιν

In this case Mark's participle is not grammatical (see p. 148).

The participle with the article is twice used for the verb, thus:

Mk. 5, 30 τίς μου ἥψατο	Lk. 8, 45 τίς ὁ ἁψάμενός μου
Mk. 11, 28 τίς σοι τὴν ἐξουσίαν ταύτην ἔδωκεν	Lk. 20, 2 τίς ἐστιν ὁ δούς σοι τὴν ἐξουσίαν ταύτην

The question τίς ἐστιν ὁ παίσας σε (Luke 22, 64) has the same form, and is perhaps an addition by Luke to Mark 14, 65 προφήτευσον, later by assimilation added to Matt. 26, 68, where it is much less suitable, since Matthew has no reference to Jesus' being blindfolded. This agreement of Matthew and Luke against Mark is, however, very puzzling. Similar, and characteristic of Luke, is the form of Luke 22, 23, τὸ τίς ἄρα εἴη ἐξ αὐτῶν ὁ τοῦτο μέλλων πράσσειν, for Mark's simple and direct μήτι ἐγώ (14, 19).

In the following cases a variety of constructions of Mark, including clauses with ἀλλά, γάρ, ἵνα, and cases of complementary infinitive, apposition, and asyndeton, are replaced by a participle in Luke:

Mk. 1, 44 ὕπαγε σεαυτὸν δεῖξον	Lk. 5, 14 ἀπελθὼν δεῖξον σεαυτόν
Mk. 5, 19 ἀλλὰ λέγει αὐτῷ	Lk. 8, 38 λέγων
Mk. 8, 36 ὠφελεῖ ἄνθρωπον κερδῆσαι	Lk. 9, 25 ὠφελεῖται ἄνθρωπος κερδήσας
Mk. 9, 6 οὐ γὰρ ᾔδει	Lk. 9, 33 μὴ εἰδώς
Mk. 10, 17 τί ποιήσω ἵνα . . . κληρονομήσω	Lk. 18, 18 τί ποιήσας . . . κληρονομήσω
Mk. 14, 10 Ἰούδας . . . ὁ εἷς τῶν δώδεκα	Lk. 22, 3 Ἰούδαν . . . ὄντα ἐκ τοῦ ἀριθμοῦ τῶν δώδεκα

But Mark 5, 25–27, had too many participles even for Luke, and by omitting some and by using a relative clause he avoids the fault of his source (Luke 8, 43, 44):

Mark		Luke	
5, 25	καὶ γυνὴ οὖσα ἐν ῥύσει . . .	8, 43	καὶ γυνὴ οὖσα ἐν ῥύσει . . .
5, 26	καὶ πολλὰ παθοῦσα . . .		
	καὶ δαπανήσασα . . .		ἥτις . . . προσαναλώσασα . . .
	καὶ μηδὲν ὠφεληθεῖσα		οὐκ ἴσχυσεν . . . θεραπευθῆναι
	ἀλλὰ . . . ἐλθοῦσα		
5, 27	ἀκούσασα . . .		
	ἐλθοῦσα . . .	8, 44	προσελθοῦσα . . .
	ἥψατο κ.τ.λ.		ἥψατο κ.τ.λ.

ἵνα and ὥστε

In dealing with clauses already dependent or semi-dependent in Mark, Luke shows a tendency to tighten the relation of the clause to the main sentence. Here he is also resisting the loose structure of post-classical Greek. The free use of *ἵνα* clauses is a feature of Hellenistic Greek, but they are distinctly looser than the infinitive with which Luke frequently displaced them. The *ὥστε* construction is notoriously loose, and this too Luke seems partially to avoid. Indirect questions are frequently modified so that their relation as substantive clauses may be made more clear. A noun, an infinitive, a relative clause, may make a good substitute; but more often Luke converts the question into a substantive by prefixing the neuter article. This of course applies also to direct questions which he wishes to incorporate in the main sentence.

ἵνα is replaced by an infinitive thus:

Mk. 3, 10	ἐπιπίπτειν ἵνα αὐτοῦ ἅψωνται	Lk. 6, 19	ἐζήτουν ἅπτεσθαι αὐτοῦ
Mk. 5, 12	πέμψον . . . ἵνα εἰσέλθωμεν	Lk. 8, 32	ἐπιτρέψῃ . . . εἰσελθεῖν
Mk. 5, 18	παρεκάλει . . . ἵνα . . . ᾖ	Lk. 8, 38	ἐδεῖτο . . . εἶναι
Mk. 5, 43	διεστείλατο . . . ἵνα μηδεὶς γνοῖ	Lk. 8, 56	παρήγγειλεν . . . μηδενὶ εἰπεῖν
Mk. 6, 41	ἐδίδου . . . ἵνα παρατιθῶσιν	Lk. 9, 16	ἐδίδου . . . παραθεῖναι
Mk. 8, 30	ἐπετίμησεν ἵνα λέγωσιν	Lk. 9, 21	ἐπετιμήσας παρήγγειλεν λέγειν
Mk. 14, 38	ἵνα μὴ εἰσέλθητε	Lk. 22, 40	μὴ εἰσελθεῖν, but cf. vs. 46
Mk. 15, 21	ἵνα ἄρῃ	Lk. 23, 26	φέρειν
Compare also:			
Mk. 1, 44	ὅρα εἴπῃς	Lk. 5, 14	παρήγγειλεν . . . εἰπεῖν

ἵνα disappears in other ways:

Mt. 7, 1	ἵνα μὴ κριθῆτε	Lk. 6, 37	καὶ οὐ μὴ κριθῆτε [Q]
Mk. 4, 22	ἐὰν μὴ ἵνα φανερωθῇ	Lk. 8, 17	ὃ οὐ φανερὸν γενήσεται
Mk. 4, 22	ἀλλ' ἵνα ἔλθῃ εἰς φανερόν	Lk. 8, 17	ὃ οὐ μὴ . . . εἰς φανερὸν ἔλθῃ [1]

[1] This construction may, however, be due to Luke's conflation of Mark with Q (Matt. 10, 26 = Luke 12, 2); note γνωσθῇ.

Mk. 10, 17 τί ποιήσω ἵνα κληρονομήσω	Lk. 18, 18 τί ποιήσας . . . κληρονομήσω
Mk. 14, 10 ἵνα παραδοῖ	Lk. 22, 4 τὸ πῶς . . . παραδῷ (but cf. Mk. 14, 11)
Mk. 15, 15 παρέδωκεν . . . ἵνα σταυρωθῇ,	Lk. 23, 25 παρέδωκεν τῷ θελήματι αὐτῶν

For the complete omission of clauses with ἵνα, see page 90.

In modern Greek the infinitive has succumbed entirely to ἵνα (νά). Luke's resistance to the growing use of ἵνα is shown in Acts, where it is comparatively infrequent, and even in its proper use less frequent than ὅπως. See J. Viteau, *Étude sur le grec du Nouveau Testament*, Paris, 1893, pp. 74, 176; Blass, *Grammar of N. T. Greek*, § 69, 2 *sub fin.*

ὥστε is removed in Luke's editing thus:

Mk. 1, 27 ὥστε συνζητεῖν	Lk. 4, 36 καὶ συνελάλουν
Mk. 2, 12 ὥστε δοξάζειν	Lk. 5, 26 καὶ ἐδόξαζον
Mk. 2, 28 ὥστε	Lk. 6, 5 omits ὥστε
Mk. 3, 10 ὥστε ἐπιπίπτειν . . . ἵνα ἅψωνται	Lk. 6, 19 ἐζήτουν ἅπτεσθαι
Mk. 4, 37 ὥστε γεμίζεσθαι	Lk. 8, 23 καὶ συνεπληροῦντο
Mt. 12, 22 ὥστε τὸν κωφὸν λαλεῖν	Lk. 11, 14 ἐλάλησεν ὁ κωφός [Q]
Mt. 23, 31 ὥστε	Lk. 11, 48 ἄρα [Q]
Mk. 4, 32 ὥστε (so Matt. 13, 32)	Lk. 13, 19 καί [perhaps from Q]

At Mark 1, 45; 2, 2; 3, 10; 3, 20; 4, 1; 9, 26, the whole clause containing ὥστε has no parallel in Luke. It is interesting that in all these passages except the last the subject is the same, — the uncomfortable results of Jesus' popularity. Luke's omission of these clauses is due probably to other reasons than those of language. The only two cases in Luke's gospel of ὥστε expressing result have a similar connection — the embarrassing effects of Jesus' miracles (Luke 5, 7 ὥστε βυθίζεσθαι αὐτὰ [τὰ πλοῖα]) or popularity (Luke 12, 1 ὥστε καταπατεῖν ἀλλήλους). See also p. 92.

ὥστε is comparatively rare in Luke and Acts, and either conveys the idea of purpose or indicates a very close connection of result. The use of ὥστε to begin a new sentence (in the sense of *quare, itaque;* see Winer-Moulton, p. 377) is not found in Luke or Acts. See Harnack, *Sayings*, p. 102; " St. Luke also avoids ὥστε in the sense of *itaque.*"

Questions

Indirect questions in Mark often receive in Luke a definite substantive construction. They are made articular thus:

Mk. 9, 34 τίς μείζων	Lk. 9, 46 τὸ τίς ἂν εἴη μείζων αὐτῶν. Cf. Lk. 22, 24 τὸ τίς αὐτῶν δοκεῖ εἶναι μείζων
Mk. 11, 18 πῶς αὐτὸν ἀπολέσωσιν	Cf. Lk. 19, 48 τὸ τί ποιήσωσιν
Mk. 14, 1 πῶς ἀποκτείνωσι	Lk. 22, 2 τὸ πῶς ἀνέλωσιν
Mk. 14, 11 πῶς παραδοῖ	Lk. 22, 4 τὸ πῶς παραδῷ (cf. also vs. 6)
Mk. 14, 19 μήτι ἐγώ	Lk. 22, 23 τὸ τίς ἄρα εἴη κ.τ.λ.

Questions are altered in other ways: [1]

Mk. 2, 25 *τί ἐποίησεν Δαυείδ*	Lk. 6, 3 *ὃ ἐποίησεν Δαυείδ*
Mk. 5, 14 *τί ἐστιν τὸ γεγονός*	Lk. 8, 35 *τὸ γεγονός*
Mk. 6, 36 *τί φάγωσι*	Lk. 9, 12 *ἐπισιτισμόν*
Mk. 9, 6 *τί ἀποκριθῇ*	Lk. 9, 33 *ὃ λέγει*
Mk. 11, 18 *πῶς αὐτὸν ἀπολέσωσιν*	Lk. 19, 47 *αὐτὸν ἀπολέσαι*
Mk. 13,11 *τί λαλήσητε*	Lk. 21, 14 *ἀπολογηθῆναι* [2]
Mk. 14, 11 *πῶς αὐτὸν εὐκαίρως παραδοῖ*	Lk. 22, 6 *εὐκαιρίαν* (so Matt. 26, 16) *τοῦ παραδοῦναι αὐτόν*
Mk. 14, 36 *οὐ τί ἐγὼ θέλω ἀλλὰ τί σύ*	Lk. 22, 42 *μὴ τὸ θέλημά μου ἀλλὰ τὸ σόν*
Mk. 14, 68 *τί λέγεις*	Cf. Lk. 22, 60 *ὃ λέγεις*

For the complete omission of questions, see pp. 81, 82.

ὅτι

ὅτι is used by Luke several times in place of *γάρ* or where in Mark there is asyndeton to secure closer relation between two sentences.

Mk. 1, 22 *ἦν γὰρ διδάσκων αὐτοὺς ὡς ἐξουσίαν ἔχων*	Lk. 4, 32 *ὅτι ἐν ἐξουσίᾳ ἦν ὁ λόγος αὐτοῦ*
Mk. 1, 27 *τί ἐστιν τοῦτο; διδαχὴ καινὴ κατ' ἐξουσίαν*	Lk. 4, 36 *τίς ὁ λόγος οὗτος ὅτι ἐν ἐξουσίᾳ*
Mk. 1, 38 *εἰς τοῦτο γὰρ ἐξῆλθον*	Lk. 4, 43 *ὅτι ἐπὶ τοῦτο ἀπεστάλην*
Compare	
Mk. 6, 35 f. *ἔρημός ἐστιν ὁ τόπος . . . ἀπόλυσον αὐτούς κ.τ.λ.*	Lk. 9, 12 *ἀπόλυσον τὸν ὄχλον . . . ὅτι ὧδε ἐν ἐρήμῳ τόπῳ ἐσμέν*

According to Hawkins, *Horae Synopticae*, the use of *ὅτι recitantis* is characteristic of Mark. The more certain cases (p. 28, following Bruder) number in Matt. eight, in Mark twenty-four, in Luke thirteen; but if some less certain cases are included, the figures become for Matt. fourteen, Mark thirty-four, Luke twenty-eight (p. 41).

[1] In view of this practice of Luke, it may be doubtful whether the difference between Luke 10, 22, *τίς ἐστιν ὁ υἱὸς . . . καὶ τίς ἐστιν ὁ πατήρ*, and Matt. 11, 27, *τὸν υἱὸν . . . τὸν πατέρα*, is due to Luke's literary method. Harnack, *Sayings*, p. 20, compares Luke's use of the direct question, *τίς ἐστιν οὗτος* and a relative clause, in Luke 5, 21; 7, 49; 8, 25; 9, 9, but in at least two of these cases the question can be attributed directly to the source, Mark 2, 7; 4, 41. Better illustrations would be Luke 13, 25, 27 *οὐκ οἶδα ὑμᾶς πόθεν ἐστέ;* 20, 7 *μὴ εἰδέναι πόθεν* (cf. Matt. 25, 12; 7, 23; Mark 11, 33), and especially Luke 8, 9 *ἐπηρώτων. . . . τίς αὕτη εἴη ἡ παραβολή* for Mark 4, 10 *ἠρώτων . . . τὰς παραβολάς*. Compare Luke 19, 3 *ἐζήτει ἰδεῖν τὸν Ἰησοῦν τίς ἐστιν.*

[2] But cf. Luke 12, 11 *πῶς ἢ τί ἀπολογήσησθε ἢ τί εἴπητε.* = Matt. 10, 19 *πῶς ἢ τί λαλήσητε.*

In the following cases ὅτι recitative of Mark is omitted by Luke:

Mk. 1, 40 λέγων αὐτῷ ὅτι ἐὰν θέλῃς	Lk. 5, 12 λέγων, κύριε, ἐὰν θέλῃς
Mk. 6, 35 ἔλεγον ὅτι ἔρημός ἐστιν	Lk. 9, 12 εἶπον αὐτῷ· ἀπόλυσον
Mk. 8, 28 εἶπαν ὅτι Ἰωάννην	Lk. 9, 19 εἶπαν· Ἰωάννην
Mk. 9, 31 ἔλεγεν αὐτοῖς ὅτι ὁ υἱός	Lk. 9, 43, 44 εἶπεν . . . ὁ υἱός
Mk. 10, 32, 33 ἤρξατο αὐτοῖς λέγειν . . . ὅτι ἰδοὺ ἀναβαίνομεν	Lk. 18, 31 εἶπεν . . . ἰδοὺ ἀναβαίνομεν
Mk. 12, 6 λέγων ὅτι ἐντραπήσονται	Lk. 20, 13 εἶπεν . . . ἐντραπήσονται
Mk. 12, 7 εἶπαν ὅτι οὗτός ἐστιν	Lk. 20, 14 λέγοντες· οὗτός ἐστιν
Mk. 12, 19 ἔγραψεν ἡμῖν ὅτι ἐάν τινος	Lk. 20, 28 ἔγραψεν ἡμῖν· ἐάν τινος
Mk. 13, 6 λέγοντες ὅτι ἐγώ εἰμι	Lk. 21, 8 λέγοντες ἐγώ εἰμι
Mk. 14, 14 εἴπατε . . . ὅτι ὁ διδάσκαλος λέγει	Lk. 22, 11 ἐρεῖτε . . . λέγει σοι ὁ διδάσκαλος
Mk. 14, 69 λέγειν . . . ὅτι οὗτος	Lk. 22, 59 λέγων . . . οὗτος
Mk. 14, 71 ὀμνύναι ὅτι οὐκ οἶδα	Lk. 22, 60 εἶπεν . . . ἄνθρωπε, οὐκ οἶδα

Similarly, Matt. 8, 2 omits ὅτι of Mark 1, 40, and so in all the other cases in Mark here cited (except Mark 14, 71, 72, where Matt. 26, 74, 75 retains the ὅτι), as well as in Mark 1, 15; 5, 28; 6, 18; 8, 4; 14, 27. As Matthew's aversion to ὅτι in this use is as strong as Luke's, if not stronger, the cases of ὅτι found in either gospel in passages based on Q are most likely preserved from that source though changed by the other evangelist. Here the balance is, as we should expect, about even.

Matt. 4, 4 γέγραπται· οὐκ ἐπ' ἄρτῳ	Lk. 4, 4 γέγραπται ὅτι οὐκ ἐπ' ἄρτῳ [Q]
Matt. 4, 6 γέγραπται γὰρ ὅτι	Lk. 4, 10 γέγραπται γὰρ ὅτι [Q]
Matt. 6, 29 λέγω δὲ ὑμῖν ὅτι οὐδὲ Σ.	Lk. 12, 27 λέγω δὲ ὑμῖν· οὐδὲ Σ. [Q]
Matt. 23, 39 λέγω γὰρ ὑμῖν· οὐ μή με ἴδητε	Lk. 13, 35 λέγω ὑμῖν ὅτι (om. ℵBD*al.*) οὐ μὴ ἴδητέ με [Q]

Yet Harnack (*Sayings*, p. 140) rejects ὅτι in Luke 4, 4 as "Lukan" (p. 45), and in reconstructing the text of Q brackets the ὅτι of Matt. 6, 29. He ignores the ὅτι which some codd. and edd. read in Luke 13, 35 (Tisch., but not Westcott and Hort, v. Soden).

But the ὅτι recitative of Mark 2, 12; 3, 11; 5, 35; 14, 72 is retained in Luke 5, 26; 4, 41; 8, 49; and 22, 61. In Luke 8, 42 the recitative ὅτι of Mark 5, 23 becomes causal (as also perhaps in Mark 6, 35 = Luke 9, 12), while in Luke 9, 22 εἰπὼν ὅτι takes the place of ἤρξατο διδάσκειν αὐτοὺς ὅτι (Mark 8, 31).

In one or two cases Luke adds the recitative to Mark.

Mk. 2, 27 καὶ ἔλεγεν αὐτοῖς . . . 28 ὥστε κύριός ἐστιν	Lk. 6, 5 καὶ ἔλεγεν αὐτοῖς ὅτι κύριός ἐστιν
Mk. 11, 3 εἴπατε· ὁ κύριος	Lk. 19, 31 ἐρεῖτε ὅτι ὁ κύριος

(Contrast the reverse in the similar passage Mark 14, 14 = Luke 22, 11; here, however, ὅτι may be causal, answering διατί; so also 19, 34.)

Mk. 11, 31 λέγοντες ἐὰν εἴπωμεν — Lk. 20, 5 λέγοντες ὅτι ἐὰν εἴπωμεν

(Here in both gospels direct quotation follows εἴπωμεν.)

ἐάν and καθώς

From the changes made by Luke in the other particles which introduce subordinate clauses few if any definite conclusions can be drawn.

Thus Harnack's repeated statement that "St. Luke, as is often the case, has written εἰ for ἐάν," can hardly be sustained on the basis of two passages derived from Q.

Matt. 17, 20 ἐὰν ἔχητε πίστιν ὡς κόκκον σινάπεως, ἐρεῖτε — Lk. 17, 6 εἰ ἔχετε πίστιν ὡς κόκκον σινάπεως, ἐλέγετε ἄν [Q]

Matt. 5, 46 ἐὰν γὰρ ἀγαπήσητε — Lk. 6, 32 καὶ εἰ ἀγαπᾶτε [Q]

For Luke nowhere appears to change the ἐάν of Mark to εἰ, so that in the above passages the alternative is quite as probable that Matthew has changed the εἰ to ἐάν. In Matt. 21, 21, which like Matt. 17, 20 has ἐὰν ἔχητε πίστιν followed by a future indicative, the ἐάν is from Matthew, not from his source (Mark 11, 22 f.). Cf. ἐάν in Matt. 6, 14, 15; 16, 26 with Mark 11, 25, [26]; 8, 36.[1] See Harnack, *Sayings*, p. 91; cf. p. 62: "The εἰ here [Luke 6, 32] and in the following verse [Luke 6, 33 D] is certainly secondary. . . . Also in other passages St. Luke has changed ἐάν into εἰ," and p. 28, "ἐάν is very frequent in Q, and St. Luke has very often changed it." So Nicolardot, *Les procédés de rédaction*, p. 149, following Harnack.

Is ἐάν to be preferred to εἰ because, as Harnack says (p. 159), "ἐάν is twice as frequent as εἰ" in Q? The same ratio holds in Mark, and no doubt in many other books. The occurrence of these words is often due to subject matter, quite apart from personal preference. The whole thought of the condition is affected by the difference, as in the parallels Matt. 17, 20 = Luke 17, 6. The only other case in point is

Matt. 10, 13 ἐὰν δὲ μὴ ᾖ ἀξία [ἡ οἰκία], ἡ εἰρήνη ὑμῶν πρὸς ὑμᾶς ἐπιστραφήτω — Lk. 10, 6 εἰ δὲ μήγε, [ἡ εἰρήνη ὑμῶν] ἐφ' ὑμᾶς ἀνακάμψει

[1] In the only other parallel with Mark that comes into consideration here Matt. 18, 8, 9, (= 5, 29, 30) may have substituted εἰ for ἐάν (Mk. 9, 43–47).

But this instance is made less significant because of the idiomatic εἰ δὲ μήγε ("otherwise"), and the wide variation in wording. Both Luke and Matthew retain ἐάν in the preceding antithetical member.

Possibly a certain preference for καθώς may be seen in the following list, though the cases again are mainly from Q, except two from Mark which cancel each other:

Mk. 1, 2 καθώς	Lk. 3, 4 ὡς
Mk. 1, 44 ἅ	Lk. 5, 14 καθώς
Mt. 7, 12 πάντα ὅσα	Lk. 6, 31 καθώς [Q]
Mt. 5, 48 ὡς	Lk. 6, 36 καθώς [Q]
Mt. 12, 40 ὥσπερ	Lk. 11, 30 καθώς [Q]
Mt. 24, 37 ὥσπερ	Lk. 17, 26 καθώς [Q]

Harnack (*Sayings*, pp. 23, 107) also thinks that ὥσπερ in the last two instances has been changed by Luke because "he is not fond of ὥσπερ—on the other hand, he uses καθώς 16 + 12 times, while in St. Matthew it occurs only three times." By similar reasoning as good a case could be made out for the belief that καθώς was in the original Q and was changed by Matthew to ὥσπερ; for ὥσπερ is a characteristic word of Matthew (Hawkins, *Horae Synopticae*, p. 7), and is actually substituted for καὶ γάρ (Mark 10, 45) in Matt. 20, 28, while Luke uses it only three times in Acts, in the Gospel once, in a passage where it comes from Q (17, 24 = Matt. 24, 27), and possibly in one other passage (18, 11 *v.l.*).

καί, δέ, μέν

The most obvious fact about Luke's use of co-ordinate conjunctions discovered by comparison with Mark is his preference for δέ over καί. Δέ belongs to the periodic form of writing; καί is characteristic of the λέξις εἰρομένη. It is colloquial, but in Mark may be due sometimes to Semitic idiom, though it is also frequent in Hellenistic and Modern Greek (see J. H. Moulton, *Grammar of New Testament Greek*, I, 12; Thumb, *Hellenismus*, 129; Robertson, *Grammar of the Greek New Testament*, p. 94.) The comparative frequency of καί and δέ in Mark and Luke has been stated in various ways, as by Hawkins, *Horae Synopticae*, p. 120 f.

But the most concrete proof of Luke's preference is shown in parallel passages where Luke has substituted δέ for καί in Mark without much other change of context:

Mark	Luke
Mk. 1, 9 καὶ ἐγένετο	Lk. 3, 21 ἐγένετο δέ
Mk. 1, 38 καὶ λέγει	Lk. 4, 43 ὁ δὲ εἶπεν
Mk. 2, 8 καὶ ἐπιγνούς	Lk. 5, 22 ἐπιγνοὺς δέ
Mk. 2, 18 καὶ λέγουσιν	Lk. 5, 33 οἱ δὲ εἶπαν
Mk. 2, 19 καὶ εἶπεν	Lk. 5, 34 ὁ δὲ εἶπεν
Mk. 2, 23 καὶ ἐγένετο	Lk. 6, 1 ἐγένετο δέ
Mk. 2, 24 καὶ ἔλεγον	Lk. 6, 2 τινὲς δὲ εἶπαν
Mk. 3, 2 καὶ παρετήρουν	Lk. 6, 7 παρετηροῦντο δέ
Mk. 3, 3 καὶ λέγει	Lk. 6, 8 εἶπεν δέ
Mk. 3, 4 καὶ λέγει	Lk. 6, 9 εἶπεν δέ
Mk. 4, 11 καὶ ἔλεγεν	Lk. 8, 10 ὁ δὲ εἶπεν
Mk. 4, 39 καὶ διεγερθείς	Lk. 8, 24 ὁ δὲ διεγερθείς
Mk. 4, 40 καὶ εἶπεν	Lk. 8, 25 εἶπεν δέ
Mk. 5, 2 καὶ ἐξελθόντος αὐτοῦ	Lk. 8, 27 ἐξελθόντι δὲ αὐτῷ
Mk. 5, 6 καὶ ἰδὼν τὸν Ἰησοῦν	Lk. 8, 28 ἰδὼν δὲ τὸν Ἰησοῦν
Mk. 5, 9 καὶ ἐπηρώτα αὐτόν	Lk. 8, 30 ἐπηρώτησεν δὲ αὐτόν
Mk. 5, 13 καὶ ἐξελθόντα	Lk. 8, 33 ἐξελθόντα δέ
Mk. 5, 14 καὶ ἦλθον	Lk. 8, 35 ἐξῆλθον δέ
Mk. 5, 41 καὶ κρατήσας	Lk. 8, 54 αὐτὸς δὲ κρατήσας
Mk. 6, 12 καὶ ἐξελθόντες	Lk. 9, 6 ἐξερχόμενοι δέ
Mk. 6, 14 καὶ ἤκουσεν	Lk. 9, 7 ἤκουσεν δέ
Mk. 6, 44 καὶ ἦσαν	Lk. 9, 14 ἦσαν δέ
Mk. 6, 41 καὶ λαβών	Lk. 9, 16 λαβὼν δέ
Mk. 8, 28 καὶ ἄλλοι	Lk. 9, 19 ἄλλοι δέ
Mk. 8, 36 καὶ ζημιωθῆναι τὴν ψυχήν	Lk. 9, 25 ἑαυτὸν δὲ . . . ζημιωθείς
Mk. 10, 13 καὶ προσέφερον	Lk. 18, 15 προσέφερον δέ
Mk. 10, 32 καὶ παραλαβών	Lk. 18, 31 παραλαβὼν δέ
Mk. 11, 4 καὶ ἀπῆλθον	Lk. 19, 32 ἀπελθόντες δέ
Mk. 11, 31 καὶ διελογίζοντο	Lk. 20, 5 οἱ δὲ συνελογίσαντο
Mk. 12, 1 καὶ ἤρξατο	Lk. 20, 9 ἤρξατο δέ
Mk. 14, 54 καὶ ὁ Πέτρος	Lk. 22, 54 ὁ δὲ Πέτρος
Mk. 15, 2 καὶ ἐπηρώτησεν . . . ὁ Πειλᾶτος	Lk. 23, 3 ὁ δὲ Πειλᾶτος ἠρώτησεν
Mk. 15, 24 καὶ διαμερίζονται	Lk. 23, 34 διαμεριζόμενοι δέ
Mk. 15, 26 καὶ ἦν	Lk. 23, 38 ἦν δὲ καί
Mk. 15, 38 καὶ τὸ καταπέτασμα ἐσχίσθη	Lk. 23, 45 ἐσχίσθη δὲ τὸ καταπέτασμα
Mk. 16, 5 καὶ εἰσελθοῦσαι	Lk. 24, 3 εἰσελθοῦσαι δέ

Similarly in Q passages we find δέ in Luke for καί in Matthew, although Matthew also often changes Mark's καί to δέ.

Matthew	Luke
Mt. 7, 26 καὶ πᾶς ὁ ἀκούων	Lk. 6, 49 ὁ δὲ ἀκούσας [Q]
Mt. 12, 26 καὶ εἰ ὁ σατανᾶς (Cf. Mk. 3, 26)	Lk. 11, 18 εἰ δὲ καὶ ὁ σατανᾶς [Q]
Mt. 12, 27 καὶ εἰ ἐγώ	Lk. 11, 19 εἰ δὲ ἐγώ [Q]

The proportion between καί and δέ is not however the same in all parts of Luke's writing, just as it varies in Mark and in the parts of the LXX as shown by Hawkins; in particular δέ is much more frequent in Acts than in the Gospel. Harnack explains this difference as due to difference of sources, or rather on the assumption that the frequent καί in Luke is due to the use of Mark, whereas in Acts the author is writing more freely (perhaps without any written sources). But our list shows that Luke considerably reduces the instances of καί in Mark when using it as a source; and we may further discover that in other parts of Luke, including some which Harnack considers to have been freely composed by Luke himself (Luke 1, 5–2, 52), the καί is relatively as frequent, or more frequent, than in parts based on Mark.

Harnack (*Luke the Physician*, p. 90, n. 1) says; "Vogel (" Charakteristik des Lukas," 2 Aufl., 1899, p. 32) has discussed St. Luke's various methods of beginning a sentence, but he has not drawn the final conclusion. If, with him, we compare 100 beginnings of sentences in the gospel with a similar number in the second part of Acts we arrive at the following result:

	καί	δέ	τε	other particles	without particle
Gospel	50	36	1	6	7
Acts	16	51	9	16	8

Accordingly καί preponderates in the gospel by three times. If, however, one subtracts all the cases in which the καί is derived from St. Mark, then the relation of καί to δέ is much the same in both writings."

The following table, illustrating the relative frequency of καί and δέ as particles introducing a sentence, is based on passages taken at random from the parts of Luke derived from Mark and those of other origin. Of course the figures are subject to some slight change by difference of opinion about division of sentences and about readings.

1. Passages the source of which is Mark

Luke	5, 17–39	6, 1–19	8, 40–56	9, 1–50	totals
καί	15	8	16	18	57
δέ	6	10	42	35	93

2. Passages of other origin

Luke	2, 1–52	14, 1–35	15, 1–32	16, 1–31	
καί	28	12	8	9	57
δέ	7	8	13	15	43

Apparently the ratio of καί to δέ is twice as great in the first class of passages as in the second; so that the greater frequency of καί in the gospel as a whole than in Acts can hardly be due to Mark, as Harnack supposed. But as Wernle (p. 21) observes regarding Luke's substitution of *δέ* for *καί* in Mark, "von einer strengen Regel lässt sich nicht reden."

In regard to *καὶ γάρ* Harnack makes a similar statement (*Luke the Physician*, p. 95): "*καὶ γάρ* occurs only once in the Acts (19, 40); in the Gospel it is more frequent, because derived from the sources." Here again his suggestion is not sustained by the facts, for only twice is *καὶ γάρ* taken by Luke from his source, viz. Luke 7, 8 (= Matt. 8, 9); Luke 22, 59 (= Mark 14, 70 = Matt. 26, 72). It occurs twice in passages peculiar to Luke (1, 66; 22, 37), the former of which Harnack believes to have been written by Luke without Greek sources, and besides these only in passages parallel to Matthew, where it is more likely that Luke has introduced it into his sources than taken it over from them. In fact, this is the view that Harnack himself elsewhere takes of these occurrences (*Sayings*, pp. 62, 65). He says: "*καὶ γάρ* is Lukan (*vide* the fifth petition of the Lord's Prayer in St. Luke, where St. Matthew has *ὡς καί*; in St. Matthew *καὶ γάρ* occurs twice, in St. Luke's gospel nine times."

The nine instances are as follows:

	Lk. 1, 66 *καὶ γὰρ χεὶρ κυρίου ἦν μετ' αὐτοῦ*
Mt. 5, 46 *οὐχὶ καὶ οἱ τελῶναι*	Lk. 6, 32 *καὶ γὰρ οἱ ἁμαρτωλοί* [Q]
Mt. 5, 47 *καὶ ἐάν*	Lk. 6, 33a *καὶ γὰρ* [ℵB; om. *γάρ* rell.] *ἐάν* [Q]
Mt. 5, 47 *οὐχὶ καὶ οἱ ἐθνικοί*	Lk. 6, 33b *καὶ γὰρ* [ℵBΛ syr. sin. om.] [Q]
	Lk. 6, 34 *καὶ γὰρ* [ℵBLΞ om.]
Mt. 8, 9 *καὶ γὰρ ἐγὼ ἄνθρωπος*	Lk. 7, 8 *καὶ γὰρ ἐγὼ ἄνθρωπος* [Q]
Mt. 6, 12 *ὡς καὶ ἡμεῖς ἀφήκαμεν*	Lk. 11, 4 *καὶ γὰρ αὐτοὶ ἀφίομεν* [Q]
	Lk. 22, 37 *καὶ γὰρ τὸ περὶ ἐμοῦ τέλος ἔχει*
Mk. 14, 70 *καὶ γὰρ Γαλιλαῖος εἶ* (cf. Matt. 26, 73 *καὶ γὰρ ἡ λαλιά σου δῆλόν σε ποιεῖ*)	Lk. 22, 59 *καὶ γὰρ Γαλιλαῖός ἐστιν*

μέν in contrasts with *δέ* may be considered a test of style, since it is a specifically Greek idiom. See Norden, *Antike Kunstprosa*, p. 25, n. 3. Luke however shows little superiority in the use of this word. It occurs in Mark five times, in Matthew twenty, in Luke ten times. Of these ten instances none is a correction of Mark or Q (except in the pronominal use of *ὃν μὲν . . . ὃν δέ* in Luke 23, 33, cf. Mark 15, 27 *ἕνα . . . καὶ ἕνα*), but, as far as those sources indicate Luke's usage, he simply keeps μέν when they supply it. Thus,

Luke 3, 16 ἐγὼ μὲν . . . βαπτίζω . . . , ἔρχεται δὲ κ.τ.λ. Cf. Matt. 3, 11 [Q]; contrast Mk. 1, 8.
Luke 10, 2 ὁ μὲν θερισμὸς πολύς, οἱ δὲ ἐργάται ὀλίγοι Cf. Matt. 9, 37 [Q]
Luke 22, 22 ὁ υἱὸς μὲν τοῦ ἀνθρώπου . . . πορεύεται, πλὴν οὐαί Cf. Mark 14, 21 (where however Luke has exchanged Mark's δέ for the less regular πλήν).

In Acts μέν occurs more frequently (nearly fifty times), but in more than three-fifths of the occurrences it is the μέν, μὲν οὖν *solitarium*, of doubtful literary excellence.

δὲ καί is a favorite combination in Luke. In the following cases it occurs in Luke but not in the parallels:[1]

Mt. 3, 10 ἤδη δὲ ἡ ἀξίνη	Lk. 3, 9 ἤδη δὲ καὶ ἡ ἀξίνη [Q]
Mt. 8, 21 ἕτερος δὲ . . . εἶπεν	Lk. 9, 61 εἶπεν δὲ καὶ ἕτερος [Q]
Mt. 12, 26 καὶ εἰ ὁ σατανᾶς (cf. Mk. 3, 26)	Lk. 11, 18 εἰ δὲ καὶ ὁ σατανᾶς [Q]
Mt. 5, 13 ἐὰν δὲ τὸ ἅλας μωρανθῇ (cf. Mk. 9, 50)	Lk. 14, 34 ἐὰν δὲ καὶ τὸ ἅλας μωρανθῇ [Q]
Mk. 10, 13 καὶ προσέφερον αὐτῷ παιδία	Lk. 18, 15 προσέφερον δὲ αὐτῷ καὶ τὰ βρέφη
Mk. 12, 4 κἀκεῖνον	Lk. 20, 11 οἱ δὲ κἀκεῖνον
Mk. 12, 5 κἀκεῖνον	Lk. 20, 12 οἱ δὲ καὶ τοῦτον
Mk. 12, 21 ὡσαύτως· 22 καὶ οἱ ἑπτά	Lk. 20, 31 ὡσαύτως δὲ καὶ οἱ ἑπτά
Mk. 13, 12 καὶ παραδώσει	Lk. 21, 16 παραδοθήσεσθε δὲ καί
Mk. 15, 27 καὶ σὺν αὐτῷ σταυροῦσιν δύο λῃστάς	Cf. Lk. 23, 32 ἤγοντο δὲ καὶ ἕτεροι δύο κακοῦργοι σὺν αὐτῷ ἀναιρεθῆναι
Mk. 15, 29–36	Lk. 23, 35 ἐξεμυκτήριζον δὲ καὶ (א *al.* om.) οἱ ἄρχοντες (cf. p. 103) Lk. 23, 36 ἐνέπαιξαν δὲ αὐτῷ καὶ οἱ στρατιῶται
Mk. 15, 26 καὶ ἦν ἡ ἐπιγραφή	Lk. 23, 38 ἦν δὲ καὶ ἐπιγραφή

Καί is used by Luke in the apodosis of relative or conditional clauses:[2]

Mk. 2, 21 εἰ δὲ μή, αἴρει . . . τὸ καινὸν κ.τ.λ.	Lk. 5, 36 εἰ δὲ μήγε, καὶ τὸ καινὸν κ.τ.λ.
Mt. 12, 40 ὥσπερ γὰρ ἦν Ἰωνᾶς . . . οὕτως ἔσται ὁ υἱὸς τοῦ ἀνθρώπου	Lk. 11 30, καθὼς γὰρ ἐγένετο Ἰωνᾶς . . . οὕτως ἔσται καὶ ὁ υἱὸς τοῦ ἀνθρώπου [Q]

[1] The *textus receptus* carries further this process in Luke. See for example 6, 6; 18, 1; 22, 68; cf. 21, 2 and Matt. 25, 22; 26, 35.

[2] In Matt. 6, 21 = Luke 12, 34 the MSS. of both Gospels read καί in the apodosis except B in Matthew.

Mt. 6, 22 ἐὰν ᾖ ὁ ὀφθαλμός σου ἁπλοῦς, ὅλον τὸ σῶμα	Lk. 11, 34 ὅταν ὁ ὀφθαλμός σου ἁπλοῦς ᾖ, καὶ ὅλον τὸ σῶμα [Q]
Mt. 6, 23 ἐὰν δὲ ὁ ὀφθαλμός σου πονηρὸς ᾖ, ὅλον τὸ σῶμα	Lk. 11, 34 ἐπὰν δὲ πονηρὸς ᾖ, καὶ τὸ σῶμα [Q]
Mt, 24, 28 ὅπου ἐὰν ᾖ τὸ πτῶμα, ἐκεῖ συναχθήσονται οἱ ἀετοί	Lk. 17, 37 ὅπου τὸ σῶμα, ἐκεῖ καὶ οἱ ἀετοὶ ἐπισυναχθήσονται [Q]

πλήν

In three cases Luke seems to introduce πλήν (cf. p. 123, note):

Mt. 6, 33 ζητεῖτε δέ	Lk. 12, 31 πλὴν ζητεῖτε [Q]
Mk. 14, 21 οὐαὶ δὲ τῷ ἀνθρώπῳ	Lk. 22, 22 πλὴν οὐαὶ τῷ ἀνθρώπῳ [Q]
Mk. 14, 36 ἀλλ' οὐ τί ἐγὼ θέλω ἀλλὰ τί σύ	Lk. 22, 42 πλὴν μὴ τὸ θέλημά μου ἀλλὰ τὸ σὸν γινέσθω

(In the last case Matt. 26, 39 also has πλήν, perhaps an independent correction made on account of the following ἀλλά.)

πλήν is a favorite conjunction of Luke's Gospel, occurring fifteen times in all. It is not found in Mark, but was probably in Q. See Matt. 11, 22 = Luke 10, 14; Matt. 18, 7 = Luke 17, 1 ℵBDL.

Bartlet in *Oxford Studies in the Synoptic Problem*, p. 332, speaking of Matt. 26, 64, says: " πλὴν λέγω ὑμῖν is a Q phrase, found also in Matt. 11, 22, 24 (where Luke 10, 11, 14 also has πλήν, a particle found only in Sayings in Luke's Gospel, while in Acts and Mark it occurs only as a preposition, save as πλὴν ὅτι in Acts 20, 23), 18, 7 (= Luke 17, 1) and 26, 39 (= Luke 22, 42)." But the influence of Q which Bartlet tries to find in Matt. 26, 39 and 26, 64 is not certain, and in the former case not πλὴν λέγω ὑμῖν but only πλήν is found.

Asyndeton

Asyndeton is perhaps even more carefully avoided by Luke than parataxis.[1] The most common method of correcting Mark is by means of καί, γάρ, δέ, and οὖν.

Mk. 1, 44 ὕπαγε,[2] σεαυτὸν δεῖξον	Lk. 5, 14 ἀπελθὼν δεῖξον σεαυτόν
Mk. 2, 11 ἔγειρε, ἆρον	Lk. 5, 24 ἔγειρε καὶ ἄρας
Mk. 4, 24 βλέπετε τί ἀκούετε	Lk. 8, 18 βλέπετε οὖν πῶς ἀκούετε
Mk. 5, 39 τὸ παιδίον οὐκ ἀπέθανεν	Lk. 8, 52 οὐ γὰρ ἀπέθανεν (*v. l.* cf. Matt. 9, 24)
Mk. 8, 29 ἀποκριθεὶς ὁ Πέτρος	Lk. 9, 20 Πέτρος δὲ ἀποκριθεὶς
Mk. 9, 38 ἔφη αὐτῷ ὁ Ἰωάννης	Lk. 9, 49 ἀποκριθεὶς δὲ ὁ Ἰωάννης εἶπεν
Mk. 9, 50 καλὸν τὸ ἅλας	Lk. 14, 34 καλὸν οὖν τὸ ἅλας [Q?]
Mk. 10, 14 ἄφετε . . . μὴ κωλύετε	Lk. 18, 16 ἄφετε . . . καὶ μὴ κωλύετε
Mk. 10, 25 εὐκοπώτερόν ἐστιν	Lk. 18, 25 εὐκοπώτερον γάρ ἐστιν
Mk. 10, 28 ἤρξατο λέγειν ὁ Πέτρος	Lk. 18, 28 εἶπεν δὲ Πέτρος
Mk. 10, 29 ἔφη ὁ Ἰησοῦς	Lk. 18, 29 ὁ δὲ εἶπεν
Mk. 11, 2 εὑρήσετε . . . λύσατε	Lk. 19, 30 εὑρήσετε . . . καὶ λύσαντες

[1] For cases of asyndeton in Luke, see 7, 42, 43, 44; 14, 27; 17, 32, 33; 19, 22; 21, 13.

[2] Also elsewhere the omission of ὕπαγε by Luke removes asyndeton; see p. 173.

Mk. 12, 9 τί ποιήσει	Lk. 20, 15 τί οὖν ποιήσει
Mk. 12, 17 τὰ Καίσαρος ἀπόδοτε	Lk. 20, 25 τοίνυν ἀπόδοτε τὰ Καίσαρος
Mk. 12, 20 ἑπτὰ ἀδελφοὶ ἦσαν	Lk. 20, 29 ἑπτὰ οὖν ἀδελφοὶ ἦσαν
Mk. 12, 23 τίνος αὐτῶν ἔσται γυνή	Lk. 20, 33 ἡ γυνὴ οὖν . . . τίνος γίνεται;
Mk. 12, 24 ἔφη	Lk. 20, 34 καὶ εἶπεν
Mk. 12, 27 οὐκ ἔστιν ὁ θεός	Lk. 20, 38 θεὸς δὲ οὐκ ἔστιν
Mk. 12, 36 αὐτὸς Δαυεὶδ εἶπεν	Lk. 20, 42 αὐτὸς γὰρ Δαυεὶδ λέγει
Mk. 12, 37 αὐτὸς Δαυεὶδ	Lk. 20, 44 Δαυεὶδ οὖν
Mk. 13, 4 πότε ταῦτα ἔσται	Lk. 21, 7 πότε οὖν ταῦτα ἔσται
Mk. 13, 6 πολλοὶ ἐλεύσονται	Lk. 21, 8 πολλοὶ γὰρ ἐλεύσονται
Mk. 13, 7 δεῖ γενέσθαι	Lk. 21, 9 δεῖ γὰρ ταῦτα γενέσθαι
Mk. 16, 6 ἠγέρθη, οὐκ ἔστιν ὧδε	Lk. 24, 6 οὐκ ἔστιν ὧδε ἀλλὰ ἠγέρθη

Anacoluthon

Hawkins has collected in the second edition of his *Horae Synopticae* (pp. 135 ff.), "instances of anacoluthon, or broken or incomplete construction, in Mark, which are altered or avoided in Matthew or Luke or both."

The cases where Luke has most plainly improved the structure of Mark are:

Mark 3, 16 f. ἐποίησεν τοὺς δώδεκα, καὶ ἐπέθηκεν ὄνομα τῷ Σίμωνι Πέτρον· καὶ Ἰακωβον κ.τ.λ.

Luke 6, 13 f. καὶ ἐκλεξάμενος ἀπ' αὐτῶν δώδεκα . . . Σίμωνα, ὃν καὶ ὠνόμασεν Πέτρον, καὶ Ἀνδρέαν κ.τ.λ.

But even Luke's form does not make a complete sentence.

Mark 5, 23 παρακαλεῖ αὐτὸν πολλὰ λέγων ὅτι . . . ἐσχάτως ἔχει, ἵνα ἐλθὼν ἐπιθῇς τὰς χεῖρας αὐτῇ, ἵνα σωθῇ καὶ ζήσῃ.

Luke 8, 41 f. παρεκάλει αὐτὸν εἰσελθεῖν . . . ὅτι θυγάτηρ μονογενὴς . . . ἀπέθνησκεν.

Mark 11, 32 ἀλλὰ εἴπωμεν . . . ἐφοβοῦντο τὸν ὄχλον.

Luke 20, 6 ἐὰν δὲ εἴπωμεν . . . ὁ λαὸς ἅπας καταλιθάσει ἡμᾶς.

Mark 12, 38–40 . . . τῶν θελόντων ἐν στολαῖς περιπατεῖν καὶ ἀσπασμοὺς κ.τ.λ., οἱ κατεσθίοντες τὰς οἰκίας.

Luke 20, 46 f. inserts φιλούντων before ἀσπασμούς, and changes the anacoluthic nominative participle to οἱ κατεσθίουσιν (cf. p. 136 above).

Mark 3, 8, the repetition of πλῆθος πολύ after πολὺ πλῆθος in vs. 7 is avoided in Luke 6, 17.

But in two of the cases Luke has not improved Mark:

Mark 6, 8 f. ἵνα μηδὲν αἴρωσιν . . . ἀλλὰ ὑποδεδεμένους . . ., καὶ μὴ ἐνδύσασθαι (*v.l.* -σησθε).

Luke 9, 3 μηδὲν αἴρετε . . . μήτε ἀνὰ δύο χιτῶνας ἔχειν, though somewhat different from Mark is equally "abrupt in his mixture of constructions." Cf. Plummer, *ad loc.*

Mark 12, 19 Μωϋσῆς ἔγραψεν ἡμῖν ὅτι ἐάν τινος . . . ἵνα λάβῃ.
Luke 20, 28 agrees, except that ὅτι is omitted.

Luke occasionally secures a better, as well as a simpler, sentence by combining two from Mark:

Mk. 10, 27 *παρὰ ἀνθρώποις ἀδύνατον, ἀλλ' οὐ παρὰ θεῷ· πάντα γὰρ δυνατὰ παρὰ τῷ θεῷ*	Lk. 18, 27 *τὰ ἀδύνατα παρὰ ἀνθρώποις δυνατὰ παρὰ τῷ θεῷ ἐστιν*

See also Mk. 3, 34b, 35 = Lk. 8, 21b quoted on p. 81 and Mt. 10, 24 f. = Lk. 6, 40 [Q].

Sentences made complete

The auxiliary verb may be omitted even in classical Greek, but in Greek dependent on Semitic thought or writing it is particularly easy to omit it, e.g., *ἐγὼ ὁ θεὸς Ἀβραὰμ κ.τ.λ.*, Mark 12, 26 and Acts 7, 32 from the Old Testament. For a full discussion of this omission, see Blass, *Grammar of New Testament Greek*, § 30, 3.

In the following cases Luke has apparently corrected his sources in this particular:

Mk. 1, 11 *καὶ φωνὴ ἐκ τῶν οὐρανῶν*	Lk. 3, 22 *καὶ φωνὴν ἐξ οὐρανοῦ γενέσθαι*
Mt. 11, 8 *ἰδοὺ οἱ* with participle	Lk. 7, 25 adds *εἰσιν* [Q]
Mk. 5, 9 *τί ὄνομά σοι*	Lk. 8, 30 adds *ἐστιν*
Mk. 6, 15 *ἔλεγον ὅτι προφήτης*	Lk. 9, 8 adds *ἀνέστη*
Mk. 8, 28 [*λέγοντες*] *ὅτι εἷς τῶν προφητῶν*	Lk. 9, 19 adds *ἀνέστη*
Mt. 24, 41 *δύο ἀλήθουσαι*	Lk. 17, 35 adds *ἔσονται* [Q]
Mk. 10, 27 *δυνατὰ παρὰ τῷ θεῷ*	Lk. 18, 27 adds *ἐστιν*
Mk. 12, 16 *τίνος ἡ εἰκὼν αὕτη καὶ ἡ ἐπιγραφή*	Lk. 20, 24 *τίνος ἔχει εἰκόνα καὶ ἐπιγραφήν*
Mk. 14, 36 *οὐ τί ἐγὼ θέλω κ.τ.λ.*	Lk. 22, 42 *μὴ τὸ θέλημά μου . . . γινέσθω*

The omission of the copula by Luke in 22, 20 is therefore difficult to understand, as all the parallels contain it; —

Luke 22, 20 *τοῦτο τὸ ποτήριον ἡ καινὴ διαθήκη ἐν τῷ αἵματί μου*
1 Cor. 11, 25 *τοῦτο τὸ ποτήριον ἡ καινὴ διαθήκη ἐστὶν ἐν τῷ ἐμῷ αἵματι*
Mark 14, 24 *τοῦτό ἐστιν τὸ αἷμά μου τῆς διαθήκης*
Matt. 26, 28 *τοῦτο γάρ ἐστιν τὸ αἷμά μου τῆς διαθήκης*

Note the addition of the participles in the following cases:

Mk. 2, 25 *ἐπείνασεν αὐτὸς καὶ οἱ μετ' αὐτοῦ*	Lk. 6, 3 adds *ὄντες*
Mt. 8, 9 *ἄνθρωπός εἰμι ὑπὸ ἐξουσίαν*	Lk. 7, 8 adds *τασσόμενος* [Q]
Mt. 11, 21 *ἐν σάκκῳ καὶ σποδῷ μετενόησαν*	Lk. 10, 13 adds *καθήμενοι* [Q]
Mk. 14, 10 *Ἰούδας Ἰσκαριώθ, ὁ εἷς τῶν δώδεκα*	Lk. 22, 3 *Ἰούδαν . . . ὄντα ἐκ τοῦ ἀριθμοῦ τῶν δώδεκα*
Mk. 15, 43 *Ἰωσὴφ . . . βουλευτής*	Lk. 23, 50 adds *ὑπάρχων*

Luke fills out the other parts of sentences where obscurity is caused by omissions. Not only are definite subjects supplied, but where the subject is already fairly obvious its identification is made certain by a pronoun, a participle, or even an article. The use of *αὐτὸς δέ* and *καὶ αὐτός* is especially frequent in Luke. The avoidance of the indefinite "they" is also secured by the addition of the subject. (Cf. p. 165).

Subject of verb added by Luke: [1]

Mk. 1, 32 *ἔφερον*	Lk. 4, 40 *πάντες ὅσοι εἶχον . . . ἤγαγον*
Mk. 1, 44 *καὶ λέγει*	Lk. 5, 14 *καὶ αὐτὸς παρήγγειλεν*
Mk. 2, 3 *ἔρχονται φέροντες*	Lk. 5, 18 *ἄνδρες φέροντες*
Mk. 2, 25 *λέγει*	Lk. 6, 3 *ὁ Ἰησοῦς . . . εἶπεν*
Mk. 3, 2 *καὶ παρετήρουν*	Lk. 6, 7 *παρετηροῦντο δὲ οἱ γραμματεῖς*
Mk. 3, 4 *λέγει*	Lk. 6, 9 *εἶπεν ὁ Ἰησοῦς*
Mt. 5, 11 *ὅταν ὀνειδίσωσιν κ.τ.λ.*	Lk. 6, 22 *ὅταν μισήσωσιν ὑμᾶς οἱ ἄνθρωποι . . . καὶ ὀνειδίσωσιν* [Q]
Mt. 11, 18, 19 *λέγουσι . . . λέγουσι*	Lk. 7, 33, 34 *λέγετε . . . λέγετε* [2] [Q]
Mk. 5, 9 *ἐπηρώτα*	Lk. 8, 30 *ἐπηρώτησεν ὁ Ἰησοῦς*
Mk. 5, 17 *ἤρξαντο παρακαλεῖν*	Lk. 8, 37 adds *ἅπαν τὸ πλῆθος τῆς περιχώρου τῶν Γεργεσηνῶν*
Mk. 5, 35 *ἔρχονται*	Lk. 8, 49 *ἔρχεταί τις*
Mk. 5, 41 *καὶ κρατήσας*	Lk. 8, 54 *αὐτὸς δὲ κρατήσας*
Mk. 5, 42 *ἐξέστησαν*	Lk. 8, 56 *ἐξέστησαν οἱ γονεῖς*
Mk. 9, 19 *ὁ δὲ αποκριθεὶς λέγει*	Lk. 9, 41 *ἀποκριθεὶς δὲ ὁ Ἰησοῦς εἶπεν*
Mt. 12, 25 *εἰδὼς δέ*	Lk. 11, 17 *αὐτὸς δὲ εἰδώς* [Q]
Mt. 5, 15 *οὐδὲ καίουσι*	Lk. 8, 16; 11, 33 *οὐδεὶς ἅψας* [Q]
Mk. 10, 48 *ὁ δὲ . . . ἔκραζεν*	Lk. 18, 39 *αὐτὸς δὲ . . . ἔκραζεν*
Mk. 11, 4 *ἀπῆλθον καὶ εὗρον*	Lk. 19, 32 *ἀπελθόντες οἱ ἀπεσταλμένοι εὗρον*
Mk. 12, 3 *ἔδειραν καὶ ἀπέστειλαν*	Lk. 20, 10 adds *γεωργοί* (so Matt. 21, 35)
Mk. 12, 12 *ἐζήτουν*	Lk. 20, 19 *ἐζήτησαν οἱ γραμματεῖς κ.τ.λ.*
Mk. 12, 23 *τίνος αὐτῶν ἔσται γυνή*	Lk. 20, 33 *ἡ γυνὴ . . . τίνος αὐτῶν γίνεται γυνή*
Mk. 13, 29 *ἐγγύς ἐστιν*	Lk. 21, 31 adds *ἡ βασιλεία τοῦ θεοῦ*
Mk. 14, 19 *ἤρξαντο λυπεῖσθαι*	Lk. 22, 23 *καὶ αὐτοὶ ἤρξαντο κ.τ.λ.*
Mk. 14, 35 *καί*	Lk. 22, 41 *καὶ αὐτός*
Mk. 15, 47 *ἐθεώρουν ποῦ τέθειται*	Lk. 23, 55 *ἐθεάσαντο . . . ὡς ἐτέθη τὸ σῶμα αὐτοῦ*

Subject of infinitive supplied:

Mk. 4, 4 *ἐν τῷ σπείρειν*	Lk. 8, 5 *ἐν τῷ σπείρειν αὐτόν*
Mk. 12, 14 *ἔξεστιν . . . δοῦναι ἢ οὔ*	Lk. 20, 22 *ἔξεστιν ἡμᾶς . . . δοῦναι ἢ οὔ*
Mk. 13, 7 *δεῖ γενέσθαι*	Lk. 21, 9 *δεῖ . . . ταῦτα γενέσθαι*

[1] Cf. Wernle, *Die synoptische Frage*, pp. 19 f.

[2] Harnack, *Sayings*, p. 19: "*λέγετε* in St. Luke is a natural correction for the indefinite *λέγουσιν* in St. Matthew." See above p. 124.

Noun supplied for adjective:

Mt. 11, 8 ἐν μαλακοῖς ἠμφιεσμένον	Lk. 7, 25 ἐν μαλακοῖς ἱματίοις ἠμφιεσμένον [Q]

Object of verb supplied:

Mt. 8, 10 ἀκούσας δέ	Lk. 7, 9 ἀκούσας δὲ ταῦτα [Q]
Mt. 8, 10 ἐθαύμασεν	Lk. 7, 9 ἐθαύμασεν αὐτόν [Q]
Mt. 11, 18 ἐσθίων	Lk. 7, 33 ἐσθίων ἄρτον [Q]
Mt. 11, 18 πίνων	Lk. 7, 33 πίνων οἶνον [Q]
Mk. 4, 3 σπεῖραι	Lk. 8, 5 σπεῖραι τὸν σπόρον αὐτοῦ
Mk. 6, 14 ἤκουσεν	Lk. 9, 7 ἤκουσεν . . . τὰ γινόμενα πάντα
Mk. 6, 41 εὐλόγησεν	Lk. 9, 16 εὐλόγησεν αὐτούς
Mk. 15, 40 θεωροῦσαι	Lk. 23, 49 ὁρῶσαι ταῦτα, cf. verse 48 θεωρήσαντες τὰ γενόμενα

In other cases Scholten suggests that Luke misunderstood or deliberately corrected the absolute use of transitive verbs:

Mk. 3, 4 ψυχὴν σῶσαι ἢ ἀποκτεῖναι	Lk. 6, 9 ψυχὴν σῶσαι ἢ ἀπολέσαι
Mk. 6, 39 ἐπέταξεν αὐτοῖς ἀνακλῖναι (*v.l.* -κλιθῆναι) πάντας	Lk. 9, 14 εἶπεν . . . κατακλίνατε αὐτούς
Compare	
Mt. 11, 2 πέμψας διὰ τῶν μαθητῶν	Lk. 7, 19 προσκαλεσάμενος δύο τινὰς τῶν μαθητῶν . . . ἔπεμψεν [Q]

The complementary infinitive is added:

Mt. 24, 48 χρονίζει μου ὁ κύριος	Lk. 12, 45 χρονίζει ὁ κύριός μου ἔρχεσθαι [Q]

More compact sentences

Luke secures a better and more compact sentence in 21, 4 by avoiding the loose apposition of Mark 12, 44, where the appositives are even separated by the verb:

Mk. 12, 44 πάντα ὅσα εἶχεν ἔβαλεν, ὅλον τὸν βίον αὐτῆς	Lk. 21, 4 ἅπαντα τὸν βίον ὃν εἶχεν ἔβαλεν
Compare:	
Mk. 4, 11 ἐκείνοις δὲ τοῖς ἔξω	Lk. 8, 10 τοῖς δὲ λοιποῖς
Mt. 25, 29 τοῦ δὲ μὴ ἔχοντος, καὶ ὃ ἔχει ἀρθήσεται ἀπ' αὐτοῦ (cf. Mt. 13, 12; Mk. 4, 25 = Lk. 7, 18).	Lk. 19, 26 ἀπὸ δὲ τοῦ μὴ ἔχοντος καὶ ὃ ἔχει ἀρθήσεται [Q]

Cf. also Mark 14, 10 (= Luke 22, 3), Mark 15, 43 (= Luke 23, 50), quoted above, p. 149.

Similarly, where a verb has two adverbial modifiers of place, Luke omits one, or otherwise avoids the double adverbial expression:

Mk. 1, 28 πανταχοῦ εἰς ὅλην τὴν περίχωρον	Lk. 4, 37 εἰς πάντα τόπον τῆς περιχώρου
Mk. 1, 38 ἀλλαχοῦ εἰς τὰς ἐχομένας κωμοπόλεις	Lk. 4, 43 καὶ ταῖς ἑτέραις πόλεσιν
Mk. 1, 39 εἰς τὰς συναγωγὰς αὐτῶν εἰς ὅλην τὴν Γαλιλαίαν	Lk. 4, 44 εἰς τὰς συναγωγὰς τῆς Γαλιλαίας

Mk. 4, 5 *ἐπὶ τὸ πετρῶδες ὅπου οὐκ εἶχεν γῆν πολλήν*	Lk. 8, 6 *ἐπὶ τὴν πέτραν*
Mk. 4, 15 *παρὰ τὴν ὁδὸν ὅπου σπείρεται ὁ λόγος*	Lk. 8, 12 *παρὰ τὴν ὁδόν*
Mk. 5, 1 *εἰς τὸ πέραν . . . εἰς τὴν χώραν*	Lk. 8, 26 *εἰς τὴν χώραν . . . ἥτις ἐστὶν ἀντίπερα*
Mk. 5, 19 *εἰς τὸν οἶκόν σου πρὸς τοὺς σούς*	Lk. 8, 39 *εἰς τὸν οἶκόν σου*
Mk. 11, 4 *πρὸς τὴν θύραν ἔξω ἐπὶ τοῦ ἀμφόδου*	Lk. 19, 32 has simply *καθὼς εἶπεν αὐτοῖς*
Mk. 13, 29 *ἐγγύς ἐστιν ἐπὶ θύραις*	Lk. 21, 31 *ἐγγύς ἐστιν*
Mk. 14, 54 *ἕως ἔσω εἰς τὴν αὐλὴν* Mk. 14, 66 *κάτω ἐν τῇ αὐλῇ* }	Lk. 22, 55 *ἐν μέσῳ τῆς αὐλῆς*

For the alteration of double adverbial expressions of time see the following:

Mk. 1, 32 *ὀψίας δὲ γενομένης, ὅτε ἔδυ ὁ ἥλιος*	Lk. 4, 40 *δύνοντος τοῦ ἡλίου*
Mk. 1, 35 *πρωῒ ἔννυχα λίαν*	Lk. 4, 42 *γενομένης δὲ ἡμέρας*
Mk. 4, 35 *ἐν ἐκείνῃ τῇ ἡμέρᾳ ὀψίας γενομένης*	Lk. 8, 22 *ἐν μιᾷ τῶν ἡμερῶν*
Mk. 10, 30 *νῦν ἐν τῷ καιρῷ τούτῳ*	Lk. 18, 30 *ἐν τῷ καιρῷ τούτῳ*
Mk. 12, 23 *ἐν τῇ ἀναστάσει ὅταν ἀναστῶσιν*	Lk. 20, 33 *ἐν τῇ ἀναστάσει*
Mk. 14, 30 *σήμερον ταύτῃ τῇ νυκτί*	Lk. 22, 34 *σήμερον*
Mk. 14, 43 *εὐθὺς ἔτι αὐτοῦ λαλοῦντος*	Lk. 22, 47 *ἔτι αὐτοῦ λαλοῦντος*
Mk. 16, 2 *λίαν πρωῒ . . . ἀνατείλαντος τοῦ ἡλίου*	Lk. 24, 1 *ὄρθρου βαθέως*

Changes in the Order of Words

Luke comparatively seldom varies the order of words that he found in his sources, and the motives for such changes as he makes are not always apparent to us and were perhaps not always clearly defined in his own mind. He allows himself considerable freedom, and pays little regard to regularity. But, if we may judge from certain kinds of cases, the changes seem to be usually in the direction of a more normal order.

Such are changes in the relative position of subject, verb, and object, e.g.:

Mk. 12, 1 *ἀμπελῶνα ἄνθρωπος ἐφύτευσεν*	Lk. 20, 9 *ἄνθρωπος ἐφύτευσεν ἀμπελῶνα*

The exceptions are frequently for emphasis, *e. g.*:

Mk. 8, 35 *ἐπαισχυνθήσεται αὐτόν*	Lk. 9, 26 *τοῦτον* [1] . . . *ἐπαισχυνθήσεται*

[1] *τοῦτον*, resuming a relative is usually put first in the clause. See vs. 24 and the speeches in Acts. Cf. p. 194.

Mk. 6, 11 ἐκτινάξατε τὸν χοῦν	Lk. 9, 5 καὶ τὸν κονιορτὸν . . . ἀποτινάσσετε
Mk. 9, 7 ἀκούετε αὐτοῦ	Lk. 9, 35 αὐτοῦ ἀκούετε

The order verb — subject is perhaps Semitic.[1]

A list of instances follows:

Mt. 4, 10 κύριον . . . προσκυνήσεις	Lk. 4, 8 προσκυνήσεις κύριον [Q]
Mk. 1, 41 αὐτοῦ [2] ἥψατο	Lk. 5, 13 ἥψατο αὐτοῦ
Mk. 1, 42 ἀπῆλθεν ἡ λέπρα	Lk. 5, 13 ἡ λέπρα ἀπῆλθεν
Mk. 1, 44 σεαυτὸν δεῖξον	Lk. 5, 14 δεῖξον σεαυτόν
Mk. 2, 10 ἐξουσίαν ἔχει ὁ υἱός	Lk. 5, 24 ὁ υἱὸς . . . ἐξουσίαν ἔχει
Mk. 2, 19 καὶ εἶπεν ὁ Ἰησοῦς	Lk. 5, 34 ὁ δὲ Ἰησοῦς εἶπεν
Mk. 9, 7 ἐγένετο φωνή	Lk. 9, 35 φωνὴ ἐγένετο
Mk. 9, 18 ἵνα αὐτὸ ἐκβάλωσιν	Lk. 9, 40 ἵνα ἐκβάλωσιν αὐτό
Mt. 6, 32 οἶδεν ὁ πατήρ	Lk. 12, 30 ὁ πατὴρ οἶδεν [Q]
Mt. 6, 21 ἔσται ἡ καρδία	Lk. 12, 34 ἡ καρδία ἔσται [Q]
Mt. 5, 25 μήποτέ σε παραδῷ	Lk. 12, 58 μήποτε κατασύρῃ σε [Q]
Mt. 23, 39 με ἴδητε	Lk. 13, 35 ἴδητέ με [Q]
Mk. 9, 42 περίκειται μύλος ὀνικός	Lk. 17, 2 λίθος μυλικὸς περίκειται
Mt. 24, 28 συναχθήσονται οἱ ἀετοί	Lk. 17, 37 οἱ ἀετοὶ ἐπισυναχθήσονται [Q]
Mk. 10, 48 ἐπετίμων αὐτῷ πολλοί	Lk. 18, 39 οἱ προάγοντες ἐπετίμων αὐτῷ
Mk. 11, 8 τὰ ἱμάτια ἔστρωσαν	Lk. 19, 36 ὑπεστρώννυον τὰ ἱμάτια
Mk. 12, 12 τὴν παραβολὴν εἶπεν	Lk. 20, 19 εἶπεν τὴν παραβολήν
Mk. 12, 13 ἵνα αὐτὸν ἀγρεύσωσιν λόγῳ	Lk. 20, 20 ἵνα ἐπιλάβωνται αὐτοῦ λόγου [3]
Mk. 12, 16 τὰ Καίσαρος ἀπόδοτε	Lk. 20, 25 ἀπόδοτε τὰ Καίσαρος
Mk. 12, 27 οὐκ ἔστιν ὁ θεὸς νεκρῶν	Lk. 20, 38 θεὸς οὐκ ἔστιν νεκρῶν
Mk. 13, 8 ἔσονται σεισμοί κ.τ.λ.	Lk. 21, 11 σεισμοὶ . . . ἔσονται
Mk. 14, 72 τρίς με ἀπαρνήσῃ	Lk. 22, 61 ἀπαρνήσῃ με τρίς
Mk. 14, 63 τί ἔτι χρείαν ἔχομεν	Lk. 22, 71 τί ἔτι ἔχομεν . . . χρείαν
Mk. 15, 2 ἐπηρώτησεν ὁ Πειλᾶτος	Lk. 23, 3 ὁ δὲ Πειλᾶτος ἠρώτησεν

The possessive normally follows;

Mk. 2, 5, 9 ἀφίενταί σου αἱ ἁμαρτίαι	Lk. 5, 20, 23 ἀφέωνταί σοι αἱ ἁμαρτίαι σου
Mt. 8, 8 μου ὑπὸ τὴν στέγην	Lk. 7, 6 ὑπὸ τὴν στέγην μου [Q]
Mt. 24, 48 χρονίζει μου ὁ κύριος	Lk. 12, 45 ὁ κύριός μου χρονίζει [Q]

Observe, however, in Luke 7, 44–50 not only ἀφέωνται αὐτῆς (σου) αἱ ἁμαρτίαι but also εἰσῆλθόν σου εἰς τὴν οἰκίαν and μου (ἐπὶ) τοὺς πόδας.

Similarly in the position of the numeral adjective Luke's changes tend toward the normal order:

Mk. 6, 38 δύο ἰχθύας	Lk. 9, 13 ἰχθύες δύο
Mk. 6, 44 πεντακισχίλιοι ἄνδρες	Lk. 9, 14 ἄνδρες πεντακισχίλιοι

[1] Wellhausen, *Einleitung*, 1st ed., p. 19: "Diese Wortstellung, von der sich bei Markus nur wenige Ausnahmen finden, ist semitisch, nicht griechisch."

[2] This word may be taken in Mark as possessive genitive depending on preceding word, χεῖρα; but cf. Mark 3, 10 = Luke 6, 19.

[3] Similarly Mark 14, 1, 10, 11 = Luke 22, 2, 6.

Mk. 6, 43 δώδεκα κοφίνων	Lk. 9, 17 κόφινοι δώδεκα
Mk. 9, 5 τρεῖς σκηνάς	Lk. 9, 33 σκηνὰς τρεῖς
Mt. 12, 45 ἑπτὰ ἕτερα πνεύματα	Lk. 11, 26 ἕτερα πνεύματα . . . ἑπτά [Q]

Dislike of Barbarous Words and Names

Many passages derived from Mark show Luke's repugnance to foreign words, a feeling that accords with the best standards of Hellenistic writing. It was because of Luke's omission of ὡσαννά in 19, 38 that Jerome calls him *inter omnes evangelistas Graeci sermonis eruditissimus* (*Ep.* 20, 4, to Pope Damasus). Latin words as well as Semitic words were considered barbarous by the cultivated Grecian, though under the Empire they were coming into general use.

In some cases Luke takes the foreign word from Mark or Q:

Mk. 5, 9 λεγιών	Lk. 8, 30 λεγιών
Mk. 4, 21 ὑπὸ τὸν μόδιον	Lk. 11, 33 ὑπὸ τὸν μόδιον (om. syr. sin. LΞ 1–118–131–209 69 *al.*) [Q?]
Mt. 5, 15 ὑπὸ τὸν μόδιον	
Mt. 10, 28 γεέννῃ	Lk. 12, 5 γέενναν [Q]
Mt. 10, 29 ἀσσαρίου	Lk. 12, 6 ἀσσαρίων δύο [Q]
Mk. 12, 14–17 Καῖσαρ	Lk. 20, 22–25 Καῖσαρ

Sometimes, while retaining the foreign word, he apologizes for it by the use of a participle meaning "named" or "called," or by ὀνόματι or some similar expression.

Thus the participle is inserted in passages taken from Mark:

Mk. 6, 45; 8, 22 Βηθσαιδάν	Lk. 9, 10 πόλιν καλουμένην Βηθσαιδά
Mk. 14, 1 τὸ πάσχα καὶ τὰ ἄζυμα	Lk. 22, 1 ἡ ἑορτὴ τῶν ἀζύμων ἡ λεγομένη πάσχα
Mk. 14, 10 Ἰούδας Ἰσκαριώθ	Lk. 22, 3 Ἰούδαν τὸν καλούμενον Ἰσκαριώτην

So also in passages not from Mark, the participle and other forms of the verb are used with foreign names, and particularly with foreign surnames:

Luke 2, 4 πόλιν Δαυεὶδ ἥτις καλεῖται Βηθλεέμ
Luke 7, 11 πόλιν καλουμένην Ναΐν
Luke 8, 3 Μαρία ἡ καλουμένη Μαγδαληνή [1]
Luke 10, 39 ἀδελφὴ καλουμένη Μαριάμ
Luke 19, 2 ἀνὴρ ὀνόματι καλούμενος Ζακχαῖος

[1] In Matthew, Mark, and John she is regularly called Μαρία (-άμ) ἡ Μαγδαληνή; cf. also Luke 24, 10 ἡ Μαγδαληνὴ Μαρία.

Acts 1, 23 Ἰωσὴφ τὸν καλούμενον Βαρσαββᾶν, ὃς ἐπεκλήθη Ἰοῦστος
Acts 4, 36 Ἰωσὴφ ὁ ἐπικληθεὶς Βαρνάβας
Acts 12, 12 Ἰωάνου τοῦ ἐπικαλουμένου Μάρκου
Acts 12, 25 Ἰωάνην τὸν ἐπικληθέντα Μάρκον
Acts 13, 1 Συμεὼν ὁ καλούμενος Νίγερ
Acts 15, 22 Ἰούδαν τὸν καλούμενον Βαρσαββᾶν
Acts 15, 37 Ἰωάνην τὸν καλούμενον Μάρκον
Acts 27, 14 ἄνεμος τυφωνικὸς ὁ καλούμενος εὐρακύλων

Even if the foreign word is omitted or translated by Luke the apologetic participle is still retained:

Mk. 3, 18 Σίμωνα τὸν Καναναῖον	Lk. 6, 15 τὸν Σίμωνα τὸν καλούμενον Ζηλωτήν
Mk. 11, 1 τὸ ὄρος τῶν ἐλαιῶν	Lk. 19, 29 τὸ ὄρος τὸ καλούμενον ἐλαιών [1]
Mk. 14, 43 Ἰούδας ὁ Ἰσκαριώτης	Lk. 22, 47 ὁ λεγόμενος Ἰούδας
Mk. 15, 22 τὸν Γολγοθᾶν τόπον ὅ ἐστιν μεθηρμηνευόμενον κρανίου τόπος	Lk. 23, 33 τὸν τόπον τὸν καλούμενον Κρανίον

In the following cases, also, the writer is probably introducing a foreign name or a Greek equivalent for one:

Acts 3, 2 τὴν θύραν τοῦ ἱεροῦ τὴν λεγομένην Ὡραίαν
Acts 6, 9 τῆς συναγωγῆς τῆς λεγομένης Λιβερτίνων
Acts 8, 10 ἡ δύναμις τοῦ θεοῦ ἡ καλουμένη Μεγάλη
Acts 9, 11 τὴν ῥύμην τὴν καλουμένην Εὐθεῖαν
Acts 10, 1 σπείρης τῆς καλουμένης Ἰταλικῆς

The use of *ὀνόματι* or *ᾧ* (*ᾗ*) *ὄνομα* makes the introduction of names less abrupt:

Mk. 2, 14 Λευείν	Lk. 5, 27 τελώνην ὀνόματι Λευείν
Mk. 15, 43 Ἰωσήφ	Lk. 23, 50 ἀνὴρ ὀνόματι Ἰωσήφ

Except Matt. 27, 32 and Mark 5, 22 the use of ὀνόματι is peculiar to Luke among the Evangelists, occurring nearly thirty times, and in the majority of cases with the indefinite τις, either in the order ἱερεύς τις ὀνόματι Ζαχαρίας (Luke 1, 5; cf. Luke 10, 38; 16, 20; Acts 8, 9; 10, 1; 16, 1), or in the order ἀνήρ τις Ἀνανίας ὀνόματι (Acts 5, 1; cf Acts 9, 33; 18, 24), or as τις μαθητής . . . ὀνόματι Ἀνανίας (Acts 9, 10; cf. Acts 9, 36; 16, 14; 18, 2; 20, 9; 21, 10). Other examples of ὀνόματι are found in Luke 24, 18; Acts 5, 34; 9, 11, 12; 11, 28; 12, 13; 17, 34; 18, 7; 19, 24; 21, 10; 27, 1; 28, 7. A few Greek names are included in this list as Αἰνέας, Acts 9, 33; Τιμόθεος, Acts 16, 1; Δημήτριος, Acts 19, 24; Εὔτυχος, Acts 20, 9, but most of them are Latin or Semitic.

Possibly the τις itself has a certain apologetic force, corresponding to the Latin *quidam*, just as ὁ καλούμενος, etc. correspond to the Latin apologetic *qui dicitur*. τις is used alone with foreign names in Luke 23, 26 (= Mark 15, 21); Acts 9, 43; 10, 6 (παρά τινι Σίμωνι βυρσεῖ); Acts 19, 14 (Sceva); 21, 16 (Mnason); 22, 12 (Ananias); 24, 1 (Tertullus).

[1] So Luke 21, 37; Acts 1, 12. From Luke 22, 39 = Mark 14, 32 it seems likely that Luke understood this to be the translation of Gethsemane.

In this connection should be compared the verbless clause ᾧ (ᾗ) *ὄνομα* used by Luke with foreign names in a similar way:

Luke 1, 26 *πόλιν . . . ᾗ ὄνομα Ναζαρέτ*
Luke 1, 27 *ἀνδρὶ ᾧ ὄνομα Ἰωσήφ*
Luke 2, 25 *ἄνθρωπος . . . ᾧ ὄνομα Συμεών*
Luke 8, 41 *ἀνὴρ ᾧ ὄνομα Ἰάειρος* (cf. Mark 5, 22 *ὀνόματι Ἰάειρος*)
Luke 24, 13 *κώμην . . . ᾗ ὄνομα Ἐμμαούς*
Acts 13, 6 *ψευδοπροφήτην Ἰουδαῖον ᾧ ὄνομα Βαριησοῦς*

In addition to the apologetic expressions mentioned many of the examples already cited still further soften the use of foreign words by adding the common or class noun, like city, feast, man, woman. Note also the explanatory phrase added in the following cases:

Mk. 1, 21 *Καφαρναούμ* (first occurrence in Mark)	Lk. 4, 31 *Καφαρναοὺμ πόλιν τῆς Γαλιλαίας*
Mk. 15, 43 *Ἀριμαθαίας*	Lk. 23, 51 *Ἀριμαθαίας πόλεως τῶν Ἰουδαίων*
Mk. 9, 4 *Ἠλείας σὺν Μωϋσεῖ*	Lk. 9, 30 *ἄνδρες δύο . . . οἵτινες ἦσαν Μωϋσῆς καὶ Ἠλείας*
	Lk. 9, 50 *οἱ μαθηταὶ Ἰάκωβος καὶ Ἰωάννης*

In the following cases Luke omits the barbarous words:

Mk. 3, 17 *Βοανηργές*	Lk. 6, 14 omits
Mk. 10, 46 *ὁ υἱὸς Τιμαίου Βαρτίμαιος*	Lk. 18, 35 omits
Mk. 11, 10 *ὡσαννά*	Lk. 19, 38 omits
Mk. 12, 42 *ὅ ἐστιν κοδράντης*	Lk. 21, 2 omits
Mk. 14, 32 *Γεθσημανεί*	Lk. 22, 39 *τὸ ὄρος τῶν ἐλαιῶν*
Mk. 14, 36 *ἀββᾶ ὁ πατήρ*	Lk. 22, 42 *πάτερ*
Mk. 14, 43 *Ἰούδας ὁ Ἰσκαριώτης*	Lk. 22, 47 *ὁ λεγόμενος Ἰούδας*
Mk. 15, 22 *Γολγοθᾶν*	Lk. 23, 33 omits
Mk. 15, 34 *ἐλωί, ἐλωί, λαμὰ σαβαχθανεί*	Lk. 23, 45 omits

See also p. 128.

In other instances a foreign word is translated:

Mk. 2, 4ff. *κράββατον* (cf. p. 46)	Lk. 5, 18 ff. *κλινίδιον, κλίνη*
Mk. 3, 18 *τὸν Καναναῖον*	Lk. 6, 15 *τὸν καλούμενον Ζηλωτήν*
Mk. 4, 15 *ὁ σατανᾶς*	Lk. 8, 12 *ὁ διάβολος* [1]
Mk. 4, 21 *τὸν μόδιον*	Lk. 8, 16 *σκεύει* [2]
Mk. 5, 41 *ταλειθά, κούμ*	Lk. 8, 54 *ἡ παῖς, ἐγείρου*
Mk. 6, 8 *χαλκόν* [3]	Lk. 9, 3 *ἀργύριον*
Mk. 12, 41 *χαλκόν* [3]	Lk. 21, 1 *τὰ δῶρα*

[1] So in Mark 1, 13 we read *πειραζόμενος ὑπὸ τοῦ σατανᾶ*, in Luke 4, 2 *πειραζόμενος ὑπὸ τοῦ διαβόλου*. But perhaps in this case Luke is following Q rather than correcting Mark, for the section evidently was in Q also, and at Matt. 4, 1 we read *πειρασθῆναι ὑπὸ τοῦ διαβόλου*. [2] See also Luke 11, 33 above, p. 154.

[3] *χαλκός* for "money" is a "vulgar" (Pollux 9, 92) if not a foreign (Latin *aes*) idiom.

Mt. 5, 26 κοδράντην[1]	Lk. 12, 59 λεπτόν [Q]
Mk. 9, 5 ῥαββεί	Lk. 9, 33 ἐπιστάτα
Mk. 10, 51 ῥαββουνεί (*v.l.* κύριε ῥαββεί)	Lk. 18, 41 κύριε
Mk. 12, 14 κῆνσον	Lk. 20, 22 φόρον
Mk. 15, 15 φραγελλώσας	Cf. Lk. 23, 16, 22 παιδεύσας
Mk. 15, 39 ὁ κεντυρίων	Lk. 23, 47 ὁ ἑκατοντάρχης

In the following cases Luke avoids repeating a foreign word by a circumlocution when it is referred to for the second time:

Luke 8, 35 τὸν ἄνθρωπον ἀφ' οὗ τὰ δαιμόνια ἐξῆλθον (cf. Mark 5, 15 τὸν δαιμονιζόμενον . . . τὸν ἐσχηκότα τὸν λεγιῶνα.)

Luke 23, 35 τὸν διὰ στάσιν καὶ φόνον βεβλημένον εἰς φυλακήν, ὃν ᾐτοῦντο (cf. Mark 15, 15 τὸν Βαραββᾶν).

Luke 24, 28 τὴν κώμην οὗ ἐπορεύοντο (i. e. Ἐμμαοῦς verse 13.).

So Luke 5, 25 ἄρας ἐφ' ὃ κατέκειτο (cf. Mark 2, 12 ἄρας τὸν κράβαττον and especially Mark 2, 4 τὸν κράβαττον ὅπου ὁ παραλυτικὸς κατέκειτο for which Luke writes (5, 19) αὐτὸν σὺν τῷ κλινιδίῳ. See above, p. 156).

With regard to ἀμήν Luke's practice varies, but he seems often to change or omit it.

He changes it:

Mk. 9, 1 ἀμὴν λέγω ὑμῖν	Lk. 9, 27 λέγω δὲ ὑμῖν ἀληθῶς
Mt. 23, 36 ἀμὴν λέγω ὑμῖν	Lk. 11, 51 ναὶ λέγω ὑμῖν [Q]
Mt. 24, 47 ἀμὴν λέγω ὑμῖν	Lk. 12, 44 ἀληθῶς λέγω ὑμῖν [Q]
Mk. 12, 43 ἀμὴν λέγω ὑμῖν	Lk. 21, 3 ἀληθῶς λέγω ὑμῖν

It is omitted in:

Mt. 8, 10 ἀμὴν λέγω ὑμῖν	Lk. 7, 9 λέγω ὑμῖν [Q]
Mt. 11, 11 ἀμὴν λέγω ὑμῖν	Lk. 7, 28 λέγω ὑμῖν [Q]
Mt. 10, 15 ἀμὴν λέγω ὑμῖν	Lk. 10, 12 λέγω δὲ ὑμῖν [Q]
Mt. 13, 17 ἀμὴν [γὰρ] λέγω ὑμῖν	Lk. 10, 24 λέγω γὰρ ὑμῖν [Q]
Mt. 5, 26 ἀμὴν λέγω σοι	Lk. 12, 59 λέγω σοι [Q]
Mt. 25, 12 ἀμὴν λέγω ὑμῖν	Lk. 13, 25 omits [Q]
Mt. 18, 13 ἀμὴν λέγω ὑμῖν	Lk. 15, 7 λέγω ὑμῖν [Q]
Mk. 14, 25 ἀμὴν λέγω ὑμῖν	Lk. 22, 18 λέγω γὰρ ὑμῖν
Mk. 14, 18 ἀμὴν λέγω ὑμῖν	Lk. 22, 21 omits
Mk. 14, 30 ἀμὴν λέγω σοι	Lk. 22, 34 λέγω σοι

But retained in:

Mk. 10, 15 ἀμὴν λέγω ὑμῖν	Lk. 18, 17 ἀμὴν λέγω ὑμῖν
Mk. 10, 29 ἀμὴν λέγω ὑμῖν	Lk. 18, 29 ἀμὴν λέγω ὑμῖν
Mk. 13, 30 ἀμὴν λέγω ὑμῖν	Lk. 21, 32 ἀμὴν λέγω ὑμῖν

Ἀμήν occurs also in Luke 4, 24; 12, 37; 23, 43, but not in Acts.

The use of ἀμήν in the Synoptic Gospels is shown by the following table (excluding doubtful readings):

[1] κοδράντης Mark 12, 42 is omitted by Luke 21, 2 as noted above.

	Matt.	Mark	Luke
In matter derived from Mark:			
retained	8	13	3
added	2[1]		
In matter derived from Q	8		0
In peculiar matter	12		3
	—	—	—
Total occurrences	30	13	6

Use of Verbs

Luke's treatment of verbs, compared with that of Mark, shows several distinct tendencies both in points of idiom and grammar and in vocabulary.

He avoids the historical present, so frequent in Mark, replacing it by an aorist of the same or similar verb.

He frequently replaces the imperfect by the aorist.

He changes Mark's periphrastic constructions with ἄρχομαι into simple verbs.

He frequently introduces periphrastic constructions with ἐγένετο, especially in the introductions to pericopes, where his recasting of Mark is most free.

Historical present

It is unnecessary here to repeat the careful table of 151 historic presents in Mark given by Hawkins, *Horae Synopticae*, pp. 114 ff., with their parallels in Matthew and Luke.

In 31 cases λέγει or λέγουσι of Mark becomes in Luke εἶπεν, εἶπον (-αν), and in a few others the participle or another verb of saying is used.[2]

In 4 cases ἔρχεται, ἔρχονται become ἦλθεν, ἦλθαν; twice the participle is used; and once Luke has himself an historical present (8, 49 = Mark 5, 35).

For an historical present, Luke substitutes an imperfect:

Mk. 5, 23 παρακαλεῖ (*v.l.* παρεκάλει) Lk. 8, 41 παρεκάλει

[1] In view of these instances of ἀμήν added by Matthew to Mark (Matt. 19, 23; 24, 2) the alternative should be left open in some of the nine Q passages above that Matthew has added ἀμήν to the source. So Harnack, *Sayings*, pp. 26, 57, etc.

[2] λέγει Luke 20, 42 for εἶπεν Mark 12, 36 is an apparent reversal of Luke's custom. Here, however, the verb is used to introduce a scripture quotation. Matt. 22, 43 also has the present (καλεῖ . . . λέγων). Cf. p. 168.

an aorist:

Mk. 11, 1 ἐγγίζουσι	Lk. 19, 29 ἤγγισεν
Mk. 11, 1 ἀποστέλλει	Lk. 19, 27 ἀπέστειλεν
Mk. 12, 13 ἀποστέλλουσιν	Lk. 20, 20 ἀπέστειλαν
Mk. 14, 13 ἀποστέλλει	Lk. 22, 8 ἀπέστειλεν
Mk. 14, 37 εὑρίσκει	Lk. 22, 45 εὗρεν
Mk. 15, 24 σταυροῦσιν	Lk. 23, 33 ἐσταύρωσαν

a participle:

Mk. 5, 22 πίπτει	Lk. 8, 41 πεσών
Mk. 9, 2 παραλαμβάνει	Lk. 9, 28 παραλαβών
Mk. 11, 4 λύουσι	Lk. 19, 33 λυόντων
Mk. 15, 24 διαμερίζονται	Lk. 23, 34 διαμεριζόμενοι

In the remaining cases either Luke has no parallel at all, or the verb as well as the form is changed.

In Q, in which there was comparatively little narrative, the historical present was consequently infrequent; but the following parallels are quite in accord with Luke's treatment of Mark:

Mt. 4, 8 παραλαμβάνει	Lk. 4, 5 ἀναγαγών [Q]
Mt. 4, 8 δείκνυσιν	Lk. 4, 5 ἔδειξεν [Q]
Mt. 4, 10 λέγει	Lk. 4, 8 εἶπεν [Q]
Mt. 4, 5 παραλαμβάνει	Lk. 4, 9 ἤγαγεν [Q]
Mt. 4, 6 λέγει	Lk. 4, 9 εἶπεν [Q]
Mt. 8, 20 λέγει	Lk. 9, 58 εἶπεν [Q]
Mt. 8, 22 λέγει	Lk. 9, 59, 60 εἶπεν [Q]

It can hardly be doubted that in these cases a present tense stood in the original source which has been retained by Matthew but avoided by Luke.

The individual and stylistic character of the historical present is shown by the statistics for ἔρχεται, ἔρχονται in the Greek Bible collected by Hawkins, *Horae Synopticae*, p. 28. These historical presents occur in Matt. 3 times, Mark, 24 times, Luke, once, not at all in Acts, in John 16 times. In LXX they occur only 27 times of which 26 are in the four books of Kings. Of the historical present in general Hawkins says (p. 114): "It appears from the LXX that the historic present was by no means common in Hellenistic Greek. . . . The only books besides Mark in which this usage is common are Job in the Old Testament and John in the New Testament. But it occurs frequently in Josephus."

See further J. H. Moulton, *Grammar of New Testament Greek*, I, p. 121, and the second edition of Hawkins, *Horae Synopticae*, pp. 213 f.

Imperfect and aorist

The imperfects ἔλεγεν (-ον), ἐπηρώτα (-ων) are frequently corrected by Luke to the aorist;

Mk. 2, 24 ἔλεγον	Lk. 6, 2 εἶπον
Mk. 4, 2 ἔλεγεν	Lk. 8, 4 εἶπεν
Mk. 5, 30 ἔλεγεν	Lk. 8, 45 εἶπεν
Mk. 6, 16 ἔλεγεν	Lk. 9, 9 εἶπεν
Mk. 6, 35 ἔλεγον	Lk. 9, 12 εἶπον
Mk. 9, 31 ἔλεγεν	Lk. 9, 43 εἶπεν
Mk. 11, 5 ἔλεγον	Lk. 19, 33 εἶπαν
Mk. 11, 28 ἔλεγον	Lk. 20, 2 εἶπαν
Mk. 12, 35 ἔλεγεν	Lk. 20, 41 εἶπεν
Mk. 15, 14 ἔλεγεν	Lk. 23, 22 εἶπεν
Mk. 5, 9 ἐπηρώτα	Lk. 8, 30 ἐπηρώτησεν
Mk. 8, 27 ἐπηρώτα	Lk. 9, 18 ἐπηρώτησεν
Mk. 8, 29 ἐπηρώτα	Lk. 9, 20 εἶπεν
Mk. 10, 17 ἐπηρώτα	Lk. 18, 18 ἐπηρώτησεν
Mk. 12, 18 ἐπηρώτων	Lk. 20, 27 ἐπηρώτησαν
Mk. 13, 3 ἐπηρώτα	Lk. 21, 7 ἐπηρώτησαν

But aside from these instances, where the imperfect was used by Mark to introduce a single and definite saying, Luke's avoidance of the imperfect is not noteworthy. Harnack (*Sayings of Jesus*, pp. 44 f, 107) has spoken of the imperfect as especially characteristic of Luke, but this also is poorly supported by a comparison with Mark. The clear cases of intentional change of tense in either direction are few. In most cases the verb as well as the tense are changed. In many cases the manuscript readings are divided, and in several the agreement of Matthew with Luke makes it uncertain what form Mark had when used by those evangelists.

The aorist takes the place of the imperfect in the following cases:

Mk. 4, 8 ἐδίδου καρπόν	Lk. 8, 8 ἐποίησεν καρπόν
Mk. 5, 13 ἐπνίγοντο	Lk. 8, 33 ἀπεπνίγη
Mk. 6, 7 ἐδίδου	Lk. 9, 1 ἔδωκεν
Mk. 12, 12 ἐζήτουν	Lk. 20, 19 ἐζήτησαν (*v. l.* ἐζήτουν)
Mk. 12, 41 ἐθεώρει	Lk. 21, 1 εἶδεν
Mk. 14, 72 ἔκλαιεν	Lk. 22, 62 ἔκλαυσεν (= Matt. 26, 75)
Mk. 15, 47 ἐθεώρουν	Lk. 23, 55 ἐθεάσαντο

At Mark 9, 38 the (conative) imperfect ἐκωλύομεν is read by ℵBDL *et al.*, and also in Luke 9, 49 by ℵBL *et al.* A number of MSS. read the aorist in both places; so AC and most minuscules. Westcott and Hort give the imperfect in both places. Tischendorf (8th ed., like D) reads the imperfect in Mark and the aorist in Luke, but says in reference to Luke "vix certo definiri potest utrum ipse scripserit."

Of the converse procedure the evidence is more scanty and unsatisfactory. There are two possible exceptions to the general avoidance of ἔλεγεν by Luke, viz.,

Mt. 3, 7 εἶπεν	Lk. 3, 7 ἔλεγεν [Q?]
Mk. 8, 34 εἶπεν	Lk. 9, 23 ἔλεγεν πρὸς πάντας

In the following cases the uncertainty speaks for itself:

Mt. 4, 1 ἀνήχθη	Lk. 4, 1 ἤγετο [Q]
Mk. 1, 28 ἐξῆλθεν	Lk. 4, 37 ἐξεπορεύετο
Mk. 1, 34 ἐθεράπευσεν	Lk. 4, 40 ἐθεράπευεν (BDW*al.*: -ευσεν *al.*)
Mk. 2, 14 ἠκολούθησεν	Lk. 5, 28 ἠκολούθει (= Matt. 9, 9, ℵD)
Mk. 3, 6 συμβούλιον ἐποίησαν	Lk. 6, 11 διελάλουν
Mk. 3, 10 ἐθεράπευσεν	Lk. 6, 18 ἐθεραπεύοντο
Mk. 11, 8 ἔστρωσαν	Lk. 19, 36 ὑπεστρώννυον (cf. Matt. 21, 8b ἐστρώννυον BC *et al.*)
Mk. 14, 54 ἠκολούθησεν	Lk. 22, 54 ἠκολούθει (= Matt. 26, 58)

The agreement of Matthew and Luke against Mark in three of these cases makes it probable that Mark itself had the imperfect there, and some MSS. of Mark still preserve it.

Thus in Mark 2, 14 (and Matt. 9, 9) ἠκολούθησεν is read in nearly all MSS., while in Luke 5, 28 ἠκολούθει apparently takes its place. Yet it is probable that either we should read ἠκολούθησεν in the latter passage with ℵAC and nearly all the other MSS. and versions, or else in Mark ἠκολούθει should be restored on the authority of ἠκολούθει in ℵD 1 21 209 in Matt. 9, 9; of C 1 258 in Mark 2, 14; and of BDLΞ 69 in Luke 5, 28.

Similarly, the aorist ἔστρωσαν in Mark 11, 8 falls under suspicion because of the ὑπεστρώννυον of Luke 19, 36. But in Mark 11, 8 the imperfect is still found in D syr. sin. *al*, and was apparently read by Matt, who first (21, 8a) changes it to ἔστρωσαν and then repeats in the form ἐστρώννυον (21, 8b, where only ℵD read ἔστρωσαν).

In Matthew the imperfect is infrequent (Hawkins, *Horae Synopticae*, 2d edit., p. 51). Probably is has been omitted by Matthew from Q (as often from Mark) rather than added to Q by Luke. But it is at least as frequent in Mark as in the parts of Luke derived from Mark. As we have seen, it rarely displaces an aorist. Luke in his revision of Mark introduces it mainly in two cases:

1. In resolution of result clauses. See Luke 4, 36; 5, 26; 6, 19; 8, 23.[1]

2. In place of the analytical imperfect,

Mk. 9, 4 ἦσαν συνλαλοῦντες	Lk. 9, 30 συνελάλουν
Mk. 10, 32 ἦν προάγων αὐτούς	Cf. Lk. 19, 28 ἐπορεύετο ἔμπροσθεν
Mk. 14, 54 ἦν συνκαθήμενος	Lk. 22, 55 ἐκάθητο
Mk. 15, 43 ἦν προσδεχόμενος	Lk. 23, 51 προσεδέχετο

[1] Quoted above, p. 138.

These cases of the removal of the analytic imperfect (and there are others less distinct) are especially noteworthy, as the analytic imperfect is undoubtedly a favorite of Luke, and yet I can find no good cases to quote where a simple verb in Mark is analyzed by Luke into its periphrastic form; nor can I find in the Q passages any support for the statement of Harnack in regard to them (*Sayings*, p. 39), that Luke "multiplies the instances where ἦν is used in construction with the participle."

ἄρχομαι

According to Allen (*St. Matthew*, pp. xxi f., xxxvii), the construction of *ἤρξατο, ἤρξαντο* with the infinitive occurs in Matthew 12 times, in Mark 26, in Luke 27. But only two of the instances in Luke are taken over from Mark, viz.

Mk. 11, 15 ἤρξατο ἐκβάλλειν	Lk. 19, 45 ἤρξατο ἐκβάλλειν
Mk. 12, 1 ἤρξατο . . . λαλεῖν	Lk. 20, 9 ἤρξατο λέγειν
One case is parallel to Matt.,	
Mt. 11, 7 ἤρξατο . . . λέγειν	Lk. 7, 24 ἤρξατο λέγειν [Q]
Compare:	
Mt. 24, 49 καὶ ἄρξηται τύπτειν	Lk. 12, 45 καὶ ἄρξηται τύπτειν [Q]

In the other 24 cases in Mark (see list in Allen, *l.c.*) Luke either has no parallel or substitutes a simple verb, e.g.

Mk. 5, 17 ἤρξαντο παρακαλεῖν	Lk. 8, 37 ἠρώτησαν
Mk. 5, 20 ἤρξατο κηρύσσειν (cf. 1, 45)	Lk. 8, 39 κηρύσσων
Mk. 6, 7 ἤρξατο ἀποστέλλειν	Lk. 9, 2 ἀπέστειλεν
Mk. 6, 34 ἤρξατο διδάσκειν	Lk. 9, 11 ἐλάλει
Mk. 8, 31 ἤρξατο διδάσκειν	Lk. 9, 22 εἰπών
Mk. 10, 28 ἤρξατο λέγειν	Lk. 18, 28 εἶπεν
Mk. 10, 32 ἤρξατο λέγειν	Lk. 18, 31 εἶπεν
Mk. 10, 47 ἤρξατο κράζειν καὶ λέγειν	Lk. 18, 38 ἐβόησεν λέγων
Mk. 13, 5 ἤρξατο λέγειν	Lk. 21, 8 εἶπεν

In these cases he has added the construction to Mark:

Mk. 2, 6 ἦσαν δὲ . . . διαλογιζόμενοι	Lk. 5, 21 καὶ ἤρξαντο διαλογίζεσθαι
Mk. 15, 3 καὶ κατηγόρουν αὐτοῦ	Lk. 23, 2 ἤρξαντο δὲ κατηγορεῖν αὐτοῦ

The use of *ἄρχομαι* with infinitive in reference to future time is found outside of Luke only at Matt. 24, 49, but in Luke it is somewhat common (3, 8; 13, 25, 26; 14, 9; 23, 30). The first case is in a Q passage, thus,

Matt. 3, 9 μὴ δόξητε λέγειν	Lk. 3, 8 μὴ ἄρξησθε λέγειν [Q]

and it is doubtful whether the μὴ ἄρξησθε is original (so Dalman, Wernle, J. H. Moulton) or substituted by Luke. See Harnack, *Sayings*, p. 2 and footnote. Peculiarly Lukan is the phrase ἄρχομαι ἀπὸ found besides in [John] 8, 9; Matt. 20, 8.

Other changes of tense

Luke makes a number of other changes in tense that do not really change the time of the action. In some cases his reasons can be conjectured.

More exact statement of future time:

Mk. 9, 31 παραδίδοται	Lk. 9, 44 μέλλει παραδίδοσθαι (= Matt. 17, 22)

Substitution of aorist for perfect (if we assume with most editors that the perfects are original with Mark in spite of limited attestation in MSS.):

Mk. 10, 28 ἠκολουθήκαμεν BCDW	Lk. 18, 28 ἠκολουθήσαμεν
Mk. 11, 2 κεκάθικεν ADX	Lk. 19, 30 ἐκάθισεν
Mk. 11, 17 πεποιήκατε BLD Orig.	Lk. 19, 46 ἐποιήσατε
Mk. 12, 43 βέβληκεν EFX	Lk. 21, 3 ἔβαλεν
Mk. 15, 47 τέθειται (*v.l.*)	Lk. 23, 55 ἐτέθη

Substitution of pluperfect for aorist:

Mk. 9, 9 ἃ εἶδον	Lk. 9, 36 ὧν ἑώρακαν
Mk. 14, 16 καθὼς εἶπεν	Lk. 22, 13 καθὼς εἰρήκει

The perfect of ἔρχομαι is used by Luke instead of the aorist.[1]

Mk. 2, 17 ἦλθον	Lk. 5, 32 ἐλήλυθα
Mt. 11, 7, 8, 9 ἐξήλθατε	Lk. 7, 24, 25, 26 ἐξεληλύθατε (but ἐξήλθατε is read in ℵA (except vs. 26) BDW) [Q]
Mt. 11, 18, 19 ἦλθεν	Lk. 7, 33, 34 ἐλήλυθεν [Q]
Mk. 5, 30 ἐξελθοῦσαν	Cf. Lk. 8, 46 ἐξεληλυθυῖαν
Mk. 14, 48 ἐξήλθατε	Lk. 22, 52 ἐξεληλύθατε (but ℵBDL *al.* read ἐξήλθατε)

The following changes of tense in other moods than the indicative affect not the time but the form of activity implied in the verb:

Mk. 5, 36 πίστευε (cf. Mk. 1, 15)	Lk. 8, 50 πίστευσον (cf. Acts 16, 31)
Mt. 10, 28 μὴ φοβεῖσθε	Lk. 12, 4 μὴ φοβηθῆτε[2] [Q]
Mk. 10, 13 ἵνα ἅψηται	Lk. 18, 15 ἵνα ἅπτηται
Mk. 12, 34 ἐπερωτῆσαι	Lk. 20, 40 ἐπερωτᾶν

[1] With some writers, for example, the author of the Revelation (*pace* the refinements of grammarians) the use of the perfects of certain verbs seems to be mainly a matter of personal taste.

[2] "μὴ φοβηθῆτε is more elegant than μὴ φοβεῖσθε." — Harnack, *Sayings*, p. 83, but see J. H. Moulton, *Grammar*, I, 122 ff.

Mk. 15, 13, 14 σταύρωσον . . . σταύρωσον	Lk. 23, 21 σταύρου, σταύρου
Mt. 5, 12 χαίρετε	Lk. 6, 23 χάρητε [Q]
Mt. 5, 42 δός	Lk. 6, 30 δίδου [Q]
Mt. 6, 11 δός	Lk. 11, 3 δίδου [Q]
Mt. 24, 45 δοῦναι	Lk. 12, 42 διδόναι [Q]

In the following cases there is simply a choice of forms:

Mt. 7, 7 f. ἀνοιγήσεται (*bis*)	Lk. 11, 9 f. ἀνοιχθήσεται (*bis*)
Mk. 2, 4 προσενέγκαι [1]	Lk. 5, 18 εἰσενεγκεῖν [2]
Mt. 18, 15 ἁμαρτήσῃ (1st Aorist is "late." See Veitch.)	Lk. 17, 3 ἁμάρτῃ [Q]
Mt. 23, 37 ἐπισυναγαγεῖν (cf. J. H. Moulton, *Grammar*, II, 10)	Lk. 13, 34 ἐπισυνάξαι (not classical, see Rutherford, *Phrynichus*, 252) [Q]
Mt. 11, 21 ἐγένοντο	Lk. 10, 13 ἐγενήθησαν ℵBDLΞ 13 33 69 (Hellenistic, see Blass, *New Testament Grammar*, § 20) [Q]

Changes in Voice and Number [3]

Luke shows considerable freedom in the use of the passive. Especially frequent is the future passive, which apparently gave the author no offence because of its length, indeed in ἀντιμετρηθήσεται (6, 38) and ἐπισυναχθήσονται (17, 37) he seems to have still further lengthened by prefixes the future passives of his source (cf. μετρηθήσεται Mark 4, 24, Matt. 7, 1; συναχθήσονται, Matt. 24, 28); and in passages peculiar to Luke we have such long forms as ἐπαναπαήσεται (10, 6); ἀφαιρεθήσεται (10, 42); ἀνταποδοθήσεται (14, 14); συνθλασθήσονται (20, 18); αἰχμαλωτισθήσονται (21, 24).

But in his parallels to Matt. and Mark, Luke's preference for the future passive is especially striking.

Mk. 2, 22 ἐκχεῖται ℵACL (= Mt. 9, 17)	Lk. 5, 37 ἐκχυθήσεται
Mt. 23, 36 ἥξει ἐπί	Lk. 11, 51 ἐκζητηθήσεται [Q]
Mt. 10, 27 εἴπατε . . . κηρύξατε	Lk. 12, 3 ἀκουσθήσεται . . . κηρυχθήσεται [Q]
Mt. 10, 33 ἀρνήσομαι	Lk. 12, 9 ἀπαρνηθήσεται [Q]
Mt. 10, 35 ἦλθον διχάσαι	Lk. 12, 53 διαμερισθήσονται [Q]
Mk. 9, 50 ἀρτύσετε	Lk. 14, 34 ἀρτυθήσεται

[1] Blass, *Grammar*, § 21.1, seems to overlook this form, supported by ℵBL *al.*, when he says of infinitives of φέρω, that only 1 Pet. 2, 5 has ἀνενέγκαι.

[2] In spite of this form and εἰσενέγκωσιν in the next verse, and εἰσενέγκῃς in 11, 4 (= Matt. 6, 13) and προσένεγκε in 5, 14 (= Mark 1, 44) and probably (so WH) παρένεγκε in 22, 42 (= Mark 14, 36), Harnack (*Sayings*, p. 69) remarks, "It is, moreover, noteworthy that neither ἤνεγκον nor any of its derivatives is found in St. Luke's gospel." First aorist forms of φέρω are found at Luke 15, 22; 23, 14.

[3] For changes in person see pp. 124 ff.

Mt. 24, 40, 41 ἀφίεται (*bis*), παραλαμβάνεται (*bis*)	Lk. 17, 34, 35, [36] ἀφεθήσεται (*bis*), παραλημφθήσεται (*bis*) [Q]
Mk. 10, 33, 34 παραδώσουσιν ἐμπαίξουσιν ἐμπτύσουσιν	Lk. 18, 32 παραδοθήσεται ἐμπαιχθήσεται ὑβρισθήσεται ἐμπτυσθήσεται
Mk. 13, 2 οὐ μὴ ἀφεθῇ οὐ μὴ καταλυθῇ	Lk. 21, 6 οὐκ ἀφεθήσεται οὐ καταλυθήσεται
Mk. 13, 12 παραδώσει	Lk. 21, 16 παραδοθήσεσθε

In some cases Luke's passive avoids an indefinite or ambiguous " they " in Mark.[1]

Mk. 3, 32 λέγουσιν	Lk. 8, 20 ἀπηγγέλη αὐτῷ
Mk. 6, 14 ἔλεγον (*v.l.* -εν)	Lk. 9, 7 λέγεσθαι ὑπό τινων (cf. p. 97)
Mk. 6, 43 καὶ ἦραν	Lk. 9, 17 καὶ ἤρθη
Mk. 9, 8 εἶδον	Lk. 9, 36 εὑρέθη
Mk. 14, 12 τὸ πάσχα ἔθυον	Lk. 22, 7 ἔδει θύεσθαι τὸ πάσχα

In others the passive avoids a change of subject in Mark, e.g.

Mk. 4, 18 οὗτοί εἰσιν οἱ . . . ἀκούσαντες 19 καὶ αἱ μέριμναι . . . συνπνίγουσι τὸν λόγον	Lk. 8, 14 οὗτοί εἰσιν οἱ ἀκούσαντες, καὶ ὑπὸ μεριμνῶν . . . συνπνίγονται

Other changes of voice:

Mk. 3, 2 παρετήρουν (AC*DΔ *al.* -ουντο)	Lk. 6, 7 παρετηροῦντο

"The middle is more frequent" (Swete on Mark 3, 2). Luke uses it again at 14, 1 but at 20, 20 uses the active.

Mt. 24, 38 γαμίζοντες	Lk. 17, 27 ἐγαμίζοντο [Q]
Mk. 10, 20 ἐφυλαξάμην (AD *al.* -ξα)	Lk. 18, 21 ἐφύλαξα (so Matt. 19, 20)

The active is classical, see Gould, *ad loc.* The middle in this sense is foreign to Greek writers but common in LXX.

Mk. 10, 49 στάς	Lk. 18, 40 σταθείς

The form σταθείς is a favorite with Luke.

Instead of Mark's plural for Jesus and his companions, Luke uses the singular, which at once focuses attention on the chief actor (Jesus) and avoids the indefinite "they" (cf. p. 150).

Mk. 1, 21 εἰσπορεύονται	Lk. 4, 31 κατῆλθεν
Mk. 1, 29 ἐξελθόντες ἦλθον (*v.l.* see below)	Lk. 4, 38 ἀναστὰς . . . εἰσῆλθεν
Mk. 5, 38 ἔρχονται εἰς τὸν οἶκον	Lk. 8, 51 ἐλθὼν εἰς τὴν οἰκίαν (cf. Mk. 5, 39, 40).
Mk. 6, 32 ἀπῆλθον	Lk. 9, 10 ὑπεχώρησεν

[1] Cf. the addition of the subject for similar reasons in cases mentioned on p. 150, and the substitution of the passive for the indefinite pronoun.

Mk. 13, 5 βλέπετε μή τις ὑμᾶς πλανήσῃ	Lk. 21, 8 βλέπετε μὴ πλανηθῆτε

Mk. 10, 46 ἔρχονται εἰς Ἰερειχώ	Lk. 18, 35 ἐν τῷ ἐγγίζειν αὐτόν εἰς Ἰ.
Mk. 11, 1 ἐγγίζουσι	Lk. 19, 29 ἤγγισεν
Mk. 14, 26 ἐξῆλθον εἰς τὸ ὄρος	Lk. 22, 39 ἐξελθὼν ἐπορεύθη
Mk. 14, 32 ἔρχονται εἰς χωρίον	Lk. 22, 40 γενόμενος ἐπὶ τοῦ τόπου

The MSS. of Mark show a similar variation between the singular and plural in certain passages. Perhaps the scribes of Mark felt the same need of correcting to the singular that Luke did. Note the following:

Mark 1, 29	ἐξελθόντες ἦλθον, ℵAC*al.* min. vers.
	ἐξελθὼν ἦλθεν, BDWΣ*al.* f g[1] arm. aeth.
Mark 9, 14	ἐλθόντες εἶδον ℵBLWΔ k arm.
	ἐλθὼν εἶδεν ACD *al.* min. latt. syr. me. go.
Mark 9, 33	ἦλθον ℵBDW*al.* pesh. vulg.
	ἦλθεν ACL*al.* min.
Mark 11, 19	ἐξεπορεύοντο ABWΔ *al.* c d syr. pesh. arm.
	ἐξεπορεύετο ℵCD *al.* min. latt. syr. sin. me. go.

Compound Verbs

Luke's changes in Mark indicate the same preference for compound verbs that is revealed both by a comparison of the passages derived from Q and by the general ratio of simple to compound verbs.[1]

Mk. 1, 29 ἦλθον	Lk. 4, 38 εἰσῆλθεν
Mk. 1, 37 ζητοῦσιν	Lk. 4, 42 ἐπεζήτουν
Mt. 7, 1 = Mk. 4, 24 μετρηθήσεται	Lk. 6, 38 ἀντιμετρηθήσεται (*v.l.*) [Q]
Mt. 15, 14 πεσοῦνται	Lk. 6, 39 ἐμπεσοῦνται [Q]
Mk. 4, 5 ἔπεσεν	Lk. 8, 6 κατέπεσεν
Mk. 5, 7 κράξας	Lk. 8, 28 ἀνακράξας
Mk. 5, 13 ἐπνίγοντο	Lk. 8, 33 ἀπεπνίγη
Mk. 5, 14 ἦλθον	Lk. 8, 35 ἐξῆλθον
Mk. 5, 27 ἐλθοῦσα	Lk. 8, 44 προσελθοῦσα (= Matt. 9, 20)
Mk. 6, 20 ἠπόρει (*v.l.*)	Cf. Lk. 9, 7 διηπόρει (cf. p. 98).
Mk. 9, 36 λαβών	Lk. 9, 47 ἐπιλαβόμενος
Mt. 11, 25 ἔκρυψας	Lk. 10, 21 ἀπέκρυψας [Q]
Mt. 22, 35 πειράζων	Lk. 10, 25 ἐκπειράζων [Q]
Mt. 12, 25 μερισθεῖσα	Lk. 11, 17 διαμερισθεῖσα [Q]
Mt. 12, 26 ἐμερίσθη	Lk. 11, 18 διεμερίσθη [Q]
Mt. 23, 34 διώξετε	Lk. 11, 49 ἐκδιώξουσιν [Q]
Mt. 10, 26 κεκαλυμμένον	Lk. 12, 2 συγκεκαλυμμένον [Q]
Mt. 10, 33 ἀρνήσομαι	Lk. 12, 9 ἀπαρνηθήσεται [Q]
Mt. 24, 28 συναχθήσονται	Lk. 17, 37 ἐπισυναχθήσονται [Q]
Mk. 10, 21 δός	Lk. 18, 22 διάδος

[1] Harnack, *Sayings of Jesus*, p. 38; p. 150: "St. Luke has about 66 per cent more compounds than St. Matthew, in which Gospel the ratio is almost exactly the same as that in St. Mark." Cf. J. H. Moulton, *Grammar*, II, 11.

Mk. 10, 30 λάβῃ	Lk. 18, 30 ἀπολάβῃ
Mk. 11, 8 ἔστρωσαν	Lk. 19, 36 ὑπεστρώννυον
Mk. 12, 3 ἀπέστειλαν	Lk. 20, 10 ἐξαπέστειλαν
Mk. 12, 18 ἔρχονται	Lk. 20, 27 προσελθόντες
Mk. 12, 18 λέγουσι	Lk. 20, 27 ἀντιλέγοντες

The contrary is less frequent, and is commonly intended to avoid unusual compounds and meanings:

Mk. 5, 36 παρακούσας (see Swete, *ad loc.*)	Lk. 8, 50 ἀκούσας
Mk. 8, 34 ἀπαρνησάσθω	Lk. 9, 23 ἀρνησάσθω
Mk. 9, 18 καταλάβῃ (see p. 60, n. 73)	Lk. 9, 39 λαμβάνει
Mt. 12, 39 ἐπιζητεῖ	Lk. 11, 29 ζητεῖ [Q]
Mk. 12, 17 ἐξεθαύμαζον	Lk. 20, 26 θαυμάσαντες
Mk. 10, 42 κατακυριεύουσιν	Lk. 22, 25 κυριεύουσιν
Mk. 10, 42 κατεξουσιάζουσιν	Lk. 22, 25 ἐξουσιάζοντες

In Matt. 12, 39 = Luke 11, 29, Harnack assumes that the ἐπιζητεῖ of Matt. is original and has been changed by Luke to the simple verb. He says (*Sayings*, p. 23), "In St. Luke the correcting hand of the stylist is here clearly traced . . . μοιχαλίς is elsewhere avoided by St. Luke as a vulgar word. Here also, contrary to his usual practice, he replaces the compound verb by the simple ζητεῖ, because he appreciates the special meaning of the compound." But the opposite is almost certainly true; for the saying again occurs in Matt. 16, 4, a doublet evidently dependent on Mark 8, 12, and there again Matthew has μοιχαλίς and ἐπιζητεῖ, while Mark has neither the adjective nor the prefixed ἐπι. It is therefore quite as likely that at 12, 39 Matthew has changed ζητεῖ to ἐπιζητεῖ (which he certainly did at 16, 4) as that Luke has reversed his usual practice (cf. Luke 4, 42 above, p. 166).

Between ἐπερωτάω and the simple verb we may judge that Luke prefers the simple verb, from these cases:

Mk. 4, 10 ἠρώτουν (-ων)	Lk. 8, 9 ἐπηρώτων
Mk. 9, 32 ἐπερωτῆσαι	Lk. 9, 45 ἐρωτῆσαι
Mk. 11, 29 ἐπερωτήσω	Lk. 20, 3 ἐρωτήσω (= Mt. 21, 24)
Mk. 15, 2 ἐπηρώτησεν	Lk. 23, 3 ἠρώτησεν

This is confirmed by comparing his use of the two verbs with occurrences in the other evangelists:

	Matt.	Mark	Luke	Acts	John
ἐρωτάω	4	3	15	7	27
ἐπερωτάω	8	25	17	2	2 (?)

If Matthew felt any objection to the use of a compound verb with the same preposition repeated in its modifying phrase, as Allen (*St. Matthew*, p. xxv f.) suggests, this objection was apparently not shared by Luke, who increases such combinations, except *ἐξέρχομαι ἐκ*, which occurs nowhere in Luke's gospel though frequent in Mark. For its correction to *ἐξέρχομαι ἀπό* see the examples on p. 202.

The occurrence of these combinations in the case of compounds of *ἔρχομαι* may be listed in the Synoptic Gospels thus:

	Matt.	Mark	Luke
ἀπέρχομαι ἀπό	1	2	4
εἰσέρχομαι εἰς	24 (27)	21 (24)	31
ἐξέρχομαι ἐκ	4 (5)	10	0
διέρχομαι διά	1 (2)	1	3
ἐπέρχομαι ἐπί	0	0	1

Notice also the following:

Mk. 6, 11 ἐκτινάξατε τὸν χοῦν τὸν ὑποκάτω τῶν ποδῶν	Lk. 9, 5 τὸν κονιορτὸν ἀπὸ τῶν ποδῶν ὑμῶν ἀποτινάσσετε[1]
Mk. 8, 31 ἀποδοκιμασθῆναι ὑπό, κ.τ.λ.	Lk. 9, 22 ἀποδοκιμασθῆναι ἀπό, κ.τ.λ. cf. 17, 25
Mk. 15, 3 κατηγόρουν αὐτοῦ	Lk. 23, 15 κατηγορεῖτε κατ' (*v.l.*) αὐτοῦ
Mk. 16, 3 ἀποκυλίσει ἐκ τῆς θύρας τοῦ μνημείου	Lk. 24, 2 ἀποκεκυλισμένον ἀπὸ τοῦ μνημείου

Verbs of Speaking

In introducing sentences of dialogue Luke shows his predilections by the changes which he makes in the diction of Mark.

Thus λέγει, which occurs over seventy times (counting λέγουσι) in Mark, is usually omitted or changed by Luke (see tables in Hawkins, *Horae Synopticae*, pp. 114 ff.). It is not used of Jesus (the exception found in most MSS. at 24, 36 is probably an interpolation from John 20, 19, for it is not found in the "Western" text of Luke), but four times of speakers in parables (13, 8; 16, 7 and 29; 19, 22), besides only at 11, 45; Acts 12, 8; 21, 37.

But in quoting scripture, Luke uses λέγει rather than εἶπεν:[2]

Mk. 12, 26 πῶς εἶπεν αὐτῷ ὁ θεὸς λέγων· ἐγὼ ὁ θεὸς Ἀβραὰμ κτλ.	Lk. 20, 37 ὡς λέγει κύριον τὸν θεὸν Ἀβραὰμ κτλ.
Mk. 12, 36 αὐτὸς Δαυεὶδ εἶπεν ἐν τῷ πνεύματι τῷ ἁγίῳ	Lk. 20, 42 αὐτὸς γὰρ Δαυεὶδ λέγει ἐν βίβλῳ ψαλμῶν

[1] Luke may be using Q here. See Mt. 10, 14 which has τὸν κονιορτὸν with Luke and ἐκτινάξατε with Mark, followed however by ἐκ τῶν ποδῶν.

[2] Cf. Acts 2, 25, 34; 7, 48; 8, 34.

λέγουσι occurs in Luke 17, 37 (though Hawkins, pp. 22, 119, fails to list it).

φησὶν occurs in Luke 7, 40 and nine times in Acts.

ἔλεγεν (ἔλεγον) occurs quite frequently in Luke, though for it also he sometimes makes a substitution (see above, p. 160). For Luke's ἔλεγεν δέ see Hawkins, p. 15.

εἶπεν is by far the commonest word for introducing sayings or speeches in dialogue and the combination εἶπεν δέ is specifically Lucan. According to Hawkins, *Horae Synopticae*, p. 15, it occurs 59 times in Luke and 15 times in Acts. The following is a list of occurrences in passages parallel to Mark or Matt.:

Mt. 4, 3 καὶ . . . εἶπεν	Lk. 4, 3 εἶπεν δέ [Q]
Mk. 3, 3 καὶ λέγει	Lk. 6, 8 εἶπεν δέ
Mk. 3, 4 καὶ λέγει	Lk. 6, 9 εἶπεν δέ
Mk. 4, 40 καὶ εἶπεν	Lk. 8, 25 εἶπεν δέ
Mk. 6, 6 ἀκούσας δὲ . . . ἔλεγεν	Lk. 9, 9 εἶπεν δέ
Mk. 6, 37 ὁ δὲ ἀποκριθεὶς εἶπεν	Lk. 9, 13 εἶπεν δέ
Mk. 6, 39 καὶ ἐπέταξεν	Lk. 9, 14 εἶπεν δέ
Mk. 8, 29 καὶ ἐπηρώτα	Lk. 9, 20 εἶπεν δέ
Mk. 9, 39 ὁ δὲ εἶπεν	Lk. 9, 50 εἶπεν δέ
Mt. 8, 22 ὁ δὲ λέγει	Lk. 9, 60 εἶπεν δέ [Q]
Mk. 10, 18 ὁ δὲ εἶπεν	Lk. 18, 19 εἶπεν δέ
Mk. 10, 28 ἤρξατο λέγειν	Lk. 18, 28 εἶπεν δέ
Mk. 12, 35 καὶ ἀποκριθεὶς ἔλεγεν	Lk. 20, 41 εἶπεν δέ
Mk. 14, 48 καὶ ἀποκριθεὶς . . . εἶπεν	Lk. 22, 52 εἶπεν δέ
Mk. 14, 71 ὁ δὲ ἤρξατο ἀναθεματίζειν	Lk. 22, 60 εἶπεν δέ

"Another test-phrase is εἶπεν δέ, frequent in Genesis and the early part of Exodus, but rare or non-existent in later books. It does not occur in Mark or Matt. In John it occurs only (*a*) in the interpolated passage 8, 11; (*b*) in 12, 6 [where D transposes δέ and syr. sin. omits εἶπεν δέ . .], (*c*) in 21, 23 οὐκ εἶπεν δέ, where δέ is supported by ℵBC and is perhaps genuine, meaning 'however.'

"In Lk. (as also in Acts) it is frequent, mostly in his Single Tradition, but sometimes in the Double or Triple *when he introduces words or arrangements of his own*. In view of these facts, Matt. 12, 47, bracketed by Tischendorf and placed by WH in marg. should be rejected as an interpolation." [Mt. 12, 47 is omitted by ℵBLΓ 3 min. syr. sin. cur. k ff^2.] Schmiedel, *Encyclopaedia Biblica*, col. 1791, note.

ἔφη is not frequent in any of the New Testament books (Matt. 13 (15) times, Mark 3, Luke 3, John 2 (3), Acts 14). Luke at times changes it to εἶπεν, e.g., Mark 9, 38 = Luke 9, 49; Mark 10, 20 = Luke 18, 21; Mark 10, 29 = Luke 18, 29; Mark 12, 24 = Luke 20, 34. On the other hand, in Luke 23, 3 and Matt. 27, 11 we read ἔφη for the λέγει of Mark 15, 2. In the following parallels ἔφη occurs in Matt. but not in Luke; Matt. 4, 7 = Luke 4, 12; Matt. 8, 8 = Luke 7, 6; Matt. 25, 21, 23 = Luke 19, 17, 19. But which reading (if either) was in the common source is not easily determined, for

Matthew appears to add ἔφη to Mark about as often as Luke omits it, e.g., Matt. 21, 27; 22, 37; 26, 34; 27, 11; 27, 23.

Luke frequently adds the participle λέγων to various expressions of saying. Thus in parallels to Mark we find these cases:

Mk. 1, 25 ἐπετίμησεν	Lk. 4, 35 ἐπετίμησεν λέγων
Mk. 2, 6 διαλογιζόμενοι	Lk. 5, 21 διαλογίζεσθαι λέγοντες
Mk. 2, 16 ἔλεγον	Lk. 5, 30 ἐγόγγυζον λέγοντες
Mk. 5, 9 ἐπηρώτα	Lk. 8, 30 ἐπηρώτησεν λέγων (om. ℵB *al.*)
Mk. 5, 41 λέγει	Lk. 8, 54 ἐφώνησεν λέγων
Mk. 9, 7 φωνή	Lk. 9, 35 φωνὴ . . . λέγουσα
Mk. 9, 17 ἀπεκρίθη	Lk. 9, 38 ἐβόησεν λέγων
Mk. 10, 17 ἐπήρωτα	Lk. 18, 18 ἐπηρώτησεν λέγων
Mk. 11, 28 ἔλεγον	Lk. 20, 2 εἶπαν λέγοντες
Mk. 12, 7 εἶπαν	Lk. 20, 14 διελογίζοντο λέγοντες
Mk. 12, 14 λέγουσιν	Lk. 20, 21 ἐπηρώτησαν λέγοντες
Mk. 13, 3 ἐπηρώτα	Lk. 21, 7 ἐπηρώτησαν λέγοντες
Mk. 14, 70 ἔλεγον	Lk. 22, 59 διισχυρίζετο λέγων
Mk. 15, 2 ἐπηρώτησεν	Lk. 23, 3 ἠρώτησεν λέγων
Mk. 15, 13 ἔκραξαν	Lk. 23, 21 ἐπεφώνουν λέγοντες
Mk. 15, 39 εἶπεν	Lk. 23, 47 ἐδόξαζεν τὸν θεὸν λέγοντες

Luke uses ἀποκριθείς with a verb of saying quite as often as do the other Evangelists, more than 30 times in its proper sense of answering questions or requests. He retains it where it is so used in his sources, and introduces it in some other passages where it was not in them.

ἀποκριθείς retained:

Mt. 4, 4 ἀποκριθείς	Lk. 4, 4 ἀπεκρίθη [Q]
Mt. 11, 4 ἀποκριθείς	Lk. 7, 22 ἀποκριθείς [Q]
Mk. 3, 33 ἀποκριθείς	Lk. 8, 21 ἀποκριθείς
Mk. 8, 29 ἀποκριθείς	Lk. 9, 20 ἀποκριθείς
Mk. 9, 19 ἀποκριθείς	Lk. 9, 41 ἀποκριθείς
Mt. 25, 12 ἀποκριθείς	Lk. 13, 25 ἀποκριθείς [Q]
Mk. 11, 33 ἀποκριθέντες	Lk. 20, 7 ἀπεκρίθησαν
Mk. 15, 2 ἀποκριθείς	Lk. 23, 3 ἀποκριθείς

ἀποκριθείς introduced:

Mt. 4, 10 τότε λέγει	Lk. 4, 8 ἀποκριθεὶς . . . εἶπεν [Q]
Mt. 4, 7 ἔφη	Lk. 4, 12 ἀποκριθεὶς . . . εἶπεν [Q]
Mk. 2, 8 λέγει	Lk. 5, 22 ἀποκριθεὶς εἶπεν
Mk. 2, 17 ἀκούσας λέγει	Lk. 5, 31 ἀποκριθεὶς . . . εἶπεν
Mk. 2, 25 λέγει	Lk. 6, 3 ἀποκριθεὶς . . . εἶπεν
Mk. 8, 28 εἶπαν λέγοντες	Lk. 9, 19 ἀποκριθέντες εἶπαν
Mk. 9, 38 ἔφη	Lk. 9, 49 ἀποκριθεὶς . . . εἶπεν
Mk. 11, 29 εἶπεν	Lk. 20, 3 ἀποκριθεὶς δὲ εἶπεν (= Matt. 21, 24)

The use of ἀποκριθείς, not in answer to a real question or request, but for the beginning of a new speech with little or no reference to the situation (perhaps a Semitic idiom, see Dalman, *Words of Jesus*, p. 24), is less common in Luke, and is habitually omitted by him when found in his sources. See Mark 6, 37; 9, 5; 10, 51; 12, 35; 14, 48; Matt. 11, 25; 22, 1.

Besides these more conventionalized and regular formulae, Luke shows a great variety in his choice of verbs to describe utterances of different kinds, frequently substituting for the common words of saying like λέγω and εἶπον verbs of more distinctive significance.[1] A careful study of the context of the following parallels will show how appropriately the substitutions have been made.

Mk. 1, 30 λέγουσιν	Lk. 4, 38 ἠρώτησαν
Mk. 10, 51 εἶπεν	Lk. 18, 40 ἐπηρώτησεν
Mk. 11, 3 εἴπῃ	Lk. 19, 31 ἐρωτᾷ
Mk. 12, 14 λέγουσιν	Lk. 20, 21 ἐπηρώτησαν λέγοντες
Mk. 4, 9 ἔλεγεν	Lk. 8, 8 ἐφώνει
Mk. 5, 41 λέγει	Lk. 8, 54 ἐφώνησεν λέγων
Mk. 15, 12 ἔλεγεν	Lk. 23, 20 προσεφώνησεν
Mk. 1, 44 λέγει	Lk. 5, 14 παρήγγειλεν
Mk. 5, 8 ἔλεγεν	Lk. 8, 29 παρήγγειλεν
Mk. 5, 43 εἶπεν	Lk. 8, 55 διέταξεν
Mk. 2, 16 ἔλεγον	Lk. 5, 30 ἐγόγγυζον λέγοντες
Mk. 12, 7 εἶπαν	Lk. 20, 14 διελογίζοντο λέγοντες
Mk. 12, 18 λέγουσι	Lk. 20, 27 ἀντιλέγοντες
Mk. 12, 37 λέγει	Lk. 20, 44 καλεῖ (= Matt. 22, 45)
Mk. 14, 70 ἔλεγον	Lk. 22, 59 διισχυρίζετο λέγων
Mk. 15, 39 εἶπεν	Lk. 23, 47 ἐδόξαζεν τὸν θεὸν λέγων

For the converse see

Mk. 6, 8 παρήγγειλεν *c.* ἵνα	Lk. 9, 3 εἶπεν. *c. orat. dir.* [Q?]
Mk. 6, 39 ἐπέταξεν *c.* inf.	Lk. 9, 14 εἶπεν *c. orat. dir.*
Mk. 8, 29 ἐπηρώτα	Lk. 9, 20 εἶπεν (cf. λέγει Mt. 16, 15)
Mk. 14, 71 ἤρξατο ἀναθεματίζειν καὶ ὀμνύναι	Lk. 22, 60 εἶπεν[2]

[1] Compare Scholten, pp. 91, n. 6, 93, n. 3, 98: "für das beständig wiederkehrende, eintönige, allgemeine λέγειν von Lc zur Abwechselung gebraucht werden παραγγέλλειν, δεῖσθαι, ἐρωτᾶν, προσφωνεῖν, διαλογίζεσθαι."

[2] For the probable motive of this change, see p. 95.

Luke's Preferences in Verbs

In regard to some other verbs Luke's preferences can be illustrated by several examples for each. In the following pages illustrations are collected to show:

1. His avoidance of θαμβέομαι (and ἐκθαμβέομαι), θλίβω, καθεύδω, κρατέω, ὑπάγω (especially the form ὕπαγε, "go thy way"), and φέρω (in the sense of ἄγω);

2. His liking for δέομαι, ἐγγίζω, ἐπιλαμβάνομαι, ὑποστρέφω, and φύω;

3. His treatment of βλέπω, ἔρχομαι, φωνέω and their compounds.

θαμβέομαι occurs in Mark 1, 27; 10, 24; 10, 32 and ἐκθαμβέομαι in Mark 9, 15; 14, 33; 16, 5, 6, but nowhere else in the New Testament.

Except the following cases, Matthew and Luke *both* omit the whole verse in which Mark uses the word:

Mk. 1, 27 καὶ ἐθαμβήθησαν ἅπαντες	Lk. 4, 36 καὶ ἐγένετο θάμβος ἐπὶ πάντας	Mt. omits this incident
Mk. 14, 33 ἤρξατο ἐκθαμβεῖσθαι καὶ ἀδημονεῖν	Mt. 26, 37 ἤρξατο λυπεῖσθαι καὶ ἀδημονεῖν	Lk. omits this point
Mk. 16, 5 ἐξεθαμβήθησαν	Lk. 24, 5 ἐμφόβων γενομένων	Mt. omits this verse

θλίβω and its compounds, as well as the noun θλίψις (see p. 186), are avoided by Luke except in the solitary instance in the New Testament of ἀποθλίβω, viz.

Mk. 5, 31 συνθλίβοντα	Lk. 8, 45 συνέχουσι καὶ ἀποθλίβουσι
Mk. 3, 9 θλίβωσιν	Lk. 6, 18 om., cf. ἐπικεῖσθαι, Lk. 5, 1
Mk. 5, 24 συνέθλιβον	Lk. 8, 42 συνέπνιγον

καθεύδω is twice retained by Luke (in words of Jesus):

Mark 5, 39 οὐκ ἀπέθανεν ἀλλὰ καθεύδει = Luke 8, 52
Mark 14, 37 Σίμων, καθεύδεις; Luke 22, 46 τί καθεύδετε;

It is not found elsewhere in Luke or in Acts, but is changed thus:

Mk. 4, 38 καθεύδων	Lk. 8, 23 ἀφύπνωσεν
Mk. 14, 37 καθεύδοντας	Lk. 22, 45 κοιμωμένους

κρατέω occurs in Matt. 12 times, in Mark 15 times, in Luke 2 (Acts 4) times. To Mark 3, 21; 6, 17; 7, 3, 4, 8; 9, 10; 14, 44, 46, 51, Luke has no parallels; κρατήσας in Luke 8, 54 is from Mark 5, 41.

In the remaining cases in Mark, Luke changes it or omits this verb:

Mk. 1, 31 κρατήσας τῆς χειρός	Lk. 4, 39 omits
Mk. 9, 27 κρατήσας τῆς χειρός	Lk. 9, 42 omits
Mk. 12, 12 αὐτὸν κρατῆσαι	Lk. 20, 19 ἐπιβαλεῖν ἐπ' αὐτὸν τὰς χεῖρας
Mk. 14, 1 κρατήσαντες	Lk. 22, 2 omits
Mk. 14, 49 οὐκ ἐκρατήσατέ με	Lk. 22, 53 οὐκ ἐξετείνατε τὰς χεῖρας ἐπ' ἐμέ

The verb *ὑπάγω* occurs never in Acts, only 5 times in Luke, though it is frequent in the other three gospels. Its intransitive use is not classical, but in Hellenistic times was common, as it is in modern Greek (Kennedy, *Sources*, p. 156). Luke frequently changes it, e.g.:

Mk. 14, 13 ὑπάγετε εἰς τὴν πόλιν	Lk. 22, 10 εἰσελθόντων ὑμῶν εἰς τὴν πόλιν
Mk. 14, 21 υἱὸς τοῦ ἀνθρώπου ὑπάγει	Lk. 22, 22 υἱὸς τοῦ ἀνθρώπου πορεύεται

The form *ὕπαγε* is especially common in Matthew and Mark, but occurs nowhere in Luke. Very likely it seemed to him vulgar. In the following cases he has probably changed or omitted it:

Mt. 4, 10 ὕπαγε, σατανᾶ (cf. Mk. 8, 33)	Lk. 4, 8 omits [Q]
Mk. 1, 44 ὕπαγε . . . δεῖξον	Lk. 5, 14 ἀπελθὼν δεῖξον
Mk. 2, 11 ὕπαγε [1]	Lk. 5, 24 πορεύου
Mt. 8, 13 ὕπαγε	Lk. 7, 10 entirely different [Q] [2]
Mk. 5, 19 ὕπαγε εἰς τὸν οἶκόν σου	Lk. 8, 39 ὑπόστρεφε εἰς τὸν οἶκον σου
Mk. 5, 34 ὕπαγε εἰς εἰρήνην	Lk. 8, 48 πορεύου εἰς εἰρήνην
Mk. 6, 38 ὑπάγετε, ἴδετε [3]	Lk. 9, 13 om. (see also p. 80)
Mt. 18, 15 ὕπαγε, ἔλεγξον αὐτόν	Lk. 17, 3 ἐπιτίμησον αὐτόν [Q]
Mk. 10, 21 ὕπαγε, ὅσα ἔχεις πώλησον	Lk. 18, 22 πάντα ὅσα ἔχεις πώλησον
Mk. 10, 52 ὕπαγε, ἡ πίστις σου σέσωκέν σε	Lk. 18, 42 ἀνάβλεψον· ἡ πίστις κ.τ.λ.

Harnack (*Sayings*, p. 109) says; "The *ὕπαγε* in all three cases of its occurrence (4, 10; 8, 13; 18, 15) is probably inserted by St. Matthew." But in passages from Mark, Matthew nowhere inserts it and Luke always omits it. Would they deal differently with Q?

With regard to another saying of Q, Harnack makes an equally unjustified statement. Matt. 10, 16 reads *ἰδοὺ ἐγὼ ἀποστέλλω ὑμᾶς ὡς πρόβατα ἐν μέσῳ λύκων*. Luke 10, 3 reads: *ὑπάγετε, ἰδοὺ ἀπο-*

[1] In Mark 2, 9 ὕπαγε is read by ℵD 33 (apparently assimilated from 2, 11), but most other MSS. of Mark and the parallels in Matt. 9, 5 and Luke 5, 23 read περιπάτει.

[2] Perhaps this verse is not from Q at all; see Harnack, *Sayings*, pp. 77, 210 f.

[3] Mark 8, 33 ὕπαγε ὀπίσω μου, σατανᾶ; Luke omits the whole verse.

στέλλω ὑμᾶς ὡς ἄρνας ἐν μέσῳ λύκων. Harnack (*Sayings*, p. 13) says: "*ὑπάγετε* is an addition of St. Luke in order to connect verse 3 with verse 2." But this connection may have been just as much needed in Q, if, as Harnack prints it on p. 134, these verses occurred in the same order there as in Luke; while Matt. could have easily omitted *ὑπάγετε* in his context.

φέρω, which in modern Greek has almost entirely replaced *ἄγω* (Jannaris, *Historical Greek Grammar*, 996,3), was already in Hellenistic times encroaching upon it, by taking the meaning "lead," "bring," of persons and cattle. So Mark uses it, but Luke corrects him thus:

Mk. 1, 32 *ἔφερον*	Lk. 4, 40 *ἤγαγον*
Mk. 9, 2 *ἀναφέρει*	Lk. 9, 28 *παραλαβὼν ἀνέβη*
Mk. 9, 19 *φέρετε*	Lk. 9, 41 *προσάγαγε*
Mk. 11, 2 *φέρετε*	Lk. 19, 30 *ἀγάγετε*
Mk. 11, 7 *φέρουσι*	Lk. 19, 35 *ἤγαγον* (So Matt. 21, 7)
Mk. 15, 1 *ἀπήνεγκαν*	Lk. 23, 1 *ἤγαγον*
Mk. 15, 22 *φέρουσι*	Cf. Lk. 23, 33 *ἀπῆλθον* (Matt. 27, 2 *ἀπήγαγον*)

In Mark, if not elsewhere, the scribe of D or its ancestor has shown the same desire for improvement as the author of Luke. The readings of that MS. for the above passages in Mark are: 1, 32 *ἐφέροσαν*, 9, 2 *ἀνάγει*, 9, 19 *φέρετε*, 11, 2 *ἀγάγετε*, 11, 7 *ἤγαγον*, 15, 1 *ἀπήγαγον*, 15, 22 *ἄγουσι*. See Wellhausen, *Einleitung in die drei ersten Evangelien*, p. 11.

ἐγγίζω occurs in Matt. 7 times, Mark 3 times, Luke 18 times, Acts 6 times. Throughout the New Testament its use in eschatological associations is common; cf. Rom. 13, 12; Heb. 10, 25; Jas. 5, 8; 1 Pet. 4, 7. So Luke uses it:

Mk. 13, 6 *ἐγώ εἰμι*	Lk. 21, 8 adds *καὶ ὁ καιρὸς ἤγγικεν*
Mk. 13, 14 *βδέλυγμα ἐρημώσεως*	Lk. 21, 20 *ἤγγικεν ἡ ἐρήμωσις*
	Lk. 21, 28 *ἐγγίζει ἡ ἀπολύτρωσις ὑμῶν*

So Matthew uses it (?):

Mk. 14, 41 *ἦλθεν ἡ ὥρα*	Mt. 26, 45 *ἤγγικεν ἡ ὥρα*

With *ἡ βασιλεία τοῦ θεοῦ (τῶν οὐρανῶν)* it is found in the preaching of the Baptist (Matt. 3, 2), in the early preaching of Jesus (Mark 1, 15 = Matt. 4, 17), and in the programme of the mission (Matt. 10, 7 = Luke 10, 9). Luke, however, repeats it in 10, 11 *πλὴν τοῦτο γινώσκετε, ὅτι ἤγγικεν ἡ βασιλεία τοῦ θεοῦ.*

In its ordinary uses, Luke's preference for *ἐγγίζω* may be seen in the following parallels:

Mt. 6, 20 *κλέπται οὐ διορύσσουσιν οὐδὲ κλέπτουσιν*	Lk. 12, 33 *κλέπτης οὐκ ἐγγίζει* [Q]
Mk. 10, 46 *ἔρχονται εἰς Ἰερειχώ*	Lk. 18, 35 *ἐγγίζειν αὐτὸν εἰς Ἰ.*

Mk. 10, 50 ἦλθεν πρὸς Ἰησοῦν	Lk. 18, 40 ἐγγισάντος αὐτοῦ
Mk. 14, 1 ἦν τὸ πάσχα καὶ τὰ ἄζυμα μετὰ δύο ἡμέρας	Lk. 22, 1 ἤγγιζεν ἡ ἑορτὴ τῶν ἀζύμων ἡ λεγομένη πάσχα
Mk. 14, 45 ἐλθὼν εὐθὺς προσελθὼν	Lk. 22, 47 ἤγγισεν

ἐπιλαμβάνομαι (found only once each in Matt. and Mark, viz., Matt. 14, 31 peculiar to Matt., Mark 8, 23 peculiar to Mark) is used by Luke in 9, 47 for λαβών Mark 9, 36; in 20, 20 for ἀγρεύσωσιν Mark 12, 13 (see Kennedy, p. 13, Schmid, IV, 267); in 23, 26 for ἀγγαρεύουσιν Mark 15, 21 (see Kennedy, p. 72). It occurs besides in Luke 14, 4; 20, 26; Acts 9, 27; 16, 19; 17, 19; 18, 17; 21, 30, 33; 23, 19.

Except in Matt. 9, 38 (= Luke 10, 2 δεήθητε οὖν τοῦ κυρίου τοῦ θερισμοῦ), δέομαι is used by Luke only among the evangelists. The following instances are in parallels to Mark:

Mk. 1, 40 παρακαλῶν	Lk. 5, 12 ἐδεήθη
Mk. 5, 7 ὁρκίζω	Lk. 8, 28 δέομαι
Mk. 5, 18 παρεκάλει	Lk. 8, 38 ἐδεῖτο
Mk. 9, 18 εἶπα	Lk. 9, 40 ἐδεήθην, cf. 9, 38

ὑποστρέφω occurs 21 times in Luke and 11 (12) times in Acts, but not in the other gospels (except Mark 14, 40, where, however, ℵBDL and the older versions read ἐλθών). That Luke should use it in recasting his sources is natural. See the following:

Mk. 1, 14 ἦλθεν	Lk. 4, 14 ὑπέστρεψεν
Mk. 5, 19 ὕπαγε εἰς τὸν οἶκόν σου	Lk. 8, 39 ὑπόστρεφε εἰς τὸν οἶκόν σου
Mk. 5, 21 διαπεράσαντος	Lk. 8, 40 ὑποστρέφειν cf. 37 ὑπέστρεψεν
Mk. 6, 30 συνάγονται	Lk. 9, 10 ὑποστρέψαντες
Mt. 12, 44 ἐπιστρέψω	Lk. 11, 24 ὑποστρέψω [Q]
Mk. 16, 8 ἐξελθοῦσαι	Lk. 24, 9 ὑποστρέψασαι

φύω and συνφύω are used of the growth of plants more properly than ἀναβαίνω and ἐξανατέλλω (Kennedy, *Sources*, p. 73).

Mk. 4, 5 ἐξανέτειλεν	Lk. 8, 6 φυέν
Mk. 4, 7 ἀνέβησαν	Lk. 8, 7 συνφυεῖσαι
Mk. 4, 8 ἀναβαίνοντα καὶ αὐξανόμενον [1]	Lk. 8, 8 φυέν

But ἐκφύῃ of Mark 13, 28 is replaced by προβάλωσιν Luke 21, 30.

Luke shares the use of βλέπω common in the Koinê as a substitute for the verb ὁράω, but in a few cases changes its more unusual combinations.[2]

[1] In the parable of the mustard seed Mark 4, 32 again uses ἀναβαίνω, while Q (Matt. 13, 32 = Luke 13, 19) apparently used αὐξάνω.

[2] The absence of the verb in Luke 7, 22 ἃ εἴδετε καὶ ἠκούσατε, parallel to Mt. 11, 4 ἃ

Mk. 8, 15 *βλέπετε ἀπό*	Lk. 12, 1 *προσέχετε* (= Matt. 16, 6), *ἑαυτοῖς ἀπό* (perhaps from Q)
Mk. 12, 38 *βλέπετε ἀπό*	Lk. 20, 46 *προσέχετε*
Mk. 13, 33 *βλέπετε*	Cf. Lk. 21, 34 *προσέχετε ἑαυτοῖς*

προσέχετε ἑαυτοῖς occurs only in Luke and Acts. The remaining instances are Luke 17, 3; Acts 5, 35; 20, 28.

For "be a respecter of persons" Luke also has a more usual form,

Mk. 12, 14 *βλέπεις εἰς πρόσωπον*	Lk. 20, 21 *λαμβάνεις πρόσωπον*

Luke usually omits *ἐμβλέψας* and *περιβλεψάμενος* when they occur in Mark, viz.: Mark 10, 21, 27 and Mark 3, 34; 5, 32; 9, 8; 10, 23; 11, 11. Each occurs once in Luke: *ἐμβλέψας*, 20, 17 (not in Mark 12, 10); *περιβλεψάμενος*, 6, 10 (retained from Mark 3, 5). *ἐμβλέψασα*, Mark 14, 67, is replaced by Luke's favorite verb *ἀτενίσασα*, Luke 22, 56, but in a later verse (22, 61) is the form *ἐνέβλεψεν*.

Note also Matt. 6, 26 *ἐμβλέψατε*; Luke 12, 24 *κατανοήσατε* [Q].

In the use of other verbs of seeing Luke has some characteristic habits.[1]

He is fond of *εὑρίσκω* in this sense and of *θεάομαι*, but frequently changes *θεωρέω*:

ἀκούετε καὶ βλέπετε, may be due to the source, or, if not, to a difference of tense, for *ἔβλεψα* scarcely occurs in the New Testament.

[1] For the omission of *ἰδών* the participle see pp. 89 f. In another series of cases Luke omits the verb of seeing but with far more radical effect on the structure of sentences. These are the cases where Luke says directly that something took place while Mark only states that something was seen to take place. Perhaps a different reason should be assigned to each case:

Mk. 1, 10 *εἶδεν σχιζομένους τοὺς οὐρανοὺς καὶ τὸ πνεῦμα . . . καταβαῖνον, κ.τ.λ.*	Lk. 3, 21 *ἐγένετο . . . ἀνεῳχθῆναι τὸν οὐρανόν, καὶ καταβῆναι τὸ πνεῦμα, κ.τ.λ.*

(Here Mt. 3, 16 has *εἶδεν πνεῦμα . . . καταβαῖνον* with Mark, but *καὶ ἰδοὺ ἠνεῴχθησαν οἱ οὐρανοί* which is more like Luke).

Mk. 5, 31 *βλέπεις τὸν ὄχλον συνθλίβοντά σε*	Lk. 8, 45 *οἱ ὄχλοι συνέχουσίν σε καὶ ἀποθλίβουσιν*
Mk. 5, 38 *θεωρεῖ . . . κλαίοντας, κ.τ.λ.*	Lk. 8, 52 *ἔκλαιον δὲ πάντες, κ.τ.λ.*
Mk. 9, 4 *καὶ ὤφθη αὐτοῖς Ἡλείας σὺν Μωϋσεῖ, καὶ ἦσαν συνλαλοῦντες τῷ Ἰησοῦ*	Lk. 9, 30 *καὶ ἰδοὺ ἄνδρες δύο συνελάλουν αὐτῷ, οἵτινες ἦσαν Μ. καὶ Ἡ. οἱ ὀφθέντες ἐν δόξῃ*
Mk. 9, 14 *εἶδον ὄχλον πολὺν*	Lk. 9, 37 *συνήντησεν αὐτῷ ὄχλος πολύς*
Mk. 14, 62 *ὄψεσθε τὸν υἱὸν τοῦ ἀνθρώπου ἐκ δεξιῶν καθήμενον*	Lk. 22 69 *ἀπὸ τοῦ νῦν δὲ ἔσται ὁ υἱὸς τοῦ ἀνθρώπου καθήμενος ἐκ δεξιῶν*

For the reverse see Mt. 8, 11 = Lk. 13, 28 and

Mk. 12, 42 *μία χήρα πτωχὴ ἔβαλεν*	Lk. 21, 2 *εἶδεν δέ τινα χήραν πενιχρὰν βάλλουσαν*

Mk. 2, 14 εἶδεν	Lk. 5, 27 ἐθεάσατο
Mk. 5, 15 θεωροῦσιν	Lk. 8, 35 εὗρον
Mk. 9, 8 εἶδον	Lk. 9, 36 εὑρέθη
Mk. 12, 41 ἐθεώρει	Lk. 21, 1 ἀναβλέψας εἶδεν
Mk. 15, 40 θεωροῦσαι	Lk. 23, 49 ὁρῶσαι (cf. θεωρήσαντες 48)
Mk. 15, 47 ἐθεώρουν	Lk. 23, 55 ἐθεάσαντο
Mk. 16, 4 ἀναβλέψασαι θεωροῦσιν	Lk. 24, 2 εὗρον

προσεφώνησεν in Luke 6, 13 seems to take the place of *προσκαλεῖται* (Mark 3, 13), and in Luke 23, 20 of the simple *ἀποκριθεὶς ἔλεγεν* (Mark 15, 12). *προσφωνέω* occurs outside of Luke (Luke 13, 12; Acts 21, 40; 22, 2) only in Matt. 11, 16 from Q (= Luke 7, 32). *ἐπιφωνέω* is peculiar to Luke (Luke 23, 21; Acts 12, 22; 21, 34; 22, 24). Simple *φωνέω* is used for *λέγω* in Luke 8, 8, 54 (= Mark 5, 9, 41), but is not specially characteristic of Luke.

Forms of *ἔρχομαι* or its compounds frequently disappear in Luke's reproduction of his sources. Not only are *πορεύομαι* and other verbs used in its place, giving greater elegance or definiteness to the description, but the (Hebraistic ?) idiom of Luke allows the use of *ἰδού* and the nominative in place of any verb at all. Further, the verb can often be omitted without great loss from Mark's narrative, especially where it is coördinate with another verb, or where several forms of the verb are gathered in a single passage.

Besides the three instances given above (p. 173) for the use of *πορεύομαι* in place of *ὑπάγω*, *πορεύομαι* (which is not found in Mark)[1] is used for *ἀπέρχομαι* in the following cases:

Mk. 1, 35 ἀπῆλθεν	Lk. 4, 42 ἐπορεύθη
Mk. 6, 36 ἀπελθόντες	Lk. 9, 12 πορευθέντες
Mk. 6, 37 ἀπελθόντες	Lk. 9, 13 πορευθέντες
Mk. 14, 12 ἀπελθόντες	Cf. Lk. 22, 8 πορευθέντες

In one instance *ἐκπορεύομαι* is used for *ἐξέρχομαι*:

Mk. 1, 28 ἐξῆλθεν (So Lk. 4, 14; 7, 17; see pp. 108 f.)	Lk. 4, 37 ἐξεπορεύετο

But for the simple *ἔρχομαι*, *πορεύομαι* appears not to be substituted. Rather are the two verbs contrasted as 'come' and 'go' in Matt. 8, 9 = Luke 7, 8.

[1] *πορεύομαι* is read by Westcott and Hort in Mark 9, 30 following only B*D and some testimony from the versions. The three occurrences in [Mark] 16, 9–20 of course cannot be considered an exception. The omission of the simple verb in Mark is the more remarkable since the compounds *εἰσ-* *ἐκ-* and *παραπορεύομαι*, are characteristic of Mark (Hawkins, *Horae Synopticae*, p. 12 n.), and are removed by Luke in rewriting Marcan passages. See Mark 1, 21; 4, 19; 5, 40; 6, 11 and their parallels in Luke.

For ἔρχομαι and its compounds Luke substitutes various other verbs:

Mk. 1, 31 προσελθών	Lk. 4, 39 ἐπιστάς
Mk. 1, 38 ἐξῆλθον	Lk. 4, 43 ἀπεστάλην (cf. pp. 97, 117 f.).
Mk. 3, 31 ἔρχεται	Lk. 8, 19 παρεγένετο
Mk. 5, 1 ἦλθον	Lk. 8, 26 κατέπλευσαν
Mt. 10, 13 ἐλθάτω	Lk. 10, 6 ἐπαναπαήσεται [Q]
Mt. 10, 34 ἦλθον	Lk. 12, 51 παρεγενόμην [Q]
Mk. 11, 27b ἔρχονται	Lk. 20, 1 ἐπέστησαν

ἰδού without a verb takes the place of ἔρχομαι:

Mk. 1, 40 ἔρχεται λεπρός	Lk. 5, 12 ἰδοὺ ἀνὴρ πλήρης λέπρας
Mk. 2, 3 ἔρχονται φέροντες	Lk. 5, 18 ἰδοὺ ἄνδρες φέροντες
Mk. 15, 43 ἐλθὼν Ἰωσήφ	Lk. 23, 50 ἰδοὺ ἀνὴρ ὀνόματι Ἰωσήφ

Compare also καὶ ἰδοὺ γυνή (Luke 7, 37) with ἦλθεν γυνή (Mark 14, 3). Note also the ἰδού of Luke 8, 41 (cf. Mark 5, 22), Luke 22, 47 (cf. Mark 14, 43 παραγίνεται). Luke introduces ἰδού elsewhere in sections taken from Mark, and in matter peculiar to his gospel, and in Acts it occurs very frequently. It is used to introduce new characters in the cases cited above and in Luke 2, 25; 9, 38 (cf. Mark 9, 17); 10, 25; 14, 2; 19, 2; Acts 8, 27; 16, 1.[1] It is also used to emphasize a large number or amount (Luke 13, 7; 13, 16; 15, 29; 19, 8) — a very peculiar and unique usage.

The following list shows how in other ways forms of ἔρχομαι are omitted, or at least reduced in number:

Mk. 1, 29 ἐξελθόντες ἦλθον	Lk. 4, 38 ἀναστὰς . . . εἰσῆλθεν
Mk. 1, 35 ἐξῆλθεν καὶ ἀπῆλθεν	Lk. 4, 42 ἐξελθὼν ἐπορεύθη
Mk. 2, 18 ἔρχονται καὶ λέγουσιν	Lk. 5, 33 εἶπαν
Mk. 3, 6 ἐξελθόντες	Lk. 6, 11 omits
Mk. 4, 4 ἦλθεν τὰ πετεινὰ καὶ κατέφαγεν	Lk. 8, 5 τὰ πετεινὰ . . . κατέφαγεν
Mk. 5, 38–40 ἔρχονται . . . εἰσελθὼν . . . εἰσπορεύεται	Lk. 8, 51 ἐλθών
Mt. 13, 32 ἐλθεῖν τὰ πετεινὰ τοῦ οὐρανοῦ καὶ κατασκηνοῖν	Lk. 13, 19 τὰ πετεινὰ τοῦ οὐρανοῦ κατεσκήνωσεν [Q]
Mk. 11, 15 καὶ ἔρχονται . . . καὶ εἰσελθών	Lk. 19, 45 καὶ εἰσελθών
Mk. 12, 14 καὶ ἐλθόντες λέγουσιν	Lk. 20, 21 καὶ ἐπηρώτησαν λέγοντες
Mk. 12, 42 ἐλθοῦσα χήρα ἔβαλεν	Lk. 21, 2 εἶδεν χήραν βάλλουσαν
Mk. 14, 16 καὶ ἐξῆλθον . . . καὶ ἦλθον	Lk. 22, 13 ἀπελθόντες
Mk. 14, 32 ἔρχονται	Lk. 22, 40 γενόμενος
Mk. 14, 45 ἐλθὼν εὐθὺς προσελθών	Lk. 22, 47 ἤγγισεν τῷ Ἰησοῦ
Mk. 14, 66 ἔρχεται . . . καὶ ἰδοῦσα	Lk. 22, 56 ἰδοῦσα

See also pp. 89 f.

[1] Especially striking is its repeated use with ἀνήρ, ἄνδρες in Luke 5, 12, 18; 8, 49; 9, 30; 9, 38; 23, 50; 24, 4 (cf. the parallels to these passages in Mark); and in Luke 19, 2; Acts 1, 10; 8, 27; 10, 19, 30; 11, 11.

For the simple verbs εἰμί and γίνομαι more definite words are substituted by Luke:

Mk. 1, 4 ἐγένετο Ἰωάννης	Lk. 3, 3 ἦλθεν (possibly from Q)
Mk. 4, 37 γίνεται λαῖλαψ	Lk. 8, 23 κατέβη λαῖλαψ
Mk. 6, 15 ἐστίν	Lk. 9, 8 ἐφάνη
Mk. 6, 15 [ἐστίν understood]	Lk. 9, 8 ἀνέστη
Mk. 8, 28 [ἐστίν understood]	Lk. 9, 19 ἀνέστη
Mk. 10, 47 ἐστίν	Lk. 18, 37 παρέρχεται
Mk. 14, 1 ἦν	Lk. 22, 1 ἤγγιζεν

Perhaps γίνομαι is preferred by Luke to εἰμί for the same reason, viz. that it is less colorless. Thus:

Mt. 7, 27 ἦν ἡ πτῶσις αὐτῆς μεγάλη	Lk. 6, 49 ἐγένετο τὸ ῥῆγμα τῆς οἰκίας ἐκείνης μέγα [Q]
Mt. 12, 40 ἦν Ἰωνᾶς ἐν τῇ κοιλίᾳ τοῦ κήτους	Lk. 11, 30 ἐγένετο Ἰωνᾶς τοῖς Νινευείταις σημεῖον [Q]
Mt. 25, 21 ἐπὶ ὀλίγα ἦς πιστός	Lk. 19, 17 ἐν ἐλαχίστῳ πιστὸς ἐγένου [Q]
Mk. 12, 7 ἡμῶν ἔσται ἡ κληρονομία	Lk. 20, 14 ἵνα ἡμῶν γένηται ἡ κληρονομία
Mk. 12, 23 τίνος αὐτῶν ἔσται γυνή	Lk. 20, 33 τίνος αὐτῶν γίνεται γυνή
Mk. 10, 43 ἔσται ὑμῶν διάκονος	Cf. Lk. 22, 26 γινέσθω . . . ὡς ὁ διακονῶν

In the following passage both verbs occur in each gospel but their position is exchanged. Harnack (*Sayings*, p. 63), attributes the change to Luke.

Mt. 5, 45 ὅπως γένησθε υἱοὶ τοῦ πατρὸς ὑμῶν τοῦ ἐν οὐρανοῖς . . . 48 ἔσεσθε οὖν ὑμεῖς τέλειοι	Lk. 6, 35 καὶ ἔσεσθε υἱοὶ ὑψίστου . . . 36 γίνεσθε οἰκτίρμονες [Q]

Compare also Luke's use of ὑπάρχω in place of εἰμί, or where words are simply in apposition:

Mk. 5, 22 εἷς τῶν ἀρχισυναγώγων, ὀνόματι Ἰάειρος	Lk. 8, 41 ἀνὴρ ᾧ ὄνομα Ἰάειρος, καὶ αὐτὸς ἄρχων τῆς συναγωγῆς ὑπῆρχεν [Q]
Mt. 7, 11 εἰ οὖν ὑμεῖς πονηροὶ ὄντες	Lk. 11, 13 εἰ οὖν ὑμεῖς πονηροὶ ὑπάρχοντες [Q]
Mk. 15, 43 Ἰωσὴφ . . . εὐσχήμων βουλευτής	Lk. 23, 50 Ἰωσὴφ βουλευτὴς ὑπάρχων

The use of γίνομαι with the dative of the person in the sense, "it happened to him," is not found in the Gospel of Luke, though it occurs thrice in Mark (and in Acts 7, 40 from LXX; cf. Acts 12, 18):

Mk. 5, 16 πῶς ἐγένετο τῷ δαιμονιζομένῳ	Lk. 8, 36 πῶς ἐσώθη ὁ δαιμονισθείς
Mk. 5, 33 ὃ γέγονεν αὐτῇ	Cf. Lk. 8, 47 ὡς ἰάθη παραχρῆμα [1]
Mk. 9, 21 τοῦτο γέγονεν αὐτῷ	Lk. 9, 42 omits the whole dialogue

ἀφίημι is a verb of so varied meaning that it is frequently ambiguous. Whether Luke consciously avoids it for this reason or not,

[1] Cf. Mk. 5, 29 ἴαται

it will be seen in the following parallels that his substitute is perfectly clear:

1. To leave heirs at death:

Mk. 12, 19 *ἐὰν . . . μὴ ἀφῇ τέκνον*	Lk. 20, 28 *ἐὰν . . . οὗτος ἄτεκνος ᾖ*
Mk. 12, 20 *οὐκ ἀφῆκεν σπέρμα*	Lk. 20, 29 *ἄτεκνος*
Mk. 12, 22 *οὐκ ἀφῆκαν σπέρμα*	Lk. 20, 31 *οὐ κατέλιπον τέκνα*

2. To leave undone, neglect:

Mt. 23, 23 *ἀφήκατε*	Lk 11, 42 *παρέρχεσθε* [Q]
Mt. 23, 23 *ἀφεῖναι*	Lk. 11, 42 *παρεῖναι* [Q]

3. To leave alone, depart from:

Mt. 4, 11 *ἀφίησιν αὐτὸν ὁ διάβολος*	Lk. 4, 13 *ὁ διάβολος ἀπέστη ἀπ' αὐτοῦ* [Q]
Mt. 18, 12 *οὐχὶ ἀφήσει* (*v. l. ἀφεὶς*)	Lk. 15, 4 *οὐ καταλείπει* [Q]

4. To allow:

Mk. 1, 35 *οὐκ ἤφιεν* (cf. 11, 16)	Lk. 4, 41 *οὐκ εἴα*
Mt. 5, 40 *ἄφες*	Lk. 6, 29 *μὴ κωλύσῃς* [Q]
Mk. 5, 19 *οὐκ ἀφῆκεν αὐτὸν* (*scil. ἵνα μετ' αὐτοῦ ᾖ*)	Lk. 8, 38 *ἀπέλυσεν αὐτόν*
Mt. 23, 13 *οὐδὲ . . . ἀφίετε*	Lk. 11, 52 *ἐκωλύσατε* [Q]

The reverse case:

Mt. 24, 43 *οὐκ ἂν εἰάσεν*	Lk. 12, 39 *οὐκ ἂν ἀφῆκεν* [Q]

is very hard to explain, especially as it is more likely that *ἐάω* is original than that Matthew has introduced it. Cf. Harnack, *Sayings*, p. 33. On Luke's use of *κωλύειν* see Harnack, *ibid.*, p. 100.

Note also the following parallels:

Mk. 4, 36 *ἀφέντες τὸν ὄχλον*	Lk. 8, 22 omits (so Matt. 8, 23)
Mk. 8, 13 *ἀφεὶς* (Matt. 16, 14 *καταλιπὼν*) *αὐτοὺς*	Lk. omits the whole section
Mk. 11, 6 *ἀφῆκαν αὐτούς*	Lk. 19, 34 omits (so Matt. 21, 6)
Mk. 12, 12 *ἀφέντες αὐτόν* (= Matt. 22, 22)	Lk. 20, 19 omits
Mk. 15, 37 *ἀφεὶς φωνὴν μεγάλην*	Lk. 23, 46 *φωνήσας* (Matt. 27, 50 *κράξας*) *φωνῇ μεγάλῃ*

Even when Luke retains the verb *ἀφίημι*, he often changes the form. Here the motive is perhaps still more obscure, but in some cases may be the varied connotation of the forms.

Mk. 2, 5, 9 *ἀφίενται*	Lk. 5, 20, 23 *ἀφέωνται* (cf. Lk. 7, 47, 48)
Mk. 2, 7 *ἀφιέναι*	Lk. 5, 21 *ἀφεῖναι*
Mt. 6, 12 *ἀφήκαμεν*	Lk. 11, 4 *ἀφίομεν* [Q]
Mt. 24, 40, 41 *ἀφίεται*	Lk. 17, 34, 35, [36] *ἀφεθήσεται* [Q]
Mk. 13, 2 *οὐ μὴ ἀφεθῇ* [1]	Lk. 21, 6 *οὐκ ἀφεθήσεται*

In Acts the verb is used only three times.

[1] In Matt. 12, 32b, B reads *οὐ μὴ ἀφεθῇ* over against *οὐκ* (*ℵ οὐ μὴ*) *ἀφεθήσεται* in all other MSS. and in the parallel Luke 12, 10.

Similarly the ambiguous verb *αἴρω* is apparently avoided by Luke:

Mk. 2, 3 *αἰρόμενον*	Lk. 5, 18 *ἐπὶ κλίνης* (Matt. 9, 2 *ἐπὶ κλίνης βεβλημένον*)
Mk. 2, 21 = Matt. 9, 16 *αἴρει*	Lk. 5, 36 *τὸ καινὸν σχίσει*
Mt. 24, 39 *ἦρεν ἅπαντας*	Lk. 17, 27 *ἀπώλεσεν ἅπαντας* [Q]
Mk. 15, 21 = Matt. 27, 32 *ἄρῃ*	Lk. 23, 26 *φέρειν*

Note that Matthew avoids *αἴρω*. Besides the passage cited above see:

Lk. 6, 29 *τοῦ αἴροντος*	Mt. 5, 40 *τῷ θέλοντι . . . λαβεῖν* [Q]
Lk. 6, 30 *τοῦ αἴροντος*	Mt. 5, 42 *τὸν θέλοντα . . . δανίσασθαι* [Q]
Mk. 4, 15 = Lk. 8, 12 *αἴρει*	Mt. 13, 19 *ἁρπάζει*
Mk. 8, 19 *ἤρατε*	Mt. 16, 9 *ἐλάβετε*
Mk. 8, 20 *ἤρατε*	Mt. 16, 10 *ἐλάβετε*
Lk. 11, 52 *ἤρατε τὴν κλεῖδα*	Mt. 23, 13 *κλείετε* [Q]

Perhaps a comparison of the use of *αἴρω* in Mark and Q can be made from the following double parallels:

Mk. 6, 8 *αἴρωσιν* = Lk. 9, 3 *αἴρετε*	Mt. 10, 9 *κτήσεσθε* Lk. 10, 4 *βαστάζετε*
Mk. 8, 34 = Mt. 16, 24 = Lk. 9, 23 *ἀράτω τὸν σταυρόν*	Mt. 10, 38 *λαμβάνει τὸν σταυρόν* Lk. 14, 27 *βαστάζει τὸν σταυρόν*
Mk. 11, 23 = Mt. 21, 21 *ἄρθητι καὶ βλήθητι εἰς τὴν θάλασσαν*	Mt. 17, 20 *μετάβα ἔνθεν ἐκεῖ* Lk. 17, 6 *ἐκριζώθητι καὶ φυτεύθητι ἐν τῇ θαλάσσῃ*

Of course it is possible that the original verb of Q is not preserved by either Luke or Matthew in any of these instances. Except in the first case, Harnack (*Sayings*, pp. 88, 145; cf. p. 134) as usual gives the preference to the form in Matthew. But *μετάβα* (Matt. 17, 20) is almost certainly secondary, for Matthew uses it five times to Luke's once, and twice (8, 34; 15, 29; cf. 12, 9) substitutes it for other verbs in Mark, who never uses the word. So apparently Matthew substitutes *λαμβάνω* for *αἴρω* in three cases given above, while *βαστάζω* may be original with Q in Luke 14, 27, as well as in Luke 10, 4 and Matt. 3, 11, where Harnack retains it.

Selection of More Literary Synonyms

More significant are the cases in which Luke substitutes a word of his own for a verb occurring only once or twice in his sources. Preference for one word for coming, saying, and the like, above a synonymous term, may merely reflect a writer's habitual mode of expression, without implying reflection or distinct motive. This is not so likely to be the case, however, with less common words, and changes in these may with greater probability be attributed to deliberate choice and thus disclose the author's sense of propriety in diction.

In some cases Luke seems to be influenced mainly by motives of style.

Thus, for the unusual ἐπιράπτει, Mark 2, 21 (the lexicons mention only this passage)[1], he substitutes the common ἐπιβάλλει (5, 36) as does Matt. 9, 16.

For σκανδαλίζονται twice in Luke, eight times in Mark and thirteen times in Matthew) Luke once substitutes the common ἀφίστανται (Luke 8, 13 = Mark 4, 17).

For κολαφίζειν (Mark 14, 65 = Matt. 26, 27, a late denominative, found elsewhere only in ecclesiastical writers) Luke 22, 63 uses δέρω, which is at least as old as the comedy in the sense 'strike.'

Similarly ἐκεφαλίωσαν (Mark 12, 4 ℵBL — ἅπαξ λεγόμενον in Greek literature)[2] disappears probably into the ἐλιθοβόλησαν of Matt. 21, 35 and the still more classical τραυματίσαντες (found elsewhere in the New Testament only in Acts 19, 16) and δείραντες, of Luke 20, 11, 12.

For προμεριμνᾶτε, Mark 13, 11, "ἅπαξ λεγόμενον in New Testament and perhaps in writers earlier than the close of the canon, Matt. [10, 19] has μεριμνᾶν, Luke [21,14] the classical προμελετᾶν, 'to prepare a speech.'" (Swete *ad loc.*)

Parallel to καταμάθετε (Matt. 6, 28, nowhere else in New Testament and not frequent in any Greek except possibly Xenophon and Plato) Luke 12, 27 has the more common κατανοήσατε, a favorite word of his, as shown by the parallels:

Mt. 6, 26 ἐμβλέψατε εἰς	Lk. 12, 24 κατανοήσατε [Q]
Mk. 12, 15 ἰδών	Lk. 20, 23 κατανοήσας

The verb ξηραίνω in the medical sense (see p. 47) is not used by Luke.

Mk. 3, 1 ἐξηραμμένην χεῖρα	Lk. 6, 6 ἡ χεὶρ . . . ἦν ξηρά
Mk. 5, 29 ἐξηράνθη ἡ πηγή	Lk. 8, 44 ἔστη ἡ ῥύσις
Mk. 9, 18 ξηραίνεται	Lk. 9, 39 omits (cf. p. 60, n. 73)

But he retains ἐξηράνθη of the withered sprout of grain, Luke 8, 6 = Mark 4, 6.

The verbs censured by Atticists, ancient and modern, and avoided by Luke form an interesting list:

Mark 15, 21 ἀγγαρεύω (a Persian loan-word not naturalized until Hellenistic times; see Norden, *Antike Kunstprosa*, p. 489, note 1, Zahn, *Introduction*, I, p. 66, note 11): Luke 23, 26 ἐπιλαβόμενοι. — Mark 12, 13 ἀγρεύσωσιν (poetical, Schmid, *Atticismus*, IV, 267): Luke 20, 20 ἐπιλάβωνται. — Parallel to ῥαπίζει (Matt. 5, 39; see Lobeck, *Phryn.* p. 175) Luke 6, 29 has τύπτω. — γρηγορεῖτε (Mark 14, 38; Lobeck, *Phryn.*, pp. 118 f.) is omitted in Luke 22, 46 (unless ἀναστάντες be a substitute for it). "Lukas hat es zweimal, aber da wo die ursprüngliche Bedeutung durchschimmert," viz. 12, 37, 39 — Norden. But the latter case is perhaps an assimilation of some MSS. to Matt. 22, 43. — For στίλβοντα (Mark 9, 3. "Dass das Wort der κοινή angehört, zeigt auch Apoll. Soph. lex. Hom., p. 145, 23 Bekker." — Schmid, *Atticismus* IV, p. 229) Luke 9, 29 has ἐξαστράπτων. — For ἐσχάτως ἔχειν (Mark 5, 23 'to be at the point of death,' a phrase condemned by Atticists, Lobeck, *Phryn.* p. 389) Luke 8, 42 has ἀπέθνησκεν,

[1] I have lately noted the word in Theophrastus, *Characters*, 16, 6.

[2] See Lobeck, *Phryn.* p. 95; ἐκεφαλαίωσαν in the other MSS. means ordinarily in Greek 'to summarize.' Cf. Scholten, p. 95, n. 5.

'was dying.' — For ὁρκίζω (Mark 5, 7; Lobeck *Phryn*, p. 361) Luke 8, 28 has δέομαι. On this change, see also above pp. 93, 175.

Certain uses of δίδωμι equivalent to the Latin *do* might be suspected of being Latinisms. Luke avoids two of them:

Mk. 3, 6 συμβούλιον ἐδίδουν ℵB *al.*	Lk. 6, 11 συνελάλουν
Mk. 4, 8 ἐδίδου καρπόν (= Matt. 13, 8)	Lk. 8, 8 ἐποίησεν καρπόν

Perhaps another Latinism is to be found in Mark's use of ἰσχύω = *valeo*. Luke uses a good Greek word in its place:

Mk. 2, 17 ἰσχύοντες	Lk. 5, 31 ὑγιαίνοντες

Luke avoids giving verbs an unusual, incorrect, vulgar, or unclassical meaning.

For θροεῖσθε, 'be frightened' (Mark 13, 7 = Matt. 24, 6, and in LXX; see Kennedy, *Sources*, p. 126; in classical Greek it meant 'raise an outcry') Luke 21, 9 has πτοήθητε, (The Western Text of Mark 13, 7 has θορυβεῖσθε). — For ὑστερεῖ, 'be wanting,' Lat. *deficere*, Mark 10, 21 (John 2, 3 *v.l.*, Dioscorides 5, 86), Luke 18, 22 has the regular λείπει. — For τρώγοντες 'eating' (Matt. 24, 38, cf. Photius p. 231, note, quoted by Norden, *Antike Kunstprosa*, p. 486 f., note 4: τρώγειν οὐχὶ τὸ ἐσθίειν ἁπλῶς, ἀλλὰ τὰ τραγήματα καὶ τρωκτὰ καλούμενα) Luke 17, 27 has ἤσθιον. — For ἐκβάλλει (Matt. 12, 35 *bis*), in its (late) colorless sense involving no notion of violence, Luke 6, 45 *bis* has προφέρει. (See also above, p. 91).

Greater definiteness and freedom from ambiguity is obtained by using for γεμίζεσθαι (Mark 4, 37, technical term for loading with cargo) συνεπληροῦντο (Luke 8, 23) when the boat was in danger of being filled with waves. For συνζητεῖν (Mark 1, 27), Luke 4, 36 has συνελάλουν ("more precise." Harnack, *Luke the Physician*, p. 89).

Improvements of literary tone may be recognized in the following:

Mk. 1, 26 σπάραξαν	Lk. 4, 35 ῥίψαν[1]
Mk. 3, 16 ἐπέθηκεν ὄνομα	Lk. 6, 14 ὠνόμασεν
Mt. 5, 39 στρέψον	Lk. 6, 29 πάρεχε [Q]
Mk. 4, 16 λαμβάνουσι	Lk. 8, 13 δέχονται
Mk. 4, 39 ἐκόπασεν	Lk. 8, 24 ἐπαύσαντο
Mt. 6, 20 ἀφανίζει	Lk. 12, 33 διαφθείρει [Q]
Mt. 10, 34 βαλεῖν εἰρήνην	Lk. 12, 51 δοῦναι εἰρήνην [Q]
Mk. 9, 42 καλόν ἐστι μᾶλλον	Lk. 17, 2 λυσιτελεῖ (Matt. 18, 6 συμφέρει)
Mk. 10, 47 κράζειν	Lk. 18, 38 ἐβόησεν
Mk. 14, 23 λαβών	Lk. 22, 17 δεξάμενος (cf. 8, 13 above)

Luke does not consistently eschew words which for one reason or another he seems to disapprove. Of those enumerated above he

[1] E. A. Abbott, *Proclamation of the New Kingdom*, p. 159, notes that in Dan. 8, 7 the Septuagint and Theodotion read ἐσπάραξεν and ἔριψεν respectively.

himself uses *σκανδαλίζω*, *γρηγορέω*, *ὁρκίζω* (Acts 19, 13), *σπαράσσω* (Luke 9, 39, 42 = Mark 9, 26), *κράζω*. But this inconsistency does not deprive his habitual improvement of the diction in such cases of its significance.

The following additional examples of such improvement may be noted:

Mt. 23, 31 τῶν φονευσάντων	Lk. 11, 48 ἀπέκτειναν [Q]
Mt. 23, 35 ἐφονεύσατε	Lk. 11, 51 ἀπολομένου [Q]
Mk. 9, 42 βέβληται	Lk. 17, 2 ἔρριπται
Mk. 11, 7 ἐπιβάλλουσι	Lk. 19, 35 ἐπιρίψαντες
Mk. 15, 22 μεθερμηνευόμενον (a late word)	Lk. 23, 23 καλούμενον

In some instances it is not obvious why one synonym is preferred to the other:

Mk. 9, 9 καταβαινόντων	Lk. 9, 37 κατελθόντων
Mk. 10, 48 σιωπήσῃ	Lk. 18, 39 σιγήσῃ
Mk. 14, 47 ἔπαισεν	Lk. 22, 50 ἐπάταξεν (Matt. 26, 51 πατάξας)
Mk. 15, 46 ἐνείλησεν	Lk. 23, 53 ἐνετύλιξεν (= Matt. 27, 59)
Mt. 5, 4 πενθοῦντες	Lk. 6, 21 κλαίοντες [Q]
Mt. 11, 17 ἐκόψατε	Lk. 7, 32 ἐκλαύσατε [Q]
Mk. 5, 38 ἀλαλάζοντας καὶ κλαίοντας	Lk. 8, 52 ἔκλαιον καὶ ἔκοπτον
Mk. 5, 39 θορυβεῖσθε καὶ κλαίετε	Lk. 8, 52 κλαίετε
Mk. 6, 17 ἔδησεν	Lk. 3, 20 κατέκλεισεν
Mk. 3, 27 δήσῃ (= Matt. 12, 29)	Lk. 11, 22 νικήσῃ (perhaps from Q)
Mk. 5, 3, 4 δῆσαι, δεδέσθαι	Lk. 8, 29 ἐδεσμεύετο
Mk. 15, 1 δήσαντες (= Matt. 27, 2)	Lk. 23, 1 omits
Mk. 15, 7 δεδεμένος	Lk. 23, 19 βληθεὶς ἐν τῇ φυλακῇ

The last nine cases may well be due to a predilection on Luke's part for *κλαίω* (used only twice in Matt.) and an aversion for *δέω* (used only twice in Luke's gospel). Except for *δεσμεύουσι* Matt. 23, 4, *δεσμεύω* occurs again only in Acts 22, 4, and *κατακλείω* only in Acts 26, 10 (where *ἐν φυλακαῖς* is used like *ἐν φυλακῇ* Luke 3, 20).

In the following cases the synonyms alternate curiously:

Mk. 5, 16 διηγήσαντο	Lk. 8, 36 ἀπήγγειλαν
Mk. 5, 19 ἀπάγγειλον	Lk. 8, 39 διηγοῦ
Mk. 6, 30 ἀπήγγειλαν	Lk. 9, 10 διηγήσαντο
Mk. 9, 9 διηγήσωνται	Cf. Lk. 9, 39 ἀπήγγειλαν

διηγέομαι occurs nowhere else in the gospels; *ἀπαγγέλλω* occurred apparently twice besides in Luke's known sources; in both cases he retains it, Matt. 11, 4 = Luke 7, 22; Mark 5, 14 = Luke 8, 34.

A few additional cases of verbs substituted for words and phrases in Mark, " not altogether polished in character," may be found in Zahn, *Introduction*, III, 136, note 13.

Harnack sees improvement in the following parallels from Q:

Luke 10, 6 ἀνακάμψει for ἐπιστραφήτω (Matt. 10, 13; 2 aor. pass. with middle ἐπιστρέφομαι used absolutely "probably belonged to the vulgar idiom." — Harnack, *Sayings*, p. 81).

Luke 12, 27 ὑφαίνει for κοπιῶσιν (Matt. 6, 28. — *ibid.*, p. 6).

Luke 7, 28 ἐστιν for ἐγήγερται (Matt. 11, 11, " too un-Hellenic." — *ibid.*, p. 16),

Luke 10, 24 ἠθέλησαν for ἐπεθύμησαν (Matt. 13, 17. — *ibid.*, p. 26).

Luke 6, 22 ἐκβάλωσιν, ' defame," for εἴπωσιν πᾶν πονηρόν (Matt. 5, 11. — *ibid.* p. 52).

Luke 6, 30, 35 ἀπαίτει, ἀπελπίζοντες (" of themselves show classical feeling." — *ibid.*, p. 60 f.) for ἀποστραφῇς (Matt. 5, 42, absolute 2 aor. pass., cf. above on ἀνακάμψει).

Luke 13, 24 ἀγωνίζεσθε (" a classical word." — *ibid.*, p. 67) εἰσελθεῖν for εἰσέλθατε (Matt. 7, 13).

Luke 6, 40 κατηρτισμένος (" a word of somewhat choice character." — *ibid.*, p. 81) compared with Matt. 10, 25.

Luke 12, 5 ἐμβαλεῖν εἰς τὴν γέενναν for ἀπολέσαι ἐν γεέννῃ (Matt. 10, 28, " bad Greek." — *ibid.*, p. 84).

Luke 17, 24 λάμπει, " a better word than φαίνεται " (Matt. 24, 27. — *ibid.*, p. 107).

With our present difficulties in fixing an exact estimate of the literary standing of a particular word in New Testament times, it is not likely that we shall be able to weigh with accuracy every pair of synonyms presented to us by the Synoptic Gospels. Nor will opinions expressed on comparative elegance always meet with the approval of all readers. Further, it is not likely that a writer, even of considerably more literary skill than his sources, will always correct their faults or recognize their excellences. Even a good stylist is a slave to his own habits of speech and may substitute them for something better. In a few cases one may perhaps be inclined to suspect that after all the rival word in Matthew or Mark is really superior to Luke's, yet I must confess that after examining all the parallels I have not found a single one in which I should be inclined to assert with any confidence that this is the case. Only the following deserve consideration:

δέω, bind, is twice recommended by an Atticistic fragment (Reitzenstein, *Griechische Etymologika*, pp. 393, 396) in preference to δεσμεύω. On Luke's use of these words see above, p. 184.

ἔλεγξον, Matt. 18, 15, is certainly no more classical, though perhaps " more original than the frequent ἐπιτίμησον," Luke 17, 3 (Harnack, *Sayings*, pp. 94 f.).

ἐμπαίζοντες, Mark 15, 31 (used in poetry and late prose) is replaced by ἐκμυκτήριζον (Luke 23, 35) not found in profane authors nor again in the New Testament, except Luke 16, 23, but frequently in LXX. Here Luke is probably thinking of Ps. 21, 8 (22, 8 Heb.), πάντες . . . ἐξεμυκτήρισάν με. In verse 36 Luke uses ἐνέπαιξαν.

ἐνείλησεν, Mark 15, 46 (LXX, Artemidorus, Plutarch, Aristotle, Philo, Heliodorus, Philostratus) is replaced by *ἐνετύλιξεν* (Luke 23, 53; Aristophanes, Athenaeus, John 20, 7). Observe, however, that Matthew also has *ἐνετύλιξεν* in his parallel (Matt. 27, 59); so that it may be doubted whether this is really a case of independent change of Mark by Luke.

Use of Nouns

In his choice and use of nouns Luke shows the same general traits as in his choice of verbs. Only a few nouns are so consistently treated that the author seems to have followed any rule about them.

Thus, he invariably avoids *θάλασσα* when speaking of the inland lake of Galilee. His substitutes are:

λίμνη 5, 1, 2 (cf. Mark 1, 16 *bis*); 8, 23, 33 (cf. Mark 5, 13 *bis*).
ὕδωρ, 8, 24, 25 (cf. Mark 4, 39, 41).

Notice the variety of expressions in other places where the word might have been used:

Luke 5, 3 *ἀπὸ τῆς γῆς ἐπαναγαγεῖν ὀλίγον*
Luke 5, 4 *ἐπανάγαγε εἰς τὸ βάθος*
Luke 5, 11 *καταγαγόντες τὰ πλοῖα ἐπὶ τὴν γῆν*
Luke 6, 17 *ἐπὶ τόπου πεδινοῦ* (Mark 3, 7 *εἰς τὴν θάλασσαν*)
Luke 8, 22 *ἐνέβη εἰς πλοῖον*
Luke 8, 26 *καὶ κατέπλευσαν* (Mark 5, 1 *ἦλθον εἰς τὸ πέραν τῆς θαλάσσης*).
Luke 8, 27 *ἐξελθόντι . . . ἐπὶ τὴν γῆν*

He omits Mark's references to the sea, to Jesus' going thither, or teaching on or by the sea (Mark 2, 13; 3, 7, 9; 4, 1; 5, 21; 7, 31).

An inclination to multiply diminutives is colloquial, and such formations are frequently censured by Atticists. Luke's more cultivated literary taste generally avoids them.

Mk. 5, 23 *θυγάτριον*	Lk. 8, 42 *θυγάτηρ*
Mk. 5, 41 *κοράσιον* (Lobeck, *Phryn.* 73 f.)	Lk. 8, 54 *παῖς*
Mk. 5, 42 *κοράσιον*	Lk. 8, 55 no subject
Mk. 14, 47 *τὸ ὠτάριον* (Lobeck, *Phryn.* 211)	Lk. 22, 50 *τὸ οὖς* (Moeris, 288)

But some MSS. of Mark read *ὠτίον* as in Matt. 26, 51. Luke also in vs. 51 uses *ὠτίον*.

In the following instances Luke substitutes more reputable words for such as are late, rare, or vulgar:

Mk. 4, 17 *θλίψεως* ("colloquial," Kennedy, p. 79)	Lk. 8, 13 *πειρασμοῦ*
Mk. 13, 19 *θλίψις*	Lk. 21, 23 *ἀνάγκη*
Mk. 13, 24 *θλίψιν*	Lk. 21, 25 omits
Mk. 3, 6 *συμβούλιον* (late)	Lk. 6, 11 omits
Mk. 15, 1 *συμβούλιον*	Cf. Lk. 23, 1 *πλῆθος*

Mt. 7, 16 τριβόλων (rare)	Lk. 6, 44 βάτου ("more choice." Harnack, *Sayings*, p. 69) [Q]
Mt. 12, 25 ἐνθυμήσεις ("rare in classics." Thayer)	Lk. 11, 17 διανοήματα (Schmid, *Atticismus* II, 94) [Q]
Mt. 24, 45 οἰκετείας (late)	Lk. 12, 42 θεραπείας (classical) [Q]
Mt. 24, 49 συνδούλους (Moeris, 273)[1]	Lk. 12, 45 παῖδας καὶ παιδίσκας [Q]
Mt. 24, 28 πτῶμα (Lobeck, *Phryn.*, 375; Thomas Magister, 765)	Lk. 17, 37 σῶμα [Q]
Mk. 10, 25 ῥαφίς (Lobeck, *Phryn.*, 90)	Lk. 18, 25 βελόνη
Mk. 10, 25 τρυμαλιᾶς ("late and rare." Swete *ad loc.*)	Lk. 18, 25 τρήματος ℵBD (classical; so Matt. 19, 24 ℵ*B)
Mk. 10, 46 προσαίτης (Swete *ad loc.*)	Lk. 18, 35 τις ἐπαιτῶν
Mk. 12, 43 ὑστερήσεως (rare)	Lk. 21, 4 ὑστερήματος (commoner)
Mk. 13, 14 βδέλυγμα (technical Jewish and rare)	Lk. 21, 20 changed entirely

ὀψία is never used by Luke. It occurs as a noun five times each in Matthew and Mark. This use is condemned by the Atticists; see Thomas Magister 102, 9; R. Reitzenstein, *Geschichte der Griechischen Etymologika*, p. 393.

Mk. 1, 32 ὀψίας γενομένης, ὅτε ἔδυ ὁ ἥλιος Mt. 8, 16 ὀψίας γενομένης	Lk. 4, 40 δύνοντος τοῦ ἡλίου
Mk. 4, 35 ὀψίας γενομένης	Lk. and Mt. have no reference to time
Mk. 6, 35 ὥρας πολλῆς γενομένης Mt. 14, 15 ὀψίας γενομένης	Lk. 9, 12 ἡ ἡμέρα ἤρξατο κλίνειν
Mk. 6, 47 = Mt. 14, 23 ὀψίας γενομένης	Lk. omits the incident
Mk. 14, 17 = Mt. 26, 20 ὀψίας γενομένης	Lk. 22, 14 ὅτε ἐγένετο ὥρα
Mk. 15, 42 = Mt. 27, 57 ὀψίας	Cf. Lk. 23, 54 σάββατον ἐπέφωσκεν

The following changes may be recorded without more particular explanation. Many of them are probably improvements in clearness, or in elegance or exactness of expression:

Mk. 1, 28 ἀκοή, 'report,'	Lk. 4, 37 ἦχος
Mt. 7, 28 λόγους	Lk. 7, 1 ῥήματα [Q]
Mt. 8, 5–13 παῖς	Lk. 7, 2–10 δοῦλος (once παῖς) [Q]
Mk. 5, 40 τοῦ παιδίου	Lk. 8, 51 τῆς παιδός
Mk. 6, 11 χοῦν, dust	Lk. 9, 5 κονιορτόν (So Matt. 10, 14; from Q?)
Mk. 6, 39 συμπόσια	Lk. 9, 14 κλισίας
Mk. 9, 3 τὰ ἱμάτια	Lk. 9, 29 ὁ ἱματισμός[2]
Mt. 10, 16 πρόβατα	Lk. 10, 3 ἄρνας [Q]
Mt. 6, 12 ὀφειλήματα, sins	Lk. 11, 4 ἁμαρτίας [Q]
Mk. 10, 1 παιδία	Lk. 18, 15 βρέφη

[1] But see p. 189.

[2] Cf. Matt. 11, 8 οἱ τὰ μαλακὰ φοροῦντες = Luke 7, 25 οἱ ἐν ἱματισμῷ ἐνδόξῳ

Mk. 12, 15 ὑπόκρισιν [1]	Lk. 20, 23 πανουργίαν
Mk. 12, 20 οὐκ ἀφῆκεν σπέρμα [2]	Lk. 20, 29 ἀπέθανεν ἄτεκνος
Mk. 12, 21 μὴ καταλιπὼν σπέρμα	Lk. 20, 30 [ἀπέθανεν ἄτεκνος]
Mk. 12, 22 οὐκ ἀφῆκαν σπέρμα	Lk. 20, 31 οὐ κατέλιπον τέκνα
Mk. 13, 7 ἀκοάς πολέμων (cf. 1, 28 above)	Lk. 21, 9 ἀκαταστασίας
Mk. 16, 5 στολήν	Lk. 24, 4 ἐσθῆτι (*v. l.* ἐσθήσεσιν)

The following differences are most likely without stylistic significance. In some cases, as the first two, the change is quite contrary to the apparent preferences of Luke:

Mk. 14, 63 μαρτύρων [3]	Lk. 22, 71 μαρτυρίας
Mk. 14, 72 τὸ ῥῆμα	Lk. 22, 62 τοῦ λόγου
Mk. 1, 27 διδαχή	Lk. 4, 36 ὁ λόγος
Mk. 3, 35 τὸ θέλημα [4]	Lk. 8, 21 τὸν λόγον
Mt. 4, 5 τοῦ κόσμου	Lk. 4, 5 τῆς οἰκουμένης [Q]
Mk. 4, 8 τὸ πετρῶδες	Lk. 8, 6 τὴν πέτραν
Mk. 6, 14 βασιλεύς	Lk. 9, 7 τετραάρχης (= Matt. 14, 1)
Mk. 13, 25 ἀστέρες	Lk. 21, 25 ἄστροις
Mk. 15, 27 λῃστάς	Lk. 23, 32, 33 κακοῦργοι

Luke adds δύναμις to ἐξουσία:

Mk. 1, 27 κατ' ἐξουσίαν	Lk. 4, 36 ἐν ἐξουσίᾳ καὶ δυνάμει
Mk. 6, 7 ἐδίδου αὐτοῖς ἐξουσίαν	Lk. 9, 1 ἔδωκεν αὐτοῖς δύναμιν καὶ ἐξουσίαν

Compare Luke 10, 19 ἰδοὺ δέδωκα ὑμῖν τὴν ἐξουσίαν . . . καὶ ἐπὶ πᾶσαν τὴν δύναμιν τοῦ ἐχθροῦ; Luke 4, 6 σοὶ δώσω τὴν ἐξουσίαν ταύτην ἅπασαν καὶ τὴν δόξαν αὐτῶν (Matt. 4, 8 has τὴν δόξαν αὐτῶν and ταῦτά σοι πάντα δώσω); Luke 12, 11 ἐπὶ τὰς συναγωγὰς καὶ τὰς ἀρχὰς καὶ τὰς ἐξουσίας (cf. Mark 13, 9 f. = Matt. 10, 17 f. = Luke 21, 12 συνέδρια . . . συναγωγὰς . . . ἡγεμόνων . . . βασιλέων); Luke 20, 20 τῇ ἀρχῇ καὶ τῇ ἐξουσίᾳ τοῦ ἡγεμόνος (not in Mark 12, 13).

He changes " father and (or) mother " to " parents," and perhaps "brother(s) and sister(s) " to " brethren,"

Mk. 5, 40 τὸν πατέρα καὶ τὴν μητέρα	Cf. Lk. 8, 56 οἱ γονεῖς
Mk. 10, 29 μητέρα ἢ πατέρα	Lk. 18, 29 γονεῖς
ἀδελφοὺς ἢ ἀδελφάς	ἀδελφούς

[1] Cf. Matt. 24, 51 ὑποκριτῶν = Lk. 12, 46 ἀπίστων, and other passages where ὑποκριτής appears in Matt. but not in Luke. Here, however, Luke has the verb (ὑποκρινομένους 20, 20).

[2] See Schmid, *Atticismus*, II, 207; III, 220: "σπέρμα = *progenies* ist mehr poetisch als prosaisch," and Norden, *Antike Kunstprosa*, p. 488, note 3: " Es ist doch sehr bezeichnend, dass Lukas das in diesem Sinn hebraisierende Wort σπέρμα nur an zwei Stellen hat, von denen die eine (20, 28) ein Citat aus der Septuag., die andere (1, 55) eine direkte Beziehung auf diese ist."

[3] Frequent in Acts; also Luke 24, 48. The change is no doubt connected with Luke's omission of witnesses (cf. pp. 102 f.) and μαρτυρία occurs in Mark 14, 55, 56, 59.

[4] Cf. θέλημα, of God's will, in Matt. 6, 10; 7, 21, but not in Luke 6, 46; 11, 2.

Mk. 3, 32 ἀδελφοὶ καὶ ἀδελφαί	Lk. 8, 20 ἀδελφοί
Mk. 3, 35 ἀδελφὸς καὶ ἀδελφή	Lk. 8, 21 ἀδελφοί
Mt. 10, 37 υἱὸν ἢ θυγατέρα	Lk. 14, 26 τέκνα [Q]

But the first passage in Luke has also (8, 51) τὸν πατέρα καὶ τὴν μητέρα and the last passage has both this combination and τοὺς ἀδελφοὺς καὶ τὰς ἀδελφάς. In two of these passages Luke (14, 26; 18, 29) makes the significant addition ἢ (καὶ τὴν) γυναῖκα. In Matt. 24, 49 = Luke 12, 45 it may be Matthew who changes into τοὺς συνδούλους (found also in Matt. 18, 28, 29, 31, 33) the τοὺς παῖδας καὶ τὰς παιδίσκας of Luke, which looks Semitic enough to be original.

The synonyms λαός and ὄχλος occur in the synoptic writers approximately as follows:

	Matt.	Mark	Luke	Acts
λαός	14 (4 from LXX)	3 (1 from LXX)	37	48 (5 from LXX)
ὄχλος	47	27	41	22

Luke uses both quite freely, but his preference for λαός, shown by the frequency of its occurrence in comparison with the other synoptists, is confirmed by the changes he makes in the wording of his sources as indicated by the following parallels:

Mk. 11, 18 πᾶς ὁ ὄχλος	Lk. 19, 48 ὁ λαὸς ἅπας
Mk. 11, 32 τὸν ὄχλον (*v. l.* λαόν)	Cf. Lk. 20, 6 ὁ λαὸς ἅπας
Mk. 12, 12 τὸν ὄχλον	Lk. 20, 19 τὸν λαόν
Mk. 12, 37 ὁ πολὺς ὄχλος	Cf. Lk. 20, 45 παντὸς τοῦ λαοῦ
Mk. 15, 11 ἀνέσεισαν τὸν ὄχλον	Cf. Lk. 23, 5 ἀνασείει τὸν λαόν (cf. p. 99).

Note the preference of Matthew, and to a less degree of Luke, for the plural ὄχλοι. It occurs only once (10,1) in Mark, in Luke 15 times, in Matt. 30 (32) times, in Acts 7 times.

Luke probably has a greater liking for ἀνήρ than has Mark, who uses it but four times (in three of which it has the more limited sense of "husband," "male"), or than Matthew who uses it eight times (four in the special sense), or than John, who uses it eight times (six in the special sense).

Mk. 3, 3 ἀνθρώπῳ	Lk. 6, 8 ἀνδρί
Mk. 5, 2 ἄνθρωπος	Lk. 8, 27 ἀνήρ τις

Note also the use of ἀνήρ in the following passages, where it is not found in the parallel:

Luke 5, 12, 18; 8, 38; 9, 30, 38; 11, 31; 23, 50*bis*; 24, 4 (cf. ἰδοὺ ἀνήρ, p. 178 n.).

In view of these facts the apparent reversal of habit is noteworthy in the following passage:

Mt. 7, 24 ἀνδρὶ φρονίμῳ	Lk. 6, 48 ἀνθρώπῳ
Mt. 7, 26 ἀνδρὶ μωρῷ	Lk. 6, 49 ἀνθρώπῳ

For *πνεῦμα* or *πνεῦμα ἀκάθαρτον* of possessing demons Luke in his gospel occasionally substitutes another expression:

Mk. 1, 23 ἐν πνεύματι ἀκαθάρτῳ	Lk. 4, 33 ἔχων πνεῦμα δαιμονίου ἀκαθάρτου
Mk. 1, 26 τὸ πνεῦμα τὸ ἀκάθαρτον	Lk. 4, 35 τὸ δαιμόνιον
Mk. 5, 2 ἐν πνεύματι ἀκαθάρτῳ	Lk. 8, 27 ἔχων δαιμόνια
Mk. 5, 13 τὰ πνεύματα τὰ ἀκάθαρτα	Lk. 8, 33 τὰ δαιμόνια
Mk. 6, 7 τῶν πνευμάτων τῶν ἀκαθάρτων	Lk. 9, 1 τὰ δαιμόνια
Mk. 9, 20 τὸ πνεῦμα	Lk. 9, 42 τὸ δαιμόνιον

But τὸ πνεῦμα is used by Luke in some passages, mostly dependent on known sources:

Luke 4, 36 (= Mark 1, 27); 6, 18 (= Mark 3, 11); 7, 21 (cf. Mark 3, 11); 8, 2; 8, 29 (= Mark 5, 8); 9, 42 (= Mark 9, 25); 10, 20; 11, 24, 26 (= Matt. 11, 43, 45).

In Acts δαιμόνιον is used of gods (Acts 17, 18), and for evil spirits πνεῦμα ἀκάθαρτον, etc. πνεῦμα πονηρόν is found in Luke 7, 21; 8, 2 and Acts 19, 12–16 (four times), but nowhere else in the New Testament.

While Luke uses both the singular and plural of *οὐρανός* (heaven) and *σάββατον* (Sabbath, week), the plurals are less frequent.

οὐρανοί occurs only in Luke 10, 20; [11, 2a]; 12, 33; 18, 22; 21, 26 (LXX); Acts 2, 34; 7, 56, where possibly some plural meaning is intended. Note that at both 12, 33 and 18, 22 the parallels to Luke's θησαυρὸν ἐν τοῖς οὐρανοῖς have the singular: Mark 10, 21 θησαυρὸν ἐν οὐρανῷ, Matt. 6, 20 θησαυροὺς ἐν οὐρανῷ, so that for this phrase the change seems intentional. For the opposite difference see

Mk. 1, 10 τοὺς οὐρανούς	Lk. 3, 21 τὸν οὐρανόν
Mk. 1, 11 ἐκ τῶν οὐρανῶν	Lk. 3, 22 ἐξ οὐρανοῦ
Mt. 5, 12 ἐν τοῖς οὐρανοῖς	Lk. 6, 23 ἐν τῷ οὐρανῷ [Q]
Mt. 7, 11 ἐν τοῖς οὐρανοῖς	Lk. 11, 13 ἐξ οὐρανοῦ [Q]

In the last two cases Matthew has his favorite plurals.

Except in the phrases ἡμέρα τῶν σαββάτων, Luke 4, 16; Acts 13, 14; 16, 13 (peculiar to Luke; cf. also ἡμέρα τοῦ σαββάτου Luke 13, 14, 16; 14, 5, also peculiar) and the more common μία τῶν σαββάτων (Luke 24, 1; Acts 20, 7; cf. Matt. 28, 1; Mark 16, 2; John 20, 1, 19) Luke never uses the plural of σάββατον in a singular sense.[1] When Mark has such a plural Luke either changes it to the singular, as in

Mk. 2, 23 τοῖς σάββασι	Lk. 6, 1 ἐν σαββάτῳ [δευτεροπρώτῳ]
Mk. 3, 2 τοῖς σάββασι	Lk. 6, 7 ἐν τῷ σαββάτῳ
Mk. 3, 4 τοῖς σάββασι	Lk. 6, 9 τῷ σαββάτῳ

or he changes other parts of Mark's sentence so that the plural if retained may be a real plural:

Mk. 1, 21 εὐθὺς τοῖς σάββασιν ἐδίδασκεν[2]	Lk. 4, 31 καὶ ἦν διδάσκων αὐτοὺς ἐν τοῖς σάββασι
Mk. 2, 24 τί ποιοῦσιν τοῖς σάββασιν ὃ οὐκ ἔξεστιν	Lk. 6, 2 τί ποιεῖτε ὃ οὐκ ἔξεστιν τοῖς σάββασι

[1] In these phrases quoted above, the singular ἡμέρα, μία, makes the phrase unambiguous. An exception may be made of Luke 13, 10 ἐν τοῖς σάββασιν (*v.l.* ἐν σαββάτῳ), but probably the ἦν διδάσκων is to be understood as in 4, 31.

[2] Whatever reading is adopted, it is evident that only one sabbath is meant.

Luke seems to make one change of gender contrary to the rules of the Atticists. Moeris distinguishes the genders of *βάτος*, " bush," thus: *ὁ βάτος ἀττικῶς· ἡ βάτος ἑλληνικῶς*. Luke not only has the feminine at Acts 7, 35, but according to the best MSS. of Mark has changed the masculine of Mark 12, 26 to the feminine Luke 20, 37. In LXX the gender is masculine (Exod. 3, 2 ff.; Deut. 33, 16).

Use of Pronouns

Nothwithstanding his inclination to fill out incomplete sentences,[1] Luke rarely if ever adds an unemphatic personal pronoun, and those which he finds in his source (possibly due to the prominence of these pronouns in Semitic idiom) he omits. The examples in the nominative are most numerous in contexts derived from Q.

Nominative:

Mt. 5, 44 ἐγὼ δὲ λέγω ὑμῖν	Lk. 6, 27 ἀλλὰ ὑμῖν λέγω [Q]
Mt. 11, 10 ἐγὼ ἀποστέλλω (LXX, Mk. 1, 2)	Lk. 7, 27 ἀποστέλλω [Q]
Mt. 10, 16 ἰδοὺ ἐγὼ ἀποστέλλω	Lk. 10, 3 ἰδοὺ ἀποστέλλω [Q]
Mt. 12, 28 ἐγὼ ἐκβάλλω	Lk. 11, 20 ἐκβάλλω [Q]
Mt. 23, 34 ἰδοὺ ἐγὼ ἀποστέλλω	Lk. 11, 49 ἀποστελῶ [Q]
Mk. 12, 26 λέγων· ἐγὼ ὁ θεός	Cf. Lk. 20, 37 λέγει κύριον τὸν θεόν
Mk. 14, 30 σὺ . . . ἀπαρνήσῃ	Lk. 22, 34 ἀπαρνήσῃ
Mk. 14, 68 οὔτε οἶδα οὔτε ἐπίσταμαι σὺ τί λέγεις	Cf. Lk. 22, 60 οὐκ οἶδα ὃ λέγεις
Mt. 7, 12 ὑμεῖς	Lk. 6, 31 ὑμεῖς (B syr. sin. *al.* omit) [Q]
Mt. 5, 48 ὑμεῖς	Lk. 6, 36 omits [Q]
Mt. 10, 31 ὑμεῖς	Lk. 12, 7 omits [Q]

Genitive:

Mk. 14, 14 κατάλυμά μου	Lk. 22, 11 κατάλυμα
Mt. 13, 16 ὑμῶν δὲ μακάριοι οἱ ὀφθαλμοί	Lk. 10, 23 μακάριοι οἱ ὀφθαλμοί [Q]
Mt. 7, 11 ὁ πατὴρ ὑμῶν	Lk. 11, 13 ὁ πατήρ [Q]
Mt. 6, 25 τῇ ψυχῇ ὑμῶν	Lk. 12, 22 τῇ ψυχῇ [Q]
Mt. 6, 25 τῷ σώματι ὑμῶν	Lk. 12, 22 τῷ σώματι [Q]

Scholten, p. 48, notices an interesting difference between Luke's use of genitive pronouns with the name of God and Matthew's. Whatever be the reason for the contrast, whether it be the Paulinism of Luke as Scholten thinks, or rather a stylistic preference of Matthew, the expression " *your* Father " does not occur in Luke except in 6, 36; 12, 30, 32. Compare the following parallels:

[1] See pp. 149 ff.

Mt. 5, 45 *υἱοὶ τοῦ πατρὸς ὑμῶν τοῦ ἐν οὐρανοῖς*	Lk. 6, 35 *υἱοὶ ὑψίστου* [Q]
Mt. 7, 11 *ὁ πατὴρ ὑμῶν ὁ ἐν τοῖς οὐρανοῖς*	Lk. 11, 13 *ὁ πατὴρ ὁ ἐξ οὐρανοῦ* [Q]
Mt. 10, 29 *τοῦ πατρὸς ὑμῶν*	Lk. 12, 6 *τοῦ θεοῦ* [Q]
Mt. 10, 20 *τὸ πνεῦμα τοῦ πατρὸς ὑμῶν*	Lk. 12, 12 *τὸ ἅγιον πνεῦμα* [Q]
Mt. 6, 26 *ὁ πατὴρ ὑμῶν ὁ οὐράνιος*	Lk. 12, 24 *ὁ θεός* [Q]
Similarly	
Matt. 6, 9 *πάτερ ἡμῶν ὁ ἐν τοῖς οὐρανοῖς*	Lk. 11, 2 *πάτερ* [Q]

Dative:

Mk. 14, 15 *ἑτοιμάσατε ἡμῖν*	Lk. 22, 12 *ἑτοιμάσατε* (cf. 22, 8 *ἑτοιμάσατε ἡμῖν*)
Mk. 1, 40 *λέγων αὐτῷ*	Lk. 5, 12 *λέγων*
Mk. 1, 41 *λέγει αὐτῷ* [ℵW1 *al.* omit]	Lk. 5, 13 *εἰπών*
Mk. 5, 9 *λέγει αὐτῷ*	Lk. 8, 30 *ὁ δὲ εἶπεν*
Mk. 5, 19 *λέγει αὐτῷ*	Lk. 8, 38 *λέγων*
Mk. 5, 41 *λέγει αὐτῇ*	Lk. 8, 54 *λέγων*
Mk. 6, 37 *λέγουσιν αὐτῷ*	Lk. 9, 13 *οἱ δὲ εἶπαν*
Mk. 8, 27 *λέγων αὐτοῖς*	Lk. 9, 18 *λέγων*
Mk. 8, 29 *λέγει αὐτῷ*	Lk. 9, 20 *εἶπεν*
Mk. 9, 19 *αὐτοῖς λέγει*	Lk. 9, 41 *εἶπεν*
Mk. 9, 38 *ἔφη αὐτῷ*	Lk. 9, 49 *εἶπεν*
Mt. 24, 45 *τοῦ δοῦναι αὐτοῖς*	Lk. 12, 42 *τοῦ δοῦναι* [Q]
Mk. 10, 20 *ἔφη αὐτῷ*	Lk. 18, 21 *εἶπεν*
Mk. 12, 16 *εἶπαν αὐτῷ*	Lk. 20, 24 *εἶπαν*
Mk. 14, 48 *εἶπεν αὐτοῖς*	Lk. 22, 51 *εἶπεν*

Accusative (contrast addition of accusative, p. 151):

Mk. 3, 2 *παρετήρουν αὐτὸν εἰ θεραπεύει αὐτόν*	Lk. 6, 7 *παρετηροῦντο εἰ θεραπεύει*
Mk. 5, 14 *οἱ βόσκοντες αὐτούς*	Lk. 8, 34 *οἱ βόσκοντες*
Mk. 9, 39 *μὴ κωλύετε αὐτόν*	Lk. 9, 50 *μὴ κωλύετε*

Examples of the apparent insertion of personal pronouns by Luke are the following:

Mk. 2, 5 *ἀφίενταί σου αἱ ἁμαρτίαι*	Lk. 5, 20 *ἀφέωνταί σοι αἱ ἁμαρτίαι σου*
Mk. 2, 9 *ἀφίενταί σου αἱ ἁμαρτίαι*	Lk. 5, 23 *ἀφέωνταί σοι αἱ ἁμαρτίαι σου*
Mk. 9, 39 *εἶπεν*	Lk. 9, 50 *εἶπεν δὲ πρὸς αὐτόν*
Mt. 13, 17 *ἰδεῖν ἃ βλέπετε*	Lk. 10, 24 *ἰδεῖν ἃ ὑμεῖς βλέπετε* [Q]
Mt. 6, 31 *μὴ οὖν μεριμνήσετε*	Lk. 12, 29 *καὶ ὑμεῖς μὴ ζητεῖτε* [Q]
Mk. 11, 29 *ἐπερωτήσω ὑμᾶς*	Lk. 20, 3 *ἐρωτήσω κἀγὼ ὑμᾶς* (= Matt. 21, 24)
Mk. 12, 35 *ἔλεγεν*	Lk. 20, 41 *εἶπεν δὲ πρὸς αὐτούς*
Mk. 14, 14 *λέγει*	Lk. 22, 11 *λέγει σοι*

The first two additions are hard to explain (see Harnack, *Luke the Physician*, p. 91); in the third and fourth cases Luke has omitted a pronoun elsewhere in the sentence (see above, and p. 191), so that the inserted pronouns are here compensations (in Luke 9, 50 possibly a mistake) for the omitted words. The next two cases add the pronoun for emphasis; the last two instances are due to a change of construction or context.

The unclassical uses of εἷς are frequently corrected by Luke:

1. As an indefinite pronoun:[1]

Mk. 6, 15 εἷς τῶν προφητῶν	Lk. 9, 8 προφήτης τις
Mk. 8, 28 εἷς τῶν προφητῶν	Lk. 9, 19 προφήτης τις
Mk. 10, 17 εἷς . . . ἐπηρώτα	Lk. 18, 18 ἐπηρώτησέν τις . . . ἄρχων
Mk. 12, 28 εἷς τῶν γραμματέων	Lk. 20, 39 τινὲς τῶν γραμματέων; cf. 10, 25 νομικός τις
Mk. 12, 42 μία χήρα	Lk. 21, 2 τινὰ χήραν
Mk. 13, 1 λέγει . . . εἷς τῶν μαθητῶν	Lk. 21, 5 τινῶν λεγόντων
Mk. 14, 66 μία τῶν παιδισκῶν	Lk. 22, 56 παιδίσκη τις

2. Meaning 'alone':

Mk. 2, 7 εἰ μὴ εἷς ὁ θεός	Lk. 5, 21 εἰ μὴ μόνος ὁ θεός

But in Luke 18, 19 it is kept unchanged (but ℵ* B* omit ὁ) from Mark 10, 18.

3. As a correlative:

Mt. 24, 40 εἷς . . . εἷς	Lk. 17, 34 [ὁ] εἷς . . . ὁ ἕτερος [Q]
Mt. 24, 41 μία . . . μία	Lk. 17, 35 ἡ μία . . . ἡ ἑτέρα [Q]
Mk. 15, 27 ἕνα . . . ἕνα	Lk. 23, 33 ὃν μὲν . . . ὃν δέ

Compare:

Mk. 4, 8 ἓν . . . ἓν . . . ἓν	Lk. 8, 8 ἑκατονταπλασίονα
Mk. 4, 20 ἓν . . . ἓν . . . ἓν	Lk. 8, 15 ἐν ὑπομονῇ

But some accented MSS. and modern editors understand εν in Mark as a preposition, rather than (with the versions) as a numeral. And at Mark 4, 8 εις is read for εν in some MSS. once (BL), in others thrice (ℵC *al.*).

4. In various other uses:

Mk. 5, 22 εἷς τῶν ἀρχισυναγώγων	Lk. 8, 41 ἀνὴρ . . . ἄρχων τῆς συναγωγῆς
Mk. 9, 17 εἷς ἐκ τοῦ ὄχλου	Lk. 9, 38 ἀνὴρ ἀπὸ τοῦ ὄχλου
Mk. 9, 37 ἓν τῶν παιδίων τούτων	Lk. 9, 48 τοῦτο τὸ παιδίον
Mt. 6, 27 πῆχυν ἕνα	Lk. 12, 25 πῆχυν [Q]
Mk. 11, 29 ἕνα λόγον	Lk. 20, 3 λόγον
Mk. 12, 6 ἕνα . . . υἱὸν ἀγαπητόν	Lk. 20, 13 υἱὸν . . . ἀγαπητόν
Mk. 14, 10 ὁ εἷς τῶν δώδεκα	Lk. 22, 3 ἐκ τοῦ ἀριθμοῦ τῶν δώδεκα

αὐτός, intensive, is a favorite word with Luke, especially in the nominative in the expressions καὶ αὐτός, αὐτὸς δέ,[2] which are often used in recasting prefaces of sections from Mark, and elsewhere.

Besides this, we find it used even for the personal pronouns of the first and second persons.

Mt. 6, 12 ὡς καὶ ἡμεῖς ἀφήκαμεν	Lk. 11, 4 καὶ γὰρ αὐτοὶ ἀφίομεν [Q]
Mt. 23, 4 αὐτοὶ δὲ . . . οὐ θέλουσι κινῆσαι	Lk. 11, 46 καὶ αὐτοὶ . . . οὐ προσψαύετε [Q]
Mt. 23, 13 ὑμεῖς γὰρ οὐκ εἰσέρχεσθε	Lk. 11, 52 αὐτοὶ οὐκ εἰσήλθατε [Q]

Cf. Luke 6, 42; 22, 71; Acts 22, 20; 24, 16 and elsewhere.

[1] See J. H. Moulton, *Grammar*, I, 96 f.

[2] See above, p. 150 f. and consult Moulton and Geden, *Concordance*, for complete lists.

More emphatic than the *αὐτός* intensive is *οὗτος* resumptive, as in *ὁ δὲ ὑπομείνας εἰς τὸ τέλος, οὗτος σωθήσεται* (Mark 13, 13 = Matt. 10, 22; 24, 13; cf. Mark 3, 35). In rewriting this passage Luke does not retain the construction, but in other parallels he adds it. Compare with Mark's explanation of the parable of the sower (4, 13-20) both Matt. 13, 20, 22, 23 (*ὁ δὲ . . . σπαρεὶς . . . οὗτός ἐστι*) and Luke 8, 14, 15 (*τὸ δὲ . . . πεσόν, οὗτοί εἰσιν*); and the following:

Luke 9, 24 *ὃς δ' ἂν ἀπολέσῃ τὴν ψυχὴν . . . οὗτος* (Mark 8, 35 = Matt. 16, 25 omit) *σώσει αὐτήν.*

Luke 9, 26 *ὃς γὰρ ἂν ἐπαισχυνθῇ με . . ., τοῦτον* (Mark 8, 38 *καὶ . . . αὐτόν*) *ὁ υἱὸς τοῦ ἀνθρώπου ἐπαισχυνθήσεται,*

Luke 9, 48 *ὁ γὰρ μικρότερος ἐν πᾶσιν ὑμῖν ὑπάρχων, οὗτός ἐστιν μέγας* (cf. Mark 9, 35; 10, 43 f. = Matt. 20, 26 f. = Luke 22, 26; Matt. 23, 11).

Compare also Acts 2, 23; 7, 35; 15, 38; 17, 6.

With Luke's *καὶ αὐτός* should be compared his *καὶ οὗτος*. The two nominatives are easily confused (especially in the feminine forms) and are often exchanged in the MSS.

Luke 7, 12 *καὶ αὕτη [ἦν] χήρα*

Luke 8, 13 *καὶ οὗτοι* (*v.l.*; Mark 4, 17 omits) *ῥίζαν οὐχ ἔχουσιν*

Luke 8, 41 *καὶ οὗτος* (BD *al.*; *αὐτὸς* ℵA *al.*) *ἄρχων τῆς συναγωγῆς ὑπῆρχεν* (cf. Mark 5, 22)

Luke 8, 42 *καὶ αὕτη ἀπέθνησκεν* (cf. Mark 5, 23)

There is a somewhat more classical tone in the use of *ἕτερος* for *ἄλλος*, even though it be not always used according to classical idiom.[1] Hence we notice here:

Mk. 4, 5, 7, 8 *ἄλλο . . . ἄλλο . . . ἄλλο* (*v.l.* *ἄλλα*)	Lk. 8, 6, 7, 8 *ἕτερον . . . ἕτερον . . . ἕτερον*
Mk. 12, 4, 5 *ἄλλον . . . ἄλλον*	Lk. 20, 11, 12 *ἕτερον . . . τρίτον*
Mk. 10, 11 = Matt. 19, 9 *ἄλλην . . .*	Lk. 16, 18 *ἑτέραν* (perhaps from Q)

In the question of John the Baptist, "Art thou he that should come or look we for another ?" the majority of MSS. of Luke read *ἄλλον* in both 7, 19 and 20. But all MSS. of Matt. 11, 3, ℵBLW in Luke 7, 19, and ℵDL with the group 1-118-131-209 in Luke 7, 20, read *ἕτερον*. In this case the original reading of Q must be considered very uncertain.

Cf. Mk. 15, 41 *καὶ ἄλλαι πολλαί*	Lk. 8, 3 *καὶ ἕτεραι πολλαί*

The possessive use of *ἴδιος* is not common in the Synoptic Gospels (perhaps altogether absent from Mark), but it occurs a few times in Luke where it is not in the parallels:

Mt. 7, 3 *ἐν τῷ σῷ ὀφθαλμῷ*	Lk. 6, 41 *ἐν τῷ ἰδίῳ ὀφθαλμῷ* [Q]
Mt. 12, 33 *ἐκ τοῦ καρποῦ*	Lk. 6, 44 *ἐκ τοῦ ἰδίου καρποῦ* [Q]
Mk. 10, 28 *ἡμεῖς ἀφήκαμεν πάντα*	Lk. 18, 28 *ἡμεῖς ἀφέντες τὰ ἴδια*

[1] See Blass, § 51, 6. Note *ἕτερος* in Luke 4, 43 for *ἐχόμενος* in Mark 1, 37, and compare *τῇ ἑτέρᾳ = τῇ ἐχομένῃ* (*sc.* *ἡμέρᾳ*) Acts 20, 15 (*v.l.*); 27, 3, and in the same sense, 'next,' (?) Luke 6, 6; 9, 56.

Luke uses the classical reciprocal pronoun for less correct expressions:

Mk. 1, 27 πρὸς ἑαυτούς (*v.l.* αὐτούς)	Lk. 4, 36 πρὸς ἀλλήλους
Mt. 11, 16 τοῖς ἑτέροις	Lk. 7, 32 ἀλλήλοις [Q]
Mk. 12, 7 πρὸς ἑαυτούς	Lk. 20, 14 πρὸς ἀλλήλους
Mk. 16, 3 πρὸς ἑαυτάς	Cf. Lk. 24, 14, 17, 32 πρὸς ἀλλήλους

Luke also omits the reflexive ἑαυτοῦ as follows:

Mk. 2, 8 ἐπιγνοὺς . . . ὅτι οὕτως διαλογίζονται ἐν ἑαυτοῖς	Lk. 5, 22 ἐπιγνοὺς τοὺς διαλογισμοὺς αὐτῶν
Mk. 4, 17 οὐκ ἔχουσιν ῥίζαν ἐν ἑαυτοῖς	Lk. 8, 13 ῥίζαν οὐκ ἔχουσιν
Mk. 5, 30 ἐπιγνοὺς ἐν ἑαυτῷ τὴν . . . δύναμιν κτλ.	Cf. Lk. 8, 46 ἐγὼ γὰρ ἔγνων δύναμιν κτλ.
Mk. 6, 36 ἀγοράσωσιν ἑαυτοῖς τί φάγωσιν	Lk. 9, 12 εὕρωσιν ἐπισιτισμόν
Mk. 9, 8 Ἰησοῦν μόνον μεθ' ἑαυτῶν	Lk. 9, 36 Ἰησοῦς μόνος
Mt. 12, 45 παραλαμβάνει μεθ' ἑαυτοῦ	Lk. 11, 26 παραλαμβάνει [Q]

The reflexive occurs in Luke and Acts with πρός only in Luke 20, 5 (from Mark 11, 31); 22, 23; with ἐν only at Luke 3, 8 (from Q, = Matt. 3, 9, though here also there is weighty evidence from fathers and versions for omitting the phrase in Luke); 7, 39 and 49, in the parables (12, 17; 16, 3; 18, 4), and in Acts 10, 17; 12, 11; never with μετά.

Use of Adjectives and of the Article

In adjectives, as in other parts of speech, Luke has well-marked preferences. His favorite ἅπας, "found only once certainly in Mark, three times in Matthew" (Scholten, p. 20, note 7), occurs certainly for πᾶς in such passages as:

Mt. 4, 9 ταῦτά σοι πάντα δώσω	Lk. 4, 6 σοὶ δώσω τὴν ἐξουσίαν ταύτην ἅπασαν [Q]
Mk. 2, 12 ἐξίστασθαι πάντας	Lk. 5, 26 ἔκστασις ἔλαβεν ἅπαντας

In the following cases ἅπας is a well attested variant reading in Luke:

Mk. 1, 32 πάντας τοὺς κακῶς ἔχοντας	Lk. 4, 40 ἅπαντες (BC *al.*) ὅσοι εἶχον ἀσθενοῦντας
Mk. 6, 39 ἀνακλῖναι πάντας	Lk. 9, 15 κατέκλιναν ἅπαντας (ABCΓΔ *al.*)
Mk. 12, 44 πάντες . . . ἔβαλον	Lk. 21, 4 ἅπαντες (ALQWΓ *al.*) . . . ἔβαλον
Mk. 12, 44 πάντα ὅσα εἶχεν, ὅλον[1] τὸν βίον	Lk. 21, 4 ἅπαντα (AWΓΔΛΠ *al.*) τὸν βίον ὃν εἶχεν

[1] Cf.

Mk. 1, 28 ὅλην τὴν περίχωρον	Lk. 4, 37 πάντα τόπον τῆς περιχώρου
Mk. 1, 39 εἰς ὅλην τὴν Γαλιλαίαν	Lk. 4, 44 τῆς Γαλιλαίας
Mk. 14, 55 ὅλον τὸ συνέδριον	Cf. Lk. 22, 66 τὸ πρεσβυτέριον τοῦ λαοῦ
Mk. 15, 1 ὅλον τὸ συνέδριον	Lk. 23, 1 ἅπαν τὸ πλῆθος αὐτῶν

Note however:

Mk. 1, 27 ἐθαμβήθησαν ἅπαντες (ℵBL) — Lk. 4, 36 ἐγένετο θάμβος ἐπὶ πάντας
Mt. 6, 32 χρῄζετε τούτων ἀπάντων — Lk. 12, 30 χρῄζετε τούτων [Q]

From parallels with Matthew, Harnack (*Sayings*, p. 80) infers that Luke has avoided for sound linguistic reasons the absolute use of ἄξιος. The passages are:

Mt. 10, 11 ἐξετάσατε τίς ἄξιός ἐστιν — Lk. 9, 5; 10, 5 no corresponding expression [Q]
Mt. 10, 13 ἐὰν μὲν ᾖ ἡ οἰκία ἀξία — Lk. 10, 6 ἐὰν ᾖ ἐκεῖ υἱὸς εἰρήνης [Q]
Mt. 10, 13 ἐὰν δὲ μὴ ᾖ ἀξία — Lk. 10, 6 εἰ δὲ μήγε [Q]
Mt. 22, 8 οἱ κεκλημένοι οὐκ ἦσαν ἄξιοι — Cf. Lk. 14, 24 [Q]

Observe also how the phrase οὐκ ἔστιν μου ἄξιος occurring three times in Matt. 10, 37 f. is replaced twice in Luke 14, 26 f. by the definite οὐ δύναται εἶναί μου μαθητής.

Luke's favorite ἱκανός appears in his rewriting of Mark 5, 11 ἀγέλη χοίρων μεγάλη as Luke 8, 32 ἀγέλη χοίρων ἱκανῶν, and in the expressions added in Luke 8, 27 (= Mark 5, 3), Luke 20, 9 (= Mark 12, 1), and Luke 23, 9 (cf. Mark 15, 4). But ποιῆσαι τὸ ἱκανόν (Mark 15, 15, said to be a Latinism, cf. Acts 17, 9) disappears in Luke 23, 24; and in Acts 13, 25 (and John 1, 27), for the Baptist's confession of unworthiness, instead of οὗ οὐκ εἰμὶ ἱκανὸς κ.τ.λ. (Mark 1, 7 = Luke 3, 16 = Matt. 3, 11), we read οὗ οὐκ εἰμὶ ἄξιος κτλ.

Literary improvement may probably be recognized in the following cases:

Mk. 2, 3 παραλυτικόν — Lk. 5, 18 παραλελυμένος
Mk. 2, 10 παραλυτικῷ[1] — Lk. 5, 24 παραλελυμένῳ (AB *al.*, παραλυτικῷ ℵCD *al.*)
Mk. 4, 16 πρόσκαιροί (late, Schmid, I. 373) εἰσιν — Lk. 8, 12 πρὸς καιρὸν πιστεύουσιν
Mk. 9, 42 = Matt. 18, 6 μύλος ὀνικός[2] — Lk. 17, 2 λίθος μυλικός [Q?]
Mk. 10, 22 ἔχων κτήματα πολλά (see Norden, *Kunstprosa*, 489) — Lk. 18, 23 πλούσιος σφόδρα (but cf. vs. 24)
Mk. 10, 47 Ἰησοῦς ὁ Ναζαρηνός — Lk. 18, 37 Ἰησοῦς ὁ Ναζωραῖος[3]

[1] παραλυτικός occurs again at Mt. 8, 6 and the equally incorrect βασανιζόμενος (see p. 59, n. 64), but neither is in the parallel of Luke 7, 2.

[2] Probably Mark's phrase would be condemned by Atticists because of their distinction between μύλος and ὄνος. See Norden, p. 488, note 2. Besides, ὀνικός is a rare word, though it has been recently found in the papyri; see *Expositor*, 7th Series, X (1910), p. 92, where three cases are cited.

[3] On the origin of the two forms, see Dalman, *Grammatik des jüdisch-palästinischen Aramäisch*, p. 141, note 7. The former is found always (4 times) in Mark, and Luke once takes it over (Luke 4, 34 = Mark 1, 24); but the latter is probably the more regular

Mk. 12, 42 πτωχή	Lk. 21, 2 πενιχράν (but cf. vs. 3)
Mk. 15, 43 εὐσχήμων, 'rich' (Lobeck, *Phryn.* 333)	Cf. Lk. 23, 50 ἀγαθὸς καὶ δίκαιος

The following cases also involve differences between Luke and his parallels in the use of adjectives:

Mk. 4, 8 τὴν γῆν τὴν καλήν	Lk. 8, 8 τὴν γῆν τὴν ἀγαθήν (cf. 8, 15)
Mk. 4, 19 ἄκαρπος γίνεται	Lk. 8, 14 οὐ τελεσφοροῦσιν
Mk. 9, 7 ἀγαπητός	Lk. 9, 35 ἐκλελεγμένος (*v.l.*)
Here Luke has in mind Isa. 42, 1; cf. ἐκλεκτός Lk 22, 35	
Mk. 10, 22 λυπούμενος	Lk. 18, 23 περίλυπος
Mt. 25, 24 σκληρός	Lk. 19, 21 (22) αὐστηρός [Q]
Mk. 12, 25 εἰσὶν ὡς ἄγγελοι	Lk. 20, 36 ἰσάγγελοί εἰσιν
Mk. 15, 27 ἐξ εὐωνύμων	Lk. 23, 33 ἐξ ἀριστερῶν

The Article

Some miscellaneous differences between Luke and his parallels in the use of the article are discussed by Scholten, pp. 22, 37, 102 f. The omission of the article four times in the saying on the lamp in Luke 8, 16 (= Mark 4, 21) he thinks shows that Luke missed the fact that in a Jewish peasant home there was just one of each piece of furniture mentioned (cf. p. 130). But a full comparison with the two other parallels makes this interpretation less probable.

Mark 4, 21	Luke 8, 16	Luke 11, 33	Matt. 5, 15
ὁ λύχνος	λύχνον	λύχνον	λύχνον
τὸν μόδιον	σκεύει	τὸν μόδιον	τὸν μόδιον
τὴν κλίνην	κλίνης		
τὴν λυχνίαν	λυχνίας (ℵD *al.* τὴν λυχνίαν)	τὴν λυχνίαν	τὴν λυχνίαν

More interesting, and with greater confidence attributable to considerations of style, are the cases where Luke removes a repeated article:

Mk. 1, 27 τοῖς πνεύμασι τοῖς ἀκαθάρτοις	Lk. 4, 36 τοῖς ἀκαθάρτοις πνεύμασιν
Mk. 4, 20 ἐπὶ τὴν γῆν τὴν καλήν	Lk. 8, 15 ἐν τῇ καλῇ γῇ
Mk. 8, 38 τῶν ἀγγέλων τῶν ἁγίων	Lk. 9, 26 τῶν ἁγίων ἀγγέλων
Mk. 3, 29 τὸ πνεῦμα τὸ ἅγιον Mt. 12, 32 τοῦ πνεύματος τοῦ ἁγίου	Lk. 12, 10 τὸ ἅγιον πνεῦμα [Q?]
Mk. 13, 11 τὸ πνεῦμα τὸ ἅγιον	Lk. 12, 12 τὸ ἅγιον πνεῦμα [Q?]
Mk. 11, 2 τὴν κώμην τὴν κατέναντι	Lk. 19, 30 τὴν κατέναντι κώμην
Mk. 13, 25 αἱ δυνάμεις αἱ ἐν τοῖς οὐρανοῖς	Lk. 21, 35 = Matt. 24, 29 αἱ δυνάμεις τῶν οὐρανῶν

form (Matt. 2, 23; 26, 71; John 18, 5, 7; 19, 19; Acts 2, 22; 3, 6; 4, 10; 6, 14; 22, 8; 24, 5; 26, 9). In Luke 24, 19 Greek and Latin MSS. are pretty evenly divided between the two.

In one reverse case:

Mk. 12, 6 υἱὸν ἀγαπητόν	Lk. 20, 13 τὸν υἱόν μου τὸν ἀγαπητόν

the later evangelist, using the first person and thinking of the application of the parable to Christ, naturally assimilates to the form of the heavenly voice ὁ υἱός μου ὁ ἀγαπητός found in Mark 1, 11 = Luke 3, 22 = Matt. 3, 17; Mark 9, 7 = Luke 9, 35 (אB *al.* ὁ υἱός μου ὁ ἐκλελεγμένος) = Matt. 17, 5. In the parable of the beam and mote the repeated article τὸ κάρφος τὸ ἐν τῷ ὀφθαλμῷ κ.τ.λ., τὴν δοκὴν τὴν ἐν τῷ ἰδίῳ ὀφθαλμῷ, occurs four times in Luke 6, 41 f. but in Matt. 7, 3–5 only once, the adjunct being usually transferred to the verb.

The differences between Luke and his parallels in the use of the article are otherwise few. In these cases he has added it:

Mk. 6, 8 = Matt. 9, 10 εἰς ὁδόν	Lk. 9, 3 εἰς (cf. 10, 4 κατὰ) τὴν ὁδόν [Q?]
Mk. 10, 13 προσέφερον . . . παιδία	Lk. 18, 15 προσέφερον . . . τὰ ('their'?) βρέφη
Mk. 15, 1 παρέδωκαν Πειλάτῳ	Lk. 23, 1 ἤγαγον . . . ἐπὶ τὸν Πειλᾶτον[1]

In these parallels it is absent from Luke:

Mk. 1, 11 ἐκ τῶν οὐρανῶν	Lk. 3, 22 ἐξ οὐρανοῦ
Mk. 2, 23 διά τῶν σπορίμων	Lk. 6, 1 διὰ σπορίμων
Mt. 12, 34 ἐκ γὰρ τοῦ περισσεύματος τῆς καρδίας	Lk. 6, 45 ἐκ γὰρ περισσεύματος καρδίας [Q]
Mk. 4, 36 ἐν τῷ πλοίῳ	Lk. 8, 22 εἰς πλοῖον
Mk. 5, 18 εἰς τὸ πλοῖον	Lk. 8, 37 εἰς πλοῖον
Mt. 7, 11 ὁ ἐν τοῖς οὐρανοῖς	Lk. 11, 13 ὁ ἐξ οὐρανοῦ [Q]
Mt. 23, 35 ἀπὸ τοῦ αἵματος Ἄβελ ἕως τοῦ αἵματος Ζαχαρίου	Lk. 11, 51 ἀπὸ αἵματος Ἄβελ ἕως αἵματος Ζαχαρίου [Q]
Mt. 6, 30 τὸν χόρτον τοῦ ἀγροῦ	Lk. 12, 28 ἐν ἀγρῷ τὸν χόρτον [Q]
Mk. 13, 16 ὁ εἰς τὸν ἀγρόν (cf. Mt. 24, 18)	Lk. 17, 31 ὁ ἐν ἀγρῷ
Mk. 11, 10 ὡσαννὰ ἐν τοῖς ὑψίστοις	Lk. 19, 38 δόξα ἐν ὑψίστοις (so 2, 14)
Mk. 12, 2 τῷ καιρῷ	Lk. 20, 10 καιρῷ
Mk. 13, 24 ὁ ἥλιος . . . ἡ σελήνη . . . οἱ ἀστέρες	Lk. 21, 25 ἐν ἡλίῳ καὶ σελήνῃ καὶ ἄστροις (cf. Acts 27, 20)

Note the variation in the use of the article in Matt. 7, 26 = Luke 6, 49 ([τὴν] οἰκίαν); Matt. 10, 35, 37 = Luke 12, 53; 14, 26, and the following:

Mk. 1, 30 ἡ δὲ πενθερὰ Σίμωνος	Lk. 4, 38 πενθερὰ δὲ τοῦ Σίμωνος
Mt. 11, 16 παιδίοις καθημένοις ἐν ταῖς ἀγοραῖς	Lk. 7, 31 παιδίοις τοῖς ἐν ἀγορᾷ καθημένοις [Q]

The omission of the article in frequent prepositional phrases is found also in classical Greek and in other languages. With the examples given compare in the Synoptic Gospels:

[1] Pilate has been mentioned before in Luke (3, 1; 13, 1; 20, 20) but not in Mark.

Matt. 9, 1 *al.* εἰς πλοῖον; Mark 2 1 ἐν οἴκῳ; 7, 4 ἀπ' ἀγορᾶς; 10, 21 (= Matt. 19, 21) ἐν οὐρανῷ; 11, 30 f. (= Matt. 21, 25 = Luke 20, 4 f.) ἐξ οὐρανοῦ; 15, 21 (= Luke 23, 26) ἀπ' ἀγροῦ; Luke 4, 13 ἄχρι καιροῦ; 12, 42 (= Matt. 24, 45) ἐν καιρῷ; 11, 16 ἐξ οὐρανοῦ; 15, 25 ἐν ἀγρῷ; 17, 29; 21, 11 ἀπ' οὐρανοῦ; 19, 38 ἐν οὐρανῷ.

See further Robertson, *Grammar of Greek N. T.*, pp. 791 ff. and note the reading of ℵB in Mark 3, 1 εἰς συναγωγήν (where other MSS. of Mark insert article with Mt. 12, 9 = Lk. 6, 6) and of John 6, 59; 18, 20 ἐν συναγωγῇ.

Use of Adverbs

Luke shows an aversion to several of the more frequent adverbs and adverbial phrases of Mark. εὐθύς so abundant in Mark (nearly fifty times) seems to occur only once in Luke, and that in a passage (6, 49) not dependent on Mark; it is found once in Acts also. Luke's commonest substitute is παραχρῆμα.

πάλιν, though frequent in Matthew and Mark, occurs in Luke but thrice, and in Acts five times. Luke rarely has any substitute, either lacking the repetition which it implies or avoiding any reference to such repetition. The following are the only passages in Mark (or Q) to which Luke has any parallel:

Mt. 4, 6, 7 γέγραπται . . . πάλιν γέγραπται	Lk. 4, 10, 12 γέγραπται . . . εἴρηται [Q]
Mk. 2, 1 πάλιν	Cf. Lk. 5, 17 ἐν μιᾷ τῶν ἡμερῶν
Mk. 2, 13 πάλιν	Lk. 5, 27 μετὰ ταῦτα
Mk. 3, 1 εἰσῆλθεν πάλιν	Cf. Lk. 6, 6 ἐν ἑτέρῳ σαββάτῳ εἰσελθεῖν
Mk. 5, 21 πάλιν συνήχθη	Cf. Lk. 8, 40 ἀπεδέξατο
Mk. 10, 32 καὶ παραλαβὼν πάλιν	Lk. 18, 31 παραλαβὼν δέ
Mk. 11, 27 πάλιν	Cf. Lk. 20, 1 ἐν μιᾷ τῶν ἡμερῶν
Mk. 12, 4 πάλιν ἀπέστειλεν ἄλλον	Lk. 20, 11 προσέθετο ἕτερον πέμψαι
Mk. 14, 69 ἤρξατο πάλιν λέγειν	Lk. 22, 58 μετὰ βραχὺ ἕτερος . . . ἔφη
Mk. 14, 70 ὁ δὲ πάλιν ἠρνεῖτο	Lk. 22, 58 ὁ δὲ Πέτρος ἔφη . . ., οὐκ εἰμί
Mk. 14, 70 μετὰ μικρὸν πάλιν	Lk. 22, 59 διαστάσης ὡσεὶ ὥρας μιᾶς ἄλλος τις
Mk. 15, 12 ὁ δὲ Πειλᾶτος πάλιν ἀποκριθεὶς ἔλεγεν	Lk. 23, 20 πάλιν δὲ ὁ Πειλᾶτος προσεφώνησεν
Mk. 15, 13 οἱ δὲ πάλιν ἔκραξαν	Lk. 23, 21 οἱ δὲ ἐπεφώνουν

See also Mark 4, 1; 10, 24; 14, 39, 40, 61; 15, 4.

Contrariwise, observe

Mt. 7, 18 οὐδὲ δένδρον σαπρόν	Lk. 6, 43 οὐδὲ πάλιν δένδρον σαπρόν [Q]
Mt. 13, 33 ἄλλην παραβολὴν ἐλάλησεν	Lk. 13, 20 καὶ πάλιν εἶπεν [Q]

The use of πολλά as an adverb or as an adverbial or cognate accusative is avoided by Luke (see above, p. 119):

Mk. 1, 45 ἤρξατο κηρύσσειν πολλά	Lk. 5, 15 διήρχετο μᾶλλον ὁ λόγος
Mk. 3, 12 πολλὰ ἐπετίμα	Cf. Lk. 4, 41 ἐπιτιμῶν
Mk. 4, 2 ἐδίδασκεν αὐτοὺς ἐν παραβολαῖς πολλά	Lk. 8, 4 εἶπεν διὰ παραβολῆς
Mk. 5, 10 παρεκάλει αὐτὸν πολλά	Lk. 8, 31 παρεκάλουν αὐτόν
Mk. 5, 23 παρεκάλει (*v.l.*) αὐτὸν πολλά	Lk. 8, 41 παρεκάλει αὐτόν
Mk. 5, 38 κλαίοντας καὶ ἀλαλάζοντας πολλά	Lk. 8, 52 ἔκλαιον καὶ ἐκόπτοντο αὐτήν
Mk. 5, 43 διεστείλατο αὐτοῖς πολλά	Lk. 8, 56 παρήγγειλεν αὐτοῖς
Mk. 6, 34 ἤρξατο διδάσκειν αὐτοὺς πολλά	Lk. 9, 11 ἐλάλει αὐτοῖς περὶ τῆς βασιλείας τοῦ θεοῦ
Mk. 15, 3 κατηγόρουν αὐτοῦ . . . πολλά	Lk. 23, 2 ἤρξαντο κατηγορεῖν αὐτοῦ λέγοντες, κ.τ.λ.

οὕτως is a word that could scarcely have given offence to Luke, yet he seems to avoid it in some cases:

Mk. 2, 7 τί οὗτος οὕτως λαλεῖ; βλασφημεῖ	Lk. 5, 21 τίς ἐστιν οὗτος ὃς λαλεῖ βλασφημίας
Mk. 2, 8 ὅτι οὕτως διαλογίζονται	Lk. 5, 22 τοὺς διαλογισμούς
Mk. 2, 12 οὕτως οὐδέποτε εἴδαμεν	Lk. 5, 26 εἴδομεν παράδοξα σήμερον
Mt. 5, 12 οὕτως	Lk. 6, 23 κατὰ τὰ αὐτά [Q]
Mt. 7, 12 οὕτως	Lk. 6, 31 ὁμοίως [Q]
Mt. 24, 39 οὕτως (cf. 24, 37 = Lk. 17, 26)	Lk. 17, 30 κατὰ τὰ αὐτά [Q]
Mk. 15, 39 ὅτι οὕτως ἐξέπνευσεν	Lk. 23, 47 τὸ γενόμενον (cf. Matt. 27, 54)

But *οὕτως* is added to Mark by Luke and Matthew (once each), as follows:

Mk. 11, 3 εἴπατε (Matt. 21, 3 ἐρεῖτε ὅτι)	Lk. 19, 31 οὕτως ἐρεῖτε
Mk. 14, 37 καθεύδεις; οὐκ ἴσχυσας	Mt. 26, 40 οὕτως οὐκ ἰσχύσατε

Twice in parallels with Matthew Luke has no equivalent for *μόνον*:

Mt. 5, 47 ἐὰν ἀσπάσησθε τοὺς ἀδελφοὺς μόνον	Lk. 6, 33 ἐὰν ἀγαθοποιῆτε τοὺς ἀγαθοποιοῦντας ὑμᾶς [Q]
Mt. 8, 9 ἀλλὰ μόνον εἰπὲ λόγῳ	Lk. 7, 7 ἀλλὰ εἰπὲ λόγῳ [Q]

According to Harnack (*Sayings of Jesus*, pp. 62 f.), "the *μόνον* of St. Matthew [5, 47] is original: St. Luke avoids this use of the word (only once in the Gospel [8, 50] — and that from St. Mark — while in St. Matthew it often occurs; it also occurs only once in the Acts."

Yet it is just as likely, or more so, that here Matthew added *μόνον* to the text of Q, as he three times inserts *μόνον* in passages taken from Mark:

Mk. 5, 28 ἐὰν ἅψωμαι κἂν τῶν ἱματίων αὐτοῦ	Mt. 9, 21 ἐὰν μόνον ἅψωμαι, κ.τ.λ.
Mk. 6, 56 ἵνα κἂν . . . ἅψωνται	Mt. 14, 36 ἵνα μόνον ἅψωνται
Mk. 11, 13 εἰ μὴ φύλλα	Mt. 21, 19 εἰ μὴ φύλλα μόνον

Cf. also Mt. 10, 42 with Mk. 9, 41. In Acts *μόνον* occurs seven or eight times.

From a variety of other differences, occurring only once or twice each, we may with less confidence suggest certain preferences or aversions on the part of Luke:

Mk. 1, 35 *καὶ πρωὶ ἔννυχα λίαν*	Lk. 4, 42 *γενομένης δὲ ἡμέρας*
Mk. 15, 1 *καὶ εὐθὺς πρωί*	Lk. 22, 66 *καὶ ὡς ἐγένετο ἡμέρα*
Mk. 16, 2 *λίαν πρωί*	Lk. 24, 1 *ὄρθρου βαθέως*
Mk. 5, 6 *ἀπὸ μακρόθεν*	Lk. 8, 28 omits
Mk. 14, 54 *ἀπὸ μακρόθεν*	Lk. 22, 54 *μακρόθεν*
Mk. 1, 26 *σπαράξαν*	Lk. 4, 35 *ῥῖψαν εἰς τὸ μέσον*
Mk. 2, 4 *χαλῶσιν*	Lk. 5, 19 *καθῆκαν . . . εἰς τὸ μέσον*
Mk. 4, 7 *εἰς τὰς ἀκάνθας*	Lk. 8, 7 *ἐν μέσῳ τῶν ἀκανθῶν*
Mk. 14 54 *μετὰ τῶν ὑπηρετῶν*	Lk. 22, 55 *μέσος αὐτῶν*
Mk. 14, 54 *εἰς τὴν αὐλήν* Mk. 14, 66 *ἐν τῇ αὐλῇ*	Lk. 22, 55 *ἐν μέσῳ τῆς αὐλῆς*
Mk. 15, 38 *ἐσχίσθη εἰς δύο ἀπὸ ἄνωθεν ἕως κάτω*	Lk. 23, 45 *ἐσχίσθη . . . μέσον*
Mt. 23, 39 *ἀπ' ἄρτι*	Lk. 13, 35 omits [Q]
Mk. 14, 25 *οὐκέτι οὐ μὴ* Mt. 26, 29 *οὐ μὴ . . . ἀπ' ἄρτι*	Lk. 22, 18 *οὐ μὴ . . . ἀπὸ τοῦ νῦν*
Mk. 14, 62 no phrase of time Mt. 26, 64 *ἀπ' ἄρτι*	Lk. 22, 69 *ἀπὸ τοῦ νῦν*
Mk. 6, 9 = Mt. 10, 10 *δύο χιτῶνας*	Lk. 9, 3 *ἀνά* (ℵBC verss. om.) *δύο χιτῶνας*
Mk. 6, 40 *κατὰ ἑκατὸν καὶ κατὰ πεντήκοντα*	Lk. 9, 14 *ἀνὰ πεντήκοντα*
Mk. 6, 7 *δύο δύο*	Lk. 10, 1 *ἀνὰ δύο* (B *al.* *ἀνὰ δύο δύο*)
Matt. 25, 21, 23 *εὖ*	Lk. 19, 17 *εὖγε* (BD Or.; *εὖ* ℵAW *al.*) [Q]

The use of *πρωί* and of combinations like *ἀπὸ μακρόθεν* perhaps seemed to him less elegant, though he uses both himself (Acts 28, 23; Luke 16, 23; 23, 49 (= Mark 15, 40). *μέσος* and adverbial expressions from it are favorites with Luke; his *ἀπὸ τοῦ νῦν* is distinctly preferred by Atticists to *ἀπ' ἄρτι*, which occurs in Matt. 26, 29, 64 (though not in the parallels in Mark [1]) as well as in Matt. 23, 39. See Lobeck, *Phryn.*, p. 21; cf. Moeris 68; Lucian, *Soloec.* 1. *ἀνά* in the distributive sense is an Atticism (Schmid, *Atticismus*, IV, 626). *εὖγε* is a good classical word (*ibid.*, IV, 173; Norden, *Antike Kunstprosa*, II, 487 — " Als Akklamation beliebter als *εὖ* ").

Below is exhibited Luke's treatment of double negatives in Mark. Matthew also frequently avoids them (Allen, *Matthew*, p. xxv).

Mk. 1, 44 *μηδενὶ μηδὲν εἴπῃς*	Lk. 5, 14 *μηδενὶ εἰπεῖν*
Mk. 5, 37 *οὐκ ἀφῆκεν οὐδένα*	Lk. 8, 51 *οὐκ ἀφῆκεν . . . τινα*
Mk. 9, 8 *οὐκέτι οὐδένα εἶδον*	Lk. 9, 36 omits
Mk. 11, 2 *οὐδεὶς . . . οὔπω κεκάθικεν* (*v.l.*)	Lk. 19, 30 *οὐδεὶς πώποτε . . . ἐκάθισεν*
Mk. 12, 14 *οὐ μέλει σοι περὶ οὐδενός*	Lk. 20, 21 omits

[1] Cf. Matt. 9, 18 *ἄρτι ἐτελεύτησεν* with Mark 5, 23 *ἐσχάτως ἔχει*; Matt. 11, 12 *ἕως ἄρτι* with Luke 16, 16 *ἀπὸ τότε*.

Mk. 12, 34 οὐδεὶς οὐκέτι ἐτόλμα αὐτὸν ἐπερωτῆσαι	Lk. 20, 40 οὐκέτι ἐτόλμων ἐπερωτᾶν αὐτὸν οὐδέν
Mk. 14, 25 οὐκέτι οὐ μὴ πίω	Lk. 22, 18 οὐ μὴ πίω ἀπὸ τοῦ νῦν
Mk. 15, 5; 14, 61 οὐκ ἀπεκρίνατο οὐδέν	Cf. Lk. 23, 9 οὐδὲν ἀπεκρίνατο

For the apparent addition of double negatives by Luke see:

Mt. 4, 2 νηστεύσας	Lk. 4, 2 οὐκ ἔφαγεν οὐδέν [Q]
Mk. 5, 26 μηδὲν ὠφεληθεῖσα	Lk. 8, 43 οὐκ ἴσχυσεν ἀπ' οὐδενὸς θεραπευθῆναι
Mk. 15, 46 ἐν μνήματι (Matt. 27, 60 ἐν τῷ καινῷ αὐτοῦ μνημείῳ)	Lk. 23, 53 ἐν μνήματι . . . οὗ οὐκ ἦν οὐδεὶς οὔπω (*v.l.* οὐδέπω) κείμενος

Probably at 4, 2 Luke is not changing, but merely retaining, the original οὐκ ἔφαγεν οὐδέν, while Matthew, with his objection to the double negative (see above) and his well known interest in ecclesiastical rites both Jewish and Christian, has substituted the technical νηστεύσας. For an opposite view, see Harnack, *Sayings*, p. 45.

Use of Prepositions

In his use of prepositions Luke [1] generally agrees with his sources. He prefers πρός with the accusative to the simple dative with verbs of speaking, so that εἶπεν πρός is a distinct feature of his style in the parts of his work which are derived from Mark as well as elsewhere. He shows some preference for ἀπό over ἐξ (a preference evidently general in the Koinê and causing the ultimate disappearance of ἐξ (see Blass, *Grammar*, § 40.2). As we should expect, he occasionally replaces μετά by σύν. He also perhaps avoids κατά with the genitive in the meaning 'against,' and ἔμπροσθεν.

Instances of ἀπό for ἐξ:

Mk. 1, 25 ἔξελθε ἐξ	Lk. 4, 35 ἔξελθε ἀπ'
Mk. 1, 26 ἐξῆλθεν ἐξ	Lk. 4, 35 ἐξῆλθεν ἀπ'
Mk. 5, 8 ἔξελθε ἐκ	Lk. 8, 29 ἐξελθεῖν ἀπό
Mk. 5, 30 ἐξ αὐτοῦ . . . ἐξελθοῦσαν	Cf. Lk. 8, 46 ἐξεληλυθυῖαν ἀπ' ἐμοῦ
Mk. 1, 29 ἐκ τῆς συναγωγῆς	Lk. 4, 38 ἀπὸ τῆς συναγωγῆς
Mk. 9, 9 ἐκ (BD33 = Matt. 17, 9; ἀπὸ ℵAC *al.*) τοῦ ὄρους	Lk. 9, 37 ἀπὸ τοῦ ὄρους
Mk. 9, 17 ἐκ τοῦ ὄχλου	Lk. 9, 38 ἀπὸ τοῦ ὄχλου
Mk. 14, 25 ἐκ τοῦ γενήματος	Lk. 22, 18 ἀπὸ τοῦ γενήματος
Mk. 16, 3 ἐκ τῆς θύρας	Cf. Lk. 24, 9 ἀπὸ τοῦ μνημείου

Compare also in compound verbs: [2]

Mk. 2, 12 ἐξῆλθεν	Lk. 5, 25 ἀπῆλθεν
Mk. 6, 11 = Matt. 10, 14 ἐκτινάξατε	Lk. 9, 5 ἀποτινάσσετε [Q?]
Mt. 24, 26 ἐξέλθητε	Lk. 17, 23 ἀπέλθητε [Q]
Mk. 14, 16 ἐξῆλθον καὶ ἦλθον	Lk. 22, 13 ἀπελθόντες
Mk. 15, 20 ἐξάγουσιν	Lk. 23, 26 ἀπήγαγον (cf. Mk. 15, 16)

[1] Cf. Scholten, *Das Paulinische Evangelium*, pp. 21, 36, 101, 191.

[2] On compound verbs see also p. 168.

Luke uses *πρός* with the accusative instead of a dative:

Mk. 1, 38 λέγει αὐτοῖς	Lk. 4 43 εἶπεν πρὸς αὐτούς
Mk. 2, 8 λέγει αὐτοῖς	Lk. 5, 22 εἶπεν πρὸς αὐτούς
Mk. 2, 16 ἔλεγον τοῖς μαθηταῖς	Lk. 5, 30 ἐγόγγυζον πρὸς τοὺς μαθητάς
Mk. 2, 17 λέγει αὐτοῖς	Lk. 5, 31 εἶπεν πρὸς αὐτούς
Mk. 2, 18 λέγουσιν αὐτῷ	Lk. 5, 33 εἶπαν πρὸς αὐτόν
Mk. 2, 19 εἶπεν αὐτοῖς	Lk. 5, 34 εἶπεν πρὸς αὐτούς
Mk. 2, 25 λέγει αὐτοῖς	Lk. 6, 3 πρὸς αὐτοὺς εἶπεν
Mk. 3, 4 λέγει αὐτοῖς	Lk. 6, 9 εἶπεν πρὸς αὐτούς
Mt. 11, 7 λέγειν τοῖς ὄχλοις	Lk. 7, 24 λέγειν πρὸς τοὺς ὄχλους [Q]
Mk. 4, 35 λέγει αὐτοῖς	Lk. 8, 22 εἶπεν πρὸς αὐτούς
Mk. 6, 8 παρήγγειλεν αὐτοῖς	Lk. 9, 3 εἶπεν πρὸς αὐτούς
Mk. 6, 37 εἶπεν αὐτοῖς	Lk. 9, 13 εἶπεν πρὸς αὐτούς
Mk. 6, 39 ἐπέταξεν αὐτοῖς	Lk. 9, 14 εἶπεν πρὸς τοὺς μαθητάς
Mk. 8, 34 εἶπεν αὐτοῖς	Lk. 9, 23 ἔλεγεν πρὸς πάντας
Mk. 9, 5 λέγει τῷ Ἰησοῦ	Lk. 9, 33 εἶπεν πρὸς τὸν Ἰησοῦν
Mk. 9, 31 ἔλεγεν αὐτοῖς	Lk. 9, 43 εἶπεν πρὸς τοὺς μαθητάς
Mt. 8, 22 λέγει αὐτῷ	Lk. 9, 59 εἶπεν πρὸς ἕτερον [Q]
Mk. 10, 32 ἤρξατο αὐτοῖς λέγειν	Lk. 18, 31 εἶπεν πρὸς αὐτούς
Mk. 11, 5 ἔλεγον αὐτοῖς	Lk. 19, 33 εἶπαν πρὸς αὐτούς
Mt. 21, 16 εἶπαν αὐτῷ	Lk. 19, 39 εἶπαν πρὸς αὐτόν [Q]
Mk. 11, 28 ἔλεγον αὐτῷ	Lk. 20, 2 εἶπαν λέγοντες πρὸς αὐτόν
Mk. 11, 29 εἶπεν αὐτοῖς	Lk. 20, 3 εἶπεν πρὸς αὐτούς
Mk. 12, 1 ἤρξατο αὐτοῖς λαλεῖν	Lk. 20, 9 ἤρξατο πρὸς τὸν λαὸν λέγειν
Mk. 12, 15 εἶπεν αὐτοῖς	Lk. 20, 23 εἶπεν πρὸς αὐτούς
Mk. 12, 17 εἶπεν αὐτοῖς (om. BD)	Lk. 20, 25 εἶπεν πρὸς αὐτούς
Mk. 14, 48 εἶπεν αὐτοῖς	Cf. Lk. 22, 52 εἶπεν πρὸς τούς παραγενομένους
Mk. 15, 12, 14 ἔλεγεν αὐτοῖς	Lk. 23, 22 εἶπεν πρὸς αὐτούς
Mk. 16, 6 λέγει αὐταῖς	Lk. 24, 5 εἶπαν πρὸς αὐτάς

Use of *σύν* in Luke in place of *μετά*:[1]

Mk. 5, 18 μετ' αὐτοῦ ᾖ	Lk. 8, 38 εἶναι σὺν αὐτῷ
Mk. 5, 37 μετ' αὐτοῦ συνακολουθῆσαι	Lk. 8, 51 εἰσελθεῖν σὺν αὐτῷ
Mk. 14, 17 μετὰ τῶν δώδεκα	Cf. Lk. 22, 14 οἱ ἀπόστολοι σὺν αὐτῷ
Mk. 14, 67 σὺ μετὰ τοῦ Ναζαρηνοῦ ἦσθα	Lk. 22, 56 καὶ οὗτος σὺν αὐτῷ ἦν (but 22, 59 καὶ οὗτος μετ' αὐτοῦ ἦν)

For the reverse see:

Mk. 2, 26 τοῖς σὺν αὐτῷ οὖσιν	Lk. 6, 4 τοῖς μετ' αὐτοῦ (so Matt. 12, 4)

Note the following pair of parallels:

Mk. 9, 4 Ἠλείας σὺν Μωϋσεῖ	Lk. 9, 30 Μωϋσῆς καὶ Ἠλείας
Mk. 11, 27 γραμματεῖς καὶ οἱ πρεσβύτεροι	Lk. 20, 1 γραμματεῖς σὺν τοῖς πρεσβυτέροις

κατά with the genitive occurs in these passages of Matthew but not in the parallels in Luke :

[1] Cf. Blass, *Grammar*, § 41, 3.

Mt. 12, 25 βασιλεία μερισθεῖσα καθ' ἑαυτῆς	Lk. 11, 17 βασιλεία διαμερισθεῖσα ἐφ' ἑαυτὴν (so Mk. 3, 24) [Q ?]
Mt. 12, 32 κατὰ τοῦ υἱοῦ τοῦ ἀνθρώπου κατὰ τοῦ πνεύματος τοῦ ἁγίου	Lk. 12, 10 εἰς τὸν υἱὸν τοῦ ἀνθρώπου εἰς τὸ ἅγιον πνεῦμα (so Mk. 3, 29) [Q ?]
Mt. 10, 34 κατὰ τοῦ πατρός κατὰ τῆς μητρός κατὰ τῆς πενθερᾶς	Lk. 12, 53 ἐπὶ πατρί ἐπὶ μητέρα ἐπὶ τὴν πενθεράν (cf. Mic. 7, 6, LXX) [Q]

Luke may have changed Q in all these passages, but the change in each case may be due to the other written form of the saying rather than to any linguistic preference of Luke.

Cases where Luke avoids ἔμπροσθεν:

Mk. 2, 12 ἔμπροσθεν (*v.l.* ἐνάντιον) πάντων	Lk. 5, 25 ἐνώπιον αὐτῶν (but cf. verse 19)
Mk. 9, 2 ἔμπροσθεν αὐτῶν	Lk. 9, 29 omits
Mt. 10, 32, 33 ἔμπροσθεν τῶν ἀνθρώπων ἔμπροσθεν τοῦ πατρός ἔμπροσθεν τῶν ἀνθρώπων ἔμπροσθεν τοῦ πατρός	Lk. 12, 8, 9 ἔμπροσθεν τῶν ἀνθρώπων ἔμπροσθεν τῶν ἀγγέλων ἐνώπιον τῶν ἀνθρώπων ἐνώπιον τῶν ἀγγέλων [Q]

In a few cases Luke secures better prepositional constructions for various place relations, resisting the encroachments in the Koinê of εἰς on ἐν and ἐπί, and using more correctly the genitive of the place where:

Mk. 1, 10 εἰς αὐτόν	Lk. 3, 22 ἐπὶ αὐτόν (= Matt. 3, 16)
Mk. 1, 38 εἰς τοῦτο	Lk. 4, 43 ἐπὶ τοῦτο (ℵBLW)
Mt. 5, 39 εἰς τὴν σιαγόνα	Lk. 6, 29 ἐπὶ (εἰς ℵDW Clem. Or.) τὴν σιαγόνα [Q]
Mk. 13, 16 ὁ εἰς τὸν ἀγρόν	Lk. 17, 31 ὁ ἐν ἀγρῷ (= Matt. 24, 18)
Mk. 11, 8 εἰς τὴν ὁδόν	Lk. 19, 36 ἐν τῇ ὁδῷ (= Matt. 21, 8)
Mk. 4, 21 ὑπὸ τὴν κλίνην	Lk. 8, 16 ὑποκάτω κλίνης
Mk. 4, 21 ἐπὶ τὴν λυχνίαν (= Lk. 11, 33)	Lk. 8, 16 ἐπὶ λυχνίας (ℵD *al.* ἐπὶ τὴν λυχνίαν)
Mt. 19, 28 ἐπὶ δώδεκα θρόνους	Lk. 22, 30 ἐπὶ θρόνων [Q]
Mk. 14, 49 ἤμην πρὸς ὑμᾶς	Lk. 22, 53 ὄντος μου μεθ' ὑμῶν

Sometimes ἐν appears to be avoided by Luke, as in certain awkward phrases:

Mk. 1, 23 πνεύματι ἐν ἀκαθάρτῳ	Lk. 4, 33 ἔχων πνεῦμα, κ.τ.λ.
Mk. 5, 2 πνεύματι ἐν ἀκαθάρτῳ	Lk. 8, 27 ἔχων δαιμόνια
Mk. 4, 2 ἐδίδασκεν ἐν παραβολαῖς	Lk. 8, 4 εἶπεν διὰ παραβολῆς
Mk. 12, 1 ἐν παραβολαῖς λαλεῖν	Lk. 20, 9 λέγειν τὴν παραβολήν
Mt. 3, 11 βαπτίζω ἐν ὕδατι	Lk. 3, 16 ὕδατι βαπτίζω [1] [Q ?]

[1] In Mark 1, 8, ADL, etc. read ἐν ὕδατι, ℵBΔ, etc. omit ἐν. The preposition is not found in Acts 1, 5; 11, 16.

Mt. 7, 2 (so Mk. 4, 24) ἐν ᾧ μέτρῳ μετρεῖτε	Lk. 6, 38 ᾧ μέτρῳ μετρεῖτε [Q?]
Mk. 9, 38 ἐν τῷ ὀνόματί σου	Lk. 9, 49 ἐπὶ (ℵBL ἐν) τῷ ὀνόματί σου

Improvements are made by the use of prepositions for the oblique cases alone or by the use of more appropriate prepositions:

Mk. 1, 21 τοῖς σάββασιν ἐδίδασκεν	Lk. 4, 31 ἦν διδάσκωκν . . . ἐν τοῖς σάββασιν
Mk. 1, 28 ἡ ἀκοὴ αὐτοῦ	Lk. 4, 37 ἦχος περὶ αὐτοῦ (cf. verse 14)
Mk. 2, 21 ἐπίβλημα ῥάκους	Lk. 5, 36 ἐπίβλημα ἀπὸ ἱματίου
Mk. 5, 22 πίπτει πρὸς τοὺς πόδας	Lk. 8, 41 πεσὼν παρὰ τοὺς πόδας
Mk. 5, 25 οὖσα ἐν ῥύσει αἵματος δώδεκα ἔτη	Lk. 8, 43 οὖσα ἐν ῥύσει αἵματος ἀπὸ ἐτῶν δώδεκα
Mk. 5, 35 ἀπὸ τοῦ ἀρχισυναγώγου	Lk. 8, 49 παρὰ τοῦ ἀρχισυναγώγου
Mk. 6, 7 ἐξουσίαν τῶν πνευμάτων τῶν ἀκαθάρτων	Lk. 9, 1 ἐξουσίαν ἐπὶ πάντα τὰ δαιμόνια
Mk. 6, 11 μαρτύριον αὐτοῖς	Lk. 9, 5 μαρτύριον ἐπ' αὐτούς [1]
Mk. 9, 38 ἠκολούθει ἡμῖν	Lk. 9, 49 ἀκολουθεῖ μεθ' ἡμῶν
Mt. 6, 30 τὸν χόρτον τοῦ ἀγροῦ	Lk. 12, 28 ἐν ἀγρῷ τὸν χόρτον [Q]
Mk. 15, 3 κατηγόρουν αὐτοῦ	Cf. Lk. 23, 14 κατηγορεῖτε [κατ'] αὐτοῦ

Compare also:

Mk. 14, 24 τὸ αἷμά μου τῆς διαθήκης (so Matt. 26, 28)	Lk. 22, 20 ἡ καινὴ διαθήκη ἐν τῷ αἵματί μου (similarly 1 Cor. 11, 25)

[1] Cf. Luke 21, 13 ἀποβήσεται ὑμῖν εἰς μαρτύριον with Mark 13, 9 = Matt. 10, 18 μαρτύριον αὐτοῖς.